THE GOOD ALLIES

Also by Tim Cook

*Lifesavers and Body Snatchers: Medical Care
and the Struggle for Survival in the Great War*

*The Fight for History: 75 Years of Forgetting, Remembering,
and Remaking Canada's Second World War*

The Secret History of Soldiers: How Canadians Survived the Great War

Vimy: The Battle and the Legend

*Fight to the Finish: Canadians in the Second World War,
1944–1945, Volume Two*

*The Necessary War: Canadians Fighting the Second World War,
1939–1943, Volume One*

Warlords: Borden, Mackenzie King, and Canada's World Wars

*The Madman and the Butcher: The Sensational Wars of
Sam Hughes and General Arthur Currie*

*Shock Troops: Canadians Fighting the Great War,
1917–1918, Volume Two*

*At the Sharp End: Canadians Fighting the Great War,
1914–1916, Volume One*

*Canada and the Korean War: Histories and Legacies of a
Cold War Conflict* [with Andrew Burtch (eds.)]

Canada 1919: A Nation Shaped by War [with J.L. Granatstein (eds.)]

Forever Changed: Stories From the Second World War [with Britt Braaten]

Victory 1918: The Last 100 Days [with J.L. Granatstein]

For King and Country: The South African and First World War

Canada in the World Wars [with Jeff Noakes and Nic Clarke]

Clio's Warriors: Canadian Historians and the Writing of the World Wars

*No Place To Run: The Canadian Corps and
Gas Warfare in the First World War*

THE GOOD ALLIES

HOW CANADA
AND THE UNITED STATES
FOUGHT TOGETHER
TO DEFEAT FASCISM DURING
THE SECOND WORLD WAR

TIM COOK

ALLEN
LANE

ALLEN LANE

an imprint of Penguin Canada, a division of Penguin Random House Canada Limited

Canada • USA • UK • Ireland • Australia • New Zealand • India • South Africa • China

First published 2024

www.penguinrandomhouse.ca

LIBRARY AND ARCHIVES CANADA CATALOGUING IN PUBLICATION

Title: The good allies : how Canada and the United States fought together
to defeat fascism during the Second World War / Tim Cook.
Names: Cook, Tim, 1971- author.
Description: Includes bibliographical references and index.
Identifiers: Canadiana (print) 20240317092 | Canadiana (ebook) 20240317130 |
ISBN 9780735248205 (hardcover) | ISBN 9780735248212 (EPUB)
Subjects: LCSH: World War, 1939-1945—Canada. | LCSH: World War, 1939-1945—
United States. | LCSH: Canada—Military relations—United States. |
LCSH: United States—Military relations—Canada.
Classification: LCC D768.15 .C6396 2024 | DDC 940.54/1271—dc23

Book design by Dylan Browne
Cover design by Matthew Flute
Cover image: First Special Service Force (CWM 19820091-001_49),
George Metcalf Archival Collection, Canadian War Museum

Printed in Canada

10 9 8 7 6 5 4 3 2 1

FOR SHARON, SARAH, CHLOE, EMMA,
PAIGE, AND BEAR, WITH LOVE.

CONTENTS

INTRODUCTION

"The secret aim of every American leader, including Franklin Roosevelt, [is] to dominate Canada and ultimately to possess the country."[1] So believed a concerned Canadian prime minister William Lyon Mackenzie King, who confessed this worry to his diary. The claim, riven with King's fear for Canada's very survival, had a basis in truth, given US invasions northward in 1775 and 1812, coupled with lesser acts of aggression in the 1830s and 1840s. Every prime minister had been aware of the precarious place of the Dominion within North America. While King admired the president of the United States, Franklin Delano Roosevelt, his comment nonetheless revealed an anxiety that ran through him and many of his generation about the growing power south of the border.

The Canadian–American relationship was shaped from its earliest days by the two nations' common origins in the British Empire in North America, as well as by their alliances with and battles against Indigenous groups. British victory over France in 1763 led to the ascendance of the British colonies in North America, albeit with a strong French-Canadian presence in what had been New France. However, that victory was soon followed by a traumatic shattering of unity during the American Revolution, which began in 1775. Through revolution and battle, the Americans carved out a new democratic republic, finally defeating the British forces stationed on present-day American soil and driving loyalists into the Canadian colonies that had remained with the Crown. With the emergence of the US as a new power—one anxious to remove Europeans from North America—the Canadians in British North America spent much of their early history worried that the headlong expansionism of the new republic would lead to them being conquered in the name of liberty and in an attempt at freeing Canadians from supposed Imperial oppression.[2] There would always be a significant population and wealth imbalance between Canada—as the confederated colonies were known from 1867 onward—and the United States. But after years of unease, conflict, and efforts at political integration, the American crusading mentality diminished in the early twentieth century. Out of two centuries of strife emerged at first uneasy friendship, then minor treaties, and ultimately fruitful partnerships that would enable the two nations to navigate living together on the continent.

Since the 1930s, few other countries in the world—especially those sharing a 9,000-kilometre border—have been so accommodating and generous to each other in matters of trade, politics, and defence. The United States is a superpower with a population nine times greater than Canada's, with the strongest military in the world, and with the most pervasive global influence of any nation, making it even more remarkable that the smaller and less populous country to its north has not only survived but thrived. A shared language and, initially, religions, a grounding in rule of law and a similar culture, a reciprocal flow of immigrants and an intermingling of people through marriages, robust trade relations and cross-border investment, and a largely undefended border and a collective vision of security have all helped to forge bonds of familiarity. The evolution of Canadians and Americans from enemies to wary neighbours to allies has a long arc, but a key turning point in that history can be traced to the Second World War, from 1939 to 1945. During that period of global crisis, the two countries put aside differences to defeat the fascists and militarists in Germany, Italy, and Japan. It was a time to battle together against the existential threat of a ruthless enemy.

This book argues that Canada became a stalwart partner to the US in defending North America during the Second World War. With its 11.5 million people in 1939 spread over a huge territory, Canada was a good ally that pulled its weight. Despite having been gutted during the Depression years, this dominion within the British Commonwealth of nations achieved success far beyond any reasonable expectation. The two countries worked closely together to secure vulnerable frontiers, stimulate wartime economies, and protect the realm of North America, a core and essential achievement that was necessary for all other military action to unfold. A fundamental objective of American defence policy, noted one US army planner, was to fashion an outer frontier to avoid "the likelihood of accepting war upon our own territory."[3] Canada had the same strategic goal. In fact, how North America was fortified and shielded is crucial to understanding the ability of the Americans and Canadians to commit to fighting overseas, for without a safe homeland, the full output of the continent's industries could never be exported to its close ally, Britain, or its ally of convenience, the Soviet Union.

Central to the Canadian–American wartime relationship was the friendship between King and Roosevelt, particularly in the period when Canada was at war and the US remained neutral, from September 1939 to December 1941. During this interlude, the two countries steadily integrated defence production, solved financial dilemmas, and constructed new ways of working together to move past seemingly intractable problems. King recorded in his diary that he found Roosevelt "exceedingly easy to talk with," just as the president confided in him that "it was great just to be able to pick up the telephone and talk to each other."[4] The president often called King "Mackenzie," even though his closest friends knew him as "Rex." In this book, he will be referred to as "King." He often preferred "Mackenzie King"—a nod to his grandfather, William Lyon Mackenzie, who was a leader in the Upper Canada rebellion of 1837 that sought to declare the colony a republic by force. It's unlikely the president was aware of the failed rebellions of 1837, or of the irony of the grandson, King, leading the country to support Britain in a time of great peril, but the future prime minister Lester B. Pearson, who served as Canada's wartime ambassador to the United States, said of Roosevelt that he "had a better understanding of the position and importance of Canada than most Americans in official places."[5] The US could have turned the screws on Canada harder and more ruthlessly (as it did on occasion to Britain)—using crisis to achieve goals of economic dominance or even the erosion of Canadian sovereignty. It did not. The American president was mindful that it was in the interest of the United States to have a strong friend on its northern border. And so the two nations came together in the face of a common enemy, surmounting many long-standing national barriers and ingrained prejudices in the collective pursuit of victory.

INTRODUCTION

Canada also kept the border with the US demilitarized because its primary goal was to support Britain, which was on the front lines in the fight against the Axis powers, an alliance consisting of Germany, Italy, and Japan since late 1940. Even though the Dominion controlled its foreign policy and pursued its own national interests, the act of standing by Britain guided the country's war effort. Canada had other strategic aims, as will be explored in this book, but none of these matched the need to aid Britain—and none of these strategies could have been achieved without closer integration with the United States. Adding complexity to the issue, Britain's weakness in the face of fascist victories early in the war reduced its ability to guarantee Canadian sovereignty, and the rapid drain on its treasury left Canada desperate for new markets.[6] As the security equation drastically changed for Canada, its leaders were required to negotiate a new relationship with the US. How the country positioned itself within North America is central to understanding the unfolding of Canadian nationhood through the rest of the twentieth century. But the complexity runs deeper. During the war, King refused to turn his back on Britain; instead, he worked assiduously to ensure that Canada would support the mother country in a war of utter necessity against the fascist powers. But it could only do so by becoming more deeply entwined with the US. Canada's freedom of action to better assist Britain was balanced by its political and military leaders who were forced to embrace closer cooperation with the US.

In 1939, the United States was an economic power, but it did not yet have the corresponding superiority of martial strength; nonetheless, it exerted control over much of the Western Hemisphere. For the Dominion of Canada to the north, this power imbalance with its neighbour did not sit easily. "Canada was regarded too often as a British colony or appendage" by the Americans, recalled one diplomatic adviser to the Canadian cabinet in Ottawa.[7] As a commercial dynamo with three times more economic power than Britain before the war, and with all of the financial and entrepreneurial potential of a population of 131 million, the United States was intellectually aligned with the democratic Western allies in their war with Germany that started in September 1939. And yet the US remained neutral in that fateful year, much to the disappointment of Britain and France. The vast majority of Americans fiercely opposed fighting another extended series of campaigns overseas just because the dysfunctional Europeans were unable to control their predatory instincts.[8] The successful enticing, courting, and inching of the Americans into the war on the side of the British Commonwealth was the single most important act towards victory achieved by officials in London or Ottawa from 1939 to 1941. Without US engagement, the German dictator Adolf Hitler would likely have ruled over a conquered Europe.

———

Out of the ashes, anger, and mass graves of the Great War rose fascist ideology. The 9.4 million soldiers killed in battle; the millions of civilians who died through direct attack, starvation, and genocide; and the 22 million combatants physically wounded had hollowed out nations. By late 1918, both the victors and the vanquished were shrouded in despair and grief.[9] One of Europe's venerable powers crumbled first: Bolshevik revolutionaries executed the Russian royal family in 1918 and waged a civil war, embarking on years of internal strife and external war. Dictator

Joseph Stalin emerged as the new leader in 1929, using terror to remake the Union of Soviet Socialist Republics (USSR) from a peasant society into an industrialized nation. He did so by deliberately starving to death millions of people, while also executing hundreds of thousands in purges and condemning countless more to isolated and brutalizing gulags. Stalin's brand of totalitarian communism was similar in ways to the fascist ideology that gripped Italy and later Germany.

Fascism was an ideology for the lost: infused with a culture of violence based on grievance and fear, it exploited vulnerable minorities within the nation as well as other identified enemies. Fascists drew upon an imagined, untroubled past to promise some version of a better future in relation to the supposedly decaying present. To create the fascist state, a hyper-nationalist and magnetic leader—his image formed, shaped, and constructed by a compliant and compromised media—manufactured and then focused the anger of his people to enact change within national boundaries and then beyond. Opposition among other political elites was suffocated. Fascism sanctified violence, and it became a means to many dire ends.

In the Far East, twentieth-century Japan conquered its neighbours to exploit natural resources and minerals to further its expansion. Ruled by a god-like emperor, the country had emerged into the modern age with an effective navy and army. In the 1920s, Japan became more aggressive and saw the United States as a natural competitor in the Pacific. Though Japan was not a classic fascist nation, as its militaristic class of soldiers and aggressive politicians took power and invoked a culture of obedience to the emperor, military, and state, the violent men of the warlike island nation became a menace to their regional neighbours. An invasion of China in 1931, provoked by a series of manufactured incidents, ultimately led to a vicious all-out war in 1937. Condemned as a pariah nation, Japan was on a collision course with the Western powers.

In Italy, following the trauma of the Great War, from which the country had emerged on the side of the victorious Allied forces, anger poisoned many who believed that the country deserved larger territorial spoils. The fascist Benito Mussolini, a journalist and politician, stoked resentments as he came to power in 1922. He rearmed Italy in the name of restoring lost grandeurs, and, after reducing the country to a dictatorship, mounted a war against Ethiopia in 1935 that turned much of the world against him. Mussolini infected the body politic with a toxic ideology of hostility and anger. So successful was Il Duce in bending the Italian people to his will that Hitler was soon an admirer.

Democratically elected in 1933 to lead a broken Germany, Adolf Hitler, a Great War veteran and agitator throughout the 1920s, had fashioned the National Socialist Party—the Nazis—into a thuggish movement with a political arm. He soon consolidated power by imprisoning and killing his opponents. Singling out the small German Jewish population as a threat, along with other vulnerable groups such as the Romani (Gypsies) and homosexuals, the Nazis created a series of fabricated crises and full-throttle propaganda that allowed for the disenfranchisement and humiliation of the weak and helpless. Germans of Jewish descent were accused of undermining the state and polluting racial purity. Ignoring the 1919 Treaty of Versailles that limited his military, Hitler rearmed with impunity as the German people increasingly saw him as the leader who would remove the stain of the last war's defeat. Western Europeans watched with apprehension, but no one wanted another war. Humiliations were swallowed, with the democracies impotently hoping that Hitler would be satisfied. He would not.

———

While Canada would become one of the US's most steadfast allies in the Second World War—and was already its number one trading partner by the 1920s—Americans have often taken Canada for granted. Perhaps that is typically the case with good neighbours. And yet trade deals, diplomatic relations, and military alliances take work: hard as they are in times of peace, they are harder still during wartime, when nations have their way of life imperilled and there is little time to formulate plans. Major-General Maurice Pope, an experienced soldier who was a key Canadian officer in wartime Washington, wrote of the challenges he faced in dealing with the Americans and standing up for the Dominion. It was never easy, he wrote, and one always ran the risk of being "big-sticked." This was a reference to President Theodore Roosevelt's intimidating phrase from the early twentieth century, in which he advocated for "speaking softly, and carrying a big stick" for possible use in bludgeoning Canadians into accepting American demands.[10]

"We shall not be a burden on anyone else—neither a burden on the States nor a burden on England," said Prime Minister King before the war.[11] He lived up to that promise. The Canadian and American joint effort to fortify the nations' shared frontiers may be the most successful alliance ever forged by the US in terms of both ease and resources expended for ultimate gain. In the context of prosecuting the war against the Axis powers, the US had a more important wartime alliance with Britain than with Canada, but it was the relationship with the Dominion that was critical for defending North America. The Soviets—a one-time enemy turned untrustworthy co-belligerent—were a different breed of ally. They had to be propped up with billions of dollars in aid and military equipment, as it was understood that if the Communists had not been bleeding the Nazis dry through bitter fighting on the Eastern Front from June 1941, there would be little hope of the war ending in anything other than a negotiated peace with Hitler in control of Europe. Though Canada was never a great power, and stayed clear of the responsibilities and challenges that are required of such nations, it emerged during the war—and because of the war—as a wealthy country better able to exploit its natural resources, harness its industry potential, and fulfill security obligations. It did so because it had largely shed its colonial past to act as an independent nation, turning to the US even as it strove to stand with Britain in facing the Axis powers.

Though much energy has been directed towards exploring Canada's military effort overseas, far less has been spent examining the defence of North America. It is a story that mattered from 1939 to 1945, and one that continues to offer lessons to this day. At the same time, most Canadian wartime histories are centred on the Canadian and British experience—not surprisingly, since the Canadians most often served with Imperial forces.[12] Ties of kith, kin, history, politics, and culture also cemented this focus. Despite its historic role in aiding the Canadian war effort, the US has rarely been the focus of a comprehensive study that examines defence, security, culture, economics, trade, politics, and diplomacy.[13] And so this book shifts the gaze from the east–west axis of the trans-Atlantic towards the north–south partnership over the border, providing a new way to understand the Canadian war effort and its profound legacy for the development of the country.

The discussion here is weighted firmly towards the Canadian war effort from a Canadian perspective. Tens of thousands of books have been written about the American experience of the war, from the standpoint of both participants and historians over several generations, and almost all neglect Canada and its considerable contributions to the Allied victory. Some of that blindness is due to the scope and breadth of the American martial mobilization; some of it too is because Canada was a dependable ally and much determined effort was made to ensure the wartime machinery worked smoothly between the two nations. Historical analysis is often drawn to crisis and conflict, and there was little of that in the profitable Canadian–American alliance. Some of the responsibility for our absence from the American historical record also rests on Canadians. Much of the literature related to North American relations is coloured by the fear of a postwar loss of independence, especially from the 1960s to the end of the century. The countries' relationship during the Second World War does not fit easily into that literature of grievance and anxiety.

The Good Allies shows that Canadians and Americans served together to safeguard North America, and that once it was protected from invasion and had its defences built up, they jointly took the war to the fascists overseas. At home, during the period of the United States' neutrality, Canada's rearmament programs on the two coasts were often driven by the need to convince the Americans that the Dominion was secure against incursion by a foreign power. "To the Americans the defence of the United States is continental defence," warned one senior Canadian general, noting that this included Canada, with or without its leaders' consent. "What we have to fear is more a lack of confidence in the United States as to our security, rather than enemy action."[14] Canadians were acutely aware of the hazard at stake if the southern behemoth felt its northern border was exposed. The King government wished to give the Americans no reason to feel they needed to liberate their neighbour from an invading force, for he worried the US soldiers might not leave after the crisis. Canada would struggle throughout the war to ensure its sovereignty was respected by the republic to the south.

Though a cross-border invasion by the US—even one to liberate Canada from a German or Japanese invasion force—was an unlikely scenario, Ottawa had to plan to avoid any such threat. The first fruit of this initiative was the promotion of mutual cooperation and military support between Canada and the US. On the east coast, Canadian naval and air forces wrestled with the German U-boat threat and led essential convoys across the Atlantic to bring war supplies to a besieged Britain. Even before the Americans formally came into the war on the side of the Allies, the US Navy was assisting in the war at sea. That action came from Roosevelt, who, as commander-in-chief of the US armed forces, slowly positioned his nation to fight, citing his obligation to protect America's coast. Indeed, in February 1942, the president watched in desperation as the Axis powers were winning on every front. He described the struggle as being "different from all the other wars of the past," and predicted it would determine the "survival of our civilization."[15]

After the Japanese attack against the West on December 7, 1941, Canada and the US were drawn closer together, with the Royal

Canadian Navy assisting the Americans along the North American east coast as enemy U-boats savaged their shipping. In the West, Canada strengthened its defences to reassure the Americans and jointly protect the long coastline, sent military formations to Alaska to stand with their allies, and even participated in a combined invasion of the Japanese-occupied Kiska Island in August 1943. These actions were done despite Canada having lost much of its influence with the US after Britain pushed the Dominion aside to have closer relations with the Americans. Led by Prime Minister Winston Churchill, the British worked in a bilateral relationship with the Americans, anxious not to have Canada present, which could dilute Britain's voice, but equally eager to continue to draw upon the Commonwealth nation's considerable military and economic resources. In early 1942, Prime Minister King complained that when the two great leaders were in conversation and jousting with one another, it "crowd[ed] both Canada and myself off the map."[16]

Canada did not withdraw in a sulk. The nation's politicians, diplomats, and service personnel shored up defences, worked with their American counterparts, and continued to fight abroad. While the country's people were galvanized to victory on farms, in mines, and from the factory floor, Canadian officials conducted the delicate dance of assisting Britain by forging closer ties with the Americans. In dealing with both Britain and the US, the Canadians grappled with exerting their sovereignty, with no area more problematic than the North, where the Americans insisted on building the Alaska Highway and air staging routes to support Alaska. Even with over 30,000 foreign soldiers and workers operating on Canadian soil, the Canucks remained accommodating allies, willing to swallow their fear of the concentrated US presence.

That did not mean there was no worry as Ottawa navigated this new relationship and learned how to stand up for itself. Robert G. Riddell, an astute observer in the Department of External Affairs, wrote in February 1943, "[W]e are letting the Americans get away with things that would have broken the Commonwealth in little pieces if London had tried them."[17]

With North America secure from enemy attack by 1943, the Canadians and Americans took their cooperation overseas, fighting side by side in Sicily and mainland Italy. This partnership found its culmination in the First Special Service Force, a unique unit consisting of Canadians and Americans. In the air war over Europe, North American bombers, often operated by crews made up of "New World" airmen, struck Germany. At least 30,000 American volunteers served in the Royal Canadian Air Force (RCAF) and the Canadian Army.[18] The multi-pronged war against the Nazis culminated in the great crusade for Europe, starting on June 6, 1944. Canadian, British, and American forces landed on D-Day, clawing their way forward in that enormous military operation to liberate the French and other oppressed people. This dangerous landing, and the grim combat to follow, was a visible demonstration of that three-way partnership. In the Pacific, Canadians and Americans rarely fought together, although 10,000 Canadians were stationed in that geographic theatre of war, and more would have served if the war had extended into 1946. Even more important, over three million Canadians were engaged in home front war industry work, mineral extraction, and food production, all of which involved deep collaboration with the American war effort, revealing that the good allyship went both ways. The massive production of weapons and vehicles pulled the Dominion from the mire of the Depression years and gave it immense resources that it directed most forcefully towards supporting Britain in its desperate battles. Sometimes the relationship between the North American nations was antagonistic, but more often it was based on mutual goals. Flying in the RCAF, New York State native Malcolm Hormats recalled that his service "left [him] with a profound respect and admiration for Canadian flyers in particular and Canadians in general."[19] Many Americans felt the same way.

In a time of great destruction, unimaginable slaughter, and genocidal actions against the people of neighbouring nations, the alliance between Canada and the US was nothing short of astonishing. Both the heroic and the ordinary are covered in this book, including presidents and prime ministers, generals and admirals, but also service personnel, war workers, and civilians on the home front. Training its focus on the history of war both in North America and beyond its borders, the narrative shifts from the strategic to the operational level and then percolates down to units and individuals. Victory would not have been possible without the Canadian and American relationship based on a common cause: to liberate the oppressed and destroy fascism.

The Second World War marked a pivotal turning point in the entwinement of these two North American nations. That did not mean that Canadians ached to be Americans. As J.K. Chapman, a RCAF navigator who enlisted early in the war, wrote in his memoirs, "We did not think of ourselves as second-class Americans. Indeed, we considered ourselves equal to or better than Americans and were inclined to pity them for having, mistakenly as we thought, declared their independence."[20] He wrote with unusual Canadian bravado, and yet in this reflection he also revealed that Canadians took pride in being members of the British Commonwealth and saw themselves as different from Americans. The war against the Axis powers nonetheless compelled closer relations. Out of that costly struggle, the two nations were forever tethered together in a remarkable alliance that altered Canada and forced the United States to take its northern neighbour more seriously.

CHAPTER I

RISE OF THE FASCISTS

"The Dominion of Canada is part of the sisterhood of the British Empire," said the much-admired President Franklin D. Roosevelt in Kingston, Ontario, on August 18, 1938. Acknowledging the place of Canada in the British Commonwealth, he also pledged, "I give to you the assurance that the people of the United States will not stand idly by if domination of the Canadian soil is threatened by any other Empire."[1] By "Empire," the president meant Germany and Japan, and as the partially paralyzed American leader stood before a large crowd of some 10,000 at the university football stadium filled with academics, students, and politicians, he was speaking to all Canadians, Americans, and the world. Those in the audience, including Prime Minister William Lyon Mackenzie King, and those who heard the speech through their radios or read about it in the papers, understood that it was a historic declaration that the North American nations would stand together in the face of a future clash of arms. It was also a threat of sorts: that the United States would trample Canadian sovereignty if it saw a foreign menace north of the border.

Europe again roiled with the possibility of war, a mere two decades after the Great War had killed more than nine million soldiers and destroyed empires. Haunted and hag-ridden by the trauma of that bloodletting, the survivors murmured "lest we forget" and prayed that it was the "war to end all wars." And yet out of the ashes of war and the economic ruin of the Depression of 1929 had emerged Nazi Germany, which had used that crisis to rearm under its Führer, Adolf Hitler. The decorated corporal of the Great War had reinvigorated Germany during the harsh Depression years, even as Roosevelt had done with the downtrodden American people. But where Roosevelt had achieved positive change through government intervention to aid the dispirited unemployed via massive construction and job creation programs, Hitler had done it through fury, grievance, and a promise to restore Germany to its rightful place by might. The Führer was in the process of strengthening his armed forces and had commenced his pitiless persecution of Jews. He had also been supporting dictator Francisco Franco in the Spanish Civil War since 1936.[2] The Soviet Union had backed the opposite side, known as the Republicans, although this was not as effective as Hitler's support of the fascist Nationalists. Joseph Stalin had been distracted by his ongoing orchestration of mass murder in the Ukraine and Eastern Russia through a deliberate weaponization of food that left millions of people starving. Comfortable with exacting genocide, Stalin also purged hundreds of thousands through executions. The terror in the bloodlands was often obscured by Soviet propaganda portraying the wonders of collectivism and communism, but the horror for those living through it was nearly unimaginable. In the Far East, Japan was engaged in its ruthless war against the Chinese. Everywhere the militarists were on the rise.

Western Europe surveyed all of this with growing terror, weary from the last war and unready for the next one, while the Americans, safe across the Atlantic Ocean, had no desire to again intervene in the mad march to war. Canadians were also safe from the maelstrom, although English Canada would stand by Britain in the coming crisis. The question was, how much blood would it cost to defeat the fascists, and would the entire country be willing to pay the price? Canadians would also come to understand that they could not do it without the United States.

———

Prime Minister King sat next to the US president during the Kingston speech and was startled to hear the promise to defend Canada if it was attacked. No one was sure about the ramifications of a foreign power invading to save Canada, and King was especially worried. The wily King, standing five feet six inches and with blue eyes and a body having long run to age, wore the scars of his long political battle since coming to power in 1921. His career had left him as a slippery centrist, given more to talk than action, happy to lead from the rear as he took the nation's pulse with his well-honed political instincts before springing ahead to surprise his opponents. Prime minister from 1921 to 1930, he returned to power again in late 1935 after winning a majority under the slogan "King or Chaos," without offering much of a way forward despite the economic misery of the Depression.

The bachelor King, educated with a PhD from Harvard unlike most of his contemporaries who chose Oxford, was a nationalist, albeit one who firmly believed in the importance of Canada within the British Commonwealth that had emerged from the old British Empire. At the same time, and without contradiction, the prime minister took great comfort in the monarchy and the traditions of the Westminster political system, while also revelling in British history and culture. Some pro-British Canadians derided King as being too friendly to the US, and their worry was not eased when one of King's first orders of business in 1935 was to solidify an agreement with Washington that reduced some protectionist trade barriers.[3] King was looking for a better trade deal, and he met with the American minister, Norman Armour, in Ottawa, where he shared his belief in stronger North American ties. In his ambassadorial role, Armour reported back to his political superiors in Washington that he felt Canada was at a crossroads between Britain and the United States, and that the new prime minister wanted to choose "the American road if we made it possible for him."[4] It was an extraordinary statement: had it been widely known, it would have been seen as nothing short of traitorous by many Canadians. King said it, but he did not believe it, and he was anxious to retain the connection with Britain to keep Canada from being fully ensnared by the United States. His stated wish to take the American pathway also shed light both on King's propensity to freely tell people things that they wanted to hear, and, perhaps less apparent, on how he planned to use the counterweight of Washington's gravitational pull to balance the centripetal force from London. King was engaging in a delicate balancing act between loyalty to Britain and the prosperity represented by the United States, hoping to find space between the two powers to carve out influence for Canada.

The trade deal signed in November 1935 was heralded by King and others as a symbol of good neighbourly relations with the Americans, especially as Europe again stormed in conflict under the aggressive dictators in Germany and Italy. President Roosevelt, who had been elected in the depth of the Depression in November 1932 on a tide of optimism and change, had sanctioned the deal with the northern dominion. He had long thought well of Canada, having vacationed for many years at a summer home on Campobello Island in New Brunswick while serving as governor of the state of New York, and he had been briefed that King and his Liberals were closer to the US than the Conservative Party.[5] The president had inherited a broken nation, with agonizing levels of unemployment and widespread hardship. In a desire to reach Americans and restore faith in the nation, Roosevelt instigated radio "fireside chats," folksy talks that were listened to by tens of millions of Americans who prayed he had a solution.[6] He did, implementing his New Deal, a series of interventionist government programs,

The wartime leaders of Canada and the United States of America:
Prime Minister William Lyon Mackenzie King
and President Franklin Delano Roosevelt.

financial reforms, and public work projects that led to a vast injection of government funding to provide jobs for the unemployed and kickstart the economy. The approach was resisted ferociously by all manner of opponents, both Republicans and even some of Roosevelt's own Democrats, who believed it was a nefarious plot to undermine American values and society while further draining the treasury. Their voices were eventually muted as the economic programs slowly brought the US out of the slough of despond. King was impressed by the president's popular appeal, writing in his diary that Roosevelt "gives the impression of strength & integrity & spiritual purpose & power."[7]

There was little money to spread around in Canada. The Depression years had, for instance, gutted the military, leaving it a wretched force, with much of the army's energy put towards policing unemployment camps for indigent men and the air force making do with outdated fighters. Only the Royal Canadian Navy had been able to make the case for some modern warships, under the pretence that they would engage in coastal security. However, even though Canada's sailors entered the war with six River class destroyers, it had only a total of ten warships. This long-term strangulation of the armed forces had also occurred because of the King government's power base in Quebec, where it had won every seat in the 1935 election. Before, during, and after the contest, Liberals claimed it was only they who stood between young French Canadians fearful of being sent to Imperial wars and the Conservatives who were too willing to enact conscription as they had when in power during the last war. Spending millions of dollars on defence was viewed with much suspicion by many Canadians still reeling from the Depression, and they were joined in this view by a constellation of intellectuals, church leaders, and journalists who warned that a stronger military would only drag the country into foreign wars. And so, for political gain and social harmony, King's Liberals left Canada's armed forces unprepared for a war that was becoming more and more probable, even from across the Atlantic, especially as Nazi Germany threatened its neighbours and brazenly rearmed for war.

———

Nazi dictator Adolf Hitler was bark, bile, and bite. His demagoguery was empowered by his shattering of the international treaties that constrained Germany's military. The Führer saw it as throwing off the shackles of the humiliating Versailles Treaty of 1919; his neighbours in Europe prayed he might be satiated without a war. In Britain, rearmament had been slow, and the hope was that diplomacy might avert conflict. France, however, did not have the luxury of protection by the Channel waters. Its cemeteries were filled with soldiers from the lost war of 1871 and the nation's more costly victory in the Great War. To protect itself, a series of concrete forts known as the Maginot Line were built along the frontier with Germany.

Prime Minister King was warned about the rising Nazi threat by the professional military staff, and he longed for the British and French to find a way to pacify Hitler. The sixty-two-year-old prime minister even took it upon himself to visit Hitler in Berlin on June 29, 1937, believing that he had much in common with the Nazi leader—a firm starting point being that both men loved their mothers. Although he had been alerted to the German dictator's seductive charm, King's mission of peace came from a place of gross naivete. During the one-hour meeting, King sensed he had

Canada's Prime Minister King at the 1936 Olympic Games in Berlin, Germany, refusing to give the Nazi salute.

a connection with the Führer, writing in fawning terms in his diary about the "liquid quality" of Hitler's piercing eyes and the smooth face of a "calm, passive man." Most egregiously, King felt that Hitler was motivated as a leader to be a "deliverer of his people from tyranny."[8] Despite his absurd misreading of the Nazi, King also said that Canada would stand by Britain in a time of war. None of it made much of an impact on Hitler, even though King deluded himself into thinking he had made a difference.

One point of common interest between Hitler and King was that they both believed that destiny controlled their fate. King went a step further, having long immersed himself in the practice of spirit rapping, seeking out mediums, and interpreting signs in dreams. Spiritualism had been stoked in the nation by the mass grief spilling from the bloody Great War battlefields, but King often turned to it as a desperately lonely man. After working crushing hours in his parliamentary office, he would return home to be alone in his large house that was gifted to him by his mentor, former prime minister Sir Wilfrid Laurier. With few people to talk to, he often sought out—and received, according to his interpretation of the signs—support, comfort, and advice from across the divide. Many political luminaries offered guidance and compliments, from British prime minister William Gladstone to Laurier. Encouragement also came from his mother, and even his dog Pat, both of whom had passed on to the other side. King often used these spiritual signals to confirm what he felt was the right way forward, although he survived more because of his well-honed political instincts.

While King's recounting in his diary of his brief meeting with Hitler is nothing short of repulsive, this too must be judged in its context, or at least by what the diary meant to the prime minister.

Lacking a partner with whom he could share his daily thoughts, King used his diary as a means to work through issues and problems. The passages alternated between a justification of his own actions—usually a self-congratulatory recording of his uncommon foresight and shrewd judgment in warding off political disasters—and a dreary regurgitation of his anxiety, outrage, and feelings of inadequacy.[9] King was a complicated man: a loner in the highest office in the land, he was often plagued by mother issues and a sense of inferiority, but he could also be hard-hearted and canny.

The Great War had nearly torn Canada apart as it deepened and created new fault lines between English and French, workers and owners, those in the cities and on the farms.[10] The extremity of the war effort that increasingly demanded more treasure and soldiers to feed the seemingly unending conflict, and that ultimately culminated in the decision to force young men to serve against their will, had damaged national unity. King had been scarred by the fractious poisons unleashed in the unfettered crusade during the war against Germany. At the same time, he also understood the need to stand by Britain if war should come again. As a British subject, King knew that most English Canadians assumed that they must back Britain, even though this impulse was much less prevalent among French Canadians and new immigrants from Eastern Europe.

The complexities and contradictions of preparing for war while not showing his hand to Canadians required that King bob and weave to obscure his intentions and buy time to find the proper path. But in the face of Germany's aggression, he had less room to manoeuvre. King claimed in September 1938 that, should Hitler and his Nazis declare war on Britain, it was his country's "self-evident national duty" to fight by the island kingdom's side.[11]

He knew that if Canada did not march with Britain, not only would he be dumped by the electorate, but the action would, in King's words, isolate the Dominion in North America and force it to cower under the Americans' defence umbrella. That was a price too high and one "much greater than we would have to pay for any other for assistance."[12] In short, support of Britain in war was the lesser of two evils, and King refused to turn his back on the nation's history and embrace the US.

In navigating the hazards of foreign policy, King was assisted by Oscar Skelton, under-secretary of state for external affairs and a close adviser to him from the early 1920s. Serving as the senior mandarin at the department, the owlish-looking Skelton, with his academic glasses and thinning hair, was incisive in his commentary, applying his sharp mind to every task. While some accused Skelton of being anti-British, he was in fact a Canadian nationalist, and one who had lived through the horror of the last war and demanded that Canada have more control over its diplomatic and defence policy. He worked assiduously at achieving this for over two decades, aware that the road to greater independence could only be achieved by loosening Canada from London's imperial grasp. This necessarily meant shifting southwards towards the US and encouraging the development of what he called a "North American mind."[13] King could never go quite so far, knowing it was political suicide to turn completely away from Britain, even though he would often ride the currents of change, scurrying between the sentiments expressed by ardently English Canadians and those of Canadian nationalists who sought to create some distance between Canada and Britain. King also understood that, from the viewpoint of London and Washington, Canada was a strange beast: a North American nation that was also a dominion within the Commonwealth.

Even as King walked the middle line in the late 1930s, saying one thing and then its opposite, he and his cabinet were aware of the threatening war. To reassure both Britain and the US, King advocated a series of rearmaments. But he faced significant opposition in his cabinet, especially from his French-Canadian ministers. He was also fearful of revealing his plans too soon and arousing pressure from the ardent English Canadians who might demand public support for Britain. Despite the growing threat, King could not convince his cabinet to buy many new aircraft or even let the Royal Canadian Air Force (RCAF) engage in joint training with the Royal Air Force (RAF), whose senior officers watched on, perplexed as to the Canadians' intentions.[14] And so he left Britain twisting in the wind.

The Imperials could not imagine that Canada would not stand by them in a major European conflict, but King's double-talk was worrisome, especially after he had refused to commit to a statement of unified defence at a Commonwealth conference in 1937. Even in the early part of the war, the British were unsure about relying on King, with one diplomatic report describing him as a "very complex character" who could not be entirely trusted.[15] Complex, yes; but so was the country, especially with its regional and linguistic cleavages. The trade-off between those interests always influenced King's political decisions. With such divisions in Canada, perhaps King's ambivalent, fretful, and compromising ways can be better understood by later generations who have the gift of knowing how history would unfold.

———

Canada remained a twilight nation in a darkening world, sensing that American influence was fully emerging just as Britain's might was waning. The country's strategic place in the Commonwealth as the senior dominion was offset by the necessity of navigating a shared North America. Though Canada had almost no contact with Mexico, it was the smaller and poorer nation in relation to the US, and its economy and culture were entangled with the Americans'. Immigration to the US had been depleting the Canadian population for decades, and the 1930 American census calculated that 1.3 million Americans were Canadian-born, behind only Germans and Italians as identifiable groups.[16] Along the immense, largely undefended border, security issues had not disturbed the free flow of tourists or immigrants, although both nations had dusty invasion plans at the ready.

Throughout the 1920s, the Canadian staff officer Colonel J. Sutherland Brown had studied American geography, taking clandestine tours to the US and buying postcards to guide his strategy for how, if war was declared, the armed forces would spring forward to invade southward across the border. These mobile columns of troops would snatch key American communities and then retreat back to Canada as time was bought for the British to send their navy to bombard US cities along the east coast.[17] Brown's Defence Scheme No. 1 verged on the ludicrous, not least for its directing of non-existent flying columns of cavalry and armoured vehicles to take the attack to the Yanks, but it was the role of professional soldiers to prepare for the worst-case scenario.

The US had a similar strategy for the invasion of Canada as part of its Plan Red, aimed at defeating the British Empire. The northern country's vast geography would be used against the Dominion. US forces would capture Halifax to deny a safe port to the Royal Navy, which it would drown in poison gas. It would also cut off east and west Canada by occupying Winnipeg. Other key cities in the east, such as Niagara Falls and Montreal, and in the west, such as Vancouver and Victoria, would all fall to American soldiers.[18] The invading force would finish off Canada by ultimately taking control of the shared Great Lakes and marching hard on Ottawa, the capital that was only 200 kilometres from the border. The plan was considered active until 1937.

In time, the two North American nations shelved their invasion plans, aware that there were far more likely enemies to face, although there remained a worrisome legacy of these machinations that sometimes revealed itself in public debate. For instance, at a 1935 congressional committee hearing about the defence of North America, several US officers testified to the likelihood of operations against Canada involving the bombing of its cities to deny safe haven to a hostile nation should one invade the Dominion to use it as a base from which to attack the republic.[19] In the aftermath of the public admission, Roosevelt publicly rebuked the irresponsible talk, and apologies were forced from the service personnel. Canadians took note, especially King, who was increasingly pressured by the president to augment defences on the east and west coast in the second half of the decade.[20] While a US invasion was highly unlikely, if Canada could not defend itself against Japan or Germany—the two nations most likely to attack the Northern Dominion—it would be subject to a liberation by force. For several years, the president had been apprised by his senior commanders of Canada's overall weak fortifications, ill-equipped forces, and scarecrow-thin numbers in the rank and file. In an ever-darkening world—with Italy at war in Abyssinia from 1936, Japan engaged in all-out warfighting in China from 1937, and Hitler threatening

Austria and Czechoslovakia in 1938—North America had to become a jointly defended fortress.

Canada's military was deeply entwined with the British through blood, tradition, history, and shared training and doctrine. Many of the senior Canadian officers had been trained at the Imperial Defence College, while almost all the senior naval officers had served on Royal Navy warships and RCAF officers had fought in the RAF in the last war.[21] Armed with British equipment and weapons, the Canadian forces prepared to march into battle alongside British units. Almost no military interaction with the Americans had occurred in the 1930s, even though Roosevelt's prodding of King, from the first to almost the last of their eighteen meetings over the course of his presidency, forced the Canadians to think more about the structures necessary to support interoperability. From late 1937, the US minister to Ottawa, Norman Armour, worked with several members of the Canadian defence establishment, including Colonel Harry Crerar, a talented Great War gunner who was on the rise in the small Canadian army. In fact, as Crerar was later to report, one American diplomat—likely Armour—confessed to him that "owing to the absence of any technical military advisors at the U.S. Legation and the consequent lack of any expert assistance in the interpretation of Canadian defence policies," the US was in the dark about how Canada might respond in a time of war.[22]

With the assistance of Armour, Colonel Crerar planned a three-day secret meeting between the countries' two chiefs of staff in Washington from January 19 to 20, 1938, with the hope of strengthening relations. As the colonel noted in one report, "our direct military contacts with the Departments in Washington were non-existant [sic], and . . . a greater interchange of ideas on military problems of mutual importance would be to joint advantage."[23] Prime Minister King had embraced closer union through trade, but in that Kingian way he had refused to commit to any sort of defence pact. King remarked in early 1938 that looking to the "US to save us" would come with worrisome commitments and fearsome obligations.[24] As always, he preferred room to manoeuvre and leave others guessing as to his real intentions. But the military had a duty to focus on continental defence, and so Major-General E.C. Ashton, Canada's chief of the general staff, sneaked out of Ottawa, to be joined later by the chief of the naval staff, Commodore Percy Nelles. The cloak-and-dagger movements revealed the Canadian cabinet's twitchiness over any sort of visible planning that would raise hackles in French Canada and with antiwar groups, as well as with the political and military leaders in London.[25]

The British concentration of governing offices and civil servants in London, known by the all-encompassing term "Whitehall," need not have worried. Little was accomplished at the Washington meeting, and initially there was much confusion on the part of General Malin Craig, the chief of staff of the United States Army, who had not been adequately briefed. Why, he wondered, were the Canadians here? When alerted to the aim of talking about continental defence, he was most interested in how the nations would jointly defend the Strait of Juan de Fuca, the west coast waterway that forms the national boundary between Canada and the United States. No doubt he was guided by the worry Roosevelt expressed on his visit to the area a few months earlier, when the president had been dismayed at the pathetic defences.[26] The senior American general also floated the idea, which had already been championed by Roosevelt, that the US would be willing to take over the defence of British Columbia to create a unified front from Washington State to Alaska should Japan ever attack that section of the west coast. General Ashton politely declined.[27] The Americans did not press the issue—which must have appeared farcical even to them given their own weak military and the notion that a sovereign nation would allow such an infringement—but the Canadians left with a better sense of the US's concerns about the northern frontier.

———

In that late summer of 1938, King was uneasy with the implications of Roosevelt's Kingston speech, and he felt compelled to publicly respond, especially with papers like the *Ottawa Citizen* writing that "the assurance of aid from the United States did not relieve Canada of the duty of defending itself."[28] King's closest adviser, Oscar Skelton, provided the prime minister with the words to convey that Canada welcomed closer relations with the US, even though it had its own responsibility to strengthen its defensive capabilities. On July 20 in Woodbridge, Ontario, two days after the president's Kingston speech, King avowed, "We, too, have our obligations as a good friendly neighbour, and one of these is to see that, at our own instance our country is made as immune from attack or possible invasion as we can reasonably be expected to make it."[29] Canada must not, through weakness, invite invasion from a stronger power that would then use the country as a base to attack the United States. "Good neighbor on one side; partners within the Empire on the other," declared King, positioning Canada between the US and Britain. "Obligations to both in return for their assistance. Readiness to meet all joint emergencies."[30] King remained wary of being painted as a warmonger, although he could no longer ignore the country's withered armed forces. Citing the need to protect Canada against potential marauders was one way to justify reinforcing the armed forces, and King had been speaking publicly since early 1937 about "the defence of our shores and the preservation of our neutrality—these are the two cardinal principles of our policy."[31] King abhorred war and was wary of the passions it unleashed, but he was among the most warlike in his cabinet; as he noted in his diary, he counselled his ministers that "we owed it to our country to protect it in a mad world, at least to the extent of police service, both on sea and in the air, alike on the Atlantic and Pacific coasts. . . . It was humiliating to accept protection from Britain without sharing on the

TWO KINDS OF FRONTIERS

"Two Kinds of Frontiers," reads this 1938 Globe and Mail *cartoon that contrasts the positive relationship between King and Roosevelt with the angry, armed borders of "any European frontier."*

costs, or to rely on the United States without being willing to at least protect our neutrality."[32]

Creating the capacity for an expeditionary force was too unpalatable for King and his cabinet, given their preoccupation with Quebec and the recent memory of the abattoir of the Western Front, but the navy could be sold to Canadians and Americans as the means to defend the coasts. The Royal Canadian Navy was commanded by Commodore Percy Nelles, who had been able to win the bureaucratic battles for limited budgets. Six modern River class destroyers had been laid down in Britain and were ready for service by the start of the war, to be joined by four coal-fired minesweepers that were smaller but also effective in multi-purpose use close to shore. These warships had come as the defence budget gradually increased: however, it was only $34.7 million in 1938–1939, less than what the government paid in pensions and medical care for disabled Great War veterans.[33] Frank Scott, an astute commentator on Canadian politics in the late 1930s, observed that King's approach to preparing for war was summed up in the phrase "postpone the evil day."[34] Delaying and dithering had worked well for King, but now that evil day was poised to arrive, and the nation could not simply materialize warships, fighters, tanks, and infantry divisions.

"Canada is the most secure of all countries," said King publicly in 1938, even as he privately noted in his diary in November that "our defence was wholly inadequate and ineffective."[35] Being a great distance from the fascists helped, with geography serving as Canada's greatest shield, but now there was likely no escaping war. What would Canada do if Britain was attacked? Despite King's misgivings, the desire of key civil servants like Skelton to sit out the fighting, and a cabinet that ached to avoid spending on defence, King knew he must lead Canada to stand by the mother country. Guiding King's thinking was the belief, as expressed in his diary in September 1938, that if Britain was defeated, "the only future left for Canada would be absorption by the U.S."[36] This was naked self interest: Canada had to stand by Britain to survive in North America alongside the US. And so he and his closest advisers worked towards a plan predicated on Canada's limited engagement in the future war, with the country preferably sending food and munitions to Britain rather than infantry battalions for the meatgrinder of combat. While those peacetime plans would not survive contact with later enemy victories, King's willingness to spend more on the military from 1937 onward was born of his belief in Canada's existential need to assist Britain in a full-scale war with Germany, to appease the US that warily watched the Dominion's weak defences, and to avoid the evil fate of being absorbed into the republic if Britain should fall. "Canada would become part of America," wrote King in his diary in January 1939, if it could not defend itself.[37]

———

It was no surprise to anyone when war exploded in September 1939. There was no slithering to Armageddon, as the failure of diplomacy in July 1914 had been described; no, Hitler had steadily menaced his neighbours with the ultimate goal of a European war. He orchestrated the annexation of Austria in March 1938, strengthening Germany's industrial base and further emboldening him when the West could muster only words in defence. After these Nazi victories, the democracies came to know that Hitler responded only to force. Many in Britain and France sympathized with the

Jews in Germany, who had been stripped of rights and hounded from jobs, businesses, and homes with the Nazi rise to power, but there was little to be done other than watch grimly, angry and unsure, as the nations' leaders sought any diplomatic solution short of war. While France rearmed in fear and looked for allies, Britain was unsure about Canada's commitment to backing them with force, and concerned about the US public call for neutrality, all of which had weakened the hand of British prime minister Neville Chamberlain in dealing with Germany.

After another show of German force, Chamberlain went to Munich in September 1938, emerging from talks with Hitler with a peace deal in hand. Though the cost was the sacrifice of German-speaking Sudetenland in Czechoslovakia to be annexed as part of the Reich, the deal guaranteed the rest of Czechoslovakia's independence. The apparently successful diplomatic trade-off was greeted with widespread acclaim, marking Chamberlain as a statesman who had found an alternative to war. Only a few lone voices objected, like British parliamentarian Winston Churchill, who, for warning that Hitler would not stop at annexing only part of the country, was widely derided as a militarist. From his seat in Canada, far from the threat, King was a vigorous appeaser, and Roosevelt, in fending off isolationists who demanded no American involvement, was no different.[38]

Though supportive of Britain and France in their stand against fascism, the Canadian prime minister and American president continued to cloak their true intentions. They had long learned the power of listening and seeming to agree with whomever was speaking with them, even if they then embraced contradictory actions. Roosevelt was accused of improvisation and an absence of guiding political ideals, but he was also an acknowledged charmer with boundless optimism. Describing his skill as an opportunist, the president noted, "I am a juggler, and I never let my right hand know what my left hand does."[39] King was adept at a similar sort of complex sleight of hand, being often willing to suffer tactical defeats to achieve strategic victories. Both leaders usually knew the end goal and understood there were many paths that could be travelled to arrive there. In the case of Hitler and his aggression, they deplored it; but they understood that another world war was nearly unthinkable to their people who were safe in North America from the gathering danger. In the aftermath of Munich, the president wrote to King in support of the British Commonwealth, declaring, "We in the United States rejoice with you, and the world at large, that the outbreak of war was averted."[40] King was ebullient about the peace purchased through appeasement; he was also pleased that Roosevelt had written to him, leader to leader.

Hitler had won again in the war of wills, and he drew the conclusion that the Western democracies were anemic and irresolute. Continuing to plot for war, which had been his goal since the fall of 1938, he sought to strike when Britain, France, Belgium, and the rest of Western Europe were unready.[41] After a brief pause, the Führer continued with his masterplan, breaking his promise as he seized the rest of Czechoslovakia in March 1939, crushing the opposition, and taunting the democracies as they helplessly watched on. While Chamberlain has gone down in history as the weak man who handed Hitler parts of other countries to appease him, he had at least secured from the German dictator a promise that he soon broke. Now the world saw Hitler for the untrustworthy warmonger that he was. Canadians were no less shocked. "A cautious foreign policy for Canada reflected the feelings of the majority of the Canadian people," recounted diplomat Lester

B. Pearson, "at least until the Nazi aggression against Czecho-slovakia."[42] King and his cabinet reeled from the invasion in March 1939, with the prime minister concluding that a world-wide war was Hitler's endgame.

The long signalled and greatly feared war came on September 1, 1939, after Hitler's diplomats forged a non-aggression pact on August 23 with Stalin's Soviet Union. It was a match made in Hell—or at least a devious diplomatic coup by two devils who put aside their ideological differences to achieve their aims. Hitler's lifelong hatred of communism was only temporarily diminished in the name of making way for the invasion of Poland on September 1. In the deal, Stalin sought time to strengthen his armed forces that he had gutted after murdering most of his senior generals. The German senior military command, long having lost its inde-pendence from the Nazi Party and being a wilful accomplice to Hitler's militaristic obsession, had prepared their fighting forces for the coming battle. That Paris and London had guaranteed Poland's security, promising war with Germany if it attacked, caused little concern to Hitler, who assumed that the West would again capitulate. It did not, although the democracies despaired as the Nazis let loose carnage.

———

In Ottawa, far from the fighting, King still believed that peace might be achieved, and he was even willing to sacrifice Poland in another act of appeasement, thinking that it might finally lead to Hitler reversing his warlike ways. For reassurance, King turned to the spirit world. A table-rapping session on the night of September 2 led to a nameless spectre reassuring King that Hitler had been assassinated.[43] The prime minister went to bed relieved. The next day he found that not only did the Führer live, but that Britain would declare war on Germany. Spiritual intervention would not save King from the terrible choice now upon him. He hoped that Roosevelt's promise in Kingston a year earlier meant that Canada and the United States would stride together into the war, to stand up for democratic ideals and to defend North America against the fascists.

CHAPTER 2

FACING THE NAZIS WITHOUT THE US

"It is what we prevent, rather than what we do that counts most in Government," wrote Prime Minister William Lyon Mackenzie King, expressing a consistent political belief—almost a mantra—that steered him throughout his long career.[1] It was, perhaps, an unheroic political principle, but in a divided country like Canada it had served him well. However, this changed after Germany's invasion of Poland on September 1, when Britain and France soon declared war, aware that there could be no more concessions to Hitler. In a period of fear and uncertainty, King would now be called upon to guide the nation forward: choices had to be made.

Canada was not automatically in the fight as it was during the Great War. After two decades of reforms, precedents, and national growth, it would be up to Parliament to decide this time. Except, of course, that Canada would almost certainly enter the war to stand by Britain due to its place as a dominion within the Commonwealth. While the North American nation was physically safe for the time being, King, his ministers, and many in Canada believed that national interests beyond the need to support Britain were at stake, as most could see that the Nazis were a scourge. At the same time, in this complex interplay of motivations, if Britain was defeated then Canada's world would be burned to the ground.

In such an apocalyptic scenario, King predicted that, to survive, Canada would be forced into a union with the US that would ultimately lead to the Dominion's assimilation. All of this and more motivated the government and Canadians to go to war, but King would have to find a way to balance interests within the country while supporting Britain. He understood that the only way to do this was with the aid of the United States in defending North America.

———

King's long-time public policy of refusing to commit to Imperial defence and of letting Parliament decide would now be tested, even as he was now firmly in support of Britain's just cause.[2] As far back as 1923, he had proclaimed that "if a great and clear call of duty came, Canada will respond, whether or no the United States responds."[3] The qualifier for King was that it had to be a major war and not an Imperial colonial adventure; his thinking had not changed in the intervening decade and a half, and now the Nazis were a threat that, without question, demanded a great and clear call of duty. The second qualifier—that Canada would support Britain even if the US did not—was perhaps a revelation to many who had listened to King's practised caution, though in fact he had believed most of his political life that a major war in Europe would require such an act. While King accepted these realities, he always argued that domestic tranquility had to trump overseas military exertion. Almost one third of the country's population was French-speaking and only loosely aligned with Britain. They had to be won over to the war effort. For without Quebec onside, the country's potential support and the full weight of

Canada's military forces (albeit a meagre heft in 1939) could never be offered to Britain.

Convincing Quebec to accept the just war that had to be embarked upon fell to the Liberal senior cabinet minister from Quebec, Ernest Lapointe. He was a bear of a man and a forceful speaker who had stood by King since the early 1920s. The prime minister, who spoke little French, had given Lapointe tremendous leeway in setting the Quebec agenda. Lapointe was joined by Great War veteran Charles "Chubby" Power, a French Canadian with Irish origins who had been wounded overseas and returned home as an ardent opponent of conscription. Well liked in the House of Commons, Chubby was known as a gregarious dealmaker and a bagman from the riding of Quebec South. He would also disappear for days on bibulous binges. Driven by a rigid moral code, King worried about Chubby, clucking like a disapproving aunt, but he had a soft spot for his wayward minister. He also needed his status as a decorated soldier of the last war. King had been condemned for shirking his duty in that great struggle because he had not served in uniform. Even worse, he had gone off to the US to be a successful labour negotiator. During heated times of conflict and when there were calls to support Britain, King was occasionally attacked in the House of Commons for not fighting in the trenches. The spectre of that war haunted him and the country, with conscription as a manifestation of how war could incubate extremes and release uncontrollable passions.[4]

King had long said that Parliament would determine whether Canada would go to war at Britain's side. Now, in this precarious time of crisis, he called what was known as a Special War Session for September 7—a day that the mystically inclined prime minister felt was lucky. Even before this, the Defence of Canada Regulations had been implemented on September 3, which gave the state authority to detain and arrest individuals, curtail free speech, and ban political organizations such as the Communist Party of Canada. And a week before that, the Royal Canadian Navy (RCN) had gone to sea. It had only ten warships and around 3,000 sailors, although its personnel would expand more than thirty-fold, ending the war with the fourth-largest navy in the world. However, in 1939, the navy was like all the service arms, and indeed the country: it was unprepared for the coming battle against the Nazis.

With Britain having declared war on Germany at 11 a.m. on Sunday, September 3, thousands of British citizens were seeking to escape the war zone in Europe. SS *Athenia*, a 13,581-ton ocean liner, was en route from Glasgow to Montreal. Captain James Cook was aware of the dire situation, but he took some solace in the fact that the ocean liner was steaming away from potential danger. At 7:40 p.m., just as the evening meal was being served, a torpedo from a German submarine crashed into the engine room. After the explosion, the ship's interior was plunged into darkness as pungent, acrid smoke was cut through with the screams of British, Canadian, and American passengers. The war had moved from Europe to the Atlantic, although this was no surprise as the German U-boats of the previous war had sunk several thousand ships in an attempt to cut the lifeline from North America to Britain.

More than 1,400 crew and passengers, including many trapped deep in the bowels of the ship, struggled to find their way out of the steel coffin. Despite their terrifying journey upwards, most made it into the 26 lifeboats. *Athenia*'s death was a slow one, and it was not until 11 a.m. on Monday the 4th that it sank stern first into the depths. When the survivors were finally counted, it was found that 112 people had died.[5] Both Canadians and Americans

The sinking of Athenia *aroused much anger in the West.*
Canadians hoped that the slaughter of civilians would bring
the US into the war. This photo shows a young survivor.

were among those who perished. In his diary, King was to write,
"I could not help but feel that this would bring home to Americans
the need for their intervention and that it was a terrible rebuke
to Roosevelt."[6]

———

President Franklin Roosevelt had spoken to the American people
on September 3 in one of his fireside chats, which had become the
preferred means of communicating White House messages, programs, and principles. On the day Britain and France went to war

with Germany, the president told Americans that he would keep the country neutral, in accordance with its laws and his own promise. "Let no man or woman thoughtlessly or falsely talk of America sending its armies to European fields," he said.[7] At the same time, the president added, "I do not ask you to be neutral in your heart," all but telling Americans where the moral authority lay in Hitler's wars of aggression. More than a few Canadians remembered the US staying out of the Great War until April 1917. American neutrality—or callousness to the cause of freedom as it was seen by many beyond the US—was a blow in Paris and London, where leaders shuddered at the profound unpreparedness of their nations. In Ottawa, King listened to Roosevelt on the radio with despair. As he noted in his diary, he experienced "an almost profound disgust. It was all words, words, words." America was the exceptional nation that had shown the world how democracy could guide a people to new heights, wealth, and ideals. And yet, King felt, in this time of crisis against fascism and wanton war on neighbouring countries, the US's mettle had been tested and found wanting. "I was really ashamed of the attitude of the U.S. Their word, at this moment, might have helped to save millions of lives . . . in the interests of humanity, justice, and life, and all that is dearest and the hearts of men."[8]

Echoing the prime minister, Canadian papers argued that the US could not remain neutral for much longer, especially in the aftermath of the barbaric assault on *Athenia* and the bloodshed in Poland. An editorial in the *Windsor Star*, the paper for the city across the border from Detroit, told its readers, "Give Hitler enough time and he will bring the United States into the conflict."[9] A few weeks later, the *Calgary Herald* noted that the *Washington Post* had predicted that "Canada's war declaration should intensify the drive to repeal the Neutrality Act because we cannot be indifferent to Canada's fate." The *Herald* wrote that even though the isolationists in Congress were a potent force—with the US having, several times in the late 1930s, renewed the Neutrality Act that limited involvement in future wars and denied the sale of weapons to belligerent nations—"judging by the overwhelming sentiment of American citizens in favor of the western democracies it seems fairly certain they will wage a losing battle."[10]

The president thought otherwise. "The country as a whole does not yet have any deep sense of the world crisis," Roosevelt mused in early September.[11] While Hitler was an odious dictator whom many Americans saw as a threat, such a feeling did not extend to going to war for the second time in as many generations, and the president certainly had a tighter grasp of prevailing sentiments in his country than optimistic Canadian papers could claim. In fact, around this time, only about 2.5 percent of Americans in one survey found that the United States should go to war, although about one in five agreed that the Allies should be aided with money and weapons.[12] Against this, at least half of Americans were strident about retaining neutrality, with no desire to send young soldiers off to fight and die on foreign battlefields. A mobilized peace movement, a desire to combat the Depression instead of Nazis, and the conviction that "Merchants of Death" and other arms dealers had tricked America into the Great War were all narratives underlying the strong sense of isolationism.[13] The death of 116,000 Doughboys in the last war was the starkest reminder of the cost to American families of the lawless ways of Europeans.[14] When the chief of staff of the US Army, General George Marshall, tried to raise the weak force from 175,000 to 200,000, the president blocked him, fearing it would provoke a political backlash.[15]

Brilliant, blunt, and a future titan of American military expansion, Marshall was new to the position (having replaced General Malin Craig) and would soon become a trusted adviser, but Roosevelt sensed that, in the prevailing antiwar climate, a rearming could be achieved only gradually, and only by, in his words, "defending this hemisphere."[16]

In the nation's capital, King bit back his disappointment over American neutrality when Secretary of State Cordell Hull called on September 5, asking about Canada's status. Was Canada at war?[17] A former senator and long-time member of the House of Representatives, Hull was an institution in Washington, respected and admired for his knowledge and experience. "The judge," as he was sometimes called, had paid far more attention to Latin America than to Canada in the late 1930s, stimulating investment in Mexico and Caribbean nations in what was known as the "Good Neighbor Policy." A key goal had been to keep Germany and other European nations from wielding influence in the western hemisphere.[18] Canada was stable, democratic, and connected through trade, and Hull had taken the northern neighbour for granted. But now Canada was on the verge of war—or perhaps already at war, as Hull and Roosevelt were unclear about the Dominion's status within the British Commonwealth. American neutrality laws forbade selling weapons to countries at war for fear that this might drag the US into the conflict. During a peculiar phone call, King explained to Hull and the president that Canada was an independent nation that would decide its own destiny. For the moment, it was not at war. Roosevelt whooped with excitement and urged his political and military leaders to support the Canadians. They did, especially in the rush sale of some much-needed sixty-five warplanes that were flown to the border and then dragged across the 49th parallel. The sneaky and supportive act was a small sign that the Americans, although neutral, would not "stand idly by" when Canada needed them. It was also a worrying indication that Roosevelt and his inner circle did not know much about the dominion on which it would rely to defend North America.

———

From September 7 onward, the debates in the Canadian House of Commons were fiercely in favour of going to war at Britain's side. Aware of the deep concern in many Quebec ridings that another war would lead to the invocation of conscription again, Minister Lapointe gave a masterful speech promising there would be no conscription of young men against their will.[19] He and his fellow Quebec cabinet ministers were the bulwark against such a dark policy, he roared in a long Church-revival-like oration, with his arms gesticulating and sweat flowing. The opposition was silenced in the face of widespread support for backing Britain, although Maxime Raymond, a Liberal MP from Quebec who broke with the party during the debates, argued on September 9 against war, using the Americans as an example of another way to proceed. "Why should we not remain neutral? We would thus take the same course that was taken by the United States, our neighbour, a country of America like our own, whose interests are about similar to ours and which has adopted a policy of neutrality. Can it be that the United States are wrong in remaining neutral?"[20] His words failed to land: Canada was not the US, and its ties to Britain were as tight as coiled steel.

The nation on the edge of war hoped that the long-serving prime minister would provide clarity and inspiration. He failed on both counts. During the debates, King was at his worst, rambling on for four hours, failing to rise to the moment, appearing uninspiring and limp. While King's speech was one of cut corners, wandering remarks, and obscured meanings, behind the scenes he had mobilized his caucus and the country, and he also understood the difference between this war and the last. "The balance of world power has shifted, and Canada has to keep its Pacific as well as its Atlantic coast in mind," said King. "From both the military and the economic aspect, the attitude of the United States would be immensely more important for the world and for us, than twenty years ago."[21] King knew the Dominion had to support Britain, and yet he hoped to do it from North American shores, and with firm agreements with the US on how to protect the hemisphere. No aid could be given to Britain without a secure hemisphere, and achieving that security demanded closer ties with the US.

When Canada declared war on September 10, a week after Britain and with the people's representatives in Parliament deciding, King was lauded for having brought the country into the struggle united.[22] His lame speech of a few days earlier was forgotten, and the isolationists were silenced. Canada would stand by Britain and France as they faced the Nazis, and there would be no conscription. Two burning questions remained: when would the Americans come into the fight with the Western Allies, and what would happen if Canada was attacked while the US was neutral? For the moment, in northern North America, one country was at war and one remained at peace.

———

Germany was in the process of annihilating the state of Poland, having been assisted by the Soviet Union since September 17 as the Red Army pounced to feast on their hated neighbour. Despite Germany's exposed flank, Britain and France failed to launch an offensive against its western front. Instead, without the support of North American troops, the Anglo-French armed forces dug in and waited to fight a defensive battle. Poland was overwhelmed in a matter of weeks, with its military losses at about 200,000 killed and wounded, and thousands of civilians slain in direct aerial attacks or as the armies swept forward over their communities. Soon afterwards came the systematic slaughter by the Germans and Russians of countless politicians, officers, intellectuals, Jews, and those who might help Poland survive the vicious occupation.

After Germany and Russia's victory in the first week in October, there was a period of relative stability in the West. The name "Phony War," by which it was sometimes called, suggested armies holed up in trenches with little fighting, although there was much activity, planning, and preparation for the coming clash. Safe across the Atlantic, Canadian political leaders began to crash-build a military force, hoping to make up for years of apathy. That the armed forces were entirely unprepared for battle did not stop tens of thousands of Canadians from flocking to the colours, enlisting in the army, navy, and air force. What motivated them to serve? There was little naivete regarding what they would face, as the last war's horrors were well known. One official report observed a "complete absence of jingoism or war excitement. Men volunteering doing so with full realization of their responsibility."[23] While some were driven to the uniform after years of unemployment or partial work, and others sought adventure or a way to live up to the ideals of fathers and uncles, many indeed believed in the cause of stopping the Nazis.

King initially had no grand vision for the Canadian war effort, other than a desire to avoid an unlimited contribution to the overseas war like that which raged from 1914 to 1918, with its assault on national unity. If the dogs of war were unleashed, he feared they would rouse the sleeping political dogs that he had soothed through years of deliberate compromise and careful inaction. And yet English Canada pressured him to send units across the Atlantic. King and his ministers could not hold the line. They ordered an infantry division overseas under the command of the charismatic Andrew McNaughton, a Great War artillery innovator and chief of the general staff in the early 1930s. The cabinet hoped the token force was enough. Canada could best aid the war effort, thought King's cabinet, not by feeding soldiers into the maw of war but by sending food, minerals, and munitions from a protected North America.

As the King government tried to manage the expectations of English Canada by rearming, while simultaneously trying not to panic Quebec, all could agree on the need for home defence. Strengthened coastal gun batteries, protective nets to keep out U-boats from vulnerable harbours, and garrison forces hastily armed were just some of the new precautions that would be essential in protecting the realm. A robust navy would be different than in the last war. While the Canadian Corps had emerged as the country's primary fighting force, led by Canadian-born Lieutenant-General Sir Arthur Currie and delivering victories at Vimy, Hill 70, Passchendaele, and during the Hundred Days campaign, the navy had done little that resonated with Canadians. In the early 1920s, the Royal Canadian Navy had barely survived being dismantled

*Canadian infantrymen of the 1st Division leaving from
Halifax, Nova Scotia, in December 1939 to defend Britain.*

as a service, and, like the rest of the Canadian military, it had survived on a threadbare budget during the Depression. But in the late 1930s the King government was able to sell to Canadians a program of building new destroyers to safeguard the country and live up to its obligations to the United States.

The sinking of *Athenia* revealed the defencelessness of vessels on the open waters, and destroyers began defensive patrols off the east coast. The RCN's high command had worked closely with the Royal Navy before the war, with most senior officers having been trained on Imperial vessels. Within two weeks of the invasion of Poland, beginning on September 16, RCN ships were protecting the grouped merchant vessels travelling in convoys. Leaving from Halifax, Nova Scotia, Canada's primary port and naval base on the east coast, the convoys would fulfill the key protective role of the navy. "There was no 'phoney war' for the navy," said one

Canadian sailor.[24] The lifeline to Britain—the logistical supply of men, war machines, weapons, food, fuel, and everything else—had to be preserved at all costs.

———

One of Canada's most significant contributions to Allied victory would be its training of future airmen. The country had a distinguished reputation for producing air warriors during the last war, when 22,000 Canadians had served in the British flying services. Those who survived the crushing losses in the air often returned home as heroes, although the Royal Canadian Air Force was not established until 1924. In the interwar years, military theorists predicted that airpower, in the form of bomb-dropping and chemical warfare–spraying aircraft, might end wars without the need for ground forces to chew each other up in attritional battles. In Britain, new radar stations had been erected in the hope of providing advance warning of the city-killers in the form of aerial armadas. Even so, there was much concern that the enemy bombers would break through to kill innocents from great heights.

British prime minister Neville Chamberlain personally appealed to King in late September 1939 to establish a massive air training plan, writing that a new legion of airmen was needed to meet Germany's overwhelming air superiority. The plan would produce aviators to serve on the new North American–produced aircraft and "might well have a psychological effect on the Germans equal to that produced by the intervention of the United States in the last war."[25] If Canada's part in the air campaign could be compared to the role of the US in the Great War, that appealed to King, as did the likelihood that a focus on the air war would dampen demands for conscription.

As part of the negotiations, the British sent over Lord Riverdale, a rough industrialist from Sheffield who seemed intent on browbeating the Canadians into submission. King disliked him from the start. He had every reason to, since Riverdale began dictating orders to the Canadians, assuming the "colonials" would jump at his command. The cost of this enormous plan, which would see the creation of dozens of new training centres and several hundred bases and airfields, was estimated at over $1 billion. Though the Canadians were inclined to help, this was several times the prewar federal budget, and King and his minister of finance, James Layton Ralston, were cautious guardians of the treasury.[26] Fiscal conservativism seemed an odd way to fight what would become a total war, but Canada was welded to its limited effort.[27] One of Ralston's worries was about the need to purchase aircraft and parts from the Americans, which would strain the balance of payments as too many Canadian dollars moved south and the US bought far less in return.

While King could work with rivals and enemies, his dislike of Riverdale made him obstinate: he was generally disagreeable in his company, and even misremembered his name in public addresses. King also felt that the British might use the crisis of the war to try to re-exert power over the Dominion. Betraying his anger at being taken for granted, King wrote that "these people . . . from the Old Country . . . seem to think that all they have to do is to tell us what is to be done."[28] The negotiations continued, and at one point a frustrated King, feeling he had already done enough for Britain with the 1st Division preparing to go overseas and the

Royal Canadian Navy engaging in convoy duties, raged that he would not pay for the entire plan because "this is not our war."[29] But it was Canada's war, and although King knew it, he had lost his temper and was perhaps showing his disdain for the British delegation. He was also practising hard negotiating tactics, which he was experienced at both in and out of politics. The Imperials were aghast and shaken, but the Canadians had signalled they would not be treated as colonials, even though they firmly supported the British-led war effort.

A deal was finally reached in mid-December and signed on King's sixty-fifth birthday, with the Canadians leveraging the agreement to ensure British pledges to purchase wheat and place war industry orders.[30] A key Canadian contribution to the Allied war effort, the British Commonwealth Air Training Plan (BCATP) trained 131,500 airmen and revealed the North American dominion to be a major leader in a multinational endeavour.[31] The Americans took note of the BCATP and realized that Canada had taken on a huge commitment, which included, over time, paying for most of the enormously expensive program. Roosevelt would flatter his neighbour with praise over its role, and he was not wrong in calling Canada the "Aerodrome of Democracy."[32]

———

As prime minister, King was the country's undisputed leader, but this did not make him de facto commander-in-chief of the Canadian military. The governor general was the symbolic commander of the Canadian military, while the minister of national defence was responsible to the cabinet and the Crown. In reality, though, the entire cabinet, led by King, shaped domestic military decisions, and it consisted of about two dozen ministers. Some were very able, others were worn out, and several were there only because they represented a region of the country or a religious group. Such was the case of cabinets before and since, and so on December 5, 1939, King established a smaller group of confidants. The Cabinet War Committee initially consisted of King (as both prime minister and his own secretary of state for external affairs), Ralston in Finance, Norman Rogers in National Defence, and a few others who would more closely direct the war. Aided by military advisers and senior civil servants, this select group of ministers hammered out most of the key decisions in long discussions, and as King was able to guide the ministers forward, they were rarely at each other's throats.[33]

King was also ably supported by a very capable public service. The most influential mandarin was Oscar Skelton, under-secretary of state for external affairs. Skelton was at the forefront in advising against sending a large expeditionary force, and, as war loomed, he advocated in an August 24, 1939, policy document that Canada should focus on providing economic support and boosting munitions production, along with protecting North America. The cabinet agreed with Skelton's assessment, and they took seriously his warning—the same one the generals had been offering for several years—that the Americans had to be reassured that Canada could defend itself against an invading force or they would likely occupy the Dominion and trample its sovereignty as they sought to drive out invaders.[34] Canada, Skelton argued, also needed to have "closer touch with Washington" and could not "ignore the Pacific" as it had done in the last war.[35] There was, for example, no alliance

TRYING TO PLEASE BOTH

*Prime Minister King is caught between the demands of the nationalists
and the imperialists in setting Canada's foreign policy and war aims
in this cartoon. Here, he is accused of "Trying to please both," with
little success. While leaders often struggle to please the electorate,
King was adept at walking between the extremes, whether through
compromise, careful measured movements, or obfuscation.*

with the US to defend their much-touted "undefended border,"
which was increasingly a concern to both nations, especially since
one was at war and one remained neutral.

The military was not absent from these discussions, but King
often tried to keep the senior officials at arm's length. He mis-
trusted the generals because he believed they would imperil

domestic unity by demanding more and more men for the armed forces. Yet he knew that they could not be ignored, and the prime minister and cabinet were much impressed by Colonel Harry Crerar, who had astutely warned before the war that Canada should tighten military relations with the United States to avoid the perception that "Whitehall was calling the tune." He noted further that when "Washington and London think alike we, in Canada, must think the same way, only more so."[36] Crerar was signalling the need to rearm effectively to placate the Americans and give Canada the capacity to assist Britain if it wished to do so. While Skelton and King would have preferred that a very limited force be sent overseas, strong public opinion in English Canada demanded that the navy, air force, and army fight beyond the country's borders. The plan for a limited engagement in the war was being increasingly tested by calls for greater commitment.

Having dextrously led a united Canada into the war, and having laid the foundations for an expanded Canadian armed force, the King government seemed well positioned for the looming election. But when appealing to the people, it always helps to have an enemy, and King had two high-profile political opponents in Quebec and Ontario. The most populous and influential province, Ontario, was led by the hawkish Premier Mitch Hepburn, who despised King. Despite being a Liberal, Hepburn was infuriated by King's tendency towards hesitation and waffling. One reporter noted that Hepburn accused King of surrounding himself with a cabinet of weak yes-men, save for Ralston—an experienced and respected battalion commander from the Great War, a veterans' advocate, and a former minister of national defence in the late 1920s. Hepburn lamented that King's "traditional policies of iner-tia, and of side-stepping every serious problem while he waits for the breaks will not work in wartime."[37] King, in turn, found the Ontario premier a boorish drinker and philanderer who rushed headlong into controversy. The two could rarely speak of each other without spewing invectives.

Almost from the start of the war, Hepburn publicly painted King as a feeble leader, a description that resonated with many in the hyper-charged war environment, especially Conservatives (and their papers) who sought a more formidable military effort. The scattershot verbal strikes came to a head in January 1940 when Hepburn stood in the Ontario legislature and condemned the prime minister for not having done his duty in the war effort: "never has and never will," he trembled with rage. It was too much for many of his Liberal provincial backbenchers, who nearly ran out of their seats in shock. The federal Liberals—King's party— could in fact point to their recent record of rearming and supporting Britain, especially with the Phony War continuing on the Western Front, but the internecine warfare between provincial and federal Liberals created a firestorm of debate.

Despite this ongoing friction, King liked his odds in an election framed around a measured response to the war overseas, especially given that Hepburn was a one-time populist who had lost much of his popularity. King also faced the electorate knowing that he had a strong foundation in Quebec, where he had bested his political enemy "Le Chef." Premier Maurice Duplessis had, since 1936, made a profitable political career out of being the foil to the Liberals in Ottawa, and in September 1939 he had gambled by calling a snap election. King's Quebec ministers, led by Lapointe and Power, had attacked Duplessis's Union Nationale relentlessly in the provincial election, and in an attempt to sway the electorate, they threatened to resign from cabinet if Duplessis won. Without the Liberal ministers in Ottawa, there would be no shield for Quebeckers against conscription. This was brass-knuckles politics from French-Canadian ministers who had learned their hard craft in the "cockpit of malodorous politics"—as one commentator described Ottawa. When the weak provincial Liberal Party in Quebec defeated Duplessis in October 1939, King and his ministers were strengthened at the federal level.[38]

With his French-Canadian power base, King also won the nation-wide March 1940 election in a landslide victory. The Conservatives had refused to embrace conscription, and, despite roaring rhetoric, they found few ways to distinguish themselves from King's party other than by advocating for a national unity party. The voters were not interested in that idea, which was similar to the platform of the Unionist Party that had run on conscription in 1917. King may have been a waffler, but the re-elected prime minister laid out where he stood in the fight against the Nazis: "If we do not destroy what is evil, it is going to destroy all that there is of good."[39]

———

As Canada prepared more vigorously for the inevitable clash of arms by raising new infantry units, training airmen, and aiding in convoy duties, Canadians continued to watch with dismay as the Americans remained neutral. Had Roosevelt's acclaimed speech in Kingston been for nought? Though King, having guided his country into the war united, now faced little opposition, his plan for Canada's limited engagement in the war would soon be spoiled by Hitler's victories. In the coming summer of despair, the Nazis were on the verge of snuffing out democracy in the West.

CHAPTER 3

A CATACLYSM

"There is of course no question about his sympathies," wrote Prime Minister King of President Roosevelt after a meeting in April 1940. "He and everyone around him are all strongly for the Allies."[1] On April 23, 1940, King joined the president at Warm Springs, Georgia, the therapeutic waters about 100 kilometres south of Atlanta. It was where the partially paralyzed Roosevelt had begun to make a recovery from polio in the early 1920s before returning to Washington. To this place of therapy, the president invited his friend, "Mackenzie," and it was another opportunity for the two leaders to talk and continue to pledge support. The hemispheric safety of North America would soon be challenged by German martial aggression.

———

The two leaders met in the aftermath of Germany's April 9 invasion of Denmark and Norway—a sophisticated combined-arms operation involving the German navy putting ashore soldiers and parachute forces that defeated the Nordic nations. These military operations shattered the complacency of the Phony War. After a plan to insert a Canadian formation in Norway was scrapped as being suicidal, the British and French watched, nearly helpless, as Denmark surrendered almost immediately and Norway fought on until June 10. The Western alliance reeled at another loss and continued to fortify their positions along the Western Front for the attack that they soon expected to confront.

Amid the crisis in Europe, the White House did not allow any reporters to speak to the Canadian prime minister for fear of what isolationists would make of the informal summit. Friendly newspapers in the US ran headlines that said the war was not discussed. Driven by different motives, journalists across the Dominion speculated about the United States supplying arms and munitions to the Western Allies.[2] The two-day meeting indeed had a focus on material support, although the discussions were interrupted by long swims, country drives, and lavish meals. During breaks in the tricky business of neutral America offering support to at-war Canada, the two leaders commiserated with one another about the fatigue of campaigning. The relationship had its boundaries, however, and King was lightly but forcefully rebuffed when he tried to convince Roosevelt to publicly state that he would enter the war if Britain and France were attacked by the German armed forces in a ground war. King felt that, for Britain's sake, he had to ask, even as he knew the president felt he could not yet face down the isolationists in his country. Seized by a pre-election fixation on North American security, the president continued to express his concern about Canada's inadequate defences on the east and west coasts, which King characterized in his diary as presenting "a real danger to the United States."[3]

Franklin and Mackenzie had become close over the years, a connection eased by the president's rare gift of making individuals feel uniquely important. King especially enjoyed the president's talent for brushing over minor issues, even as the Canadian fretted over his slip-ups in conversation or the ramification of refusing drinks when he was on one of his teetotalling crusades. They would develop a richer relationship in the coming months, paving the way for the good alliance that would be cemented by the catastrophe that was soon to be unleashed.

———

The twilight war on the Western Front came to a lightning-fast end when the Germans launched their blitzkrieg warfare on May 10, 1940. With more than half a year to prepare for the onslaught, the Western Allies deployed over a hundred infantry divisions for the expected assault on their trenches: dug-in forces would defend against limited infantry advances within the protective range of shellfire. To the Allies' surprise, however, German armoured formations plunged ahead, assisted by divebombing Stukas, driving relentlessly through the heavily wooded Ardennes forest. This steel spearhead cut deep, struck fast, and pushed ahead at a crushing pace, slicing like a rapier into vital organs. The vaunted Maginot Line of forts and gun emplacements was bypassed without a frontal assault, and the French garrisons collapsed or were left behind.[4] It was not a one-sided slaughter, as thousands of invading soldiers were killed, but the French morale wilted as commanders in the rear were left confused and blinded by the swift advance and the chaos that reigned. Retreats turned into routs.

The start of the war in the west was almost the end. Had the British not arranged for the miracle at Dunkirk—the evacuation at the end of May of 224,686 British and 129,942 French soldiers by a flotilla of brave ships that took the vulnerable off the beaches—

the Nazis might have achieved complete victory.[5] As it was, within a month, Hitler ruled most of Western Europe. France surrendered, and the invasion of Britain seemed imminent.

But the British people refused to buckle under the weight of their losses, and they were now led by the pugilistic wordsmith Winston Churchill. Neville Chamberlain had been forced out on May 10, having been judged the wrong man to lead the nation through the dark days ahead. The new leader was known for his long political career that stretched back decades, encompassing multiple political offices and frequent misadventures. Few would have predicted that he would emerge as the saviour of the Western world. A cigar-chewing and heavy-set aristocrat who was always short of money, Churchill was given to bouts of depression even as he was able to lift the spirits of millions with oratorical brilliance. Like King in Canada, he was a complex man to say the least. And yet he was indomitable. His courage was tested when, during his first six weeks as war leader, he oversaw one of the greatest disasters in British history as the ruined army fled France. Undeterred and unbowed, Churchill faced the enemy defiantly, even as doomsayers in his new cabinet pressed him to surrender. Scrambling for options, Churchill bought time, pleading, cajoling, and praying for a victory. Nor was he certain about the backing of King in Ottawa or Roosevelt in Washington.

The Canadian prime minister did not like his British counterpart, who he believed was a dangerous swashbuckler because of his imperialist ideology and his warmongering calls for rearmament in the late 1930s.[6] King also worried that, just as Churchill had unseated Chamberlain, the steady, stoic, and reliable Great War veteran J.L. Ralston, who was admired by the military, might dethrone him. It was a misplaced fear. Ralston was loyal and he had no support in French Canada or influential allies in the party who were willing to plot King's ouster. In fact, in the dark days of 1940, Ralston felt King was the right man to lead the nation, telling journalist Grant Dexter, who was close to the Liberal elite, that King had no defeat in him and that his friendship with Roosevelt was an asset.[7] King also knew how to use talent. Ralston had been cautious as minister of finance, keeping funds ready for what he expected would be a "long grinding economic struggle," but he was promoted to a more crucial role when Canada's minister of national defence, Norman Rogers, died in an aircraft accident on June 10.[8] King made the widely esteemed Ralston responsible for the expansion of the armed forces; in this role, he was less guarded and was eventually unable to control the senior brass, who planned a large and multi-service expeditionary force to fight around the world. His finance role was taken over by J.L. Ilsley, who, though a dour and quiet Nova Scotian, was a good man for channelling the innovative work of gifted civil servants. The prime minister was safe for the moment because of the massive electoral win that made it difficult for usurpers to shuffle him off to the Senate, the place where political careers went to die.

Canada's war fundamentally changed with France's collapse. Before this cataclysm, the Dominion was engaged in a relatively restricted effort. Now Canadians understood that they faced a total war environment, with the very survival of the British Commonwealth at stake. A new infantry division of around 20,000 soldiers was raised and ordered to be equipped on May 17 to send overseas, along with the RCAF's only modern fighter squadron. In the face of the shocking German victories, on May 23 the RCN also sent its four best destroyers across the Atlantic to fight alongside the Royal Navy in British waters. By early June, HMCS

OUR JOB NOW

*An optimistic July 1940 cartoon by Les Callan, who later served
overseas, about the Allied war effort. The fresh-faced worker, "Canada,"
is seen rolling up his sleeves to pick up the load after France's defeat.
The youthful Canada will stand with the older Britain against
their shared enemy. The US is nowhere to be seen.*

Restigouche and HMCS *St. Laurent* were off the French coast
assisting in evacuating Imperial soldiers and assaulting German
field batteries. Canada's limited war was thus buried in the same
mass grave of French pride, freedom, and dreams.

Attesting to the continuing importance of hemispheric defence
and the need for Ottawa to always keep one eye on Washington,

a key worry of King's cabinet was what the Americans would think about Canada sending its best forces overseas. The neutral Yanks were advised of the movement of Canadian formations to fight on the front lines of the European war. This was both good politics and a sign that Canada could not act without concern for US sensibilities and fears. The Americans understood the Dominion's need to order its armed forces to the battle zone, but they monitored the situation cautiously. They were little calmed by the fact that, beginning in late 1939, the RCN had sent clandestine buyers to the US to purchase private American yachts that would be armed for coastal defence duties. The last of fourteen vessels—all of which bore animal names—was incorporated in the RCN by May 1940. While these armed yachts, with their 12-pounder gun and light machine guns, would be no match for the U-boats when they came to North American waters, the fortified ships were a symbol of Canadian resolve.[9] And since the purchase of the yachts ran counter to US neutrality laws that disallowed the sale of weapons to any belligerent countries, they were a sign that the American authorities were sympathetic to their North American neighbour. However, the sympathy only went so far. A June 1940 public poll found that just 8 percent of Americans supported the US going to war.[10]

———

"It is right we should strike with her the last blow for the preservation of freedom," wrote King of sending Canada's modern destroyers to Britain, which was now in the desperate struggle against Hitler's forces that were preparing to invade the island.[11] And yet he also worried that the vessels might not ever return and "we may find our own coasts left bare."[12] With Britain vulnerable to invasion after losing much of its army's weapons, mechanized vehicles, and equipment in the retreat from France, it would struggle to repel the coming amphibious force. But Germany was a land power. Any crossing of the English Channel would first have to sink the Royal Navy, whose warships would wreak havoc among the unarmed landing craft carrying the invaders. As Hitler's generals, admirals, and air marshals prepared for the assault, Churchill warily eyed France's navy, which had escaped the ruin.

The downfall of France created a complex situation, as its colonies in North Africa were separate from the mother country that was now occupied. The powerful French navy had sought refuge in the port of Mers-el-Kébir near Oran in Algeria. If it fell into German hands, Britain would be imperilled. Churchill tried to convince Admiral Jean François Darlan to order his navy to join British warships in the fight against the Nazis, but the admiral was decidedly anti-British and was too proud to place his navy under control of another nation. The danger to Britain was existential, so Churchill gave the brutal but necessary order to attack on July 3. Hitler watched gleefully as the two former allies turned on each other. The Royal Navy damaged several French ships, sinking the battleship *Bretagne* and causing more than 1,500 casualties.[13] The French convulsed with rage, ordering an aerial strike against Gibraltar. The relationship plunged to new depths in the face of rumours sweeping through France that said the nation's defeat had been hurried along because Britain had failed as an ally in the ground war.

Even though the Canadian government offered little in the way of public opinion about the Royal Navy's attack on France's navy, King was thankful for Churchill's grit as he had been warned that a German-controlled French fleet could be the weapon to attack Canadian shores in 1940.[14] Nonetheless, there remained great disquiet in the West. Beginning in late May, Canadian and American senior civil servants and politicians met, talked, and exchanged notes in the hope of strengthening ties between the countries through wartime production and the defence of North America. But King was not turning his back on Britain, and he felt compelled to help London by working through Washington. There remained no small amount of bad blood between the two economic competitors, with the Americans also remembering the uneasy history with Britain that stretched back to the Revolution, the War of 1812, and a series of diplomatic disagreements and near military clashes. Now, in the early summer of 1940, for Britain to survive it needed American support. The neutral US wanted to help keep Britain in the war, but it did not mind if its global rival was humbled a little in the fight. King, despite being wary of getting caught in the middle, felt it was his duty to step up as mediator to bring the two nations closer together.

In Washington, Roosevelt's administration was cautious about its growing closeness to Canada. King's cabinet also tread carefully, warned that there was no shortage of British and German agents of influence trying to draw the United States and Britain together in a military alliance or pull them apart through the stoking of grievances. One of the most successful agents, code-named "Intrepid," was the Manitoba-born spymaster William Stephenson, who was one of the inspirations for Ian Fleming's James Bond. A decorated airman from the Great War, Stephenson had lived a life of intrigue and adventure while amassing a small fortune in business deals. As head of the British Security Coordination in the US, before the war Stephenson had passed information to Churchill on the rise of the Nazis, and he was instructed in June 1940 to win over Americans to the Commonwealth war effort. Well connected with journalists and politicians, Intrepid planted positive stories about Canada and Britain while playing up the heinous acts of the fascists.

As King's cabinet sought a special role in influencing the United States, a Canadian Information Office was soon established in the country's legation in Washington. The office acted with much caution since the prime minister became wary about disseminating propaganda after the president told him that he would look unkindly on any overt influence to drag the United States into the war.[15] King settled on working towards his goal of reconciling the two great English-speaking powers via quiet personal diplomacy instead of a noisy blitz. As wartime reporter Blair Fraser remarked, Canada had some impact because, he noted mischievously, "we can speak English and American with equal fluency."[16] King and Canada had every reason to bridge the chasm between the Anglo-Saxon nations because Ottawa's aim of supporting Britain in the war could only be achieved if the US more forcefully backed Britain as it faced imminent invasion.[17]

———

President Roosevelt was alarmed by Hitler's stunning conquests, and more so when advisers predicted that Britain would likely not survive the coming air and amphibious assault.[18] After Dunkirk, Escott Reid of the Department of External Affairs spoke for many of his fellow Canadians in Washington when he remarked, "I sense a feeling not merely of defeatism, but of frustration and impotence." Only the overly optimistic in the US believed that Britain could hold out, and Reid described "a feeling of almost panic hysteria at the defencelessness of the United States if faced this summer by a victorious Germany."[19] Roosevelt did not want to see Britain go under. But he was more concerned about the United States' hemispheric security, being well aware of the perilous shortages of his country's modern weapons. Even worse was the spectre of Hitler taking control of France and Britain's combined navies, which he would use to overwhelm US warships and bring the war to North America. As Roosevelt warned the Canadian envoy, Hugh Keenleyside, who had been sent by King to talk to the president and share how Canada would respond to the threat, this unstoppable super fleet would be "the end of hope."[20]

On May 26, 1940, Roosevelt turned to his friend, Mackenzie, asking him to impress upon Churchill the need to sail the warships of the vaunted Royal Navy to Canada or Bermuda if Britain was conquered and occupied. King blanched at taking part in such discussions, realizing that the American president was transparently only concerned about the United States. "I would rather die than do aught to save ourselves," anguished King in his diary.[21] The prime minister refused to write off the British homeland, even if it meant risking his own political survival. Instead of playing it safe, King threw himself into the fray, living up to a promise he had made to the president years earlier that he could be of "service" in bringing the British Commonwealth closer to the US.[22] King appealed to the White House to free up aircraft to replace some of the more than 1,000 Royal Air Force fighters and light bombers lost during the Battle of France.[23] But the Americans were also militarily feeble, and unlike the Canadians, who sent their destroyers across the Atlantic, they refused to weaken their defences.

After agonizing over the president's request that he advocate for a ruthless plan, King sent a May 31 telegram to Churchill, as the president had hoped, tuning up the language to show that he had faith in Britain, although still asking about plans to keep fighting from North America if the worst should occur. Having fretted so deeply, King assumed that Churchill would understand the impossible situation in which he had been placed in trying to bridge the gap between the US and Britain.[24] In London, the British leader was not amused when he received the message since he was already dealing with many of his own wobbly ministers and members of Parliament who were pressuring him to capitulate as France went into a death spiral. Snarling at the Roosevelt administration that had failed not only Britain but democracy, along with the Canadian weakling who was complacent in the request to protect North America with the Royal Navy while the British became Nazi slaves, he considered his response.

Churchill stood in the House of Commons on June 4 to rouse his people, to defy the Nazis, and to tell those quivering in North America that Britain would not go down without a fight. His "We shall fight on the beaches" speech was hammered home with the resounding cry, "We shall never surrender." The fierce rhetoric "has stirred all Canada, and it has brought equally fervent response from the United States," claimed an editorial in *The Globe and Mail*.[25] Churchill had also said—almost pleaded—that his country's military would "carry on the struggle, until, in God's good time, the New World, with all its power and might, steps forth to the rescue and liberation of the Old." Britain, he made clear, could not survive without North American aid, money, and armed forces.

A day after the bulldog's inspirational speech, a fanged telegraph arrived in Ottawa warning King that he should be careful about letting the Americans think that they could do nothing in defence of democracy and then pick up Britain's fleet on the cheap. Churchill told King that even though Britain was on the verge of toppling, "no practical help has yet been forthcoming from the United States."[26] It was a bitter accusation, but Churchill saw the need to put the president's feet to the fire. He also told Roosevelt bluntly in a separate communiqué that if Britain surrendered, he could not guarantee that the warships would not fall into Hitler's hands. Once the Nazis had mauled the British, the US would be next. Amid the public adulation for his defiant speech, Britain's warlord fired a warning shot across the American bow.

———

As Canadians lurched about in shock after France's defeat, new rallying cries rang forth to double Canada's efforts to support the British. The *Toronto Daily Star* was among the many papers that warned of the Nazi cruelty meted out to the enslaved French: "It is a dagger which stabs individual liberty, which crushes individual initiative, which makes of man a creature who acts and thinks only as the state tells him to act and think."[27] With the US still holding out, only Britain, Canada, and the Commonwealth could reverse that which had been snatched at the point of the sword.

Faced with the encroaching threat to North America, the Liberals rushed through Parliament the National Resources Mobilization Act (NRMA), passing it on June 21, 1940.[28] The act, wrote Jack Pickersgill, a close adviser to King, was "a fresh expression by Parliament of its intention to support prosecution of the war wholeheartedly."[29] It would mobilize the country's resources—military, industry, and people—to prosecute the war more vigorously. In a radical reversal of policy, the act put an end to King's promise of voluntary enlistment by legislating that a limited number of able-bodied men would be conscripted for home defence while women would be encouraged to serve in wartime industry.[30] This shift reflected the shock induced by France's downfall, which, according to senior External Affairs mandarin Hugh Keenleyside, brought home to Canadians the "possibility of defeat. . . . It was

Canada's war industry, soldiers, and finance stand shoulder to shoulder against gigantic Nazi forces, as represented by Hitler, who menaces from across the Atlantic.

now evident not only that our participation was going to demand heavy sacrifices but also that to a greater degree than any of us had realized we were going to have to rely upon support that only the United States could supply."[31]

Thousands of Canadians, awakened to the grim situation, enlisted across the country. "On the day that France capitulated I remember thinking, 'My God, now the Brits are the only ones left!'" recounted Lieutenant Vladimir Ignatieff, who had left Russia when he was thirteen and served throughout the war in the infantry.[32] However, while the NRMA was lauded in much of English Canada, its inclusion of home defence conscription was a dangerous signal to many in French Canada. It took the full weight of Ernest Lapointe's reputation to calm Quebec. The respected politician told his French-Canadian colleagues and all Quebeckers, "our first duty at this time is to provide for our own defence. Preparedness is essential."[33]

In this charged environment, Canadians became more fearful and susceptible to stories of German agents in the United States who were keeping the Americans neutral and preparing for nefarious acts of sabotage. A rumour of a supposed German–American military operation being carried out across the 49th parallel drew its inspiration from stories of Fenian raids after the Civil War. The Fenians had emerged as cross-border boogeymen, with Irish-American veterans invading Canada successfully in the summer of 1866 and then retreating back to the republic. Their goal had been to capture parts of British North America and then ransom it back to Britain after London gave Ireland its independence. Even though the American authorities suppressed the movement, the Fenians had stoked fears that the republic had always coveted the Dominion.

These rumours circulated freely, but Canadian and American authorities were forced to respond when the unstable Ontario premier, Mitch Hepburn, brazenly accused the Americans of plotting an invasion. Fearmongering on June 10, 1940, that a horde of German-American Nazis were preparing to strike through the Niagara region, he urged local communities to arm themselves and prepare for a bloody battle to defend "their homes and factories, their wives and children."[34] Hepburn was widely condemned, and some MPs suggested that perhaps he should be imprisoned for his reckless statement. The Americans were more than a little disturbed that the political leader of Canada's wealthiest and most populous province had accused the US of harbouring Nazis for an incursion. Even General George Marshall, the chief of staff of the US Army, was forced to address journalists on the issue. While the general acknowledged that there were fascist sympathizers in the US, he queried, not so innocently, "Does the premier think anybody of this ilk could organize a strong force in the U.S. without the government knowing about it?"[35]

Hepburn's incendiary and inaccurate comments did not find traction among Canadians, who, despite their fear of saboteurs, understood that the country would likely have to turn to the US as an ally if Britain fell. This period, from May to August 1940, was one of the darkest of the war for the two democratic nations. There were calls for drastic measures to be taken in every field of endeavour. Everything had changed. To secure North America, Canada's *Financial Post* noted on June 15, 1940, there was a need for "Joint Defense," even though "politicians both in this country and in United States have long been terrified of the subject."[36] A few days later, a group of prominent Canadian academics, public intellectuals, and experts in international affairs called for stronger political and military ties with the US "to determine the extent of Canada's zone of defence and her function in the strategic sense."[37] In the face of this new menace, old prejudices needed to be set aside. The Nazification of Europe and the possibility of war coming to North America required that Canada seek greater unity with the United States.

———

American secretary of war Henry L. Stimson called France's defeat in June 1940 "the most shocking single event of the war."[38] The Roosevelt administration had based its grand strategy in Europe on France fighting as it had in the Great War. For more than four years, the French had stood their ground, battling stolidly at the Marne and Verdun, in the Arras area, and at other sites of carnage. Now, almost inexplicably, the French had folded in six weeks. Britain had a tough scrapper at the helm in Winston Churchill, but no one could be certain the nation would survive. In the US, the isolationists remained strong and vocal, using the words of the founding fathers to warn against becoming re-embroiled in European wars, or pointing to the last painful disaster in the human grinder of the Western Front. In a more pragmatic vein, others drew attention to America's relatively weak military, telling politicians to mind their own business and to focus on the economy, which was finally revving up again after a decade of Depression.

On June 10, the situation darkened as Italy entered the war on the side of Germany, with the fascist dictator Mussolini leading the Italian goose-stepping soldiers towards what he believed was the side of the victors. Mussolini's feverish and foolish dream of a new Roman Empire was soon delivered a heavy blow by military reversals in North Africa, as the British struck hard and fast. Nonetheless, Italy was another authoritarian nation to join the fascist alliance, further weighting the war against Britain, Canada, and the Empire.

With Britain teetering on the edge of defeat, Roosevelt warned that the United States could not survive as "a lone island in a world dominated by the philosophy of force."[39] Even if most Americans did not want war, the country had to rearm. When Belgium fell in late May 1940, by default the US now had the eighteenth largest army in the world, only slightly ahead of Bulgaria. Congress finally understood the dire situation and the defence budget expanded to $1.5 billion in May 1940. Another $1.7 billion was appropriated the next month to expand the army to 375,000 men.[40] Roosevelt publicly talked of building a fleet to achieve a "two-ocean navy," while exhorting that the production of aircraft had to reach the unlikely goal of 50,000 machines a year. As in Canada, this was sold to the public as a matter of home defence, although the president and his leadership team continued to eye the fascists in Germany and Italy, while Japan remained aggressive in fighting its own war with China.

Fierce opposition in the US to expanding the armed forces led to a constellation of groups coalescing around the charismatic Charles Lindbergh, the famous aviator who had flown solo in a non-stop flight across the Atlantic in May 1927. Lindbergh spoke for many when he openly questioned the drumbeat signalling a clash of arms and the "hysterical chatter of calamity and invasion that has been running rife."[41] Preparing for war would only bring war, said Lindbergh. His critics scoffed that the right to deny reality died when Hitler made Europe a land of the subjugated and enslaved. That Lindbergh had expressed an open appreciation for some aspects of Nazi Germany, especially its technological advances in air power, led many to wonder if he was a Nazi agent. Roosevelt certainly thought he was in the Führer's back pocket. Lindbergh became the spokesperson for the America First Committee, a non-interventionist organization, and his radio addresses reached millions. He was an influential voice, and the president knew that he represented the many Americans who did not want their sons and daughters dragged into the vortex of war for the second time in a generation.

———

A keen observer of Canadian and American relations, journalist Bruce Hutchison took a trip to Washington in the aftermath of France's defeat and wrote of the widespread concern in the American capital. "Endangered for the first time, this nation looks around, counts its friends, wonders which it can depend on. . . . First of all, it counts on Canada. And it realizes as it has never realized in the past that no friend is so important to it, none so close and dependable, as its northern neighbor. It was never like this before." As an expert on American politics and culture, Hutchinson knew that, before the Nazi victory, few in Washington had much interest in what happened above the 49th parallel and there was little support in the idea of fighting fascism overseas. Now, however, "they have realized that Canada is their northern frontier, an essential part of their own defense and safety."[42]

Both the United States and Canada's real war thus began with France's collapse and Britain's retreat to its island. Though Canada became Britain's ranking ally, Canadians feared that the tattered British armed forces would not be able to hold off the Nazis. If defeated, they asked, would the surviving Royal Navy warships steam to Canada, carrying the royal family and whatever gold reserves could be smuggled out of the country to continue the war? Or would Britain surrender, as France had done, and be forced to eke out an existence with the Nazi jackboot pressing heavily on its people's windpipe? If that doomsday scenario came true, Canada would join with the United States in fortress North America, surely losing much if not all of its independence. Even if Churchill and his military kept the fascists at bay, King, his cabinet, and his generals would have to thread the needle on leaning into the US to better stand by Britain. Canada would not let Britain down, but to offer the nation's full military and financial support it needed American assistance, which would likely lead to the erosion of bonds with the mother country. The predicament was summed up by Frank Scott, a McGill University professor of law: "We are in the curious position that the more we do to assist Great Britain . . . the more we are obligated to co-operate with the United States."[43]

CHAPTER 4

COMING TOGETHER

"The G.O.C. stated that we are a mobile reserve with a 360 degree front," wrote Major-General Andrew McNaughton on June 25, 1940, noting that his force "may have to operate anywhere in Great Britain from the South coast, to Scotland, or in Wales." The 1st Canadian Division arrived in Britain in the last days of 1939 and, after the fall of France, was ready for battle against the coming Nazi invasion. After the retreat of Britain's army from Dunkirk, McNaughton's warriors were one of the few infantry formations in England that was combat ready. The Canadians, as McNaughton observed, had been entrusted with a "serious responsibility" by the G.O.C., the senior British military commander.[1] Indeed, Canada was Britain's ranking ally, and during the course of the war, much would be asked and expected of the senior Dominion. The Canadians gave that effort freely, all the while sustaining their important balancing act with the United States, aware that aid to Britain could only be accomplished by forging an alliance with the Americans.

—

With all parties focused on the defence of the island kingdom, Britain remained desperate to rearm its withered forces. The soldiers of the British Expeditionary Force had been rescued from Dunkirk, but they had left behind most of their tanks, vehicles, and weapons. Whereas Britain had been stingy in its allocation of contracts in Canada in 1939 and early 1940, it now turned in desperation to the Dominion to help replace its destroyed weapons.[2] It needed everything, especially artillery, trucks, and munitions, with Britain placing hundreds of millions of dollars in contracts in Canada: from $11.6 million in April to $31 million in May to $148 million in October.[3] Throughout 1940, the British asked for more than 300 tanks, 72,000 vehicles, 3,450 artillery pieces, 100,000 rifles, and 42,600 Bren light machine guns.[4] Only six months earlier, Canada had possessed no capacity to make any of these weapons or military vehicles. "Britain's need for supplies from overseas jumped," said Canada's war production czar, Minister of Munitions and Supply Clarence Decatur Howe, in the House of Commons in November 1940. "Canada was requested to go full speed ahead."[5]

Overseeing the massive and expanding war industry was the American-born Howe, a blunt, talented, and energizing businessman. A graduate of the Massachusetts Institute of Technology, he had a good eye for business, having made his global reputation as an engineer in constructing grain elevators. Howe would emerge as Canada's most successful businessman-politician of this period. Elected in 1935 to represent Port Arthur, Ontario, he was recognized for his talents by King, who made him minister of transport the next year. As a minister, he proved a practical leader who got things done and earned the respect of Liberals and Conservatives alike. Before the war, the lingering effects of the Depression still clogged industry, like sand in an engine. The 1940 Royal Commission on Dominion–Provincial Relations had reported, "Canada is one of the least self-sufficient countries in the world."[6] Anticipating the need to transform Canada's nascent industry, in April 1940 King made Howe minister of munitions and supply, a mammoth conglomerate that positioned the nation into becoming a major supplier of weapons and war matériel.[7] There was no little irony that Minister Howe, a free-market entrepreneur, now assumed unparalleled interventionist control of the economy on behalf of the state. War creates unexpected opportunities and legacies.

Canada had ramped up wartime industrialization during the Great War, producing over 100 million shells for the British and dominion forces, and yet these plants had been shut down and the expertise lost over time. Now, with Britain reeling, Howe faced nearly unimaginable challenges in stoking the forge of production in the poor and underdeveloped country. He used the power of the state to spend heavily to aid factories and industry in shifting from civilian to military goods. "In many cases, however, the necessary plants did not exist, or, if they existed, their capacities were inadequate, and extensions of existing plants, or the construction of wholly new plants, has been necessary," said Howe about how the government was called upon to intervene to charge the war economy.[8]

In the name of victory, Howe recruited wealthy businessmen, both Conservatives and Liberals, who were known as the "dollar-a-year" men in reference to their nominal salary, although most continued to draw pay from their companies.[9] This mobilization of industry was far more effective than the country's industrialization during the Great War, as Howe's rapidly growing empire took

This colourful poster depicts the Canadian war effort, with the worker
supplying ammunition to the soldier going into battle. The Tommy
machine gun depicted here, and made famous in Hollywood gangster
movies, was rarely used by the Canadians in combat.

control of strategic minerals to more effectively produce the weapons that were needed to battle the Axis powers. Howe urged more: department officials were told to find ways to ease bottlenecks in production, spend money, and support industry. In King's go-slow government, Howe was a whirlwind of activity. "If we lose the war nothing will matter," argued the minister in the summer of 1940, "if we win the war the cost will still have been of no consequence and will have been forgotten."[10] What followed was an unprecedented industrial revolution for Canada, which transformed it into "the arsenal of the Empire."[11] This weaponization of business would forever change the industrial landscape, but to achieve these goals Canada needed American financial assistance and a more integrated war economy. In fact, one late 1940 report from External Affairs argued for greater integration of the North American economies, insisting, "this is the most important problem now before the Canadian Government."[12] It was necessary to fully draw upon the United States' raw material, expertise, and wealth, which would propel the Canadian war industry forward and shape the country's "future development." Some in Canada did not want to hear this, fearing that the country would be drawn further into the American orbit. Britain also worried about the ramifications for the Commonwealth. But there was no denying that for the Dominion to assist its monarch and the brave people facing the Nazi threat, Canada would have to fashion new ties to the US.

———

"The long period of sophistry, intellectual bewilderment and moral evasion which has been such an unworthy episode in the story of

U.S. life seems to be ending," wrote journalist Beverly Baxter in a June 1940 issue of *Maclean's*.[13] It was an overly optimistic assessment of the United States' readiness to enter into the war on the side of Britain and Canada. Roosevelt was appalled by the German victory that transformed the geopolitical balance of power in Europe, but he believed that he would need to manoeuvre carefully to persuade his country to support Britain because a majority of Americans still had no wish to fight in another European war.[14] Even though only Congress could declare war, the president strengthened his hand in June 1940 by removing two committed isolationists from his cabinet and replacing them with internationalists. Secretary of War Henry Stimson and Navy Secretary Frank Knox were firm supporters of rearming the American military and standing by Britain as part of the US's forward defence, and both were Republicans who might sway some of their party members to support the Democratic president. Nonetheless, this would be a long process, and the defence of North America remained the White House's priority despite the threat to Britain.

Speaking at the Reichstag on July 19, Hitler raged that Britain's desire to keep up the struggle would only bring ruin upon the island. He mocked Churchill and the monarchy for believing that "even if Great Britain should perish, they would carry on from Canada."[15] But although Hitler's battle-hardened army would likely overrun Britain, it first had to cross the English Channel. With the Royal Navy having savaged the German Kriegsmarine in the invasion of Norway in April 1940, and the British warships now waiting to tear up vulnerable flat-bottomed river barges carrying the invading force, the Germans understood that Britain's navy would first have to be defeated if there was to be any hope of success. And the only way for that to occur was through command of the air. The Luftwaffe had proved its value in the campaign against Poland and in Western Europe as its bombers pounded cities like Warsaw and its fighters attacked ground forces. As part of this choreographed operation, an extended air battle had to destroy the Royal Air Force (RAF) before the Luftwaffe could knock out the Royal Navy to clear the way for invasion.

In the Battle of Britain, the RAF would have the advantage of fighting on the defensive, with radar stations providing early warning of incoming squadrons. Though the force was outnumbered, with fewer than 600 fighters facing four times that number of German aircraft, including 864 high-performance single-seater Messerschmitt Bf 109s, the RAF, aided by two Canadian squadrons and Polish fighters, knew they were going into combat for Britain's survival. The air campaign began on July 10. Vast air battles of fighters and bombers cut the sky with vapour trails. Crashed aircraft soon pitted the fields along the eastern part of England. Even as casualties gutted the squadrons, the British factories were producing Hurricane and Spitfire fighters to meet the threat and replenish losses. Airmen were in short supply, however, and more than 100 Canadian flyers contributed to holding off the Luftwaffe. Victory came at the end of October 1940 after a total of 1,900 Luftwaffe aircraft were destroyed.[16] Journalists like Ed Murrow, and dozens of other reporters, provided engrossing newspaper and radio stories—accompanied by the sounds of aerial assault and crackling flames from downed aircraft—along the transatlantic radio for North Americans. Some US citizens fought in the front lines with the RAF, having made their way overseas on their own. Arthur Donahue, who had grown up on a Minnesota dairy farm and who had taken to flying in the interwar period, enlisted in the RAF and fought in the Battle of Britain, writing later,

"I felt it a duty as a follower of the civilized way of life to throw my lot in."[17] The plucky underdog British proved their mettle, and opinion polls revealed that Americans were increasingly supportive of Britain in its clash with the Nazis.[18]

The RAF handed Hitler his first decisive defeat and Britain stayed in the fight, backed by factories pumping out aircraft under the watch of the brilliant Lord Beaverbrook. The expatriate Canadian millionaire press baron had found ways to energize the moribund system, using his friendship with Churchill to destroy his enemies, stoke production, and restore some of his reputation as a scoundrel. A rebuffed and infuriated Hitler rethought his strategy, looking eastwards to invade the Soviet Union, although he remained vengeful towards the resilient British. Beginning in September 1940, he ordered bomber strikes in a series of night-time operations against the cities known as the Blitz. This calculated terror campaign would kill 43,000 people, mostly civilians, and wound and maim another 139,000 in the coming six months. "If we fail," said Churchill, "then the whole world, including the United States, including all that we have known and cared for, will sink into the abyss of a new Dark age."[19] The British would hold out against the Nazi menace, but Churchill's primary strategy for victory involved dragging the US into the war on the side of the democracies.

———

"A man who had sold himself to the lower depths of hell could not have expressed himself more damnably," was King's visceral response to Hitler's brutal speech of July 19, in which he had promised to destroy Britain.[20] Many Canadians felt the same way, and the fall of France and the Battle of Britain galvanized the country to action. However, the cautious prime minister, who supported Britain to the hilt and hated Hitler with much ferocity, continued to walk a fine line between the war's most ardent supporters and the more cautious nationalists. The former, who supported enacting conscription, demanded that Canada be willing to pay almost any price to support Britain, while the nationalists—often associated with Quebec, but in fact found across the country in universities, churches, women's organizations, and almost all walks of life—sought voluntary commitment, believed in protecting North America first, and questioned the necessity of sending armed forces overseas to be ground away in battle. As with all issues, most Canadians were not for only one position or the other: they could be fully supportive of sending forces overseas while also defending North America, although the extreme ends of the spectrum were polarizing. King was most comfortable in the middle. He also felt, and had felt for many years, that Canada could act as a middleman between the US and Britain, with the Dominion both a North American nation and a firmly established member of the Commonwealth. In fact, during King's meeting with Hitler on June 29, 1937, he had told the dictator, "in Canada we were continuously explaining to the English what the Americans really meant, in certain things, and to the Americans, what the English really meant."[21] Though the British rarely saw the value of Canada operating as the third point in a triangle that connected the three countries, even Churchill, who disliked King because of his prewar evasions that diminished Imperial defence, asked him in June 1940 to apply pressure on Roosevelt to assist with military support.[22]

In the aftermath of the fall of France, the Canadians and Americans conducted rushed diplomatic and military talks on the joint defence of the hemisphere. The Americans had their own contingency plans if the northern dominion were to be invaded. The Canadians might have been more concerned if they had been aware of a July 3 meeting among senior American leaders, including Chief of Staff of the US Army General George Marshall, about how to strengthen Canada. On the table was a suggestion that the US send arms to the Canucks, but Marshall argued that a better response would be to prepare to rescue Canada with up to 30,000 soldiers if the Germans should land in the Maritimes.[23] No decision was made, perhaps because of an awareness that the Canadians would no doubt wish to be involved in any discussion about an armed foray across the border. In the face of these grim prospects, it was agreed that both the Canadian and American military high commands would benefit from a committee to discuss joint defence plans and priorities.

Less than a fortnight later, a meeting was held in Washington, with senior Canadian service heads going south to consult with General Marshall and others. Much productive work was done, with the Canadians at pains to make it clear, as one report indicated, that "our visit was in no sense dictated by panic, but, on our part, was intended to explore the possibilities of common action in the similar problems of defence that confronted both countries."[24] The Americans reacted positively to this message; however, Marshall stressed the need for the "maintenance of the strictest secrecy," as any leaking of the talks would be damaging to the Roosevelt administration with its attempt to shift the US away from its fiercely neutralist stance. The Canadian senior brass returned home feeling they had made progress by securing new weapons, especially anti-aircraft guns and coastal artillery. They also impressed on the Americans that Canada could protect itself, though it would welcome stronger common defence of the east coast if the US entered the war.

A month later, Roosevelt invited King to talk in Ogdensburg in upstate New York, where he was taking a brief pause in his presidential campaign for an unprecedented third term. Roosevelt was exhausted, but he felt the need to reach out to the Canadian prime minister to further discuss matters of continental defence. Given France's collapse and Britain's vulnerability, this was a time for the US to shore up allies and find new ones. Though Canadians were a proud British dominion, the president knew he could work with them as North Americans. King readily accepted the invitation, anxious to continue cementing his positive relationship with the president. Roosevelt had that seductive quality of making it easy for people to like him, with his comfortable ways and bright spirit that attracted supporters. That he seemed to have a real friendship with King was surprising for many since the two leaders seemed to be polar opposites, although there were certainly connections as mundane as both men having attended Harvard and as intangible as the shared loneliness of leading their respective countries. While King lacked the oratorial powers of the president and his radiating charisma, he hadn't held power for over fifteen years by being an awkward social pariah. It was common for him to ingratiate himself to others with compliments and charm, and he stoked the president's ego with much agreeable conversation and storytelling.

King slipped out of Ottawa on August 17, with the pressmen missing his departure even as he and his driver picked up Jay

Pierrepont Moffat, the US's senior official in Canada. Moffat's arrival in June had made news across Canada, with journalist Bruce Hutchison writing that he was "Uncle Sam's Ottawa Ace." A gifted professional diplomat with considerable experience both in foreign legations and at the White House, the aristocratic-looking Moffat would be kept busy with explaining Canada to the US, and Americans to Canadians. Carrying the official gilded title of "Envoy Extraordinary and Minister Plenipotentiary," Hutchinson suggested that the minister "must understand and be able to interpret the restless, soaring mind of Franklin Roosevelt."[25]

Even though Major-General Harry Crerar, the newly appointed chief of the general staff, had reported to the cabinet that the Canadian armed forces should be more closely linked to their American counterparts to properly defend North America, King must have been a little shocked to learn that the American First Army of seven divisions of regular and National Guard troops was training in upper New York State.[26] Such a massive assembly of tens of thousands of soldiers near the border would have sent the Canadians fearfully scurrying in the past, but for King this was another sign that the US was awakening to the idea that the viability of neutrality as a strategy was fast fading.

Aboard Roosevelt's special campaign train, the leaders discussed how Canada and the United States should work more closely together, with King no doubt reflecting on Roosevelt's historic pledge made in Kingston two years earlier to the very day. The two warmed to closer military integration between the nations. Stirred by the possibilities, the president fished a piece of paper out of a waste basket and jotted down an agreement. And so the Permanent Joint Board on Defence (PJBD) was born, a committee of service personnel and diplomats that would study and devise new policy solutions for "the defence of the north half of the western hemisphere." While talk shops are rarely radical, this board was unique for isolationist America, just as it was for Canada, which had now entered a defence pact with a country that not only had adopted a neutral stance in the war but had only

Cartoonist John Collins depicts Canada and the US working together to strengthen hemispheric defence by using a "Joint Defence Board" to construct a wall. Hitler looks on, dismayed by the cooperation. Canada hoped to unite with the US in building a wall of defence in North America so the Dominion could more safely send aid to Britain.

shelved its northward invasion plans in 1937. The Ogdensburg agreement, in theory, gave the two countries an equal voice in the defence of North America and established a path, as King penned in his diary, "to help secure the continent for the future."[27] A monumental victory for King and Canada, the six sentences in the forthcoming press release would be the foundation for more intense military cooperation. Forged in war, the PJBD continues to this day.

King returned to Canada triumphant. His cabinet was delighted by their leader's breakthrough. Canada's security had been radically strengthened with the creation of the PJBD, and the US had been drawn further into the war by agreeing to the shared protection of North America with a belligerent nation. The country's military leaders could also now send more units and formations to Britain without worrying about home defence. Newspapers responded with unreserved praise for this new coalition. The *Toronto Daily Star* published an editorial on August 19 about the significance of the new joint defence board for planning "unified action" and funnelling key decisions to "make common cause against a possible foe."[28] The American minister in Ottawa, Moffat, reported that an anti-Americanist reaction to the announcement was almost entirely absent and that, instead, "Canada believes that such cooperation would tend to bring Britain and the United States closer together."[29] Though there was some criticism among American politicians and in the press over linking the neutral US to warring Canada, Roosevelt's response was to frame the agreement by emphasizing how it would assist in the protection of North America.[30]

Even as Canada's Conservatives had been hammering the government for not acting with more urgency in rearming the nation or rushing forces to Britain's side, some were now sickened by how the PJBD tied the two countries together in what appeared to be a "permanent" defence pact. While the new body's structure was influenced by the successful and ongoing 1909 International Joint Commission that advised on water rights between the two countries, King's mantra of "Parliament will decide" had been silenced, and elected officials had not even been consulted on the action. Fellow members of Parliament would have been even more horrified if they'd had access to the prime minister's diary, in which he wrote that success had come from hidden forces that he described as the "Hand of Destiny."[31]

King could be rightly pleased with the results of his mission, which included having skilfully rebuffed the president's request to station American soldiers in Nova Scotia. That was a bridge too far for King.[32] With this deal, the fussy prime minister, who was sometimes afraid of his own shadow, emerged into the light as an influential statesman, proclaiming in the House of Commons that the agreement would lead to the "defence of the British commonwealth of nations as a whole."[33] He was correct in what he told MPs, Canadians, and the people of the Commonwealth: that this defence pact with the US would allow the Dominion to better support the British people on the front lines. Left unsaid was that this action drew Canada closer to the US. Was there any other viable option? Not likely. King knew he had to ally with the Americans to assist the British, who were perched on the knife's edge between defeat and survival. Churchill was less pleased. Upon hearing about the agreement, the British bulldog grumbled that Ottawa was turning away from London in a time of great need and embracing "Canada and America's mutual defence" at the Empire's expense.[34] Churchill wrote meanly to King that, while public opinion was with him, history might judge him more harshly. For the imperialist Churchill it appeared that North America was again hedging its bets on Britain's survival. London's authorities had long wondered if the Americanized King was too pliable in allowing the White House to decouple the Dominion from the Commonwealth.[35] Though he was hurt by Churchill's insinuation, King saw it differently: Canada could only assist Britain if it secured closer military and diplomatic ties with the United States. This was an act of necessity in the war against the Nazis.

———

As the terrible summer of 1940 was waning, the democracies could only hope for time to survive and arm themselves against the Nazi threat on land, in the air, and at sea. Hitler's odious ally, Stalin, continued to oversee the occupation of his part of Poland and the Baltic states that had been invaded and swallowed in June 1940. Finland had also finally been defeated in battle after inflicting heavy losses on the poorly equipped and terribly trained Soviet soldiers. The Nazis occupied France, Belgium, the Netherlands, and other Western European nations, draining their treasuries to feed the German war machine and subjecting their people to wanton brutality. The Gestapo, along with traitors and ordinary people who joined the internal security forces, were soon identifying Jews, rounding them up, and sending them to concentration camps where death awaited them. Within two years, mass murder would become industrialized genocide to eradicate Jews and others deemed as undesirables. Britain had survived the Battle of Britain, but it was being pummelled in the aerial Blitz. Thousands were dying in the smoking ruins of the nation's cities, and by late 1940, after months of punishment, it remained unclear if the British might not still buckle under the onslaught. "If Great Britain goes down, the Axis powers will control the continents of Europe, Asia, Africa, Australia and the high seas—and they will be in a position to bring enormous military and naval resources against this hemisphere," President Roosevelt told the American people. If that were to happen, he warned, "it is no exaggeration to say that all of us in the Americas would be living at the point of a gun."[36] Most Canadians already understood this in their bones, but Americans were at last coming to the realization that the fascists could not be reasoned with and only understood force.

CHAPTER 5

DESPERATION ON
THE FINANCIAL FRONT

"Our Canadian economy is so enmeshed with that of our neighbor that we shall prosper or hunger with them."[1] Such was a Canadian journalist's observation in November 1940, and the emerging entanglement between Canada and the US also extended to hemispheric defence and wartime industrial production. President Roosevelt was a friend to Britain and Canada—with one adviser to Prime Minister King observing that the president's "popularity in Canada was all but universal." Yet he continued to assure Americans that the United States would not be drawn into the war. In a campaign speech at the end of October at the Boston Garden, he promised, "Your boys are not going to be sent into any foreign wars."[2] Was that pledge only for public consumption in the heat of election speech-making, or had Roosevelt's goodwill towards Britain, Canada, and the other beleaguered Allies reached its limit? Canadian politicians, civil servants, service personnel, and citizens from all walks of life studied the tea leaves and hoped that the president was on their side.

Closer to the battle front, the plucky English had survived months of bombing, with large parts of London, Manchester, and Coventry blasted to rubble and burned to ashes by the unending aerial attacks. "We can take it" was a rallying cry for many among the ruins, even as they wept and dug out the corpses of women, men, and children from the blackened carcasses of their neighbourhoods. Americans and Canadians watched with no little admiration for the British people's fortitude in withstanding the assault. Canadians, though, had reason to feel much more anxious than their continental neighbour, with their loved ones in uniform on the warships defending against Germany's invasion, in Hurricane fighters that sniped at the German bombers in the defence of British air space, in the army that dug in along the coast to repel an invasion, and in the small but growing bomber force that was beginning to strike back against German-occupied Western Europe.

———

In the summer of 1940, US public opinion polls indicated that more and more Americans understood that a German and Italian victory in Europe would endanger the republic, with over 70 percent agreeing upon the need for compulsory military training for young men.[3] And yet, on Capitol Hill, the Republicans were at daggers drawn over Roosevelt's selective service bill to introduce the first peacetime draft of young men into military service. The opposition came at them with feverish warnings and accusations that the president was a liar who was clearly leading the nation towards that inexorable goal of war far from North America. In one exchange that revealed the tenor of the debate, Senator Burton K. Wheeler said that the forced impressment of the young would "slit the throat of the last democracy still living."[4] Despite the rhetoric, on September 16, 1940, Roosevelt signed the Selective

Training and Service Act, which was framed as a response to the need to defend North America. This was the foundation that would allow the US military to expand rapidly; by war's end, 49 million men would be registered for service and over 16 million would serve in uniform.

Believers in American neutrality were shaken on September 27, 1940, when the Axis powers of fascist Germany, Italy, and Japan signed the Tripartite Pact, loosely aligning these nations against the Western democracies of Britain and the Commonwealth. Another diplomatic coup for the Germans, the "Pact of Steel" also freed up the Japanese to pick away at the European colonies and the exposed Dutch and French in the Pacific and Southeast Asia. As formidable as the pact appeared, the Axis powers never forged a unified strategy of defence, trade, or diplomacy.[5] Still, few could imagine the British Commonwealth surviving a coordinated onslaught.

The Axis pact was met with alarm in the West, with some seeing it as a reaction to Roosevelt's generosity three weeks earlier when, on September 3, 1940, he had announced the destroyers-for-bases agreement. Finally responding to Churchill's desperate pleas of the past six months, the American administration transferred fifty Great War–era destroyers to Britain in exchange for ninety-nine-year territorial leases in eight British colonies and dominions in the western hemisphere, including several Caribbean islands, Bermuda, and—much to the worry of Canada—Newfoundland.[6] The president presented the deal to the American people as a means to aid a friend, insisting that it in no way infringed on the country's neutrality and that the bases, when they were built, would form a more robust US military frontier.[7] At the same time, chief of staff General George Marshall declared in October 1940 that the Royal Navy was "fundamental" to North American defence, noting that the fifty new destroyers (seven of which were sent to the Royal Canadian Navy) would keep the Axis naval powers at bay.[8] Churchill was unhappy with the loss of territory, feeling that this was not the generous gift that Roosevelt claimed it was, and that it had been extracted at a heavy price when his people were at their most vulnerable. But he was thrilled with the bolstering of the fleet, calling the American action "a decidedly unneutral act."[9] He was playing a long game in enticing the US slowly into an alliance.

On November 5, 1940, after months of campaigning, President Franklin Roosevelt was once again elected. Running against Republican Wendell Wilkie, a political outsider who also urged a strong military effort to stop the fascists, the president won a landslide victory, carrying 38 states to Wilkie's 10 and securing 27.3 million votes to Wilkie's 22.3 million.[10] Roosevelt stood behind his record of taking the nation out of the Depression and keeping it out of the war, even though it was evident that he stood with the Allies. Both candidates were in fact sympathetic to a stronger US effort in support of Britain and Canada, leaving isolationists without much of a choice. "The satisfaction Canadians should feel in Roosevelt's re-election will be measured in the terms of the rage and chagrin with which Rome and Berlin will hail the result," wrote the *Winnipeg Free Press*.[11] While Roosevelt had campaigned against intervention in the war, his electoral victory, enthused one Canadian journalist, was a "bastion of hope for all who yet endure beneath the tyrant's heel or in the path of despotism."[12] The president's position on Britain and Canada's war effort was seen around the world as decidedly unneutral. Having forged a strong relationship with the president, King was obviously pleased with Roosevelt's victory, noting it ensured that "we have the United States with us for the next four years."[13]

———

"The defence of our shores and the preservation of our neutrality—these are the cardinal principles of our policy," said King before the war.[14] Although no plan survives contact with the enemy, as the military maxim goes, King's focus was on North America, even as he was also acutely aware that English Canada expected his government to do more to aid Britain after the fall of France. But he worried about repeating history, or at least helplessly watching it rhyme. He had witnessed how an extreme war effort had torn apart the country in the Great War, pitting English against French, region against region, farmers against city dwellers, new Canadians against those with deeper British connections. His mentor, Sir Wilfrid Laurier, had been defeated in the 1917 election for opposing conscription, and King had lost his riding. Though King had stayed loyal to Laurier, parlaying that connection into becoming the leader of the Liberal Party in 1919 and then prime minister in 1921, he was vehemently against conscription. Entering the war in 1939, King was resolute in his support for Britain, but he also remained watchful of threats to national unity. He moved gradually towards standing with Britain, hoping that Canada's wartime industrial contributions, its air training program, and its limited overseas forces would be enough to satisfy English Canadians. As one British diplomat noted in May 1938, remarking on King's cautious ways: "political life had taught him that any success he had attained had been due far more to avoiding action rather than taking action."[15]

But action was necessary to expand the war effort. The mobilization of human, political, and manufacturing power under the National Resources Mobilization Act (NRMA) revealed a new urgency. On the industrial front, many of the factories had begun the onerous work of converting from civilian to military production, for which the Canadians relied on American expertise, machinery, and tools, as well as trade contracts to pay for the transition. Progress was slowed by US neutrality and by the Americans' focus on their own shift to war production. However, to assist the Canadian war effort before the production lines were working at top speed, the Americans had made some obsolete weapons available, including 80,000 Enfield rifles, 250 First World War 6-ton M1917 light tanks, and a few outmoded aircraft.[16] This was something akin to the dregs of the barrel, but the shipment helped the weakly armed Canadian forces, with the tanks proving especially useful in training new armoured regiments. King played up the American support in the House of Commons, stressing that the "aircraft and tanks for training purposes, and destroyers for active service, are outstanding among the many essentials of warfare which the United States has so generously made available to Canada."[17] This was an overt tribute to the Roosevelt administration. It was also King at his best: his positive remark contained a subtext reminder to the American people that, by providing aid to Canada, they were increasingly moving away from neutrality.

In February 1941, the army high command put on paper what everyone in Canada already knew: "Canada's front line lies in and around the British Isles."[18] This strategic reality, made vivid when Nazi Germany attacked in May of the previous year, was what had motivated King's cabinet to send its best RCAF squadrons and RCN warships to British waters, along with the three infantry

*American M1917 tanks arriving in Canada to
bolster the Dominion's weak armed forces.*

divisions that were now defending Britain. Though King was uncomfortable with the expanding armed forces, he had few ways to curtail it, given that his minister of national defence, J.L. Ralston, advocated for a large army. Always timid around the generals, King wrote at one point in his diary, "I did not like to assert my view against those of the military authorities, not having the technical knowledge and did not wish to go contrary to military advice."[19] King's cabinet was losing control of the war effort

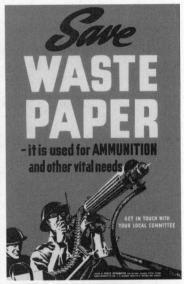

These posters capture some of the images and messaging that
urged Canadians to support the war from the home front.

that was bursting forth in all directions, and the prime minister was left insisting, time and time again, that he would support the expansion of the fighting services only if it would never lead to overseas conscription. Promises were duly given by his military staff, who showed him charts and graphs assuring that there were enough men who would volunteer willingly. And so by early 1942, Major-General Harry Crerar, chief of the general staff, had convinced the cabinet to grow the army to its full strength of five divisions (two of them armoured) and two independent tank brigades. While Canada's prewar senior commanders had made little impact on King, the clever and articulate Crerar had made his mark, and would continue to do so throughout the war.[20]

To fill the ranks, Canadians enlisted from across the country: from the nine provinces and two territories, and from nearly every city and town, all classes, and most religions. It was a great coming together of Canadians, and it included Americans who had been crossing the border to enlist since the start of the war. Skirting neutrality laws, Americans had already enlisted in French and British units, although it was far easier for them to do so in the northern dominion. News stories in American papers explained how to enlist across the border, and a robust series of rumours instructed young men to testify at Canadian units that they had lived in Canada before September 1939. The isolationist movement in the United States worked against the idea of Americans serving in Canadian forces, and Charles Lindbergh made several references to Canada as a foreign and warlike power enticing his innocent countrymen to their likely deaths. For good measure, he accused Canada of being a mere agent of the British Empire, a lackey-nation that perched dangerously atop the US, wreaking havoc on its neighbour. "Have they the right to draw this hemisphere into a European war simply because they prefer the Crown of England to American independence?"[21] That might have cut too close to the bone for some in the Dominion and Britain, with journalists and politicians striking back. In but one of many broadsides, the *Sunday Express* in October 1939 described Lindbergh as an "honored and decorated visitor of Hitler's [and] fervent admirer of Nazi strength."[22]

Lindbergh had his supporters, but his message did not prevent thousands of young Americans from enlisting in the Canadian army and air force. The numbers are difficult to determine with full precision because many Americans lied about their place of birth; and yet at least 18,848 Americans served in the army alone, most of them before the inflexion point of December 1941.[23] They served for all the reasons that Canadians did (save for, presumably, a sense of loyalty to the British Crown): honour, adventure, pay, and the belief in standing up for oppressed people. Ben Brinkworth, born in Chicago and taken on strength with the Essex Scottish, fought at Dieppe on August 19, 1942, where he was captured and spent the better part of three years in a prisoner-of-war camp. After the war, he recounted that he had enlisted to be on the "right side of history."[24]

———

"Well boys," announced Britain's ambassador to the US, Lord Lothian, speaking to American journalists upon his arrival at New York's LaGuardia Airport on November 23, 1940, "Britain's broke; it's your money we want." It was a staggeringly open revelation of Britain's state of financial desperation, a situation especially dire as the country had weathered the Battle of Britain and was still facing the threat of invasion. The Imperial reserves of gold and sterling were all but gone, and without them war supplies could not be purchased to defend the island kingdom or launch a strategic counterattack to liberate Western Europe. To date, Britain had been paying for food, weapons, and materiel in the United States through securities and gold that were sold in New York to raise American dollars. These Yankee dollars were then spent by the hundreds of millions in the crash-purchase of war supplies, minerals, tools, and weapons. Churchill and his ministers had hoped that the Americans would show generosity by supplying a fellow democracy with weapons free of charge, but the neutral Americans did no such thing. Congress saw the war as an opportunity to put their traditional economic competitor to the screws and bleed the old country of its properties, securities, and gold.[25] Canada's political and financial elite watched with disgust as the US was "cleaning Britain out," although King's government also had to charge the motherland for goods if it was to keep its industry churning.[26] The gloomy situation came to a head at the end of 1940, when the British were forced to suspend payments to Canada, an act that threatened the burgeoning domestic war industry.

The drain on Ottawa's treasury continued because most of the new weapons of war—from artillery to planes and from trucks to small arms—required American parts, as well as steel or other minerals, all of which had to be paid for using US dollars. However, as these dollars left the country, they did not flow back to Canada through US purchases because the Americans did not buy as much in return. In the first half of 1940, Canada had dealt with this imbalance by offsetting British and European acquisitions of Canadian civilian and military goods. But now that the European markets were closed and Britain's war chest was nearly empty, Canadian officials watched as the nation's reserves drained away.

By February 1941, Ottawa's Department of Finance examined the books and determined that the British deficit with Canada was $795 million; the Dominion would soon have no money left to pay for the American materials it urgently needed to supply its war industries, most of which were to be sold to Britain.[27] Even after King's cabinet agreed to devalue the dollar to 90 cents in relation to the American greenback and impose a tax on all imports (save for those bought with British sterling), Canada and Britain urgently needed a solution to this dollar crisis.

Secure in his electoral victory and refreshed by a brief Caribbean holiday, Roosevelt turned his mind back to matters of defence and security. His military planners, primarily Admiral Harold Stark, had advised him that if Britain were defeated and the US were left facing the Axis powers alone, there would be no avoiding war: "While we might not lose everywhere, we might, possibly, not win anywhere."[28] Several options were available, but the best of these was to keep Britain in the war. Having ruminated on the problem, Roosevelt told Americans in his folksy way on December 17, 1940, that he planned to lend Britain and other allies war supplies and weapons, as opposed to selling them. The president compared this unprecedented and extraordinary act to an individual lending their neighbour a hose to fight a fire started by "a gang of outlaws"—his term for the fascists, who were burning down the neighbourhood. A gamechanger, the program was commonly known as Lend-Lease. The Senate passed the bill on March 8, 1941, after the president had thrown his full weight behind it. Introduced as "An Act to Promote the Defense of the United States," the Lend-Lease Act was framed around arming Britain and other Allied countries as part of the forward defence of the United States.

The Lend-Lease program, eventually resulting in the transfer of $36.5 billion of war supplies to all the Allies (about 15 percent of the total US war budget), showed the awesome economic might of the United States and would become the foundation of what Roosevelt called "the great arsenal of democracy."[29] On taking advantage of the program, Churchill recalled, Britain aimed to "order everything we possibly could and leave future financial problems on the lap of the Eternal Gods."[30] Lend-Lease was clear economic warfare against the Nazis and a notable milestone in the steady march of the US towards entering the war as an ally. The *London Economist* described the aid program as the "Declaration of Interdependence."[31]

———

Though Lend-Lease was celebrated by Canadians for its assistance to Britain, the program had the potential to ruin the Dominion's wartime industry. What was the point of Britain paying for Canadian war materiel and weapons if the Americans were handing over these supplies free of immediate charge, to be paid later? King raced southward for another in-person meeting with Roosevelt. The British were pressuring him to take the deal because it would make finance and payment easier, but the prime minister, well advised by his diplomats and financial mandarins, believed that he could not sign Canada on for Lend-Lease.[32] For King, the subtle chains of American generosity were too likely to come with the consequences of permanent indebtedness and threats to Canadian sovereignty. He needed a better deal, and, confiding his fear privately to his diary, he declared, "We do not intend to avail ourselves of the Lend-Lease Bill but to allow its advances wholly to Britain. . . . I have no doubt the U.S. will undoubtedly keep the obligations arising under the Lend-Lease Bill hanging pretty much over her head to be used to compel open markets or return of materials, etc. It is a terrible position for Britain to be in."[33]

King mulled over this devil's choice as he prepared to go to Washington. What could he say or trade to secure American financial aid? Though he talked to key cabinet members, he felt the absence of his most trusted adviser of almost two decades, the man who had done much to give him the argument, and often the words, to negotiate successfully with the Americans. As undersecretary of state for external affairs since 1925, Oscar Skelton, a gifted academic turned senior diplomat, had provided expert support to King and gifted him the ways and means to stand up to the British imperialists demanding Canadian acquiescence. Skelton had worked relentlessly in guiding the country's foreign policy, and when the senior mandarin died of a heart attack on January 28, 1941, some accused King of riding him into the grave. It was a great loss for King and the country. Skelton was occasionally labelled a dangerous man: while accused of being disloyal to the Crown or a lapdog to the Americans, other critics feared his intellect, influence, and vision for a more independent Canada. Now he was gone, and King felt further adrift.

In mid-April 1941, King travelled again to the White House. Yugoslavia had just surrendered to Germany, marking another defeat in a long line of routs for the Allied forces. Unbeknownst to King, as the bombs continued to fall on London during the last gasp of the Blitz, the president told his advisers that he wanted to assist the Canadians. In Washington on April 18, Secretary of State Cordell Hull and Secretary of the Treasury Henry Morgenthau met with King, who spoke of the looming disaster: the Canadian war industry would grind to a halt, he warned, if Britain stopped purchasing goods. The Americans offered to include Canada in Lend-Lease, but King politely refused. Instead, the canny King asked for a more reciprocal program tailored to Canada's needs, including a requirement that the US buy as many Canadian goods as the Dominion was purchasing in the United States. This balance of trade would allow both nations to manufacture at a frenzied pace while selling raw materials and finished products to one another, and especially to Britain.

Hull and Morgenthau believed that Canada should not be precluded from signing on to Lend-Lease, and that the country could perhaps be squeezed for more assets and gold. But the president refused to authorize such ungenerous action. Aware of the need to assist his good allies, he invited King to extend his trip and travel to Hyde Park, some 140 kilometres north of New York City. After Roosevelt drove King around his estate and the prime minister stayed the night in a room previously occupied by King George VI, King and Roosevelt continued to talk on April 20. The president asked the prime minister to draft a few lines to capture his view of the situation. Thinking for a beat and likely waiting for his heart to settle, King wrote, "In mobilizing the resources of this continent, each country should provide the other with the defense articles it is best able to produce." To right the existing imbalance of trade, the US agreed to purchase $300 million a year in Canadian raw materials for war production and other supplies, and Canada agreed in return to purchase goods made in the US. "Done by Mackenzie and F.D.R. at Hyde Park on a grand Sunday, April 20, 1941," wrote the president on the typed-up agreement, using typical chummy phrasing.[34] Forged without the pressures of wrangling advisers or zero-sum gains, the Hyde Park Declaration was one of the most integrative trade agreements in Canadian and American history: it would aid both countries through increased trade, and would improve assistance to Britain and other allies in their desperate struggle on the front lines. Roosevelt could have held King's feet to the fire; instead, he chose the route of cooperation. The importance of King's friendship with Roosevelt in bringing about this deal should not be overlooked, and nor should his subtle negotiating skills honed over decades, but it was the president who made the Hyde Park agreement happen. The moniker "good allies" applied to both Canada and the US.

———

Britain's strategy after Dunkirk was simply to hold on and not to lose; it was far more difficult for those in the fight to know how to win. However, two crucial elements on the road to victory were finance and the mass production of war weapons. Canada would play an outsized role in both fields in supporting Britain, but only because of its close entwinement with the US. After returning to Ottawa, King wrote to Roosevelt on April 24, gushing about how past visits, and especially their historic summit at Hyde Park, created memories that "will always be among my most cherished possessions." In banding together to assist one another, and to aid beleaguered allies, King enthused that their deed was another "declaration of independence on the part of good friends and neighbours."[35] He might also have noted that this deal would allow Canada to fully arm Britain in the coming years of attritional warfare against a skilled and resilient enemy.

King had achieved a monumental victory in the economic war. Despite the allure of easy Lend-Lease dollars, the prime minister

*This cartoon shows Uncle Sam proposing to Canada, represented as a
young woman, with an engagement ring revealing a tag that reads,
"Hyde Park Declaration." Keeping a watchful if seemingly unconcerned
eye is J.B. (John Bull, or Britain). In reality, Whitehall was very worried.*

sought a different route—by working as a partner with the Americans and not as a client joining the lineup waiting for US largess.
While King repeatedly spoke of the Hyde Park agreement's role in
empowering Canada to provide "maximum aid to Britain," others
worried about how the new defence and trade arrangements would
fundamentally transform the Dominion.[36] King downplayed the

continentalist shift towards the United States, although he was candid in telling the House of Commons that "the Hyde Park declaration will have a permanent significance in the relations between Canada and the United States. It involves nothing less than a common plan for the economic defence of the western hemisphere."[37] In those expedient days of 1940, no one could have predicted the long-term ramifications of those braided economies that were forged in the crisis of war.

CHAPTER 6

WAR PRODUCTION
FOR THE WORLD

In July 1941, the American Legion held its annual convention in Toronto, the largest city in Ontario and the one whose citizens were among the most publicly supportive of the war against Hitler, Mussolini, and their fascist minions. In what was described as a mission of goodwill, American veterans came north to be feted on the Fourth of July. These survivors of the Great War served as a powerful symbol of the partnership between the two nations in the fight against the Kaiser's Germany in 1917 and 1918. Though some Canadians sneered that the Americans had arrived three years late to the party when they declared war in April 1917, less well known was the role of an estimated 40,000 Americans who had served in the Canadian Expeditionary Force. Hundreds, possibly thousands, of these American soldiers lie under the maple leaf emblem in Commonwealth War Graves Cemeteries.[1] For a few days in the heat of July, the Union Jack, the Red Ensign, and the American Stars and Stripes flapped together in the breeze, with Doughboys marching, singing, and celebrating alongside aged Canadian Tommies. The Legion also used the occasion in Toronto to recognize the thousands of Americans in the ranks of the Canadian armed forces in this new war against the Axis powers.[2] These veteran-led commemorative events were another sign that the neutral United States was drawing closer to the at-war Canadians. A mid-May 1941 survey in the US had, for instance, indicated that if Canada were invaded, 90 percent of Americans believed the US should deploy military might and come to its aid.[3] At the moment, however, most North Americans, save those relatively few Canadians in the armed services, remained an ocean away from the worst of the fighting, as they watched the German and Italian fascists, joined by Japan's militaristic class and the Soviet Union's communists, carving up the world.

———

Canny, tough, and homicidal, Soviet dictator Joseph Stalin had scratched his way to the top over the backs of his assassinated enemies and friends. Ruthless in his application of communist ideas, Stalin implemented collectivism in the early 1930s, taking farms away from landowners and forcing them to till the state's land, a practice that led to mass starvation among Russians, Ukrainians, and others within the USSR. Stalin's cruel policy involved seizing wheat, grains, and other foods from the starving dispossessed and then selling them abroad for profits that would then be invested in the industrialization of Soviet society. The resulting malnourishment, disease, and death took an unthinkable toll as the extermination of millions through these means was added to Stalin's murderous legacy. Carrying out purges throughout his terrifying reign, Stalin ordered mass murders that were conducted most heavily beginning in 1936, when in his pathological paranoia he killed hundreds of thousands of so-called "enemies of the state" and sent more than a million others to isolated forced-labour camps known as gulags, which held horrors beyond the imagination.

Most world leaders found Stalin threatening and repugnant, with some, like Churchill (who was in the political wilderness through the 1930s), publicly calling out his murderous ways. Hitler, too, considered communism a cancer to be annihilated. A Germany at the centre of a new Europe could not share continental power with the Soviet Union. It was therefore a profound shock to the world when, in August 1939, Stalin and Hitler came together, pledging to avoid conflict in a non-aggression pact that allowed them to turn their fury on others. This they did, first in Poland, where both German and Soviet forces attacked in September 1939. In victory, Stalin's Red Army, especially its brutal political officers, executed thousands of Polish officers and the elites of society, long before the Germans more systematically carried out the Holocaust against Jews. The next year, Germany's conquests in the west were matched by the Soviets' crushing opposition in the east, where Stalin's forces defeated the resilient Finnish people in a vicious winter war and, as of June 1940, oversaw the occupation of the Baltic States of Latvia, Lithuania, and Estonia. The malevolent dictators of Russia and Germany had carved up Europe, but now they faced one another. Would it be trade and mutual security that guided future action, as in North America, or would it be something more aligned with the inherent violence of fascism and Soviet totalitarianism?

With the aerial Blitz unable to break the British people's spirit, Hitler called off his bombers in May 1941. The frustrated but still blood-thirsty dictator turned his sights on the Soviet Union, his Nazi beliefs driving him to wipe out the ideology of communism and the millions who were, in his mind, infected by it. He would acquire Russian lands to populate with German people who would oversee a new society of the enslaved, and then continue to enact his genocidal policies against Jews, the physically disabled, and others that he deemed undesirable. Tens of millions would be killed. Operation Barbarossa, the first strike in this campaign of terror, would hurl 3.5 million soldiers at Russia on June 22, 1941, in the largest military invasion in human history.

Few predicted the Russians would survive the Nazi onslaught, but the German offensive was diverting massive resources away from Western Europe, and both Roosevelt and Churchill understood the value of the Nazis and communists bleeding each other white for as long as possible. The West had to ensure that the communists survived, although it would take time to send weapons, food, and resources to the beleaguered empire. Despite deep German advances and the capture and killing of several million Soviet soldiers, Stalin's forces did not collapse. Tough Russian soldiers preferred to face the invading enemy, aware that communist political officers would shoot them if they retreated. Huge spaces across the Russian grasslands also swallowed up the German forces, and General Winter froze the Wehrmacht in place in December, short of its goals. Soldiers and civilians suffered from the intense cold, shortages of food, and unthinkable ferocity. But the wounded communists endured the onslaught. Within a few months, the United States began to send supplies, food, and weapons to its former enemy turned ally, furnishing billions in aid.[4] Canada also provided support to the Soviets through what became known as the Canadian Mutual Aid program, which would include over $167 million in food and weapons.[5] The most effective way for the North Americans to hurt the Nazis was by stoking the forges and factories red hot to deliver weapons to arm the Soviets in their death struggle against Hitler's marauding hordes.

———

The stipulation in the Hyde Park agreement that "each country should provide the other with defence articles which it is best able to produce" guaranteed that the US would purchase hundreds of millions of dollars a year in Dominion wartime supplies and raw material. Unshackled, the Canadian industry was exploded into action in late 1940 to fill the industrial capacity. Building on the prewar integration of sectors in their economies to further their industrial output, these North American good allies worked together to support Britain and stand against the Axis powers.

Widely called the "Minister of Everything," C.D. Howe was a whirling dervish of action. Quick to temper but with the foresight necessary for long-term planning, he was more of a corporate CEO than a traditional member of Parliament with a law background. Howe moved fast in making decisions, empowered his reliable lieutenants—the "dollar-a-year men" drawn from the industrial class of tycoons—and then moved on to the next problem. Unlike Minister of National Defence J.L. Ralston, who was brilliant and relentless but struggled to delegate, Howe carried out his work by finding effective leaders and authorizing them to run the hundreds of components in the interconnected spiderweb of war industry. In August 1940, Howe was given nearly unparalleled power to mobilize, control, and regulate industry and trade that would create thousands of factories and jobs for hundreds of thousands of Canadians.

The staggering complexity of creating a vast war industry was made more difficult by the shortages of supplies as war disrupted trade. Canada's rubber and silk came from the Far East, and war

"Do your share in the War Weapons Drive," this poster demands. Canadians are urged to buy War Savings Certificates so the state can produce more bombers, ships, and armoured vehicles.

between Japan and the West was becoming more and more likely, especially as the United States tightened the sanction screws. In response to these shortages, and the immense disorder of occupied Western Europe, Howe and his able lieutenants established Crown corporations. These government-owned corporations would operate outside of many bureaucratic restraints, have more access to special funds, and meet specific demands for the entire wartime industry. The creation of several corporations in the summer of 1940—Plateau for silk and Citadel Merchandising for machine tools, for instance—relieved pressure in these sectors and established protected industries. Citadel was vital in securing machine tools in the US to help Canadian industry convert to a war footing as of mid-1940, and it achieved an early victory by convincing the Americans to give the Dominion many of France's tools that had been ordered before the country collapsed. The want of these tools had been a major stumbling block for the Dominion's wartime industry, especially since the Depression years had shut down so many factories. Through favourable deals like this, Canada was able to purchase 40,000 machine tools in the US.[6] The Polymer Corporation in Sarnia, Ontario, was a Crown corporation that met the new need for synthetic rubber, with the country's output growing from nothing in 1939 to over 80,000 tons in the last two years of the war.[7] Some 28 corporations were eventually chartered to provide greater flexibility for Canadian industry to bypass bottlenecks and constraints. However, private industry, under the supervision of the Department of Munitions and Supply, produced most of Canada's goods. On the industrial front, Canada increasingly embraced a total war footing that also included the control of profits and high taxes to further pay for the all-out effort against the fascists.

—

"Their battle sounds were the clatter of riveting guns, the humming of turbines, the screech of saws, the roaring of mines, the clangorous din of shops and foundries, the rhythmic pounding of great machines," enthused a 1944 publication, praising the efforts of Canada's army of war workers.[8] At the war's start, as much as 20 percent of the Canadian workforce was unemployed, but the country's factory workers soon kicked off the rust of the Depression years. Average annual income in Canada rose from $956 in 1938 to $1,525 in 1943, with a private in the army making only $1.30 a day by comparison.[9] The "army of the industrial front" included women, who were employed far more effectively in the Western wartime economies than in Germany or Italy.[10] In Canada, by 1943, some 261,000 women were contributing in factories. They were part of the 1.2 million Canadians in direct war industry jobs. Another 2.1 million more men and women were in the supporting industry, with about half of the country's adult men and women directly or indirectly involved in the war economy.[11] Women were often singled out for their support of industry. Employed at the John Inglish Company in Toronto, Veronica Foster, known as Ronnie the Bren Gun Girl, was captured in a series of photographs, provocatively smoking as she stared at her completed machine gun. Foster became an icon of the Canadian weapons industry, a counterpart to Rosie the Riveter to the south.

Less widely publicized was the hazardous work of munitions production, which involved the handling of and exposure to myriad chemicals. Over time, and to avoid poisoning these skilled labourers, new precautions were devised, including decontamination procedures and the requirement to wear resistant suits. It was

*Ronnie, the Bren Gun Girl, was Canada's alluring and
hard-working counterpart to the US's Rosie the Riveter.*

still not uncommon, however, for men and women to have their
skin and hair burned or for them to take on a yellow, sickly hue
as they suffered from toxic jaundice. Though working in less cor-
rosive environments, the "bomb girls" were forbidden from wearing jewellery for fear it might cause a spark and set chemicals
ablaze. Posters were plastered on the walls of factories, warning
of potential doom if safety was neglected. Stringent quality control
was exerted in the manufacture of shells, fuses, and other intricate
weapons. Carol LeCappelain, who was employed at the GECO
factory in Scarborough, Ontario, was uncompromising in her
inspections and recounted later in life, "I didn't want any soldiers
killed due to a faulty fuse."[12] With workers playing such a key role
in the war, by 1944 organized labour fought for and received the
right to organize and engage in collective bargaining in federally
regulated industries.[13]

Little of this wartime industry would have been possible without Canada's abundance of hydro-electricity. "This is our strength," claimed a state-issued poster revealing a strong hand through which water flowed to create hydro-electric power. Canada had among the largest reserves of fresh water in the world, and the Department of Munitions and Supply extended its control to

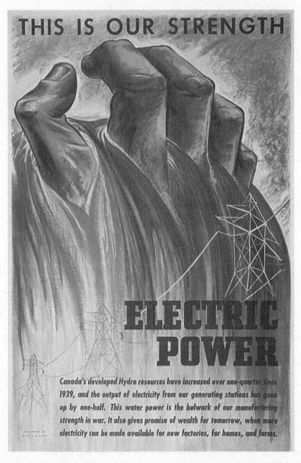

THIS IS OUR STRENGTH

ELECTRIC POWER

Canada's developed Hydro resources have increased over one-quarter since 1939, and the output of electricity from our generating stations has gone up by one-half. This water power is the bulwark of our manufacturing strength in war. It also gives promise of wealth for tomorrow, when more electricity can be made available for new factories, for homes, and farms.

The war led to the development of Canada's hydro-electric power for its industry. Electric power, as this poster shows, was indeed a strength for the Allied war effort.

harnessing this power. Concentrated in Ontario and Quebec, waterpower was captured through updated and new grids, becoming one of the country's fundamental exports to the US. The resource's necessity led to a 40 percent increase in production, which would stimulate a revolution in hydro-electricity to power Canada after the war.[14]

"The United States, as well as Britain, look to Canada for a part of their supply of essential base metals," said the prime minister in the House of Commons on January 26, 1942. "Canadian production of aluminum, copper, nickel, lead and zinc has grown steadily in volume."[15] Generating but one of the many new areas of the mineral war, Canada's aluminum was crucial to the multinational effort. Output increased a thousand-fold during the course of the war as the country provided one third of the material that was used in Allied aircraft production.[16] The light-weight and non-rusting aluminum may have been the single most important Canadian strategic asset in the war. Most of the country's aluminum went to other nations, with 3,674,284,000 pounds generated in total and a third of it going to the US.[17] Aluminum was of such great magnitude in the global war that when labourers went on strike in late July 1941 at the country's largest factory at Arvida, Quebec, Minister Howe demanded that the army be called in to forcefully put it down.[18] King and Ralston disagreed, and avoided escalating the strike. But even after the dispute was settled, precious anti-aircraft gun batteries were moved to Arvida to protect it from possible—although surely fanciful—long-range bombers operating from German aircraft carriers.[19] "If there was one thing Canada had to do to save the war," wrote Herbert Symington, the Canadian production czar responsible for hydro-electricity, "it was to make aluminum."[20]

To supply the war of materiel, Canada extracted and forged mountains of resources: 3,499,746,000 pounds of copper, 2.5 billion pounds of lead, 1.6 billion pounds of nickel, 10.2 billion short tons of pig iron, 27.9 billion board feet of lumber, and 106.5 billion short tons of coal.[21] Half the world's supply of asbestos came from Canada, and over 90 percent of the nickel used by the Allies (excluding the Soviet Union) was dug out of the Dominion's mines.[22] In high demand in the US, nickel was used in all manner of goods, including the production of artillery pieces. To conserve supply, in 1943 the Royal Canadian Mint introduced a new five-cent piece that contained no nickel, substituting instead a type of brass. Called the "tombac," the twelve-sided coin featured a V for victory. So valuable was nickel that American experts in procurement pleaded with their Canadian counterparts to increase the exploitation of its extraction, and Canada duly complied, with the amount of refined nickel rising from 137,000 pounds in 1939 to 194,000 pounds in 1944.[23]

Much of the country's steel was redirected towards ship production. As the United States charged its war industry through contracts worth tens of millions of dollars, American companies placed large orders for the raw minerals of steel and aluminum, as well as finished aircraft and ships. Canada's small navy also needed to expand to meet the U-boat threat. Commodore Percy Nelles and the RCN senior staff hoped for more destroyers, but the domestic shipbuilding industry—equipped with only 2,000 skilled workers and four shipyards at the start of the war—was not able to immediately construct these large, complex warships.[24] The relatively simple British-designed Flower class corvette was the compromise, and 64 were ordered by the British and Canadian navies in February 1940, with 206 eventually built in Canada.

Unlike the British ships named after flowers, those ordered for the RCN were known by the names of Canadian cities, and were often adopted by those communities. These anti-submarine warships, only 58 metres long and 10 metres wide, were lightly armed with a single 4-inch gun, a few machine guns, and depth charges. Meant as a stop-gap and for shore protection, the corvettes would be pressed into Atlantic convoy duty, providing service throughout the war and becoming critical to victory in the Battle of the Atlantic. Quick and nasty, Churchill called the corvettes, and they were. They were also "wet," described as such by sailors on the tough ships that rode the waves across the Atlantic, with the sea washing over the deck.

The corvettes were built in yards along the Great Lakes and the upper St. Lawrence River, as well as on the British Columbia coast. On the lakes that were divided by the international border, the Americans were supportive of Canadian warship construction even though they could have raised hell. The Rush-Bagot agreement from 1817, which helped keep the peace after the War of 1812, had ensured that both countries restrict the construction of warships on the Great Lakes. The pact had been modified before the Second World War, but the Americans might still have strangled the Canadian shipbuilding industry. They did not, and the first corvettes were in service by late 1940, with Bangor class minesweepers and larger frigates to follow. Merchant vessels were in particularly short supply, with the U-boats targeting these ships. To keep Britain in the war and to prepare for the eventual invasion of Europe, Canada set to producing the standard-design 9,300-deadweight-ton ships with their deep cargos. In 1942, seventy-two were built with another eighteen in service by 1943. SS *Fort Romaine* was constructed in just fifty-eight days during

Montreal's Vickers Yard finishes U.S.S. Danville *on November 14, 1942, with the sign reading, "Take her away U.S.A."*

the summer of 1943, as labourers heaved day and night—a point of pride for the Canadian industry. As a further sign of the intensity in the shipyards, on September 18, 1943, twelve vessels were launched from Canada on that single day.[25] By war's end, over 300 Canadian companies employing 30,000 workers were involved in shipbuilding. The output was 410 merchant ships.[26] These joined the 2,710 American-produced Liberty ships, the 134-metre cargo vessels that carried supplies in the war of grand logistics. Canadian naval manufacturing lived up to the claim of Minister Howe, who told the House of Commons in March 1941, "We are going all out on ships."[27]

The merchant navy seamen were the unsung heroes of the war. Known as the Fourth Arm, the merchant navy steamed through the enemy-infested waters.[28] These civilian sailors—who later fought for and won official veterans' status—oversaw the passage of all manner of supplies, including grain and food for the British people. "Wars can be won over the battle for food," intoned the 1943 NFB film *Thought for Food*, a truth that allowed Canada to leverage its agricultural power. In October 1943, some 245,000 men and women were employed in the field of agriculture, harvesting the wheat or raising the poultry that was essential to Britain.[29] Bacon was much desired in the British market, with over 400,000 tons moved each year from 1940 to 1944, and that amount only dipping to 365,000 in 1945.[30] Great storehouses of foodstuff, as it was called, also went to the US, with sales reaching $1.8 billion in 1944. The integration of Canadian and American wartime industry extended to agriculture, and the wartime trade agreements saw Canadian farmers gain new access to American markets. Canada's production was also sent to other nations, especially Russia and China, to help ease the grim shortages leading to malnutrition and starvation that killed about 20 million people during the war years.[31] "Food will win the war," exclaimed a popular slogan, but it was also a weapon of war.

———

Meanwhile, across the Canadian landscape, the British Commonwealth Air Training Plan (BCATP) took on its first airmen for training in early 1940 and continued to expand through the next three years. Hundreds of new schools and airfields were created, a subject that will be addressed in more detail later in the book. Experienced airmen were needed to train the new recruits, but an equally urgent immediate concern was to find aircraft. The initial plan was to use the British Anson twin-engine, which, although obsolete for combat, was still important for getting pilots into the air, but the Imperials clawed these back in order to train airmen in Britain. The mother country also stopped exporting aircraft parts to Canada, leaving the Dominion in the lurch. Ottawa insider and journalist Grant Dexter noted in late May 1940 that "our airplane industry which is based on British engine and frames not produced here, was brought permanently to a dead stop."[32] It would not be a lasting halt because the cabinet, with Howe in the lead, ordered business leaders to design and make their own machines, while new deals were struck in the US to purchase the intricate engines that were beyond the ability of Canadian industry.

Federal Aircraft Limited was established as a Crown corporation to oversee this new manufacturing sector, and its purchasing agents scoured the US for engines and planes. They would eventually buy hundreds of Cessna Cranes, light twin-engine aircraft used by the United States Army Air Corps, and North American Yales that were made in the US for France but then diverted to Toronto after that country's fall in June 1940.[33] Many agents worked out of Washington, learning to navigate the groups and committees that formed, collapsed, and were reborn—an ever-changing pattern that one contemporary observer described as having a "kaleidoscopic quality."[34] Howe and his staff were no strangers to complexity, and the minister travelled in the US frequently, moving from meeting to meeting as he paved the way for Canadian success, leaving behind his buyers so he could gallop on to the next emerging crisis or opportunity.

American experts assisted the nascent Canadian industry, in which some 116,000 skilled labourers in aviation would eventually produce a stunning number of aircraft: 2,269 Ansons and over 2,000 Harvard (both trainers); 1,451 Hurricane fighters and almost as many Mosquitos; and 894 Curtiss Helldivers and 676 Catalina flying boats. The Helldiver carrier-based bomber was used by the US Navy, and the twin-engine Catalina was a good weapon against the U-boats because of its long-distance flying capability.[35] By 1943, some 3,000 aircraft had been supplied by the United States, although Canada was also manufacturing a significant number, reaching a total of 16,418 over the course of the war.[36] Aircraft construction was exceedingly complex, with the designs going through constant modifications. In one example, the Helldiver had some 60,000 changes and modifications to its models during the course of the war, all of which had to be implemented by the two Canadian firms manufacturing the fighter bombers for the Americans who unleashed the "Big-Tailed Beast" in battle.[37] Canadian engineer Elsie MacGill, who played a heralded role in adapting the Hawker Hurricane at the Canadian Car and Foundry plant in Fort William, Ontario (now Thunder Bay), remarked on the intricacy of improving the aircraft's performance, as changes to one part of the aircraft impacted others: "Aeroplanes are not like baby carriages."[38]

Canada even committed to building the British-designed, four-engine Lancaster bombers, which were hideously complex and expensive in relation to the fighters or trainers. Delays and problems slowed the output, even with the creation of the Crown corporation Victory Aircraft Limited in Malton, Ontario, but when the bombers left the production line, they were touted as a major Canadian contribution to the air war. For public consumption and pride, the inaugural Lancaster went to the RCAF's No. 6 Bomber Group. The Ruhr Express, as it was named, first flew in a November 1943 operation. Its experiences were captured on film for wide consumption across Canada, with an emphasis on the war industry in North America having built a weapon that was used against Germany overseas. Eventually, 430 Lancasters were produced, and most were flown in RCAF bomber squadrons.

Canada had almost no munitions industry before the war, with only a federally owned arsenal in Quebec City that made small arms ammunition and a subsidiary factory in Lindsay, Ontario. In the early part of the war, British officials were skeptical of Canada's ability to contribute to the production of small arms and munitions. They were wrong. Throughout the Commonwealth,

A seemingly endless supply of Canadian-made Bren light machine guns.

rifles for the expanding armies were in short supply, and Canadian industry turned to the British Lee Enfield No. 4, manufacturing more than 905,000 during the war, along with 186,000 Bren light machine guns and 126,703 Sten guns.[39] The Dominion's rifles and machine guns were used in battle throughout the Commonwealth.

Canada also became a colossal producer of munitions and shells, hitting its peak in 1943. "Munition production on a nation-wide plan is a four-years' task," wrote Winston Churchill. "The first year yields nothing; the second very little; the third a lot, and the fourth a flood."[40] The flood in 1943 came from 130 plants manufacturing 59 million shells in that year alone.[41] The Crown corporation War Supplies Limited oversaw the risky work in several dozen plants—retooling machines, finding experts to operate them, and managing the supply line of minerals, infrastructure, and transportation. A civilian army of contractors, experts, lawyers, and agents also travelled extensively to the United States to sell munitions, supplies, and weapons. By war's end, Canada had churned out 132 million rounds of filled ammunition and 64 million rounds of unfilled ammunition.[42] The Americans outproduced all the Allied nations, generating about 61 percent of all munitions to Britain's 33 percent, but Canada was third with 5 percent (excluding Russia). To put the Dominion's figure into context, it was five times that of the combined yield of all the other minor Allied powers, from Australia and New Zealand to South Africa and India.[43]

To make sure those shells could be fired, Marine Industries Limited at Sorel, Quebec, became adept at producing the British and Canadian primary field artillery piece, the 25-pounder. Almost all of the British army's guns had been lost in the retreat from Dunkirk, and they were desperately needed in the Commonwealth

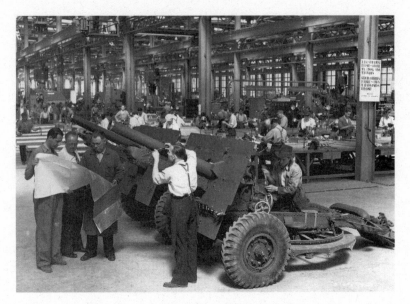

Workers assemble the 25-pounder field artillery piece.

armies. In July 1941, the first guns came off the assembly line. With its standard carriage, the 25-pounder had 1,286 parts, and, for expediency, the work was sub-contracted to over 60 firms in a process known as "bits and pieces," with this time-saving lesson learned from Chrysler's car factories.[44] One of the many hidden efficiencies included in the Hyde Park Declaration allowed for Canada and the US to ensure that that the larger nation would manufacture more complex weapons of war, especially aircraft engines, thus freeing up the Dominion to focus on small arms, munitions, and artillery pieces.

Less successful was tank production, in which the Canadian industry had no experience. With Canada's armoured forces in pathetic shape at the start of the war, Canada had turned in desperation to purchasing 265 6-ton tanks from the United States. Though these Great War tanks were completely outdated, the

Americans had, with a wink and a nod, cut the Canadians a deal, selling the weapons as scrap metal to circumvent American neutrality laws. One of the tanks had painted on its steel hull the encouraging message, "Good luck, Canada! Take 'em away."[45] They would be put to use in training until Canada could secure or manufacture more modern tanks. In January 1940, Britain kickstarted tank production in Canada by ordering 100 hulls for the Valentine tank. It was a small tank and its three-member crew operated a weak 2-pounder gun and several machine guns. Though there was much confusion over the order, with the British slow to send the designs for security reasons, the CPR's Angus Shops in Montreal were converted to make the tanks. And yet inexperience compelled one inspector in June 1941 to wail that the lack of innovation in the plant betrayed "no realization of the magnitude of the task."[46] Eventually, the factory modernized and made 1,420 Valentine tanks, but the assembly lines stopped in May 1943 as the tank was no match for German armour. Most of the Valentines were sent to Britain as trainers or to the Soviets, with one of the Russian generals writing to officials in Ottawa, "We have always been great admirers of Valentine tanks . . . which has contributed so much our common cause, the final destruction of our enemy, the German Fascists."[47] This was an overly generous testament to the effectiveness of the Valentine, but it acknowledged that the Soviets needed every weapon they could get to wield against the invading Nazis.

A next generation tank, the M-3 Grant, was also manufactured in Canada at Montreal Locomotive Works. Experts, parts, and machinery were brought north from the US to assist the Canadians in producing the medium tank armed with a 75mm gun; unfortunately, its main weapon was in a fixed position, rendering it inferior to more mobile gun platforms. The Canadians coordinated with the British and Americans to make the Ram, a modified Grant with a revolving turret and gun. The five-man, 30-ton tank had two versions: one armed with a 2-pounder barrel and the second, the Ram II, with an up-gunned 6-pounder. Twelve Canadian firms were eventually involved in its complicated manufacture.

Given the rapid advancement of armoured vehicle design, the Ram would soon be outclassed by the American-conceived M4 General Sherman tank—named after the Union Civil War general—with its superior engine, better crew accommodation, rotating 75mm gun, and more robust cross-country performance. It was manufactured in the United States at an astonishing rate: almost 50,000 were produced from 1942 onward. Montreal Locomotive Works built 188 of the Grizzly I, the Canadian version of the Sherman, but the Canadian Army's armoured formations regiments used American Shermans to fight in Sicily, Italy, and through Northwest Europe. Though the German tanks were generally better than the Allied ones, especially because of their thicker armour and deadlier guns, the high standards made them labour intensive and therefore slower to come off the assembly lines.[48] The Ram was ultimately a failed element of the country's wartime industry, though Montreal Locomotive Works was able to pivot into the manufacturing of the Sexton self-propelled gun (a 25-pounder artillery gun on a mounted Ram chassis), and it was a valuable weapon used by the Canadians in Europe. Canada's tank production relied heavily on American expertise, much of which was initially drawn from the automobile sector. As the complicated tank production process strained the Canadian industry, all the engines and most of the transmissions were made in the US, although 5,794 tanks of various types were eventually finished in Canada.[49]

Canadian-produced Sexton mobile artillery on the assembly line.

Though most eyes were on the armour, a far more important national contribution was the manufacture of Canadian Military Pattern (CMP) trucks. These workhorses of the army were made in several classes that were compliant with British specifications. Before the war, senior officers at the Department of National Defence had asked the integrated Canadian and American auto industry to produce a series of vehicle designs. The most valued of these proved to be a three-ton truck, although there were at least ninety types.[50] In support of the industrial war, the established

Canadian branch plants of General Motors, Chrysler, and Ford put aside their natural rivalries to expedite output.[51] Some 90,000 passenger cars and 47,000 commercial vehicles were produced in 1939 alone, with the wartime assembly speeding ahead along the established supply chains and electrical grids.[52] The Allied armies were far more mechanized than those of the Axis powers, and they were greedy for every vehicle that came off the factory lines. An astonishing 815,729 trucks were made in Canada, as well as 50,000 armoured vehicles, tanks, and self-propelled guns.[53] The CMP trucks were one of the greatest contributions of Canadian industry and were used in most theatres of war, from the Eastern Front to Italy, and from Burma and North Africa to Northwest Europe and the Netherlands.

———

"We must face the fact of a hard war, a long war, a bloody war, and a costly war," said President Roosevelt in January 1942. The industrial might of the United States had to be mobilized to stave off defeat that would lead to a "world of tyranny and cruelty and serfdom."[54] American war production dwarfed every other nation, with factories across the republic making overwhelming numbers of weapons: 1,500 naval vessels, 88,000 tanks, nearly 300,000 aircraft, 6.5 million rifles, and 40 billion bullets.[55] Even though weapons alone do not win battles, it is an understatement to note that the side with more tanks, aircraft, and shells has significant advantages in wars of attrition.

"No people in the world should appreciate Canada's war service more than we Americans," pronounced the *Pittsburgh Sun-Telegraph* in August 1943.[56] Its ability to complement the US's output—and feed it with vast sums of raw material—was Canada's greatest wartime contribution to Allied victory. Manufacturing 800 naval and cargo vessels, 16,400 aircraft, 815,729 trucks, 50,663 armoured vehicles, 1.5 million firearms, and over 4.6 billion rounds of ammunition, Canada ranked fourth among the Allies in war production, only behind the United States, Britain, and the Soviet Union.[57] It was also a net supplier, with about 70 percent of Canada's military yield going to its allies: Britain received the largest share, although there was also much cross-border trade, sharing of natural resources, and sale of finished goods to the United States.[58] Not only did Canada pull its weight in the continental military alliance, but it was the only country dealing with the US that paid its own way. That Canada stood as an equal ally with the Americans in the industrial war was, said Prime Minister King, "a legitimate source of pride to all Canadians."[59] In a secure North America far from the invading armies and armadas of bombers wrecking industry, the US and Canada engaged in nearly $5 billion of bilateral trade during the war, leaving Canada in 1945 to have a trade surplus with the US for the first time in its history.[60] A midwar report from Kenneth Wilson in *Maclean's* summed up the interwoven industry between the two countries. "It is realized with some astonishment that so far as the war effort is concerned the forty-ninth parallel has virtually disappeared."[61]

CHAPTER 7

A MULTI-FRONT WAR

If Imperial Japan should attack British or Dutch possessions in the Far East, President Roosevelt told the British ambassador, Lord Halifax, in early December 1941, "we should obviously be all together."[1] Such a hostile action would trigger the necessity for the US to come into the war on the side of the British Commonwealth, thought the president, who had been steadily if slowly working against isolationism as he prepared his country for the seemingly inevitable clash with Nazi Germany and militaristic Japan. Though the US believed itself relatively safe from Japan's military reach, save for the Philippines, in late 1941 Roosevelt and his generals understood that a war with Japan was all but certain. The collision course had been years in the making, and it would transform the war into a global conflict.

The island nation of Japan had been intimidating its neighbours and broadening its influence throughout the Pacific and Southeast Asia as it sought to dominate regional trade and monopolize the region's natural resources. In Tokyo, a growing segment of militant officers demanded the removal of the shackles that were holding down Japan, imposed on them by treaties with the United States in the early 1920s. Expansion was the only future for these warmongers. In 1931, a group of rogue Japanese officers launched a war in Manchuria in northern China—the country that had been Japan's hemispheric competitor for centuries. The fighting there set in motion the occupation of the area, the creation of a puppet state, and the eventual displacement and death of millions of Chinese people. With the West lurching from crisis to crisis during the Depression, all the teetering democracies could muster was public outrage. When the toothless League of Nations condemned the action, Japan, like Germany and Italy after it, simply withdrew from the international body. Japan was fast becoming a pariah state, an impression that only intensified after the full-fledged Sino-Japanese war of 1937. The Japanese unleashed their forces against the poorly led and wretchedly armed Chinese, who were at the same time engaged in their own civil war between nationalists, communists, and regional warlords. War came to the Far East before the shooting in Europe broke out between the great powers.

American foreign policy–makers had been tightening the screws on Japan since the late 1930s. Military and financial support for the Chinese, who had a strong and effective lobby in Washington, was combined with a strategy of imposing painful trade embargos on Japan, freezing its assets, and, as of 1941, interrupting the flow of oil to slow the manufacturing base.[2] Canada also joined in, prohibiting the export of key minerals like nickel to Japan beginning in February 1940, to align with American policy.[3] With Japan reliant on the import of metals and oil, sanctions were thought to be effective in curbing its militaristic aggressions. However, while the Americans and Japanese engaged in negotiations, machinations, and threats, the Japanese military continued to deepen its authority over small nations in the Pacific. The dilemma for the Emperor's Empire was evident: it was stalemated in China, finding its military unable to conquer the vast land or its great number of people, and it would likely face inevitable defeat in any war with the larger, more industrialized, and wealthier United States, which appeared bent on suppressing Japan's ambitions. And yet, strangely, diplomacy was increasingly eschewed as a sign of weakness by Japan's military leaders, who were driven by cultural norms that demanded action and force. Military officers argued for a martial solution against the Americans before the US set to fully arming itself. When all one has is a hammer, everything looks like a nail.

———

Early in 1941, as Roosevelt was rallying support for Lend-Lease, American and British senior military staff officers came together in Washington to coordinate Allied strategy. This was no easy thing since Britain was at war and fighting for its very survival while the US remained neutral. Nonetheless, from January 29 to March 27, fourteen intense meetings established a series of principles about how the two nations might coordinate if the US declared war on the Axis powers. These secret meetings became known as the US-British Staff Conference, and the final report of these meetings was ABC-1 (with the "C" not representing Canada, which was left out of the discussions, but instead "Conversations"). Neutral American staff officers were fully aware that the British were aching to have them join the war effort, with the Imperials particularly transparent in advocating for US naval assets to reinforce their fortress at Singapore, the major naval base in the east. The Americans refused as they continued to build up their under-strength protectorate of the Philippines. Furthermore, the US had a long-term strategy of pressing for the dismantling of the far-flung

British Empire, and the White House was struggling with how to support Britain but avoid encouraging its colonial reach. President Roosevelt's much heralded speech on January 6, 1941, proposing a world after the war founded on "Four Freedoms"—the freedom of "speech and expression" and of "every person to worship God in his own way," as well as "freedom from want" and "freedom from fear"—had been a clarion call to many of the oppressed and colonized people of the world to throw off the shackles of European dominance. The Americans and British were at odds over the future of Britain's colonies, even as they worked together to forge important strategies, including securing control of sea lanes, defending neutral countries against invasion by the Axis powers, and, most importantly, working to defeat Germany rather than Japan first should the United States enter the war. "Collapse in the Atlantic would be fatal," commented chief of staff General George Marshall on the plan, whereas "collapse in the Far East would be serious but not fatal."[4]

Canadians were dismayed to hear that they had not been included in the ABC-1 talks, and became even more so as Imperial officers assumed their usual habit of speaking for all the dominions. The chief of general staff, Major-General Harry Crerar, had warned that the country's exclusion would not only influence the "conduct of the present war" but also shape Canada's "future as a nation."[5] Whether this was fair warning or gaspy hyperbole, King's cabinet understood it would need to rely on the Permanent Joint Board on Defence (PJBD) to leverage the Americans effectively. The board had been struck by King and Roosevelt in August 1940, and it became an organization for sharing intelligence, grappling with issues and problems, and easing the natural tensions of conflicting priorities in the defence of North America.[6] The PJBD was to study problems and recommend solutions, although the politicians and senior military officers in the two countries would ultimately accept and implement policy as they saw fit.

Two national sections formed the board, with the Americans led by the fiery, skilled, and brash Fiorello La Guardia. The combative New York mayor was known throughout the US for his work as a reformer fighting exploitative labour practices. Though La Guardia was not in uniform, he had ample natural aggression. By instinct, he went for the throat. The squat little man was decisive, influential, and lacking in pomposity. He also seemed to value Canada. However, in the name of mounting an effective hemispheric defence, under his guidance the Americans were keen to take control of the Dominion's military. Canada's side was headed by Colonel Oliver Mowat Biggar, a distinguished lawyer who served his country in multiple fields of public service. "Spare in person, trim in dress, quiet in speech, he was meticulous, careful, precise, and reserved," wrote one observer.[7] The even-tempered Biggar was ably supported by Brigadier Maurice Pope, who would later play a critical role in Washington, where he sought to represent Canadian interests. Together, the two representatives from the Dominion countered the idea of neutral Americans commanding Canadian forces in war. But that is what the Canadians had permitted in the dark days after France's defeat, when both countries' leadership teams were panicking. Canada had agreed that, in the event of the doomsday scenario of Britain surrendering to the Nazis in the late summer of 1940, its armed forces would be placed under American "strategic direction" in the defence of North America as part of Basic Plan No. 1—code-named "Black."[8] Had it come to pass, the defeat and enslavement of the British would have been an existential crisis for Canada, and US command over its forces at the strategic level would have been the least of its worries, especially with its two best divisions annihilated in the fighting on the island kingdom, along with most of its destroyers and modern fighters. But the situation had now changed, and the Canadians wanted to make the two countries equal in coordinating the defence.

In late August 1940, only a week after the board was established by Roosevelt and King, the first PJBD meetings were held in Ottawa, with a reunion following up in Washington from September 9 to 11. The initial report reiterated the importance of the "exchange of information," but also addressed challenges such as strengthening the military forces of the US and Canada in Newfoundland, specified steps to improve the "defence of the Maritime Provinces," and called for the "preparation of a detailed plan for the defence of North America."[9] By early 1941, after the Battle of Britain was won and as the British people were heroically weathering the Nazis' aerial bomber blitz, the Americans sought to develop a new strategic plan for joint operations beyond North American shores. The Canadians were in agreement, especially with regard to defence of the Atlantic sea lanes, and they aimed to shift the Americans off the code Black plan and re-exert more control over North American strategy.

The Americans pressured their Canadian counterparts, preferring the original plan and seeking to augment it with operational control over Dominion forces. This would mean that US commanders would have the power to direct and deploy Canadian units in accordance with their own operations. The Canadians were appalled by the idea of this obvious loss of sovereignty, and they refused the proposal. La Guardia wrote to Biggar on May 2, 1941, "it seems to me that it is far better to trust to the honor of the United States, than to the mercy of the enemy."[10] But the Canadian representatives remained obstinate, believing that their country could not call itself an independent nation if its military was under US strategic command. Furthermore, as Biggar was to write to La Guardia, "Canada is all out in the war: the United States is not—yet." Canada could not "surrender to the United States what she has consistently asserted vis-à-vis Great Britain."[11]

As these negotiations continued, King's cabinet also studied what should be done to better protect Canada's borders, understanding that stronger defences were necessary to placate the Americans and fend off their demands for unity of command. Over the years, Roosevelt had communicated his thinking to King on the need to reinforce the country's fortifications and its ability to repel an invasion, and he publicly announced in May 1941, "The United States not being an active belligerent is, nevertheless, virtually ready to undertake the defense of Canadian eastern coast, including the land and waters of Newfoundland and Labrador. . . . Canada is really devoting its war effort to sending as much in the way of men and materials across the ocean as possible. In the active carrying out of war plans the strategic responsibility ought to rest with the United States, in view of the fact that in actual defense nine-tenths of the total effort will fall on the United States."[12] Ironically, it would be Canada that was forced to come to the US's defence on the east coast when the Americans were drawn into the war. Nonetheless, Roosevelt's statement would have chuffed the Canadians for its acknowledgement that they were sending their best armed forces to Britain to stand in the front lines. His casual mention of taking over the defence of Newfoundland and Canada would, however, have given them great cause for worry.

The Canadian prime minister was always willing to enforce home defence because strong borders were necessary for a sovereign nation. Hemispheric security was also a means by which to calm any doubts emerging in the White House or Pentagon about what might be done if Canada's weakness invited invasion from Germany or Japan. "If the Americans felt that security required it," King wrote, they would "take a peaceful possession of part of Canada."[13] In effect, if the US believed it was vulnerable because Canada could not defend itself, he suspected there would be no stopping the Americans from occupying the country. The spectre of what to do if the Yanks refused to go home also haunted the cabinet. King knew that despite friendly relations with Roosevelt, both leaders much preferred an agreement in advance than rushed action in the middle of a crisis when frenzied panic would override reasoned thought. And thus a major supporting truss of King's wartime strategy was to defend North America against both the Axis threat and the more subtle American menace to sovereignty.

The Americans remained anxious about leaving the defence of their contiguous border areas to another nation.[14] Before the war, the undefended Canada–US border had been celebrated as a sign of a lack of militaristic antagonism; now, given that Canada was at war and was potentially the site of coming conflict, the Americans felt the need to coordinate and control the overall security of North America. Multiple meetings at the PJBD were rife with heavy pressure and led to deep disquiet on the Canadian side about the American desire to re-exert control over Canadian forces. The Ottawa men held fast to their principles, even though La Guardia went twice to Roosevelt to see if he would intervene with King. The president declined, refusing to force the Canadians against their will.

Stalemated, the board agreed only on "mutual cooperation" of the armed forces. Beyond the board's discussions, the US military's desire to have a base on Canada's Atlantic coast, preferably in Halifax, garrisoned by American soldiers and sailors, was also quashed. The Canadians convinced La Guardia to assist in killing the idea. Despite the fierce debate within the international organization, La Guardia supported his Canadian colleagues, noting that the PJBD was a "Defence Board, not a real estate board."[15] The feverish plans for American soldiers to be stationed on Canadian soil were kept at bay, at least for a while. When the ABC-22 plan was finalized in late July 1941, it was a victory for the smaller northern nation, though friction would remain during the war—over how to balance the control of naval forces; what to do with peripheral countries like Newfoundland, Greenland, and Iceland; and how to coordinate limited resources.[16] And yet the fact that Canada would engage in all of these discussions as a nominal equal with the United States through the PJBD reflected the importance that Washington placed on hemispheric defence, as well as its understanding that it had to work with the Canadians, not dictate to them.

———

President Roosevelt, who had slowly shifted his divided country from isolation towards a position of more openly siding with the Commonwealth, declared on May 27, 1941, a state of unlimited national emergency because of the fascist threat that he characterized as having a goal of overthrowing the "existing democratic order."[17] Canada had played a role in bridging differences, with Prime Minister King, who had helped to bring the two giants of

Roosevelt and Churchill together in 1940, taking pride in his actions but suffering bruises as he was caught in the middle. While King knew he had done good work with the defence and trade agreements that would allow the Dominion to support Britain, he was soon to find that with the British desperate to win over the Americans, Canada would be pushed aside. This was revealed starkly at the Atlantic Conference in August 1941, when Churchill crossed the ocean to meet with Roosevelt at Argentia, Newfoundland. Not only did he not invite King to attend, but he also informed the Canadian prime minister of the meeting only at the last moment. Churchill wanted no distractions as he sought to forge a close relationship with the president.

On August 2, President Roosevelt left Washington for New London, Connecticut, telling reporters he was going on a fishing trip. Journalists scrambled for information when General George Marshall also disappeared. A few days later, the president's yacht was met by USS *Augusta*, the heavy cruiser flagship of the US Atlantic Fleet. With its escort of four destroyers, the convoy churned at high speed to Placentia Bay, a remote cove in Newfoundland's southeastern coast that had been awarded to the US as part of the destroyers-for-bases deal. The fishing people of the small village at Argentia watched in amazement as five warships lay at anchor through two days of rough weather, including sleet, rain, and fog. Such was the unpredictable weather off Newfoundland, even in high summer. Equally stunning, the enormous HMS *Prince of Wales*, one of the Royal Navy's newest battleships, arrived from across the Atlantic for the historic meeting.

Dressed in a naval uniform and peaked cap, Churchill met the president for the first time since the start of the war, and for only the second time in his life. As the ship's band played "God Save the King," Churchill and his entourage came aboard *Augusta*. The two leaders fast became friends, with both putting on the charm offensive while leaving the military staff to work out the details over four days of meetings. Churchill often owned the room with his great knowledge, loquacious oration, and unbridled optimism. A heavy cigar smoker, and heavier drinker—starting early with champagne and working his way up to whisky during the day—he was almost never seen to be tipsy. And this even though he drank all day, much to the amazement of everyone who ever met him, leading one observer to quip that he was no alcoholic, "for no alcoholic could drink that much."[18]

Churchill, it seems, was fuelled by an inner fire. With both leaders given to poetry and a love of the navy, Churchill was also sure to remind Roosevelt of his American mother and how that gave him insight into the US. It really didn't, but the two men were looking for connections in fraught times, and Churchill often referred to the two nations as the "Anglo-Saxons." Roosevelt did not need much prodding to like the British prime minister, with their active minds and penchant for storytelling drawing them together. The two would exchange some 2,000 pieces of correspondence during the course of the war.[19] Like all crisis leaders, they had to find ways to overcome their differences—including, on Churchill's side, the belief that Roosevelt should have stood by the democracies more firmly, and on Roosevelt's, his dislike of Britain's tendency to lord over its far-flung empire. Their relationship was crucial to Allied victory.

The rich texture of the leaders' friendship emerged over the coming days, but behind the scenes, the military staffs engaged in a different dance that carried with it the occasional flash of the blade. The British senior military officers were well briefed and ably supported, and in discussing the strategic direction of the coming war, the Americans soon realized they were outclassed by the crisp replies that deflected the US goal of rapidly taking the war to Germany should the United States enter the conflict. The Americans talked unwisely of invading Europe as soon as possible, with the British more cautious and aware that any force would likely be destroyed on the beaches of occupied France. There was, however, more agreement than friction, and both Britain and the US agreed to send considerable aid to the Russians to keep fighting the Nazis on the Eastern Front, while Roosevelt promised essential aircraft to the British. The ever-anxious Churchill hoped for more, but the president was constrained in his actions since it was only the US Congress that had the power to declare war.

Churchill pressed his new friend for a public declaration of Anglo-American unity. Even though Roosevelt could not be drawn into any announcement of war against Hitler, he offered an eight-point statement that would be known as the Atlantic Charter. A foundational document, the charter laid out a vision of a future defined by self-determination for peoples, economic development and trade, and "freedom from fear and want." These noble sentiments were a beacon of light in a world dominated by fascism, war, and conquest. When the Atlantic Charter was presented publicly on August 12, 1941, it laid out the principles of the struggle and an idealized postwar system, and it further tied the United States and Britain together in the implementation and enforcement of this new global order. Hitler found it deeply troubling and saw it as another sign that he would soon face an Anglo-American military alliance.

The conference is best remembered for the forging of the Atlantic Charter, but in terms of Canadian and American relations in the name of North American defence, it led to a new protection of the sea lanes in the Battle of the Atlantic. On Roosevelt's order, the US Navy, though still technically neutral, took over control of the northwestern Atlantic, escorting the fast convoys from North America to Iceland, which was now occupied by US military personnel. This was pushing the bounds of neutrality, and Roosevelt talked about the possibility—some felt his hope—that the Germans would fire on American ships. His administration publicly presented this naval engagement as an act of ensuring "freedom of the seas."[20] There were some German attacks on US warships later in 1941, but Roosevelt did not think this was enough to convince the isolationists that the nation should go to war. He further committed his navy, ordering it to act aggressively, although he was anxious to keep the U-boats from North American waters, as well as the Royal Navy, whose presence he feared would challenge the Monroe Doctrine.

The American protection of these convoys freed up several dozen British warships to focus on defence of their home waters against the German surface raiders and U-boat threat. In all of this, Canada was pushed aside, and the American control of the convoys was a blow to the Royal Canadian Navy. Matters were made even worse as the RCN was assigned the slow convoys consisting of older merchant vessels. Since a convoy could travel only as rapidly as its slowest ship, it made sense to divide them up, keeping the fast ones together. But that left the smoke-belching clapped-out rust buckets for the Canadians. These were easier victims for the U-boats, and in the coming months, this would be a huge burden to the Canadian sailors. Aware of the pressing need to accept any and all convoy support to stave off the U-boats, the RCN's senior brass agreed to the US Navy's overall command under Hemisphere Defense Plan No. 4, but behind the scenes senior RCN commanders like Rear-Admiral Leonard Murray continued to manoeuvre for Canadian control and influence in the hope of making a name for the RCN.[21]

As the warships steamed away from Argentia, Canadians learned of the momentous meeting and wondered where their leader had been. Prime Minister King raged at his exclusion by the Downing Street dominators whom he viewed as the culprit for cutting him out as their go-between with the president. A mortified King stewed about the insult for days, spewing sulphurous phrases to advisers and journalists, and writing in his diary about the "extraordinary" insult to Canada, with the British "simply saying that we would be told what had been done, though having no voice in the arrangements."[22] Refusing to blame the Americans, even though Roosevelt was also unyielding about not including King, the Canadian leader refused to be mollified. He warned the British high commissioner, Malcolm MacDonald, a steadying force in Ottawa since April 1941, that underhanded actions like this would be the way that the "British lost their friends, wanting them in foul weather and ignoring them in fair."[23] In his embarrassment, King was most disgusted by the optics of the exclusion and was little concerned that the RCN was under the strategic guidance of a neutral nation. How the RCN negotiated this will be explored later in the book, but the Canadian sea captains did not respond well to being ordered about by a neutral power.

With all eyes on the east coast as the German U-boats ranged deep across the Atlantic, the west coast remained poorly defended. The primary American base for the Pacific Fleet was at Pearl Harbor, Hawaii, some 4,000 kilometres from the US mainland. It was also 6,600 kilometres from the Japanese islands, and so thought to be safe. As a series of American embargos bit hard into Japanese reserves, Tokyo's war leaders ordered their navy and army to expand influence against the exposed French and Dutch colonies that had a wealth of resources like rubber and oil. The British understood their empire was vulnerable, especially Hong Kong, although the Imperial fortress at Singapore was expected to hold in the face of any attack. Roosevelt was under no illusions about Germany and Japan's plans for aggression, describing their pact as an "unholy alliance" with a goal to "dominate and enslave the entire human race."[24] The Americans were in danger too: their military base in the Philippines was unlikely to survive a full-scale assault. And yet for the Americans and British to do nothing, and thus continue to show weakness against flagrant Japanese belligerence, was viewed as inviting an attack. The failed appeasement of Hitler also shadowed these strategic decisions.

The Japanese military high command had struggled with how best to strike at the United States, with its much larger and distant land mass, population, and industrial power. Even in the face of such realities, military officers who harboured a long sense of grievance felt that any concession or diplomatic solution would be a humiliation. Options narrowed. It was decided that the goal of expanding the new Japanese empire could not be achieved unless a knock-out blow was delivered against the American navy to restrict its ability to project power across the Pacific. Furthermore, the Japanese high command predicted that if the US was driven to its knees, the other colonial powers would similarly fall and the

Americans would sue for peace. This was a significant misreading of the American people's will, rooted in a grossly misshapen idea that the US was corrupted and weakened by its wealth, having grown soft with opulence. In October, the appointment as prime minister of Hideki Tojo—a general known as the Razor who had blood on his hands from the China war—all but sealed the case for an offensive against the United States.

Even though the Americans had deciphered encrypted dispatches from Tokyo's Foreign Office, resolute discipline and radio silence shrouded the coming Japanese operation. The Americans believed in late November 1941 that war was inevitable, given evidence of Japanese manoeuvres against Singapore, the East Indies, and the Philippines, but the primary assault on Pearl Harbor was a complete surprise. Why? Naval air power was untested, and unimaginative American officers did not anticipate the potential threat from the air by a Japanese fleet so far from home.[25] As the defences at Pearl Harbor remained unready for battle, the commander-in-chief of the Japanese Combined Fleet, Admiral Isoroku Yamamoto, mobilized six fleet carriers armed with four hundred dive bombers, torpedo planes, and Zero fighters to take the war to the United States.

The assault came on December 7, 1941, as Japanese dive bombers with the rising sun emblem on their wings flew in from the north. Radio silence was broken at 7:53 a.m. by the call of "*Tora! Tora! Tora!*" (Tiger! Tiger! Tiger!). The Japanese punished the American warships that, being tied up, were almost impossible to miss as targets. The US military had felt the need to keep them close together to guard against possible fifth columnist saboteurs. Similarly grouped aircraft on the ground were easily destroyed.

Amid the fire, smoke, and screams of the wounded, two American battleships were sunk and lost, while others were damaged. Three others were sunk but raised, and they would serve again against the Axis powers. Over 2,400 Americans were killed and almost half that number wounded. But the three American aircraft carriers were not in harbour, and the smashed warships were repaired with astonishing speed. The strike left the victors hoping that the US would wilt and surrender.

As Americans reeled in shock, the isolationists were doomed as a political force, realizing that the nation's mass grief would be channelled into actionable fury. When Winston Churchill heard of the surprise Japanese attack, he nearly bounced with joy, knowing that the Americans would have no choice but to finally join the alliance. "Dreamed of, aimed at, and worked for, and now it has come to pass," said the British warlord.[26] However, US wrath was directed at the wrong enemy. As the Americans licked their wounds and planned for a total war in the Far East, the challenge for the British was to keep them focused on the Nazis.

Adolf Hitler solved Churchill's problem with one of his greatest strategic blunders of the war. The dictator declared war on the United States on December 11, 1941, believing it was the time to strike at the Americans when they were down. Having raged about Roosevelt's aid to Britain, Hitler obsessed over fantastic visions of Jewish cabals controlling the US government and, in his words, weakening its "mongrel society."[27] He had placed Germany in a multi-front war: against the Soviet Union in the east; against the British and the Commonwealth in North Africa and, to a lesser extent, in western Europe; and now against the United States.

The US was deeply unready for a two-front war, but Canada was quick to action. With news of Pearl Harbor reaching Ottawa on the night of the 7th, the cabinet signed an order-in-council declaring war against Japan for having "wantonly and treacherously attacked British territory and British forces, and also United States territory and United States forces."[28] The order boldly noted that this was a decision of the Parliament of Canada and that it was completed without consulting London. In a strange quirk of fate, Canada went to war with Japan before the United States moved to do so, a deliberate measure by King to act fast and stand by the country's wounded ally.[29] And yet there was every reason for the Dominion to do so. For even though the devastation at Pearl Harbor eclipsed other Japanese offensives, about 2,000 Canadians were in fierce combat with Japanese soldiers in the British colony of Hong Kong.

––––

Despite military appraisals by the British that they could not hold Hong Kong against a sustained assault, Churchill felt he needed to make a show of force in the hope of dissuading the Japanese from attack.[30] After two years of loss and setbacks, Churchill feared another series of potential defeats. The Commonwealth must fight. He and other senior generals came to believe that if the garrison were strengthened, it might have a chance until reinforcements arrived by sea, an appreciation partially shaped by contempt for the fighting abilities of the Japanese based on their supposed racial inferiority. This was wishful thinking masquerading as a strategy, but there were no good options. Britain certainly couldn't simply abandon the colony, as it was a key port through which military aid flowed to the Chinese, who were resisting the Japanese. Thousands of British subjects also resided in Hong Kong. Were they to be abandoned to the same fate as those massacred by the Japanese in other occupied Chinese cities? The only viable course appeared to be choosing this lesser evil and praying that the defence would hold.

In the early fall of 1941, Canada was asked to contribute soldiers to this fight in the Far East. At the time, Major-General Harry Crerar advocated forcefully for the army to send two battalions to the colony to assist in its defence.[31] Both Crerar and Ralston pushed for the inclusion of Canadian soldiers since the army had not been engaged in much action, with some grumbling in Britain (and even in the Canadian army) that the Dominion's soldiers seemed to be sitting out the war in the pubs. They were not, having defended the island kingdom from potential invasion, but some journalists had begun to squawk that it was King's cowardly government that was holding back the army. As the Canadian military had little intelligence-gathering ability and Britain was unwilling to share its dire assessment of the garrison's slim chances of surviving a Japanese attack, the cabinet lacked access to information on the ground. Though King worried that the demand had the whiff of an Imperial plot, Ralston was adamant, invoking the need to stand by the United States and noting that, in his view, the US was "none too ready to come in [to the war], and anything which would either defer or deter Japan from coming in would be highly desirable."[32] King relented.

About 2,000 members of the Winnipeg Grenadiers and Royal Rifles of Canada, forming a unit known as C Force, were sent to the Hong Kong garrison, arriving approximately three weeks before the Japanese offensive. As the Canadians settled in, their officers worked with the British commander, Major-General Christopher Maltby, to understand his plan of defence. The

Canadian infantrymen training for battle in Hong Kong.

British colony consisted of the island of Hong Kong and the New Territories on the Chinese mainland, with the core of the population concentrated in the port city of Kowloon. Maltby aimed to meet the enemy in battle on the mainland, fight a delaying action of about two weeks, and then fall back slowly to the island. There, the troops would hold out until Royal Navy reinforcements arrived.

The battle for Hong Kong went poorly from the start, with the Japanese catching the garrison forces unprepared. The assault was timed to coincide with the attack on Pearl Harbor, though it landed on the 8th because of the colony's position east of the international date line. Furthermore, General Maltby had poorly situated his defenders on the mainland, spread out over a wide front and with little central reserve. Japan had been at war since 1937, and their battle-hardened soldiers knew how to hit hard and fast. They soon crashed through the Allied defences and destroyed the few RAF aircraft on the ground that might have aided in aerial observation. Within a week, Maltby's force—including British, Scottish, Indian, and Hong Kong militia—retreated to the island, where the 2,000 Canadians were situated. On the mainland, the Japanese murdered, raped, and pillaged, with the burning buildings throwing up a dark cloud that wafted over the island.

In addition to Hong Kong, the Japanese struck throughout Southeast Asia, overrunning independent Thailand and British-ruled Malaya (modern-day Malaysia), and, in a few months, the oil-crucial Dutch East Indies (modern-day Indonesia). Nothing was more shocking to the British than the sinking of two capital ships, *Prince of Wales* and *Repulse*, off of Malaya by Japanese dive and torpedo bombers on December 10. These were crippling losses to the Empire's prestige and its ability to protect colonies and outposts. It also meant there would be no support for the Hong Kong defenders. That same day, the first Japanese soldiers came ashore at Luzon, the primary island in the Philippines. American general Douglas MacArthur's headquarters remained strangely passive in the face of this all-out assault, and as on other fronts, the Japanese air force of Mitsubishi bombers and Zero fighters destroyed many American aircraft that were left exposed, almost wing-to-wing, on Clark Field.

At Hong Kong, the Japanese soldiers grouped for an amphibious storming on December 18 to capture the island. Maltby had done little to reinforce the most obvious landing site, and with the Japanese forces traversing the open water in small boats in a gutsy night attack, Indian positions were overwhelmed. On the 19th, the Japanese surged ahead, taking the high ground that Maltby had

The graves of Canadian soldiers who were
killed during the battle for Hong Kong.

failed to strengthen with defenders. Plumbing the depths of failed generalship, Maltby even neglected to guard the island's water supply, which was soon captured. From this point, the defenders were fated to defeat. The Canadians nonetheless fought day and night, striking and retreating, gathering together reinforcements and hurling themselves again at the enemy. "The situation is getting worse," wrote Corporal George Verreault, a Canadian signaller from Montreal. "We are trapped like rats. We can't escape. We've been told that the Japs do not take prisoners. What a way to die."[33]

The fighting continued until Christmas Day, when the last of the Allied forces surrendered. The Canadian brigadier, John K. Lawson, was among the slain, his position overrun as he met the enemy with two pistols drawn, blazing away until he was cut down. He was among the 290 Canadians killed. Another 493 were wounded.[34] The Japanese treated those who had laid down arms savagely, beating and humiliating the captured, executing some of the injured. They also abused and raped army nurses and civilian women on the island. The survivors of the garrison were marched into captivity, where they would face a new war of endurance in brutal conditions.

———

"War comes to North America," was just one of many grim headlines in Canadian newspapers after Pearl Harbor, with a prediction in Toronto's *Globe and Mail* that now "it will be a total war for every man and woman who can help. It will mean in reality a total war for Canada, whose southern boundary, for war purposes, will no longer exist."[35] While there remained a border, continental defence became even more vital, with the two nations feeling a new urgency to coordinate military action and economic productivity. At the same time, as King observed worriedly in his diary a few days after Pearl Harbor, the Japanese had struck a heavy blow upon the British, which might drive Canada further into the arms of the US. "As one who loved the Empire, and felt strongly about belonging to it as against belonging to the [United] States," he wrote, "we had to be careful to see that our moves did not lead the people in that latter direction instead of the former now that a hemisphere war was on."[36] The new Japanese threat would test Canadians. In this fight for survival, they were forced to balance security with sovereignty, aware that either military defeat or uninhibited martial cooperation in the pursuit of victory might lead to assimilation by the United States.

CHAPTER 8

DOMESTIC VICTIMS OF HEMISPHERIC DEFENCE

"Vancouver is fighting with its back to the wall!" reported one British official, referring to the expected Japanese invasion of Canada's west coast in early 1942.[1] The Japanese conquests had convulsed the United States and shattered the notion of European supremacy. Victories against the British and American fleets and the occupation of Hong Kong, Wake Island, and Guam were all devastating. The lowest point for the Allies was the collapse of Singapore on February 15, 1942, a cataclysmic and baffling defeat that led to the surrender of 130,000 British soldiers to a numerically inferior Japanese force. Churchill nearly wept at the humiliation. Amid this calumny of defeat and disgrace, the west coast of North America seemed open to attack.

———

Canada's declaration of war against Japan was, according to a *Winnipeg Tribune* reporter in Washington, "hailed as an expression of solidarity in the common interests of American nations," and now it was anticipated that the two countries would liaise even more closely in matters of defence.[2] In response to the immediate danger in the Pacific, American and Canadian fighting forces were rushed to populate dilapidated coastal guns and strongholds, although this did little to stop the speculation, rumour, and worry about whether the defenders, with little training in tactics or combined-arms fighting, could be battle-ready before the invasion came. The frantic Americans pressured the Canadians to place their military forces in British Columbia under US command to create a unified front from Alaska to California.[3] Canadian authorities refused, even as they understood that the Americans needed to be reassured with action. At this time, one Department of External Affairs report warned that the US was in no mood to consult Canada on its plans and programs, revealing perhaps that it too had something to learn about being an ally. Nonetheless, the author of the warning, Hugh Keenleyside, a scholar of the US who was well respected by the Roosevelt administration, felt that Canada must act with boldness to avoid any sense in Washington that the Dominion was little more than "a colonial dependency."[4] Canada had to pull its weight, and separate from Britain. It would do so, with new infantry formations joining RCAF squadrons already stationed in the West to confront the "mounting menace," as the *Ottawa Citizen* called the wave of invaders in the Pacific that was rolling towards North America.[5]

Newspapers across the country, but especially in British Columbia, with its astonishingly long and jagged coastline of 25,725 kilometres, worried readers by imagining the many ways that the Japanese could take the Americans and Canadians by surprise.[6] Japanese army and navy victories in the Far East created a hysteria in BC, with civilian leaders and members of the public offering widespread predictions that an invasion was coming and that the coast's defences were grossly inadequate. Ottawa was repeatedly and roundly condemned for its inaction. Writing in her diary, journalist Gwen Cash described the widespread panic in Victoria, made worse by the rushing about of poorly equipped soldiers, the sight of obsolete aircraft flying up and down the coast searching for enemy forces, and the issuing of gas masks to some but not all because there were not enough to go around. Describing the prevailing attitude towards the treatment of Japanese Canadians—how the federal government had allowed them to remain free when it was believed they would likely aid an invading force—Cash raged, "The island is of course filled with rumours and seething with indignation."[7] As news emerged of the Japanese atrocities in the Pacific, Cash all but resigned herself and others to being sacrificed by out-of-touch officials in Ottawa who were moving too slowly to respond to the coming battle for North America. Officials in BC, and later in the capital, were disquieted too, especially by the possibility of internal assistance being provided to an attacking force, as had been the case in most of the Japanese victories in the first months of the war. With 23,000 Japanese Canadians and Japanese nationals living in British Columbia, one provincial intelligence report noted that "while it is difficult to know the precise feeling" of these people who looked like the enemy, it is not unreasonable to suppose that they have a "natural predilection towards the country from which they spring." The report concluded that "from a military point of view," in the event of a war between Canada and Japan, "these people offer a problem of the first magnitude."[8]

Long before the Japanese threat, the state had branded some Canadians as internal enemies. With powers under the War Measures Act, federal authorities had the right to restrict or remove civil liberties, to impose censorship, and to curtail freedoms. After Stalin sided with Hitler in August 1939, and with the Canadian government aware that orders had been sent to communists around the world to undermine democratic society, a number of known traitors or communist agitators had been detained. Some, like high-profile communist campaigner Tim Buck, fled to the United States; he had consistently spoken about how Canada should withdraw from the "Imperialist War."[9] But this was no blanket prosecution, and only eighty-seven communists had been arrested by January 1941.[10] A relatively small number of Italian Canadians were also viewed as enemies of the state when Mussolini's fascist Italy entered the war on the side of the Axis powers. Italian-Canadian fascists had for many years spread their odious ideology, although the "Blackshirts"—usually aggressive young men strutting about in black uniforms that mimicked those worn by Mussolini's forces—remained a minority within the larger loyal Italian Canadian community. With Canada at war with Italy, police rounded up and imprisoned many of the most vocal thugs, along with some unfortunate innocents. About 600 were put behind bars or barbed wire.[11] No widespread campaign of harassment or imprisonment was carried out on Italian Canadians, or on the 800 interned German Canadians, many of whom had been identified in Nazi movements, like the Swastika clubs in Manitoba, Ontario, and Quebec.[12] Far more Italian and German Canadians served in the armed forces than ever agitated for fascism.

———

The fall of Hong Kong on Christmas Day 1941 left thousands of Canadians agonizing over the fates of their fathers, sons, and brothers in uniform. The Japanese delayed the mail from surviving prisoners so that loved ones waited months to hear whether the garrison had held. Other Canadian civilians living in Asia were also captured and interned in camps where systemic deprivation led to tremendous suffering. One was Ethel Mulvany, a prewar teacher in Singapore who was imprisoned and starved in Changi Prison. To stay alive, she organized some of the women to hold imaginary dinner parties where they talked about their favourite recipes. The malnourished women found that reflecting on prized meals brought a crumb of solace. At one point, Mulvany was reduced to eating the glue along the spine of her Bible for some sustenance. Diminished in health, Mulvany returned to Toronto, where she compiled those recollected recipes and published a cookbook, with the proceeds from the sale of some 20,000 copies assisting her fellow prisoners left behind.[13]

Though several thousand civilian and military personnel were captured in the first months of Japanese victories in the Pacific, King and his cabinet were more concerned with the weak state of the BC coastal defences. Even the major naval base at Esquimalt on Vancouver Island was ill-equipped. Efforts were made to rapidly build airfields and lay defensive systems, although workers looked over their shoulder at the vast Pacific and wondered if they would finish before the invaders struck. A tally of units stationed in the province in late 1941 revealed a paltry six militia infantry battalions, twenty-five warplanes, and three minesweepers.[14] The military was particularly lacking in anti-aircraft guns, without which it would be impossible to stop the Japanese bombers and fighters from killing at will. Speculation focused on an assault in which massive Japanese naval and aerial bombardments would plaster the coastal area in preparation for an amphibious landing of crazed infantrymen. The Canadian defenders would be swept aside in an orgy of destruction and those in the coastal communities would be put to the sword.

The BC newspapers were filled with agitated letters from the public demanding protection from the coming horde that was expected to be assisted by fifth columnists who would sabotage the defence or provide information to the enemy.[15] In this hyperfearful environment, a senior Canadian military officer on the west coast warned of "inter-racial riots and bloodshed" directed against Japanese Canadians and Japanese nationals in the province, who were being singled out as disloyal because of their race.[16] Ian Mackenzie, minister of pensions and national health, and an inveterate racist against those of Japanese origin, argued in cabinet for sending more military forces to defend BC and to remove the threat of potential fifth columnists. In contrast, the Canadian military believed it was highly unlikely that Japan could further invade North America as its forces were overextended.[17] The Japanese menace was questionable; the fear among Canadians was incontrovertible.

Aware of his duty to protect all Canadians and support the Americans, the prime minister insisted that the new chief of the general staff, Lieutenant-General Kenneth Stuart—an intelligent and articulate Quebec-born general who had risen to the top military position after General Harry Crerar went overseas for new command positions—order that two new infantry divisions immediately be stationed in BC.[18] They would defend against any potential invasion while calming the vulnerable people of BC, and they could be used to help the Americans, who were reeling from the sneak attack. Stuart initially objected, but King kept at him, refusing to be put off. "Not to be able to send planes and ships into American territory, as for example Alaska, and islands that lie beyond," wrote King, "is to risk much in the way of additional co-operation by the United States in the defence of our country."[19] The Americans had to be backed in this time of need, and the Canadians had to show their neighbours that they could defend their realm. In early June 1942, reflecting on the U-boat war in the Atlantic, King anguished in his diary, "We have been directing all our attention toward fighting the battle on another front, and left the back door completely opened for the enemy to come in from that side."[20] King was adamant in standing tough on the Pacific because he felt that the Americans, in their rage over Pearl

As part of the west coast defences, the Canadians installed an 8-inch gun position at Christopher Point, British Columbia.

Harbor, should be given no pretext for crossing the border to garrison forces on Canadian soil if they felt that the northern dominion could not repel a Japanese assault.

———

Even as the Americans built up their armed forces, especially through the Victory Program that would see eight million soldiers in uniform within 215 divisions, the US turned to Canada for assistance in May 1942.[21] With the Americans facing a multi-front war, they needed help in the north. Ottawa agreed to assist, and two RCAF squadrons were soon operating out of Annette Island, at the south end of the Alaskan Panhandle, with two more to follow.[22] Canadians and Americans would serve together on that front, and although the RCAF would be under American command, there were few worries in Ottawa since it was on US territory. In fact, these were the first Canadian forces ever to be based on US territory, and their presence on American soil required that US secretary of state Cordell Hull designate all personnel as "distinguished foreign visitors" to skirt troublesome customs and import issues.[23]

To further bolster North American defences and assure British Columbians and Americans that an invasion could be repelled, No. 1 Armoured Train was formed. A mobile gun battery with two 75mm artillery pieces, four Bofors anti-aircraft guns, two searchlights, and 15mm armour plating, the train ran from Terrace in the interior to Prince Rupert as of late July 1942. The train added to the firepower of the growing garrison on the west coast, though its use also seemed to reveal the severity of the situation. The deep harbour at Prince Rupert was already an essential port for moving supplies to support Alaska, and in early 1942 the Americans had installed two 8-inch railway guns. The Canadians insisted on being in overall command.[24] Furthermore, to defend the long coastline, the Pacific Coast Militia Rangers were formed. Eventually, 115 companies of some 14,000 militiamen were charged with defending their communities against any incursion.[25] The soldiers— wearing khaki denim uniforms with a distinctive armband labelled "P.C.M.R."—were another response to the serious threat, and the creation of this force showed how Canada had turned to its own citizens to patrol for enemy subversives, bolster its defences, and stave off invasion.

After the shock of the Pearl Harbor attack, the Royal Canadian Navy, operating out of its base at Esquimalt, ensured that about half a dozen warships would guard the Pacific waters and protect inshore convoys running north to Alaska.[26] That northern territory was closest to Japan and the Soviet Union, and, as explored later in the book, it was a crucial route in delivering aircraft to the Russians in their fight against the Nazis on the Eastern Front. Closer to population centres, American and Canadian warships and coast guard vessels patrolled together along the Juan de Fuca Strait, the site of the international boundary between the two countries. With so few armed vessels, however, the Canadians turned to experienced sailors to shore up the weakness. The Fishermen's Reserve had been created in 1938, and this loose naval militia numbering some 475 volunteers on 48 vessels sailed the waters they knew. They were on the lookout for the enemy and occasionally took breaks to pull in their nets.[27] The Reserve created their own informal uniforms and embraced very relaxed discipline, though the "gumboot navy" added much needed naval presence to the vast waters where the enemy was believed to lurk.

There were few in BC who scoffed at the threat, and fewer still when they saw the rapid build-up of armed forces that seemed to signal a looming offensive. Nine Japanese submarines were indeed prowling along the North American west coast in the two weeks after Pearl Harbor, although they were very cautious in their actions, sinking only five merchant ships. The most spectacular assault involved the shelling of Los Angeles oil installations in the early hours of February 25, causing a panic that led to the drawing in of aircraft squadrons, garrison soldiers, and barrage balloon defences. The Japanese submarines were nonetheless largely ineffective, causing little but deep disquiet. Admiral Ernest King, the US Navy's chief of naval operations, said of the new enemy, "Thank the Lord they did not understand or learn much about managing U-boats from the Nazis."[28]

———

Along with Canada's poorly prepared defences in the initial stages of the war, the military had weak intelligence-gathering capabilities. This lack of a way to gauge the enemy's strength or intentions had already constrained the cabinet's ability to adequately probe the military's request to send soldiers to Hong Kong. The bitter defeat there had soured King and his ministers on the prospect of other expeditions in the Pacific, but it was also disastrous for Japanese Canadians and Japanese nationals in Canada. Both military intelligence and the RCMP had investigated these ethnic groups before Pearl Harbor, reporting that, other than a very small number of radicals, no overt disloyalty had been discovered. But there were nonetheless some radicals. Furthermore, the RCMP suggested that "Many of the Japanese communities, if not the majority of them, are culturally, socially and ethnically Japanese," and that some were closely aligned with the Imperial Japanese Consular in Vancouver. "There can be no doubt that the actual standards of loyalty of at least some of these Japanese is questionable," concluded the RCMP.[29] An added problem for the police forces was that they had no officer on staff who spoke Japanese and they could therefore not be sure if covert acts were being conducted.[30] In this vacuum, the US shared intelligence intercepts (code-named "Magic") with the Canadian cabinet, consisting of instructions from the Foreign Office in Tokyo to North Americans of Japanese descent to gather intelligence, especially on Pacific coast defences.[31] By revealing potential orders for an uprising, these intercepts fuelled new fears—even though there was no way to know how widely distributed the directives were, or even if they made it into the Japanese-Canadian community. This revelation added to the terror inspired by the fall of Hong Kong, the seemingly unstoppable Japanese forces in the Pacific, the weak Canadian coastal armaments, and sinister rumours of imagined internal terrorist groups. When these factors were mixed with racist, anti-Asian convictions that were long ingrained in Canada, the resulting heady broth supported the views of many white British Columbians that the Japanese Canadians and Japanese nationals who lived in their midst were a danger to security.

The American fury over the surprise Japanese attack was channelled into a frenetic energy infused with revenge. The enemy was to be crushed. But what about those who looked like the enemy? "What happens to enemy aliens in wartime?" asked the *Daily Independent* out of Illinois on December 12, 1941. "We don't want any witch-burnings, or lynchings and on the other hand we don't want to be foolishly complacent."[32] The 120,000 Japanese

This Victory Bonds poster reveals the German
and Japanese menace to Canada's coasts.

Americans, two thirds of whom were born in the United States or were already American citizens, would experience much more prosecution than complacency in the weeks to follow, even as President Roosevelt pleaded with Americans not to turn on one another.

The widespread fear included stories of enemy agents being aided by members of the Asian community, who would destroy military facilities and key infrastructure. No evidence of planned sabotage was found; and yet on February 19, 1942, on the recommendation of the military, the president signed Executive Order 9066, calling for the removal of resident "enemy aliens" from areas along the west coast to interior prisoner-of-war camps. In the newly created military zone, Japanese Americans were singled out as the main threat, although the prosecution also extended to some Italians and Germans.[33] This mass forced incarceration was made easier because Japanese Americans were often culturally isolated, while Italian Americans and German Americans, as the two largest immigrant groups in the United States, were far greater in number and more scattered across the country. The racism towards those of Japanese ancestry during this time cannot be minimized, as these exposed Americans were ordered to barbed-wire-enclosed camps where they were treated as prisoners of war. Forced to live without most of their possessions, they were labelled "the enemy" and "aliens" by their own country. As one conscientious objector lamented in response to seeing his fellow beaten-down Americans: "It was too terrible to witness the pain in people's faces, too shameful for them to be seen in this degrading situation."[34]

The Canadian cabinet watched the developments in the US closely, especially the ramifications of Executive Order 9066.[35] King had made a radio appeal in the aftermath of Pearl Harbor, asking Canadians to treat members of the Japanese-Canadian community with respect and noting that the authorities did not believe these individuals were a security concern. But intense pressure came from officials in British Columbia who were calling for action.[36] About two thirds of the 23,000 Japanese Canadians in

1942 were Canadian-born, although there were 7,200 Japanese nationals who were not yet British subjects. Even with questions of citizenship being complex during the war, this large number contributed to the feeling within Canada that Japanese nationals were not legitimate Canadians. The alignment of continental defence sealed the fate for Japanese Canadians and Japanese nationals. Because of hemispheric security concerns and the establishment of the Permanent Joint Board on Defence, the Canadians had agreed to mirror American actions on the "enemy alien" issue.[37]

Following the Americans' lead, King's cabinet authorized the forced removal of all "persons of Japanese racial origin" from the BC coast with order-in-council P.C. 1486 on February 24, 1942. Labelled "Enemy Aliens," as in the United States, Japanese Canadians and Japanese nationals were rounded up, given only a few days to decide what limited possessions to bring with them, and driven under armed guard to camps in the interior of BC, or even further east to beet farms in Alberta. Uprooted from their homes, they were dumped in isolated communities with crowded housing and poor sanitation. Those who were openly pro-Japanese or who protested the action based on their loyalty to Canada were treated harshly, with some being imprisoned at Petawawa and Angler in Ontario.

As the worry about a Japanese invasion subsided in late 1942 (though it would flare up intermittently for at least another year), political authorities in BC plotted to find a way to ensure that the relocated Japanese Canadians did not return to their homes. Even though these Japanese Canadians and Japanese nationals had been removed without trial or even charges, authorities found a ruthless solution to the "problem" by selling off their homes, fishing boats, and possessions. This could not be done under existing Canadian

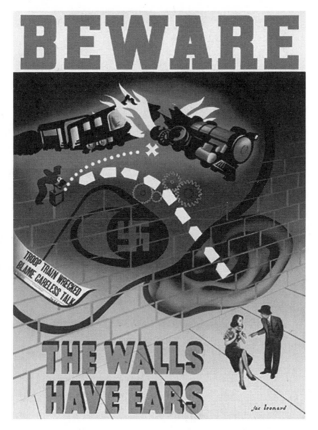

One of many posters warning against spies in Canada who were
working against the war effort. In this case, a troop train has been
sabotaged because of "careless talk." In the wartime environment
of heightened fear, the enemy was thought to be everywhere.

law, so the cabinet created a Custodian of Enemy Property that
sold the property at below-market prices and without the owners'
consent. The proceeds of this corrupt and disgraceful action went
into the government's coffers, but detailed records of the actions
were kept, which would provide evidence for a future reckoning.

Canadians and Americans of Japanese ancestry suffered under the stigma of being singled out as untrustworthy enemies. As in Canada, Japanese Americans were placed in barren sites, with many families crammed into insufficient housing in places such as Manzanar and Tule Lake, although, unlike in Canada, they were enclosed within barbed wire and surveilled by armed sentries. No community wanted them. Governor Nels Smith of Wyoming threatened that if these Americans were moved into his state, they would "be hanging from every tree."[38] In an act of absurd callousness, Japanese Americans, though prevented from returning to their communities, lost their businesses because they could not operate them or pay taxes. These prisoners were also exploited for low pay and pressured into working for the war effort or for local farmers.[39]

Even those who had served their country in previous wars were not immune. At least 220 Japanese Canadians had served in the Great War, and over 50 were killed. The survivors now pointed to their service medals as they were accused of disloyalty, asking how they could be disloyal when they had fought for Canada. One of them, decorated veteran Masumi Mitsui, was swept up in the forced relocation. He had used his veteran's status after the war to overturn the racist laws that denied Asians the right to vote in British Columbia, achieving that long-denied goal in 1931. Despite having received the Military Medal for gallantry on the battlefield and being a known veterans' rights activist, Mitsui endured his farm being seized and sold without his consent. He and his family were relocated to Greenwood, the formerly abandoned town in the interior of British Columbia.[40] During this dark period,

Tsurukichi Takemoto, another who was forced from his home and relocated to Greenwood, wrote of the injustice, "Isn't the method you're using like the Nazis? Do you think it is democratic? No! I certainly think you're just like the Fascists."[41]

In both countries, those forcibly relocated or imprisoned pleaded their innocence, although they received no trials through which to refute any alleged evidence against them. As one displaced person wrote to authorities, Japanese Canadians were "no less loyal to Canada than any other Canadian."[42] Their appeals were ignored. Some of these targeted individuals nonetheless offered to serve in uniform. At least thirty-two Japanese Canadians had enlisted before Pearl Harbor, overcoming racial barriers despite the obvious value of having soldiers with some affinity for the Japanese language serving in uniform. Late in the war, over a hundred Japanese-Canadian men enlisted to serve in the Canadian Intelligence Corps.[43]

In the United States, several thousand Japanese Americans came together to serve in the 442nd Regimental Combat Team. "Go For Broke" was the unit's motto, which summed up the desperation of these soldiers who fought for the republic even as their loved ones were being prosecuted. Beginning in June 1944, the 442nd battled in Italy, where these Americans engaged in fierce combat on June 26 at the village of Belvedere in Tuscany. A skilled tactical manoeuvre drove the German defenders to flee, and the 442nd received a rare Presidential Unit Citation. Known for its high morale and fighting effectiveness, the 442nd had 18,000 soldiers pass through it over the course of the war, with individuals awarded some 4,000 Bronze Stars, 560 Silver Star Medals, and 21 Medals of Honor (the US equivalent of the Victoria Cross).[44] Bill Maudlin, the American soldier and famed cartoonist, said of

An American poster demanding vengeance for
the December 7, 1941, attack on Pearl Harbor.

the Japanese Americans he witnessed, "No combat unit in the army could exceed them in loyalty, hard work, courage and sacrifice. . . . [We] used to scratch our head and wonder how we would feel if we were wearing the uniform of a country that mistreated our families."[45]

———

In the United States and Canada, neither Roosevelt nor King was much troubled by their governments' actions against these vulnerable citizens. Though both leaders faced a multitude of pressing and urgent issues, neither used his power to intervene or reverse the odious policy once the threat of invasion passed in 1942. When the president's wife, Eleanor Roosevelt, tried to appeal to her husband, he bluntly told her not to mention it again. King had no such better angel to help guide him along the moral path, and his truest companion, the diary in which he recorded his impressions of the day and his ongoing worries, reveals an unsympathetic attitude towards Japanese Canadians. King was a political animal. He allowed these Canadians and Japanese nationals to be sacrificed, comforting himself with the justification that he was protecting them from violence by removing them from the vengeful white community.[46]

In 1944, the US Supreme Court ruled that the restrictions on where Japanese Americans could live were unconstitutional, and many returned to their communities late in the year. A corresponding move did not occur in Canada. As the war was coming to an end, the federal government hounded Japanese Canadians with pressure to leave the country and threats of deportation to Japan. One Canadian minister, E.C. Carson, felt the "best solution" was that those "who do not want to go back to Japan should be placed on a South Pacific island under mandate to the League of Nations."[47] There had been little overt sympathy for Japanese Canadians in early 1942, but journalists now caught wind of the threatened deportations. A few raised awkward questions about how the nation was fighting tooth and nail against oppression and tyranny overseas, only to violate the rights of the most helpless at home.[48]

David Suzuki and his siblings during the war: victims of
fear, racism, and the unified defence of North America.

Surprised by the emerging public sympathy, King's cabinet referred the deportation plan to the courts. It then used the bought time to accelerate the pressure on disillusioned Japanese Canadians and Japanese nationals. Some families, like the Suzukis, withstood the pressure but were denied a return to the West, resettling instead in London, Ontario; a young David grew up to become a scientist and a famed environmental advocate, rightly describing the forced relocation as "one of the shoddiest chapters in the tortuous history of democracy in North America."[49] The awful capstone to the despicable wartime action was that almost 4,000 Japanese Canadians and Japanese nationals—about one in six of the prewar population—were ultimately intimidated into leaving the country. Most of these exiles arrived in Japan after August 1945. The defeated Japanese were bewildered to have these boatloads of refugees from Canada arrive on their shores. In an ultimate irony, they categorized them as "aliens."[50]

———

In this war of liberation, it was a painful truth that some of the most defenceless in North America faced oppression. Racism had been present before the war, but it was the Japanese sneak attack and the extreme fear of an invasion off the west coast that led to the harsh campaign of displacement and imprisonment against these Canadians and Americans. Equally damaging for those of Japanese descent in Canada was the fact that Ottawa had linked its security policy to the Americans'. The fate of North Americans was entangled during the war, and no one felt this more keenly than those of Japanese descent who were victims of irrational deep-seated racism and a justifiable dread of invasion of the northern hemisphere.

CHAPTER 9

TREADING CAREFULLY
WITH THE AMERICANS

With Hitler's reckless declaration of war on the United States having solved Britain and Canada's problem of how to draw the Americans into the swirling melee of combat, many challenges remained for the three countries in forging a military alliance. The Soviets had barely survived the 1941 fighting year, and there was a pause as Stalin's greatest weapon—the Russian winter—unleashed misery on soldiers of the Wehrmacht. An emerging sympathy in the West for the sturdy Soviet people was inspired by their resilience. The Allies also eventually sent billions in munitions and weapons to help Stalin continue to chew up German forces, understanding the importance of supporting this war of attrition that was buying time for the Western democracies to mount a counter-strike.

While the Soviets were struggling in their own war for their very existence, the Anglo-American alliance was strengthened through formalized joint military planning in the aftermath of Pearl Harbor. But before this, the Americans, British, and Canadians weathered several storms of negotiation over how to deal with Greenland, Iceland, and two French colonies off the coast of North America. When the Americans were neutral, they were adamant about keeping Britain out of the western hemisphere, as dictated by the 1823 Monroe Doctrine and by generations of presidents demanding that the Europeans stay clear of the New World. Though the US had long opposed European action in the western hemisphere, the desperate circumstance produced by the war now called for some compromise. Diplomacy, goodwill, and the shared strategic interests served by fighting the fascists were tested in these discussions, which were sometimes dangerously charged. As Norman Robertson, the undersecretary of state for external affairs and Prime Minister King's chief diplomatic adviser, warned two weeks after Pearl Harbor, the Americans were "turning everywhere to more direct and forceful methods of exerting . . . influence." Authorities in Ottawa, he warned, had to be on guard against the American inclination "to take Canadian concurrence and support entirely for granted."[1] In short, Canada would need to work hard to avoid being steamrolled in the alliance.

———

An early clash between Canada and the United States occurred over the status of the colony of Greenland. Denmark had colonized and occupied the ice-covered island since 1721. No one in London, Ottawa, or Washington had thought much about Greenland, but, jutting southward into the sea lanes, the country soon became a strategic site in the Battle of the Atlantic. When Denmark was invaded and occupied by Germany in April 1940, Greenland was cut off. New air bases there would be safe haven for aircraft flown from North America to Britain, as these machines often did not have the ability to fly the full distance across the Atlantic. Equally important, bombers increasingly were ordered to provide aerial cover for convoys running the gauntlet of German U-boats, further increasing Greenland's importance to the Allies. Alternatively, if occupied by Germany, Greenland would be a forward base for the Nazis to refuel U-boats and further harass the convoys through airpower. London understood that such a threat, leading to the strangulation of war supplies, would be unthinkable: Greenland had to be occupied by the Allies.

Though there were fewer than 20,000 Greenlanders and Danes on the island, the small colony also rose to prominence because of a cryolite mine at Ivigtût (now Ivittuut). Cryolite was essential in the production of aluminum, which was used in the manufacture of most aircraft and other weapons of war. The risk of losing access to this rare mineral immediately became a concern for Britain and Canada.[2] And so, in April 1940, Minister of Defence J.L. Ralston gave the order to occupy Greenland with Force X—a company of infantry and supporting artillery. Surprisingly for Ottawa, the Americans reacted furiously, all but accusing Canada of plotting to annex the mineral-rich land as part of the spoils of war. Major-General Maurice Pope, Canada's best soldier-diplomat, recalled that US secretary of state Cordell Hull "told us in no uncertain terms to stay the hell out of Greenland."[3] Not only did the Americans want to keep Canada from carrying out this apparent act of expansion, but they worried—before the surprise attacks of December 1941—that the occupation might set a precedent for the Japanese to seize the Dutch East Indies and other vulnerable European colonies in the Pacific and Southeast Asia.

"Greenland," wrote King in his diary, "becomes an issue of balancing relations with Britain, who wants a proactive occupation of Greenland, and the United States who do not want an occupation."[4] While few in Ottawa wished to alienate the Americans, King's willingness to appease Washington was aroused by Lord Lothian, Britain's ambassador to the United States, who had fumbled his response to journalists' questions when he suggested that, to avoid complications under the Monroe Doctrine, Canada would occupy Greenland. Known for talking freely, Lothian had, alas, not consulted with anyone in King's government, and Ottawa's ministers and diplomats raged about his "apparent assumption of a right to speak for Canada." One briefing note to the Canadian cabinet labelled his speech as "one of the most incredibly stupid and embarrassing interviews ever given by a public representative."[5]

After a witch's brew of messages, meetings, and correspondence with Canadian diplomats in Washington, King ordered the abandonment of the Force X operation, deciding he preferred to keep the Americans sweet rather than stand with the British. The Canadians nonetheless continued to press Washington on what was to be done if the Germans took control of Greenland. Constrained by the isolationist sentiment at the time, Roosevelt's administration dithered but eventually sent US Coast Guard vessels to patrol the waters and bring supplies. Roosevelt also promised that if the Germans ever occupied Greenland, he would order an American carrier, with its full complement of aircraft, to "bomb them to Hell."[6]

After incrementally moving his country onto a more warlike footing, in April 1941 Roosevelt announced that the United States would send troops to Greenland to extend North America's security frontier. By July, a consular team was in place there and some 700 Americans were building military installations, including an airfield at Narsarssuak (now Narsarsuaq) in the southern part of the country. In late 1941, as Greenland—described in one briefing to the Canadian government as the "future crossroads of the air"— took on more importance as a strategic base in the Battle of the

Atlantic, the US forces entrenched further and engaged in construction projects.[7] To monitor the rugged east coast of the island, the US Army, the Coast Guard, and Greenland authorities established dog sled patrols that were more successful in covering ground than aerial surveillance, as the wretched weather often grounded aircraft. An early dog sled victory was the discovery of a German trawler attempting to establish a radio and weather station in the Mackenzie Bay area, and the dog teams later received military status as a unit in the US Army.[8] In extending out the frontiers of defence from North America, US occupation also brought wealth and modern infrastructure to Greenland. US service personnel and officials worked closely with the Greenlanders to ensure a steady stream of goods, and no little financial gain poured into the small colony in exchange for the right to purchase its cryolite. This was an Allied victory achieved without the clash of arms, and King felt that his tactical retreat had ultimately led to a strategic win.

———

The northern volcanic island of Iceland was also important in the North Atlantic, and it, like Greenland, presented problems for the Allies after the fall of Denmark. The British felt compelled to invade because of Iceland's expected future importance in the naval war, and they decided to do so a day after Denmark capitulated on April 9, 1940. Warships carrying an invasion party of about 800 Royal Marines met no resistance when they captured the capital of Reykjavík a month later, on May 10. The Icelanders calmly watched the uniformed foreigners, and sailors even asked a local Icelandic police officer to push back the crowd a bit so that the armed Marines could come ashore. He replied, "Certainly."[9]

Royal Canadian Navy warships protecting a convoy in the North Atlantic.

While the invasion was bloodless, it engendered hostility among many of the island's 120,000 souls. A formal protest from the Icelandic government changed little, as the British all but shrugged off the occupation and promised to pay for damages at the war's end. Though the Germans eyeballed Iceland for its strategic placement, and freely used Viking imagery in much of their wartime iconography, they were unable to project power that far into the North Atlantic. But that did not diminish Iceland's importance. It sat on the sea lanes running from North America to Britain and would become a key base for ships in rough weather and for bombers supporting the convoys. "Whoever possesses Iceland," wrote Churchill, "holds a pistol firmly at England, America and Canada."[10]

With Britain needing troops to defend the island kingdom, Canada sought ways to assist.[11] The Dominion's Z Force landed in Reykjavík on June 16, with the Royal Regiment of Canada in the vanguard. Its soldiers, drawn from Toronto, were soon joined by other infantry and machine-gun formations. "Reykjavik presented a city unlike any Canadian city," noted the war diary for the Cameron Highlanders of Ottawa. "The view from the boat reminded one of many coloured shoe boxes set around and on a hill."[12]

Ensuring proper accommodation was a challenge for the garrison, especially as temperatures dropped in the later months of 1940. Half the Canadians still lived under tents that were periodically swept away by high winds and heavy rain. Next to the harsh weather, boredom was the worst enemy for the more than 3,000 Canadians who served on the island. Cameron Highlander Fred Hicks believed that the strange volcanic landscape drove a few of his comrades "stark raving mad."[13] Relations with the Icelandic people also remained frosty. In January 1941, *Time* magazine ran a critical article that drew upon testimonies from over a dozen Canadians who complained of open antagonism that saw Icelanders refuse the soldiers entry into their homes, and of foreign food that consisted of mutton "in nearly every dish, stewed, boiled, broiled, roasted, fried."[14] This was no easy posting, and to pass the time, soldiers turned to a potent local drink that went by the name Black Death.

A rise in alcohol-fuelled incidents left the high command worried, and so in that time-honoured army tradition of keeping soldiers out of trouble, officers devised all manner of back-breaking work projects. In addition to protecting the coastline and sending out patrols to keep watch for any German landings, the Canadians built new harbours, roads, and facilities, along with warehouses, freshwater filtration systems, hospitals, and defensive positions.[15] In gratitude for the prosperity the Allies brought, some Icelanders called this occupation "the Lovely War," but others loudly protested the invasion. They resented the horde of North Americans, and Icelandic women were pressured by journalists, police, and community members to avoid consorting with the strangers.[16] Hal Lawrence, who served on several RCN ships that made port in Reykjavík, recounted that he knew of no Canadian "who ever had a hospitable word said to him by an Icelandic man or woman."[17]

In June 1941, the Americans sent the first of thousands of soldiers to Iceland, and eventually some 41,000 Americans would serve there.[18] The Canadian soldiers had mostly left by that point, but six remained, buried on the island, victims of accidents, disease, and possibly a suicide. Later in the war, other Canadians would die in and around the Icelandic waters, especially when, during a freakish storm in October 1944, HMCS *Skeena* was lost while at anchor near the coast. Fifteen sailors were drowned.

As the convoy battles became more desperate throughout 1941 and into 1942, Iceland emerged as a crucial base from which Allied patrol aircraft would provide aerial coverage for the warships and merchant vessels crossing the rough Atlantic. Other constructed bases and airfields were used by Ferry Command pilots flying

Soldiers of the Royal Regiment of Canada stationed in Iceland.

newly built bombers and fighters from North America to Britain. Beginning in early 1944, RCAF No. 162 Squadron flew out of Iceland, providing important air support and being credited with destroying six German U-boats from Iceland and Scotland.[19] All the while, the port of Hvalfjörður was a cold, bleak, and lonely outpost for Allied ships. Though Iceland remained technically neutral, its people generally supported the Allies, even if they were forced to do so by a friendly but still invading force that occupied their land.

———

While the Americans, Canadians, and British sorted out complex alliance questions regarding the control of Greenland and Iceland, they found a greater challenge in dealing with France's colonial outreach. Germany's rapid victory compelled the American administration to rethink its grand strategy. Though the quisling government of Vichy France obsequiously supported the Germans—blaming the collapse of France on internal subversives like Jews and Communists, and on the British, who were accused of having poorly supported them in battle—the collaborators nonetheless curried American favour. Vichy French officials were not completely prostrate as they still controlled the North African colonies of Algeria, Morocco, and Tunisia, in addition to a modern navy that could be a factor in any Allied invasion of the continent. Washington tried to maintain open relations with Vichy, even as it watched France being pillaged of much of its treasure, art, and resources to feed the German war machine while the Gestapo executed members of the resistance and rounded up Jews for mass murder.

The Americans flailed in their attempts at finding a suitable policy towards Vichy, even when a new champion of the Free French emerged. General Charles de Gaulle, a wounded and decorated veteran of the Great War, as well as a first-rate military thinker in the interwar period, had fought his armoured division effectively against the Germans before he had escaped his country's collapse. De Gaulle was given airtime on the BBC on June 18, 1940, to provide hope to the French. Using his moment wisely, he broadcast a fiery speech to his beloved France, vowing that he would keep up the fight as the de facto head of government in London. Extraordinarily brash, confident, and prickly, the gangly giant who stood six foot five became the leader of the Free French movement. Intransigent to the point of arrogance, he never wavered from seeing France as a great power even as it was occupied, humiliated, and woefully diminished. While his stubbornness was born of his determination not to appear as an Anglo-American puppet, his brash confidence bordered on megalomania. Roosevelt and most of his administration despised the insufferable general, even as he proved to be the most competent of the French leaders. Judging that de Gaulle had dictatorial aspirations, Roosevelt was reported as saying, "I can't imagine a man I would distrust more."[20]

With the fall of France, the leaders in French colonies had been forced to decide if they would support the collaborationist administration in Vichy France or navigate independent action. Most followed Vichy, including St. Pierre, Miquelon, and Langlade, the small islands forming an archipelago off the coast of Newfoundland. An anomaly resulting from the fall of New France in the Seven Years War of 1763, these three islands clustered together had a total land mass of only 242 square kilometres. Given their proximity to North America, the islands, with their 4,400 French citizens, could become forward bases and supply centres for German U-boats to strike North America.

The US State Department made it clear that Britain and Canada should avoid antagonizing Vichy France.[21] Washington did not like the Vichy officials working with the Nazi occupiers, but it did not need another enemy. For the King administration, navigating these difficult waters was made all the more challenging because in Quebec there was significant sympathy for Vichy France, which was conservative and Catholic. As a result, Canada had preserved diplomatic relations with the Vichy regime.[22]

For the Canadians, remaining neutral allowed room for flexibility, but Ottawa's stance had more than once attracted British anger, most pointedly in June 1940, when the French cruiser *Émile Bertin* was docked in Halifax. The warship carried in its hull some $300 million in gold that officials in Paris had been able to save before the country fell, and it was to be stored in the vaults of the

Bank of Canada. This fortune was enticing to the British, as they urgently needed gold to pay the Americans for weapons. They asked the Canadians to seize it. Forced again to make a hard decision that would alienate French-speaking Canadians, King pondered his options and refused to be rushed.[23] Even in the face of a direct appeal from Churchill, King decided not to give the order to the Royal Canadian Navy. On June 21, *Émile Bertin* steamed away from potential danger to Martinique, much to the displeasure of Churchill, who felt King had lacked the will to make the necessary hard calls. The Canadians, who still had diplomatic ties to the French, were undoubtedly correct in their assessment.

———

Exiled to England, General de Gaulle needed a win. Always anxious to show his influence, and driven by a pathological desire to twist the tiger's tail when he felt the Allies were taking him for granted, he decided on a Free French liberation of the islands. The order was given, and a French flotilla of three corvettes and a submarine sailed from Halifax, landing some 230 soldiers and sailors to capture St. Pierre on Christmas Eve 1941. When the Cross of Lorraine was hoisted without a shot being fired, de Gaulle was rightly thrilled at the victory.[24]

Despite this casualty-free operation by the Free French Forces, US secretary of state Cordell Hull wanted blood. The Americans had maintained a delicate relationship with Vichy France, even though the quislings had already firmly supported German forces in North Africa. Now they feared de Gaulle's brazen invasion-liberation might be enough to fully tip Vichy against the Allies, although the British believed such a shift would become inevitable as the craven Vichy officials gradually lost independence from their Nazi overlords. The stress of the immediate aftermath of Pearl Harbor and then Hitler's declaration of war on the US had also left many in Washington with little patience for their allies.

Raging against de Gaulle, the British, and even the Canadians—who were dealing with the shock of their surrender of the Hong Kong garrison on the same day that the islands were liberated—Hull all but accused the three of skullduggery in a conspiracy to embarrass the Roosevelt administration. The Free French leader was easy to hate as an opportunist, and the British had long pushed for the islands' occupation, but neither the British nor the Canadians were complicit in the operation. What to do with these accusations? Canada did not like to anger its friends to the south, but when the secretary of state accused the Canadians of breaking their promise not to invade the islands, he overstepped the bounds of decency and diplomacy. Hull went even further by issuing a press release that instructed the Canadians to reverse the action of the "so-called Free French" forces and called into question de Gaulle's legitimacy. Some saw it as an order to invade the islands and return it to Vichy. That view, frankly, verged on the insane. The American envoy in Ottawa, Jay Pierrepont Moffat, who, though he could be prickly, had a warmth of feeling for the Dominion, warned Washington that Hull's temper tantrum had Ottawa politicians and senior diplomats in a lather. In describing Hull's order, one Canadian diplomat remarked that he was treating the Dominion as a "banana republic to be pushed around."[25]

To make matters worse, the British and the Americans had organized a critically important strategic meeting in Washington to hammer out the details of the two-front war against Germany and Japan. The Arcadia conference, which included Churchill,

Roosevelt, and their staffs, was initially soured by the news of de Gaulle's independent action, and Prime Minister King, who was invited by the president to act as an observer, arrived in Washington on Christmas Day with no little trepidation.[26] The Americans' concern came partially from a sense of their own weakness, as they now faced a two-front war and were not anxious to add Vichy France to the mix of belligerents. However, after a series of threats failed to move de Gaulle, the Americans backed down as Roosevelt refused to waste any more energy on the incident.

De Gaulle took the victory, his status raised among his own people, but he was much diminished in Washington, where the White House viewed him as a deceitful rogue. Churchill was nonplussed by it all, rightly noting that the French general was bothersome even at the best of times, but the invasion was an utterly minor event in the world war that swept across oceans and continents—and which could scarcely be going worse for the Allies as they suffered defeats on nearly every front. Vichy France seethed with anger but failed to launch any operations of consequence against the Allies. Ottawa stayed silent, happy that there was little collateral damage, but King and his cabinet bristled at Canada being treated by Hull as a colonial lackey to be ordered about. There had been enough of that from the British over the decades.

———

Over the waning days of 1941, Churchill and Roosevelt, along with their military staffs, established a new, unified strategic front. With the US joining the British Empire and Commonwealth at war, this would become the Western democratic Allied war effort. The Soviets were an ally of a different kind—absolutely crucial, but fighting their own war. Canada was the third ranking member of the Western alliance, albeit a distant third. King had almost no say in matters of strategy in Washington, or indeed throughout the war. During the Arcadia conference, he was politely tolerated, largely because the Canadian knew his place, offering only cautious observations. One of his close advisers, Jack Pickersgill, was little impressed with his political master, describing King's quiet watching from the wings as "humiliating."[27] While neither the president nor the British prime minister wanted King to weigh in seriously, the Canadian quietly lamented being a mere onlooker, reduced to twirling his reading glasses as he often did in meetings as he listened to others and planned his rebuttals. In his diary, he angrily blamed Churchill's "supercilious English attitude," although, as usual, he was unable to say a bad word about Roosevelt, whom he fawned over for much of the war.[28] Perhaps a more dynamic Canadian political leader might have carved out a better position for Canada in this war, although that is likely promoting fantasy over fact.[29] With the two titans in the room jousting and circling each other, their forced smiles and cautious suggestions masking the strain of achieving their strategic goals, King's accomplishment was simply to be invited to be in the room.

Over several weeks of discussion, the British were anxious to ensure that the Americans, enraged by Japan's attack on their bases and territory, would not turn their full might to the war in the Pacific and abandon the fight against the Nazis. Roosevelt remained committed to the Germany-first policy, although he was much aided in maintaining this focus by Hitler's declaration of war on the United States a few days after Pearl Harbor. However, a significant point of contention was when the Allies should strike Germany in a cross-channel invasion: the Americans wanted to go early and hard in 1942. The British demurred, with some panic in their eyes, believing that the Nazis were too strong, that there were not enough landing craft to get the soldiers ashore, and that the available firepower from bombers and destroyers' guns was not enough to keep the counterattacking panzer divisions at bay. U-boats were also harvesting the merchant ships in the Battle of the Atlantic, with precious weapons and supplies sunk in staggering amounts even before they reached the potential battleground. The US plan was so reckless it verged on the criminal, and the British planners deflected it at every turn, preferring instead to mount a campaign in North Africa. This, the Americans complained, was too far from Europe and a foolish waste of resources.

As the weeks wore on, the British skilfully put off any talk of invading France until 1943. Instead, and to continue pressuring the Germans in 1942, they promised the Americans a heavier bomber campaign against occupied Western Europe, a series of raids along the coast, accelerated ship production to secure the sea lanes in the Battle of the Atlantic, and a continued push against the fascist forces in North Africa, where the British had been fighting since 1940. Though the American generals did not like the compromise, they went along with the British—while also gathering forces for their second war in the Pacific, where they would largely go it alone. The present was a disaster, with the fascists winning everywhere, but a workable alliance was being forged for a better future.

———

Speaking before the House of Commons on December 29, 1941, Churchill acknowledged, "Canada occupies a unique position in

British prime minister Winston Churchill giving his rousing speech
to the Canadian House of Commons on December 30, 1941.

the British Empire because of its unbreakable tie with Britain and
its ever-growing friendship and intimate association with the United
States." The British prime minister, having taken a few days to
travel from Washington to Ottawa, was there to thrill Canadians
with his pugnacious words, razor-sharp wit, and glowing tributes.
"The contribution of Canada in the Imperial war effort in troops,
in ships, in aircraft, in food, and in finance has been magnificent,"
he enthused.[30] Indeed it had been, although Churchill betrayed
himself by calling it the "Imperial" war effort. This view did see
Canada fighting as an ally, though a junior one. Churchill could be
forgiven, perhaps, because he needed Canada's strength and influence to be co-opted within the Imperial effort for Britain to stand
as something closer to an equal with the US. The Americans, while

also impressed with the Dominion's contributions, were now seeking to build a closer relationship with Britain as it faced its two-front war, and they were increasingly willing to push their northern neighbour aside in most matters save for continental defence.

How should Canada position itself? King was not de Gaulle, with his ravenous desire to bite all the hands that fed him. The Canadian never had such appetites. Still, as a sharp political operator, King knew when to retreat and when to fight, and he did the latter during the St. Pierre and Miquelon affair. The divisive issue soon died away amid far worse crises. While there were difficulties and differences among alliance members, they never proved fatal. More challenging for Canada was the need to find a voice in the Anglo-American talks about grand strategy. King was left to the side, but he would continue to work from the flanks to aid Britain and the US against their common foe; in turn, both countries needed the support of Canada's domestic wartime industry and, to a lesser extent, its overseas fighting forces. All the while, the Americans and Canadians would stay the course in defending North America. It was in the pursuit of this security goal that the Americans would also learn how to work closely with their northern ally. Greenland, Iceland, and the French islands proved a distraction at times, but more friction was to follow—in particular, a wrestling over control of Newfoundland that threatened to affect matters of security and sovereignty off Canada's east coast and drive a wedge between the Dominion and the United States.

CHAPTER 10

FORTRESS NEWFOUNDLAND

"The integrity of Newfoundland and Labrador," declared Canadian prime minister William Lyon Mackenzie King, was "essential to the security of Canada."[1] The large island off the east coast of Canada was a fortress in the war against the Nazis because of its position between the sea lanes in the Northern Atlantic and the entrance into the heart of Canada, the mouth of the St. Lawrence River. As a British dominion, Newfoundland was separate from Canada. Though Canada had courted Newfoundland for decades, urging it to become part of the confederated provinces, the distinct people of "The Rock" had rebuffed Ottawa at every turn. The Americans were also interested in the sixteenth-largest island in the world, with both North American nations understanding the strategic importance of the land mass as a safe harbour for the warships and merchant vessels supplying Britain. The value of air power—especially long-range bombers that would fly top-cover for naval convoys crossing the Atlantic through the U-boat gauntlet—made Newfoundland even more important to the war effort. Newfoundlanders would serve in Canadian, British, and American formations, but the island's primary role in the global war was as a forward base in the Battle of the Atlantic. Not only would these British subjects find the fascist war coming to them, but they would face two friendly invasions—one by Canadians and the other by Americans. Newfoundland would be forever transformed by the war effort.

———

All countries that fought in the Great War carried scars, with Newfoundland's running deep and jagged. The small dominion of around 240,000 had contributed mightily to that war effort: over 8,600 served in the Royal Navy, forestry units, the Canadian Expeditionary Force, and the Royal Newfoundland Regiment.[2] The regiment epitomized the unwavering support of the islanders, who fought for King and country at Gallipoli and on the Western Front. After hollowed-out communities had buried their 1,656 dead, the economy never recovered from the weight of wartime debt.[3] In 1934, Newfoundland suffered a colossal reversal when its bankruptcy led to Britain suspending its democratically elected government and replacing it with an unelected commission chaired by a governor. Canada, Australia, and other dominions had emerged from the war with a stronger sense of identity and more confidence in their place within the British Empire; Newfoundlanders could look back on the wartime sacrifice and see how they lost democracy, reverting to colonial status.

At the start of the new war, Newfoundland's now 300,000 people were spread among small outports because of the island's historic fishing economy, and were grouped in only a few major cities, especially the capital of St. John's with its protected port. Newfoundlanders served during the Second World War in home defence units—with another 700 in the Royal Air Force and some 4,000 in British and Canadian naval forces. Two artillery regiments fought overseas: the 166th (Newfoundland) Field Regiment in North Africa and Italy, and the 59th (Newfoundland) Heavy Regiment engaged in defending England and then in the liberation of Europe. Close to 600 women served in the three Canadian women's formations, in forestry units, or in the merchant navy. In total, about 12,000 Newfoundlanders were in uniform during the war, but almost all others were affected by the fundamental changes wrought by the Allied forces who arrived at the island fortress.[4]

Newfoundlanders had long believed that the "Canadian wolf" had been licking its chops in anticipation of devouring the island. Though there was no active annexation campaign in Ottawa, it was always assumed there that the two dominions would continue to be drawn together through trade, the movement of peoples, and a shared history, and that perhaps one day they would join in union—not dissimilar to how some nineteenth-century Americans believed that Canada would likely be enticed into their republic. Most proud islanders, deeply connected to Britain and with a strong culture and identity of their own, wanted no part of Canada despite the undeniable economic benefits that would come with provincehood. Time or opportunity, it was thought in Ottawa, might alter opinions. And so Canadians were worried when the destroyers-for-bases deal in September 1940 gave the Americans ninety-nine-year leases to establish select military outposts, airfields, and bases in sites at St. John's, Argentia, Stephenville, and other smaller communities. Newfoundlanders were even more anxious. With no diplomatic voice, they watched the British give away parts of the island to the United States. After the deal was done, Churchill pleaded that the islanders' sacrifice was in the name of "strengthening cooperation between the two great democracies in this struggle for the freedom of mankind."[5] Newfoundlanders accepted the appeal.

The Canadian military had studied the ugly scenario of what would happen if Germany occupied the island, but officers were also concerned about the US setting up base there. Alarmed at the possibility of the Americans becoming a permanent occupying force, and dealing with the shock of the fall of France in June 1940, Canada negotiated with Britain to bolster Newfoundland's defences. They erected gun batteries on Bell Island (a key source of iron ore for the steel industry at Sydney, Nova Scotia) and sent a small garrison there to repel an invasion.[6] At the same time, RCAF bombers from No. 10 Squadron were ordered to the Gander air-field in the centre of the island, arriving in mid-June 1940. Other airfields were built near St. John's, and long-distance aircraft, first Douglas Digbys and later Consolidated Liberators, were soon conducting anti-submarine patrols that ranged some 1,000 kilo-metres into the Atlantic.[7] The RCAF and RCN commitment gath-ered in size as a new naval base was constructed at St. John's. It was known affectionately as "Newfyjohn." Leading to the ocean, a rocky and broken coastline was gashed by the entrance to the harbour: the Narrows. At only 700 metres wide at its mouth and roughly 2 kilometres long, the harbour was far smaller than that at Halifax. But the frenzy of convoy crossings demanded that it become a haven from the sleet, fog, driving waves, and enemy warships. Some twenty-five to thirty vessels sheltered there at any given time, with that number rising in 1942 to seventy vessels, leaving the harbour dangerously congested.[8] Throughout the war, a sizeable part of the RCN called St. John's home, launching anti-submarine patrols from its shores and escorting the vulnerable merchant naval ships across the Atlantic. Even as Newfoundlanders welcomed the Canadian soldiers, airmen, and sailors, one wary administrator noted, "It is one thing to let them in, but it would be another thing to get them out."[9]

———

"The city of St. John's looks like the slum district of Chicago," noted Private Cecil Hutchens, a nineteen-year-old soldier from Iowa who arrived on the giant troopship *Edmund B. Alexander*. "They have streetcars and automobiles. The people drive on the opposite side of the road." Hutchens seemed to be writing about an exotic locale as he and his shipmates sailed into St. John's Harbour. Arriving on January 29, 1941, they were welcomed by a large crowd of cheering Newfoundlanders. However, the Americans were forced to live for several months on the massive ship that had been captured from the Germans at the end of the First World War, waiting while engineers frantically threw up buildings and living spaces. When the Americans came ashore, they rapidly forged a positive relationship that would be strengthened by the regular invitation of Newfoundlanders to the US bases to partake in rich food and to watch the latest films. The Americans also spread around their high pay with no little abandon. In contrast, the Canadians—said to start more fights and be less generous with their cash—had a rougher reputation, although they too would transform the island through the arrival of thousands of army, air force, and naval personnel.

American journalists, like Canadian ones, portrayed Newfoundland as the perimeter of the North American defence system. *The New York Times* told its readers in late September 1940 that the fortified island would "protect any northeastern approach of the United States."[10] Fort Pepperrell, along the north shore of Quidi Vidi Lake, about 2 kilometres from St. John's, became the largest American base at 93 hectares. Permanent structures, hangars, a firing range, and recreational facilities were soon constructed on the site. The costs of these bases were staggering, with the US spending tens of millions of dollars in Newfoundland, and over $200 million for all the bases on the land received in the swap for their fifty destroyers.[11] Several thousand Americans were stationed at Fort Pepperrell, along with some 200 Canadian women in uniform serving with the Women's Division of the RCAF. Canadian corporal Kitty Hawker, who worked in the American operations room that coordinated and tracked aircraft, recounted after the war, "Just about every navy in the free world was there, and one felt very close to all the action."[12]

Across the island, land was appropriated from farmers in the name of building defence projects. This seizure led to a muted outcry that was drowned out by the promises of work for over 5,000 Newfoundlanders, who would be gainfully employed on the American bases.[13] Stephenville witnessed the emergence of an airfield, after which squadrons flew in support of the inshore and transatlantic convoys that were transporting war-winning supplies to Britain. Gander's airport—roughly in the centre of the island—was a hub of the aerial transatlantic route. On November 10, 1940, seven Lockheed Hudson bombers manufactured in Burbank, California, flew from Dorval Airport near Montreal to the island and then set off to cross the Atlantic.[14] Flying nearly 3,400 kilometres, they arrived on Remembrance Day in Aldergrove, North Ireland. This route would become an essential means of transporting the newly made aircraft coming off North American assembly lines to serve in Britain, and it also helped to ease the burden on supply convoys that could be sunk. The sky bridge across the Atlantic led to a fury of building. Developing new modes of planning and working together, Canada and the United States honed the complicated process, eventually establishing an airfield at Goose Bay, Newfoundland, and other aerial routes that used landing strips in Iceland and Greenland as refuelling sites. The transatlantic flight was long and dangerous, and yet the brave and largely civilian pilots—including many Canadians, Americans, and British, both men and women—eventually delivered some 9,000 warplanes at the loss of only 100.[15]

——

"We became fast friends in the idea of keeping the war on the other side of the Atlantic," said the RCN's Commodore Leonard Murray, deputy chief of the naval staff, speaking in the summer of 1940 about how the Canadian and American navies were anxious to create a forward combat zone to ward off the German U-boats.[16] Though King was wary of overcommitting the Canadian forces, he recognized the value of the RCN for impressing upon the US that his country could be responsible for the "joint defence" of North America. The prime minister wanted the Americans to know that "we could bear our share of the burden of naval defence."[17] And the threat was coming. The obstacle of the Atlantic had kept the U-boats from North American waters throughout 1940, but by the next year, as the Nazis established new bases on the French coast and churned out more U-boats in shipyards, the subs would hunt their victims closer to Canada and the United States.

There were never enough Royal Navy and Royal Canadian Navy warships to fully protect the convoys, although grouping

An ice-encrusted Royal Canadian Navy warship that has braved the Atlantic crossing and the gauntlet of U-boats.

the vulnerable merchant vessels together reduced the number of targets and made them harder to locate for the enemy marauders.[18] Maritime patrol bombers flying out of Newfoundland provided air cover, which frequently pushed back the submarines, but the dense fog of the Great Banks allowed the enemy ghosts to lurk closer to shore. Crucial to survival was the Royal Navy's integrated system of sharing intelligence on the location of U-boats, information that was gathered through the periodic breaking of German signal codes. This allowed for the steering of convoys away from known concentrations of wolfpacks. In the war against the U-boats, it was better to run than to fight.

At the end of 1940, as the U-boats savaged vessels in the eastern Atlantic around Britain, one ominous naval study concluded that the Germans had sunk 3.5 million tons of shipping that year, and that only 1 million tons of new shipping was being built.[19] As unsustainable as this was, it was also chilling to hear the ghastly losses described in terms of tons. Instead of emphasizing the number of sailors killed or the agony they faced in the rough, icy Atlantic waters, the report measured the tonnage, referring to the size of the ship and what it could carry. Whichever way the sinkings were tabulated, Britain would be starved into submission without North American supplies, and the weapons created through massive exertions in the factories would indeed be sent to the dark depths before they even reached the fighting front. In this desperate clash, the human cost was staggering. One Canadian sailor observed that tonnage lost meant little to him, and instead he could never shake the "sight of a lifeboat full of merchant sailors rowing frantically from the side of a burning tanker, and the sound of their screams as the flames engulfed them."[20]

The most dangerous area in the rough seas was known as the Black Pit—located a distance of around 2,000 kilometres from land in the mid-Atlantic, where even long-range bombers could not reach. The establishment of naval and airbases in Iceland helped to close the gap, enabling more coverage of the northern Atlantic, as did the allocation of long-range bombers in late 1942, but there were not enough aircraft until the next year because of a struggle among the navy and the air force over whether the bombers should be used to protect the convoys or be unleashed against German cities.[21] Bombing the cities won out, partially because it was one of the few ways to strike at the Germans, and pledges had been made to Stalin to keep up pressure on the enemy. But looking back on this perilous time in 1941 and 1942, Churchill reflected on the agony inflicted by the U-boat war on Britain's sea supremacy, writing that "this mortal danger to our life-lines gnawed my bowels."[22]

With the RCN in Halifax and St. John's stretched to the break-ing point and providing escorts only to the Grand Banks, the senior naval officers in the RN and RCN worked to create a new force to meet the U-boat menace. In March 1941, Britain and the US agreed to a formal protocol recognizing that Newfoundland was integral to the defence of Canada. This was no minor act, espe-cially given the presence of US bases and soldiers on the island.[23] Two months later, in May 1941, the Newfoundland Escort Force (NEF) was formed under the command of Commodore Leonard Murray, a Canadian naval officer who was respected by both the British and the Americans (and who sat for a time on the PJBD). Murray gathered together warships to deploy in coastal defence patrols and in the ocean escort of convoys.[24] This was Canada's first major operational task in the naval war, and maritime bomb-ers were folded into the force through No. 1 Group of Eastern Air Command, under the leadership of Air Commodore C.M. "Black Mike" McEwen. RCAF Digbys, Cansos, Catalinas, and Hudson patrol aircraft flew in support of the convoys. The NEF's Canadian warships, soon to be joined by Royal Navy corvettes and destroy-ers, would lead the convoys out of the harbour across the entire Atlantic Ocean. Eventually some 23 RCN destroyers and cor-vettes, along with 11 Royal Navy warships, would be engaged in nearly constant convoy work, crossing the 3,000 kilometres of the stormy Atlantic, fending off U-boat attacks, briefly refuel-ling in the British Isles, and then returning for another turn at the "North Atlantic Run."[25]

While it was always better to stay clear of the U-boats, often the enemy could not be avoided. When the killers struck in the night under a clouded moon, the corvettes and destroyers sprang to action amid the exploding merchant ships. Relying on their

Making the link between ship production, the merchant navy,
and the Royal Canadian Navy, this poster reads,
"Give Us the Ships, We'll Finish the Subs!"

rudimentary radar to detect the low-lying U-boats on the water's surface, the Allied warships steamed outside or even within the convoy, seeking the German vessels illuminated under hastily fired flares that lit the sky in ghostly colours. But the Canadians were always a technological generation behind the British since they could not pull their warships from their relentless convoy duties to carry out the necessary refit. And the Royal Navy, it should be noted, almost always outfitted its warships before those of the Canadians. And so the RCN at this stage was so poorly served by its surface-detecting radar that even when sailors visually spotted a U-boat on the surface, the radar often failed to detect it in the choppy Atlantic waters.[26]

If a U-boat was sighted, the RCN ships steamed ahead at full speed into the attack. The corvettes' single 4-inch main gun and the destroyers' more effective armaments could sink a U-boat, but this rarely happened as the German boats dove under to escape any surface battle where they would be at a grave disadvantage. But that too was good, as the U-boats were slower under water, which provided time for the merchant ships to speed ahead and escape the ambush site. In keeping up the attack, RCN warships rolled depth charges filled with hundreds of pounds of explosives off the stern of the warship, sending them downwards to explode on contact or at a predetermined depth. These blind attacks occasionally damaged or sank a U-boat, with the sub's fate sometimes revealed by a pooling oil spill on the surface, which looked much like black blood rising from the deep.

Allied corvettes and destroyers learned that the most effective technique for attacking a U-boat was by ramming the sub to damage it, often rendering the enemy sailors vulnerable thousands of kilometres from their home base. These tactics became more refined as the war stretched on, with the development of better armaments—particularly the hedgehog mines, which exploded on contact, and the squid mortars, which had a greater range—and the advent of the Leigh Light, an aircraft-mounted searchlight that brilliantly lit up the sea below. More effective and sensitive radar was important, especially in evolving tactics that involved method- ically searching for a submerged U-boat and then dropping depth charges as other vessels attempted to hold the target's location with radar. But those sophisticated sub-killing tactics were still some two years off, and in early 1941 the U-boats had all the advantages, even if most convoys made it through unscathed. Facing long odds, Murray would not back away from the fight, and in his mind, the RCN's reputation would be forged in "the success or failure of the NEF."[27]

Through all of these grim convoy battles, the North Americans learned to fight together. In April 1941, Roosevelt ordered the US Navy to conduct aggressive sweeps within an extended "security zone" extending outward from Newfoundland to the 25-degree longitude line. This zone included Greenland, and both American air and naval patrols freely shared information with the Royal Navy when U-boats were spotted. Though the August 1941 Argentia conference had given the Americans strategic command over the RCN, Murray actively resisted US operational control over naval and air assets. Admiral Ernest J. King of the US Navy agreed and restrained himself, putting into place a system of "coordinating supervision."[28] This was, in effect, the lightest of control, and King refrained from issuing direct instructions to the Canadians, opting instead for higher-level organizational guidance. Nonetheless, there remained a good deal of struggle and strife between the Canadians and Americans over the application of maritime air squadrons. This friction created problems in providing high cover for the convoys—including poor coordination between the American aircraft flying out of Gander and Argentia and the RCAF's bombers and Catalina flying boats. For the most part, the RCAF refused to put itself under US control since the Canadian commanders had more experience than their American counterparts and the Americans did not have many aircraft on the east coast, with only four US squadrons to the RCAF's ten.[29] US senior military officers continued to argue for unity of command to best coordinate naval and air defences, but the RCAF air marshals refused to go along.[30] The cabinet backed the RCAF, although it gave this support quietly, hoping to make no stink. The chief of the air staff wrote in November 1941 to Minister of Air Chubby Power, "We have held them off, so far!"[31]

Even after the Americans entered the war, the thorny issue of command and control in Newfoundland was not improved, with the discord continuing until late 1942, when the two allies improved intelligence sharing and coordination of resources. Added to this stew of national units on the island, Canada's army had thousands of soldiers safeguarding fortifications, and it commanded the Newfoundland Militia. Eventually, a workable series of compromises between the Yanks and Canucks was forged, as minor grievances and sources of friction were subsumed within a cooperative system of protecting the convoys. Some of this Canadian obstinance was driven by the desire to keep the Americans from gaining permanent influence over Newfoundland.[32]

———

Warships and merchant vessels routinely limped into the welcoming sanctuary of St. John's Harbour through the Narrows. Most showed evidence of being battered by the Atlantic, while others revealed gaping, jagged, black holes because German torpedoes or cannon shells had torn open their hulls. Injured seamen were carried off ships to hospitals, many with skin blackened by dreadful burns or by the oil-saturated water in which they floated after their original ship had gone down. Sailors draped in blankets and still recovering from hypothermia wore the haggard appearance of young men who had faced death and had not yet emerged from its shadow. Attesting to the violence at sea, some 6,000 wounded sailors of all nationalities were cared for in the island's military hospitals.[33] It is no wonder that Ruth Gray, serving in the Women's Royal Canadian Naval Service as one of at least 568 Wrens stationed in bases on the island, recalled that "being in Newfoundland was just like being in Britain. We felt under fire."[34]

As the naval war continued to grow in intensity, evolving into an all-out battle for survival in 1941, more sailors, soldiers, and airmen converged on the Rock. St. John's was swollen as thousands of North Americans joined the 40,000 residents of the city. There were about 7,600 Canadians in uniform, although this figure fluctuated with the coming and goings of ships and units.[35] The Yanks outnumbered the Canadians on the island, and while no exact figure has been established, tens of thousands of Americans either served or passed through Newfoundland and Labrador.[36] The Newfoundlanders were generally accommodating, willing to do their bit for the war, trying to create entertainment for the sailors, soldiers, and airmen of the Allied forces. "The redeeming feature of Newfoundland was the nature of the inhabitants," wrote one grateful Canadian sailor. "Kind, friendly, generous and decent,

MEN of VALOR
They fight for you

MERCHANT NAVY——Fourth Arm of the Service.

Outfighting submarines and dive bombers in a three day battle, Capt. Fred S. Slocombe, M.B.E., and his heroic crew succeeded in delivering the icebreaker **MONTCALM** to Murmansk as a gift from Canada to the U.S.S.R.

The Men of Valor series highlighted key aspects of the Canadian war effort. This poster presents the brave work of the merchant navy, which was labelled the "fourth arm of the service."

rich and poor alike, they could not have been more supportive of all these strangers who had descended upon them."[37]

To support these young men, patriotic and religious groups formed drop-in centres, dance halls, and theatres. In "Newfyjohn," eligible women rarely lacked a long queue of suitors. For the majority of sailors without a date, the search for screech—the potent rotgut rum for which the island was infamous—enlivened shore leave. Movement and song rippled through St. John's, along with laddish behaviour, public drunkenness, and fierce brawls. For those officers who wished to escape this hustle and bustle, the RCN's officers established the Crow's Nest, known officially as the Seagoing Officers' Club, a refuge as naval and merchant mariner officers were obliged to climb fifty-nine steep and rickety stairs to reach its dark and quiet confines. A stiff drink and a good meal awaited the weary sailors who had braved the Atlantic and the U-boats, and all paid homage in thought or toasts to the RCN's ship's crests that festooned the walls, including badges for those vessels that never returned from their voyages.

"The Yanks are pouring in with weapons as well as tools," wrote an American journalist struck by the charged energy in Newfoundland. "You might call it an invasion. But instead of looting the country they are pouring money into it."[38] Newfoundland was never so prosperous, and the good people extended much friendship to the free-spending sailors, airmen, and soldiers, while also being wary of the rise in petty crime and the cost of living, as well as the lack of affordable housing. The night-time blackouts to protect against enemy bombers that never came or, more likely, against U-boats prowling the coast and coves, led to accidents and robberies. They also provided a convenient cover of darkness for the men to be with girlfriends or prostitutes.[39] Venereal disease

became a problem as it led to the hospitalization of service personnel and a fear of widespread degeneration. Young Newfoundland
men were frequently angry that they could not compete financially
with those in uniform, and occasionally this resentment led to ill
will and street battles. The invaders were also known to do battle
with each other, with booze, adrenaline, and ego spawning a potent
mix. Reflecting on the rough atmosphere, Paul O'Neill, a young
Newfoundlander, recalled, "[O]ne night in Bannerman Park, a fight
broke out between the Americans and Canadians. And we all
rushed over—we kids—and the Americans and Canadians were
punching each other and banging each other until the police
arrived." O'Neill and his mates were cheering on the Americans,
whom they liked better: "Come on, Yanks. Come on, Yanks. Kill
them. Kill them."[40]

The fear of German raiding parties coming ashore periodically
troubled the American commander Major-General Gerald C.
Brant, who warned on Christmas Eve 1941 that such attacks were
"not only possible . . . but very probable."[41] There were in fact
no raids, although anxiety and unease were stoked by rumour,
blackouts, and the return of combat-scarred warships and vessels.
Graveyards were filled with those mariners whose bodies washed
ashore or sailors who succumbed to their injuries sustained in
the attacks. A robust defence was planned should St. John's be in
danger of falling, but if the city could not be held, it would, per
the Allies' scorched-earth policy, be razed to deny the strategic
position to the Germans. Authorities were to destroy gas and oil
stocks, smash the harbour's docks, scuttle ships that could not be
sailed away, and burn anything of value to the enemy.[42] The same
was true of other major Maritime ports, since these orders had
been received from Britain; however, Canadian authorities would

decide if Halifax or Sydney, the other two major Canadian naval bases in the Maritimes, were to be burned to the ground to deny the positions to the enemy. Such action was a frantic last measure to be considered only after the warships, bombers, gun batteries, and thousands of soldiers had been defeated or driven back, and it was about as likely as the US plans to invade Canada back in the 1920s. The scheme was nonetheless an indication of Newfoundland's front-line importance in the Battle of the Atlantic.

———

"The war has wrought strange changes in the life of North America's outer bastion," wrote wartime journalist Leslie Roberts.[43] The American bases in Stephenville, St. John's, and Argentia had new buildings and structures with indoor plumbing and central heating. In noticeable contrast, many of the Canadian buildings were less permanent and constructed of flimsier material. After the war, most of the Canadian-constructed buildings were demolished, although some of the warehouses were sold at low prices to local merchants, while the US-built airfields were a means to connect the island with the rest of North America. The sacred space of the Crow's Nest, a site of respite and maritime history, lives on to reveal the storied naval war and the illustrious part St. John's played in it. Wartime legacies abounded. Newfoundlanders abandoned the British practice of driving on the left-hand side of the road, shifting to align with the norm in Canada and the United States. This was symbolic of the dominion's drift into the North American orbit, away from Britain and ultimately into the arms of the Canadians. The invaders were generally liked and almost always tolerated, but Newfoundlanders worried that their lives would never be the same.

CHAPTER 11

U-BOATS IN NORTH AMERICAN WATERS

"Your people," Admiral Ernest King, the US commander-in-chief of the fleet, told the Canadian naval brass, "have as yet had little opportunity to conduct the work involved on the scale required."[1] This statement rubbed the Canadians raw: they had, of course, been at war for two years while the Americans remained a neutral nation. But the RCN understood the importance of gradually bringing the US into the alliance against the Nazis, and of dispersing the load of the relentless escort duty. Admiral King had no concern about offending the Canadians: his daughter was later to comment that he was remarkably even tempered, being perpetually in a rage! Canada's two primary naval groups on the east coast— the Newfoundland Escort Force operating out of St. John's, and a smaller grouping of warships deployed from Halifax, Nova Scotia—were controlled by Canadian admirals and their staffs but guided strategically by the United States Navy (USN). Though ABC-22 was still foundational for establishing operating rules between the two nations through the principle of "mutual cooperation," the RCN's senior commanders were bitter about the suzerainty of US command, even if it was lightly applied. However, with the Japanese and Germans declaring war on the United States in December 1941, the U-boats soon came to North America, and the USN and the RCN would stand together in the fight against the submarine threat.

———

In the aftermath of Pearl Harbor, the USN moved most of its fleet from the Atlantic to the Pacific, leaving its ships there even after the Nazis went to war with the United States. It would thus be the RCN that emerged to take over much of the inshore and mid-Atlantic escorts. Through late 1941, the RCN had been pressed hard for months as the U-boats ravaged the convoys; this included a mauling of convoy SC 42 in early September 1941, which led to the loss of fifteen ships in running battles that lasted over a week.[2] In addition to 203 sailors killed, the cargo that went down included over 21,000 tons of high-grade iron ore and steel; 21,617 tons of wheat and other food; and almost 30,000 tons of lumber, fuel oil, and chemicals.[3] If the U-boats could sever the strategic lifeline from North America, Britain might be starved into submission and the Allies' invasion of Europe strangled in the cradle before it was ever launched.

The RCN corvettes were overused in the desperate struggle for mastery of the Atlantic, and yet still their crews fought courageously against the sea and the enemy. The zig-zagging convoys, often consisting of fifty to seventy-five ships, were thrashed by ferocious storms, with vessels slowed in winter by the ice that encrusted them as the blistering winds raked sailors to the bone. And amid the violent storms lurked the U-boats. To fend off the stalking enemy, the Newfoundland Escort Force was combined in February 1942 with British-based Royal Navy warships to form the Mid-Ocean Escort Force. This new group would continue to shepherd convoys across the entire Atlantic, from the Grand Banks to Londonderry, Northern Ireland. It was a long run, especially for the corvettes, which were never meant for mid-Atlantic duty. But the urgency of the naval war of attrition demanded that all warships be thrown into the line. As Frank Curry of the RCN was to write of his comrades' experience at sea, "Day by day, we gained in knowledge and experience."[4]

When Germany declared war on the US, the U-boats were ready to strike, unleashing Operation *Paukenschlag* (drumroll). Despite the presence of a dozen U-boats off Newfoundland, the Canadians had developed a system of coordinating and routing shipping in the western hemisphere that was tied into the Royal Navy's global organization.[5] Moreover, the defences around major ports like Halifax, Sydney, and St. John's had all been radically strengthened by new artillery, bunkers, and anti-submarine nets. High cover by aircraft extended further into the mid-Atlantic, providing a new threat to the U-boats, and the convoys had small escorts of warships that ran about the pack like sheepdogs. In this hostile environment, the German captains were increasingly wary of attacks from warships or the air, fearing even limited damage to their vessels so far from their home bases. In January 1942, twenty Allied merchant ships were sunk off Canada and Newfoundland, in waters that were crawling with submarines, but the German captains preferred easier targets. They found them along the US east coast.

The convoys had been very effective in narrowing the targets for the U-boats and reducing the potential carnage; sadly, however, the Americans had taken few precautions along their eastern seaboard against the coming onslaught. Most egregiously, Admiral King saw little value in using defensive convoys to protect merchant ships, with the American approach being to aggressively seek out the enemy in battle. The problem was that the US had neither the warships, the weapons, nor the training to kill the U-boats. And so the vessels filled with supplies continued to steam mostly unprotected along predictable routes, using open radio frequencies that the Germans listened in on and blaring fog horns. The US almost invited attacks on ships that were silhouetted against America's coastal cities that had not enacted blackout strategies. Their leaders worried about the impact the shuttering of lights would have on tourism and the number of automobile accidents.

It was a welcome change for the Germans, who had faced much privation in crossing the Atlantic, enduring the harsh winter weather off Canada, and then avoiding the American and Canadian air and sea defences in Newfoundland and Nova Scotia. Now they would feast upon the reckless and the naive. On January 14, 1942, *U-123* surfaced undetected in New York City's Lower Bay under the shadow of darkness. From the U-boat's bridge, Kapitanleutnant Reinhard Hardegen watched illuminated Manhattan, its twinkling brightness calling to him as they had to countless millions. "I have a feeling the Americans are going to be very surprised," he was to write.[6]

Two nights earlier, on the 12th, *U-123* had taken its first victim, the British freighter *Cyclops*, 450 kilometres east of Cape Cod. The vessel, carrying cargo and Chinese sailors bound for Britain, was sunk by a torpedo, with eighty-seven passengers and crew killed. The winter winds lashed them as spray coated them in ice, and those who made it off the doomed ship huddled in lifeboats for twenty hours before being rescued, all survivors close to death. Others were not so lucky. Would-be rescuers came upon the haunting site of open lifeboats that were filled only with frozen corpses. On the 14th, before sneaking into New York City's waters, *U-123*

Desperate sailors in a life raft, their ship
having gone down into the depths.

also sank the *Norness*, a tanker carrying 12,200 tons of crude oil from New Jersey to Liverpool. Only thirty-nine got off the ship alive, with many later suffering from the effects of the tar-like oil in the water that matted their hair and fouled their skin. The U-boat sailed away, unharried by bombers or warships.

Despite the German subs' limited fuel, food, and torpedoes, and their need to sometimes use tourist guidebooks to navigate along the coast, the U-boat scourge was devastating. With few American warships to keep them at bay, the long-range Type IX U-boats sailed up and down the coast killing almost at will. The best merchant ship tactic was to flee if the crew spotted a U-boat, with the hope of hiding in fog or the darkness. The hunted lived in terror. As the unarmed ships went up in flames, the Germans labelled this the Second Happy Time or, more brutal still, the American Shooting Season.[7]

The US Navy had no modern warships on the east coast, relying instead on Coast Guard cutters, a few dated gunboats, and wooden sub chasers. As a further sign of American unpreparedness, though about a dozen older destroyers were in New York Harbor, they were not deployed because of a shortage of sailors and inadequate preparation. Interservice rivalries also hampered an effective response to the threat. While there were more aircraft along the east coast, they were controlled by the air force and not the navy, and they had little experience in seeking out subs. The reign of error continued. Over a period of four months, Axis submarines sank 198 ships, killing thousands and denying Britain critical supplies, food, and weapons.[8] Half of these vessels were tankers that exploded with oil needed for the industrial war effort.

———

As the Canadians were shuddering at the extended massacre to the south, in March 1942 RCN warships out of Halifax steamed to assist the hard-pressed Americans by guarding inshore convoys. Five warships were peeled off the North Atlantic run to protect grouped vessels from Halifax to St. John's; other merchant ships were taken from there to Boston; and still more convoys were guided from Boston to Halifax. This was known as the Triangle Run, and a few months later the Canadian convoys were extended to New York, which was a great attraction for the Canucks who took shore leave and encountered the unending parties, jazz clubs, and steamier entertainment. Wily RCN officers found much profit in interacting with their American counterparts, with whom they traded Canadian whisky for better victuals. As the RCN's Hal Lawrence recalled, when US officers came aboard RCN warships to partake in shared festivities, "the conversations would grow heated about the relative advantages of kings and presidents and we invariably found ourselves in that peculiar Canadian position of explaining the English to the Americans."[9] Though the run was an added burden for the overtaxed RCN, it was necessary for assisting the out-classed Americans.

Finding fewer targets along the northeastern seaboard, more U-boats drifted south into the Caribbean Sea, through which crucial supplies passed. In May 1942, eight U-boats sank fifty-eight ships of more than 255,000 tons in the warm waters, and in the first six months of the year, a total of 2.34 million tons of shipping (397 ships) were sunk along the eastern seaboard, in the Gulf, and in the Caribbean.[10] Admiral Karl Dönitz, commander of the U-boats, was delighted by the success of his fleet, crowing that "By attacking the supply traffic—particularly the oil—in the U.S. zone, I am striking at the root of the evil."[11] As the crisis deepened, and the scarcity of fuel was felt across the Canadian war economy that imported 82 percent of its oil (with the great Alberta oil fields not being discovered until after the war), Canada's high-revving war industry was in danger of seizing up.

Though American pride was hurt, the USN acknowledged it needed help and time to set up inshore convoys. This process included pulling US warships from their role of protecting convoys across the Atlantic and removing tankers from the waters for a few weeks. The last measure further dried up oil coming to Canada, with stocks of fuel in Halifax falling to drastically low levels.[12] The RCN's Vice-Admiral Percy Nelles, hearing that the Americans were retreating back to safety, and being unwilling to let oil-filled tankers steam northward, declared, "To hell with that, we'll get our own."[13]

As of early May, RCN warships were heading south to the Caribbean, picking up oil tankers, and shepherding them safely back to Canadian waters. RCN sailor Frank Curry, who served on HMCS *Kamsack*, remembered that "scattered through the inner convoy were the most vulnerable of all—the tankers, some carrying crude oil, many with high-octane aviation fuel. We corvette sailors stood in awe of the merchant sailors who rode the tankers."[14] With the RCN escorting tankers from Trinidad to Halifax from May to July, not a single one of the oilers was lost in thirty-seven voyages.[15] The RCN's growing professionalism was revealed again in this operation, despite the fraught conditions.

Canadian warships also continued to support the Americans, with the US often providing important air cover. They worked well together. Off Cuba on August 28, HMCS *Oakville* was aided by an American PBY patrol aircraft in confronting *U-94* when it attacked a twenty-nine-ship convoy. The Type VII C U-boat had already sunk twenty-six Allied ships since its commission in August 1940, but its fate was soon sealed. The Catalina first sighted and dropped multiple 650-pound depth charges around the sub, even as it crash-dived in desperation. When the depth charges forced the wounded boat to the surface, the Canadian corvette pounced, using its 4-inch gun to hammer the sub with shellfire while the captain skilfully advanced on it. In parts of the battle, the two vessels manoeuvred so close to each other that some of the Canadian sailors threw Coca-Cola bottles across the expanse at some of the Germans manning their deck gun. Soon, Canadian shellfire and the damage effected by ramming the U-boat three times left the enemy vessel dead in the water.

As the U-boat crew was abandoning ship, the quick-thinking Canadian sailors, led by Sub-Lieutenant Hal Lawrence and Petty Officer Art Powell, formed a boarding party to capture intelligence documents. *Oakville*'s captain, Lieutenant-Commander Clarence King, a Great War veteran decorated for sinking a U-boat, eased the corvette alongside the enemy warship and Lawrence led the raiders onto the damaged sub. A chaotic fight ensued, and explosions threw Lawrence and his crew into the water. They rapidly scrambled back on the ship. In the blast, Lawrence lost his shorts, and the now naked sailor led the Canadians down through the conning tower that had been ripped open by the corvette's ramming action. Shooting two Germans in the descent, Lawrence entered the dark confines of the U-boat. Gas choked the air and water flooded into the dying vessel. Cowing the terrified enemy sailors who were desperate to escape, Lawrence searched for an Enigma code machine and codebooks, but the crew had already disposed of them. The Canadians made their escape with twenty-six prisoners, and the action of *Oakville* was celebrated in the North American press.[16] The heroes, Lawrence and Powell, received their own war poster meant to inspire others (with Lawrence's shorts depicted in the fight). Less visible because of censorship and the need not to reveal information to the enemy was the

MEN of VALOR
They fight for you

**Two-man boarding party from the
Canadian corvette 'Oakville' subdues
crew of German sub in Caribbean**

*The attack by HMCS Oakville was used to publicize the
Royal Canadian Navy and its struggle against the U-boats.*

importance of cooperation between the Canadian and American fighting forces in the Caribbean.

———

In the first half of 1942, as the Allies battled through crushing defeats and a costly stalemate, there was growing pressure in English Canada for the government to bring in overseas conscription to meet the demands of an all-out war. The U-boat attacks along the eastern seaboard also stirred up apprehension and anger. Though the army was not yet in sustained battle and reinforcements were in ample supply, enacting conscription would match what the Americans and British had done in terms of managing their manpower (to use the military term), and would also ensure an equal commitment to the war across the country. Prime Minister King, aware that such an action would likely single out Quebec and some parts of the country that were home to new immigrant groups, did not like the idea. He feared that instead of drawing the country together in a galvanized crusade, as some proponents claimed, conscription would tear it apart. English Canada condemned him for indecision and—in bouts of rising hysteria—for disloyalty. In a heated war of words, comparisons to the US were hurled, including in a January 1942 debate in the House of Commons, where an MP drew attention to how Roosevelt made a solemn pledge that draftees would not be sent overseas and then changed his position, telling Congress, "We cannot wage this war in a defensive spirit."[17] The call for conscription became one of the Progressive Conservative Party's cudgels for battering the government.

King remained unconvinced of the need to end the voluntary war effort, often talking of his August 1941 trip to Britain, where he met Churchill. The two leaders found some common interests, closing the gap on their previous distance. At the time, the British prime minister, aware of King's concern about disunion, had told him it "was not a war of men but a war of specialized machines."[18] The observation was partially true, although King swallowed the statement as a drowning man clings to a lifeline. He repeated it often, even if it was clearly a war of the big battalions as much as one of weapons' technology. In early 1942, the Liberal cabinet was riven over conscription, with Minister of National Defence J.L. Ralston ready to resign unless the draft for overseas service was enacted. King struggled to find a compromise, eventually settling on a national plebiscite. It would pose the question to Canadians as to whether they would support freeing his government from its 1939 promise of an exclusively voluntary war effort.[19]

In April 1942, English Canada voted 75 percent in favour of releasing the government, while Quebec was firmly against, with 72 percent. Although English Canada made up more than two thirds of the country, King worried about Quebec and decisively chose to do nothing. He promised caution with the memorable phrase "not necessarily conscription, but conscription if necessary." Even after the government had, via the plebiscite, been released to bring in conscription, King invoked his incantation that it was not yet "necessary." And indeed it was not. Recruitment was strong in early 1942, and casualties minimal. French Canadians were also registering in identifiable numbers, with about 17 percent of the armed forces eventually consisting of enlistees from Quebec or French-speaking areas of the country.[20] Though more were joining up than in the previous war, it was less than the

John Collins of the Montreal Gazette *ridicules Canada's little man as King attempts to stand with Churchill and Roosevelt but is not singing from the "Victory Song Book." The jab "Better Not Rush into This—Let's Take a Vote" is directed at King's plebiscite.*

near-third of the country that identified as French-speaking. The English press assaulted Quebec's lack of patriotism, as they characterized it, and went berserk over King's refusal to invoke conscription, viewing it as a sidestepping of his duty as a leader. Ralston tendered a resignation letter, further endangering King.

While the prime minister talked him into staying as minister, their relationship was irrevocably damaged. French Canada, however, breathed easier.

In the aftermath of this tumult, President Roosevelt wrote to his friend, Mackenzie, suggesting that the French Canadians were a troublesome bunch and that the Canadian state should hasten their assimilation, perhaps with the assistance of the US.[21] King ignored the advice, breaking his general habit of fawning over the president's words. In fact, King's faith in Roosevelt was shaken by the president's poor understanding of Canada as a bi-cultural country. The suggestion also confirmed for King his belief that while the Americans were staunch allies, the US remained a country far different from Canada.

———

In May 1942, a fearful distraction from the war of words between English and French Canada erupted when the emboldened U-boats crept into Canada's most important commercial waterway, the 1,200-kilometre-long St. Lawrence River. The U-boat invasion had been expected, but Canadians were shocked when the enemy warships slipped into the country's riverine heartland. The U-boats would eventually penetrate as far as Rimouski, some 300 kilometres east of Quebec City, with the danger made real as ships were sunk and bodies washed up on the shores. Eastern Canadians who believed that they were far from the European war found that the killing had come home. This was almost the equivalent of U-boats steaming down the Thames into London, sinking ships along the way.

En route from Montreal, the British merchant ship SS *Nicoya* was the first to die. It was hit at 11:52 p.m. on May 12, 1942, by a torpedo off the Gaspé Peninsula.[22] The crew evacuated the vessel, and nineteen minutes later *U-553* fired a second fatal torpedo. Six crewmen were killed. Captained by Karl Thurmann, *U-553* struck again only two hours later, when it encountered the freighter SS *Leto* that was also sailing without convoy protection. It had no observers on deck, as the crew assumed they were safe on the St. Lawrence. A torpedo took *Leto* down in minutes, killing twelve of the forty-three crew members. The Type VIIC U-boat would go on to sink thirteen ships before mysteriously disappearing with all hands on January 20, 1943.

Prime Minister King had previously warned Canadians of a possible attack, speaking in the House of Commons on March 25, 1942, about the U-boats marauding up and down the east coast of the United States—but now the threat had arrived. Despite Canada's censorship laws, journalists reported on the slaughter in the country's interior, with some even taunting French Canadians for having recently voted against releasing the government in the plebiscite. It didn't help that the minister of national defence for the navy, Angus Macdonald, who was a proud Maritimer, said that French Canadians' calls for greater protection were depicting the "Quebec populace as a simpering pressure group."[23] For good measure, he added that no one in the Maritimes had complained about the onslaught they had faced since the start of the war.

The RCN's professional sailors, long aware of the value of convoys, immediately ordered inbound and outbound vessels to sail with protective warships. The RCAF contributed low-flying aircraft, hoping to trap U-boats on the surface or force them to dive to a depth where they were slower and less effective against shipping. But there was fear that the enemy vessels would sail to the major ports along the St. Lawrence—Montreal, Trois-Rivières, and Quebec City—which were all vital in the movement of goods, supplies, and people. The building of corvettes and merchant vessels occurred in giant dockyards along the St. Lawrence, and Canadians were troubled by apocalyptic visions of U-boats shelling vulnerable workers and firing unfinished warships.

On July 6, 1942, near Rimouski, Quebec, *U-132* tracked QS-15, a convoy of twelve vessels on its way to Sydney, Nova Scotia. Kapitänleutnant Ernst Vogelsang's U-boat torpedoed three ships, though he and his crew were nearly killed when RCN warships scrambled to catch them. The U-boat dove for cover, but the tricky waters of the St. Lawrence—with a layer of dense, cold seawater lying about 60 metres down—prevented them from going any further. HMCS *Drummondville*, a Bangor-class minesweeper, dropped depth charges, damaging the U-boat. It only escaped via the desperate manoeuvre of flooding the forward torpedo tubes, which allowed the sub to push deeper through the resisting water before stabilizing by blowing ballast.

Two more vessels would fall victim to *U-132* after it made improvised repairs and began patrolling off Cap de la Madeleine, Gaspé. On the 19th, the U-boat spotted a convoy and fired two torpedoes; one found its mark in the 4,367-ton British freighter *Frederika Lensen*. The RCN warships used their sonar to search for the U-boat and dropped depth charges in defined patterns. Nothing but dead fish rose to the surface. Four crew members were killed, but the freighter was saved and towed to Grande Vallée, Quebec, although it was later deemed unsalvageable.

To protect the convoys and calm the Canadian population, the RCN diverted more naval resources to this Dominion battleground. Air power was deployed to hunt the hunters. This combined-arms approach drove the U-boats eastward out of the seaway into the Atlantic. With the inland waters of the St. Lawrence becoming too dangerous, the enemy subs returned to patrolling off Newfoundland, along the Greater Northern Peninsula and up and down the Labrador coast. And yet the shipping butchery continued, with Canadian and American convoys being attacked.

Convoy SG-6, sailing on August 27 from Sydney to Greenland, was savaged by several U-boats. The slow convoy, which included three merchant ships, an old oiler, other aged vessels, and the troop transport *Chatham* (carrying 428 Canadian and American labourers), was protected by the US Coast Guard cutter *Mojave*. Between the two components of the American convoy were two merchant ships escorted by RCN corvette HMCS *Trail*. Air cover was sporadic and stretched thin, with No. 10 Squadron, RCAF, devoting only a single Douglas Digby to fly above the American section of the convoy. It was not enough.

In the Belle Isle Strait, at 8:48 a.m. on the 27th, a *U-517* torpedo caught the troopship *Chatham*. It was a kill shot, and a secondary explosion ripped through the ship as cold seawater detonated the boilers. Somewhat miraculously, most of the crew and passengers escaped, as the sturdy ship took half an hour to sink. *U-517* slipped away. Per orders not to fight the sub or stop for survivors, HMCS *Trail* escorted the two terrified merchant ships to their destination in a bay on the Labrador coast, before returning a few hours later to the scene of the battle, where it picked up eighty-eight sailors. None of the Canadian or American vessels located the submerged U-boat with their radar because of the riptides and shifting water temperature. The final losses for the *Chatham* were low, with seven crew and seven passengers killed, but it was the first American troopship sunk in action.

These naval ambushes demonstrated the bold nature of the U-boats that struck protected convoys sailing close to shore, and also the poor quality of the radar on the American and Canadian warships that could not detect the U-boats whether they were submerged or on the surface. Though ships were lost, the close interactions of Americans and Canadians saved the strategic bulk of the convoys. The outgunned RCN warships, always reacting to German attacks, were much assisted by RCAF aircraft, which increasingly made it more difficult for the U-boats to strike as they were forced to dive for cover to escape the hawks circling in the sky.

On September 7, several Allied ships were sunk by the Germans, including Canada's HMCS *Raccoon*, one of the yachts purchased early in the war from the Americans. *U-165* struck it with a torpedo and it exploded, with its entire crew of thirty-eight sailors lost. Two days later, the Canadians closed the St. Lawrence to all Allied shipping, marking a significant victory for the U-boats. This was a defeat for Canada, although little known at the time was the extent of the RCN's self-sacrifice in ordering seventeen corvettes (sixteen RCN and one British) to assist the American invasion of North Africa known as Operation Torch.[24] The act of sending off much of its corvette force in the midst of this domestic crisis was quite remarkable, but it was a sign that the Canadians understood the importance of supporting their Anglo-American allies who were striking the fascists far from North America. The

RCN had engaged in similar supportive action in early 1942 by assisting the US to staunch the bleeding along its east coast. In the name of assisting primary allies, Canada's navy was spread thin in the global war. Though the U-boats had forced the closure of the St. Lawrence, they had been steadily pushed back to the Atlantic by effective air power and convoy work, with the relatively modest cost of twenty-three ships sunk over six months.[25]

———

As the U-boats pulled back to the eastern Atlantic, fearful of the RCN and RCAF's coordinated response, they nonetheless continued to search for targets. Particularly effective in harassing the U-boats, the RCAF's 113 Squadron of Eastern Air Command made multiple sightings of *U-517*. Flying Officer M.J. Bélanger, a twenty-three-year-old Québécois enlistee who had come through the British Commonwealth Air Training Plan, made two attacks on the U-boat, including a near hit on September 29, when his Lockheed Hudson bomber swooped down and dropped depth charges all along the submarine's hull. Amid the churning water, the robust U-boat dived and fled, having been damaged and shaken. Bélanger—who received the Distinguished Flying Cross—and his crew embodied the ever-growing impact of air power in the war against the U-boats.

In a vicious last-gasp assault, on the night of October 14, 1942, *U-69* sent a torpedo into the civilian ferry SS *Caribou*, which was carrying 237 passengers and crew from Sydney to Channel-Port Aux Basques.[26] The single escort, the armed minesweeper HMCS *Grandmère*, went after the sub, dropping depth charges and manoeuvring to ram it. After a two-hour chase, the U-boat writhed free and slunk away. Left behind in the dark water, the survivors of *Caribou* endured a grim struggle for life, crying out for help, their voices slowly being silenced as the lethal cold took hold. Two nursing sisters clung to a capsized lifeboat after having survived the suction of being pulled underwater when *Caribou* went down. Nursing Sister Margaret Brooke, a specialist medical dietician, encouraged and helped her comrade Nursing Sister Agnes Wilkie as they both grew weaker from hypothermia. Wilkie eventually fell unconscious, after which Brooke held her friend's head above water even as her hands grew numb. As Brooke too was near death, she lost the unconscious Wilkie when a wave swept her away. The icy water also nearly took Brooke before she was rescued by the returning crew of *Grandmère*. There was little joy when she later received the MBE (Member of the Order of the British Empire) for her courage. The captain, Lieutenant James Cuthbert, later recounted the anguish he suffered as, following orders to chase the U-boat, he left the helpless victims in the water. "Oh my God. I felt the full complement of things you feel at a time like that. Things you had to live with. You are torn. Demoralized. Terribly alone."[27]

The sinking of the *Caribou* brought home the reality that Canadian and Newfoundland civilians were in the front lines of the war. It was a fitting disaster to end a hard year on the seas. Though the destruction of vessels was strategically inconsequential in the world war—especially given statistics revealing that over the six-month period, only 1.2 percent of the shipping lost was sunk in the St. Lawrence—the limited casualties were amplified by widespread fear in eastern Canada.[28] The public's alarm over-shadowed the success of the RCN and the RCAF. The naval forces had reacted with growing expertise and kept the reaping to a minimum, but there were still about 400 dead—a harsh reminder to many Canadians that Hitler's U-boats could strike directly against them in North America.

———

The RCN was at the breaking point in 1942, grappling with its three-pronged commitment to fight in the Battle of the Atlantic, defend the east and west coasts, and protect convoys from the Caribbean and in the St. Lawrence. The German thrust into the country's innards along the St. Lawrence led to death and mayhem, revealing to complacent Canadians and Americans that the hemisphere was not safe. While the closing of the St. Lawrence was a blow to Canadian prestige, the North Americans had survived the onslaught, and the convoys continued to steam across the Atlantic. The Canadians' commitment of seventeen warships to the Torch landings at this juncture demonstrates the painful trade-off they faced in balancing the responsibility for defending North America with the need to taking the fight to the Axis overseas. Canada often sacrificed its own safety and security to serve on multiple fronts in support of its allies, Britain and the United States, in the common war against the Axis powers.

CHAPTER 12

SOVEREIGNTY AND STRATEGY

"It seems odd to me to think of myself as a war leader," wrote Prime Minister King late in the conflict. "Nothing could sound to me more remote."[1] Ever the conciliator and compromiser, King was careful with every step he took. While Churchill burst forward demanding "action this day" and Roosevelt manoeuvred relentlessly as the cheerful, master manipulator of the Washington carnival, with spotlight on him for full effect, King could never match the spirit and verve of these two titans. Given to seeking the safe road that was usually much travelled, his natural desire to avoid sensation and embrace restraint left others slightly contemptuous of him. In this regard, however, he was a much safer actor than Churchill, who was given to all manner of flights of fancy, including not only his fascination with eccentric strategy and superweapons but also the excesses in his personal life. King was also more careful than Roosevelt, who, as a showman, seducer, and breezy optimist, left many close aides believing that he rarely thought through his momentous decisions. But as a leader with little flash, King was always tougher than his few friends and many foes gave him credit for. Optimistic about Canada's ability to stride forward during the war and emerge from Britain's shadow, King was nonetheless aware that he governed a nervous union of two cultures and many jealous regions. He therefore moved with caution, often crab-like in this war of falcons.

The limited war that King hoped to wage was lost amid the cataclysm of defeat in June 1940 and the urgings of a majority of Canadians for the government to raise numerous fighting formations to defend the country and take the war to the Axis powers overseas. King's government responded to the call, while also ensuring the home front economy was churning at top speed. It made no sense to feed the armed forces but starve the wartime industry. And so the work in the factories, farms, and mines, as well as the cross-Canada air training plan, were all huge endeavours, in addition to raising a million-man army, navy, and air force. On closer examination, King's strategy aimed to do more than just balance interests and prevent a schism within Canada. A second major goal involved supporting Britain in the war against the fascists, while also fending off periodic Imperial attempts to reverse some of the constitutional changes achieved by Canada over the previous three decades. King worried that an unrestrained war effort might allow Whitehall to re-exert control over Canadian political autonomy. Third, King understood that Canada's aid to Britain was essential to achieving victory, as the island kingdom was on the front lines. However, providing this support—be it military units or vast storehouses of supplies—would require American backing, and gaining that first required committing to the defence of the continent, the mobilization of industry, and the strengthening of financial systems. The need of King and his cabinet to negotiate the complex relationship of standing with Britain, fending off its overreach, and at the same time guaranteeing that the Americans felt secure on their northern border would require the Canadians to continually assert their independence as an

*This impish cartoon has the little boy King attempting to
take his seat with the real leaders, Roosevelt and Churchill.*

ally—to make it clear that the Dominion was a vassal state to
neither empire. Not to do so, warned Escott Reid of External
Affairs, was to risk Canadians "being treated as children because
we have refused to behave as adults."[2]

—

The Axis juggernaut continued throughout the first half of 1942, with the alliance boasting a nearly unbroken series of victories in the global war. The primary German battle front against the Soviets saw additional military triumphs as horrendous losses were inflicted on the communists, who hung on by their bloodied fingernails. In North Africa, the tough, battle-hardened, and charismatic German general Erwin Rommel, wielding far fewer forces, drove back the British in the desert war, advancing dangerously close to Cairo. On the oceans, the U-boats were inflicting ghastly losses on merchant ships, while production in Germany was rising despite the bomber war that was picking up speed and ferocity. In the Pacific, the Americans stemmed the bleeding with the critical victory at Midway in June 1942, and then took to the offensive in further campaigns at Guadalcanal, making an amphibious landing there on August 7. The island invasion saw three land battles and seven naval battles, as well as nearly continuous aerial combat above the ground forces. For six awful months, the battle raged, producing shockingly heavy casualties from combat and disease.

Canada had little influence over the Allied grand strategy in any of these theatres of war. King was not inclined to be involved, even though he sometimes expressed his frustration at being locked out of the decision-making process. While he took offence at the affront of Churchill and Roosevelt meeting nearby in Newfoundland in August 1941, he was also aware that neither they nor their staffs believed that the war could be waged by a large committee. King contented himself with the knowledge that he had aided Britain through his talks with the president in 1940, clinging to that ever-distant act of meaningful support that was now all but forgotten within the solidifying Anglo-American alliance. Even on occasions when Churchill invited King to London along with other dominion leaders, the Canadian was fearful of leaving Ottawa for extended periods of time. He remembered how Prime Minister Borden had gone overseas for months on end during the Great War, becoming detached from the day-to-day events at home and further ensnared in the Imperial war effort. King's caution was also based on his long experience and his attendance at multiple Imperial meetings over two decades, which led him to believe that if he was seen as a part of a British committee of war leaders, Canada's independence of action as a North American nation would be compromised. "Each part of the Empire must direct completely its own affairs," wrote King. "The relationship must be one of co-operation not centralization."[3] When potential influence came with the shackles of obligation, King preferred to opt out.

For Churchill and Roosevelt, King's mediation, useful early in the war, was a thing of the past, although the president remained friendly towards King, and Churchill came to despise him less. One realistic Canadian briefing note from External Affairs observed, "It is probably an inevitable consequence of the increasing involvement of the United States in the war and of its acceptance of leadership of the democratic cause that the President should tend more and more to deal directly with the Great Powers and find less time to spend on the specifically Canadian aspects of American international relations." Canada, the briefing declared, had the greatest influence on its southern neighbour when the two nations were engaged in "hemispheric defence."[4] However, now that the Americans were in a global war, they increasingly took Ottawa's cooperation for granted. The Canadians had to find a way to insert themselves into the Anglo-American alliance. Politicians and mandarins studied how they might capitalize on the country's fighting forces, its wartime industry, and its value as a trading partner. This would be no easy task.

Canada's war effort was now virtually unlimited, with massive armed forces and most of the economy geared towards' weapons' production, mineral extraction, and transport of foodstuffs to Britain. Testy debates swirled among the key ministers Howe, Ralston, Power, and Lapointe over the allocation of the workforce among war industry, farms, and the fighting formations.[5] Howe was probably not wrong when he argued that if Britain had to choose between soldiers and aluminum, its leaders would select the metal over the men.[6] But that would never satisfy Canadians seeking to take the war to the enemy. One of the most respected voices, besides the prime minister, was Lapointe, King's chief political lieutenant who had unified the party by winning over the Quebec wing to the Dominion's full role in the war. The two men understood the importance of Canada supporting Britain, although they agreed this aid must stop short of imperiling the country through the invocation of conscription.

Lapointe's death in November 1941 from cancer ended this two-decade partnership. While King grieved, he needed an influential advocate to smooth relations with Quebec. Louis St. Laurent, an experienced Quebec lawyer, was brought into the cabinet as minister of justice. He too opposed conscription, albeit less stridently than Lapointe. And yet with the expansion of the armed forces, Ralston's nation-wide impact and visibility as minister of national defence grew, with the experienced colonel, respected friend of veterans, and tough individual championed by English-Canadian journalists as a possible replacement for King. But Ralston was a good soldier, rarely seeking to undermine the long-serving prime minister even as he grew to dislike his propensity for prevarication and delay. Even with an army, navy, and air force that would see more than a million Canadians in uniform, King and his cabinet's strategic goals were essentially political in nature and not usually grounded in military issues—particularly anything like carving out independent commands for the Canadians or even determining where they would fight. The cabinet's strategy remained focused on achieving unity within Canada, fending off Britain's overreach, and finding favour with the Americans.

———

"What three things matter most in the world?" was a question for British Foreign Office candidates sitting the exam. A cheeky response, and one much repeated among successive British ambassadors to the United States, was "God, love and Anglo-American relations."[7] The latter surged to the foreground in the dark aftermath of Pearl Harbor. After the Christmas 1941 Arcadia conference in Washington, a Germany-first strategy was repledged, which allowed the British to breath easier. Also emerging out of the conference was the Combined Chiefs of Staff, consisting of the American and British military brain trust who worked together to hammer out strategy. There were few problems that could not be solved through the skill of these leaders, even as they addressed seemingly countless issues, from supply and strategy to the selection of Allied commanders and the theatres to which forces would be sent. The Canadians were not even formally told of the establishment of the Combined Chiefs of Staff, and so it is no surprise that they were not invited to sit in the meetings, just as they manoeuvred for inclusion via politicians, diplomats, and senior officers pleading the case.

General George Marshall was a diplomatic soldier of the highest order, having won the confidence of Roosevelt and other political leaders and the admiration of most of the senior British generals. As chief of staff of the US Army, Marshall understood the importance of the Anglo-American commanders coordinating their nations at war, and in support of this goal he fast-tracked the career of one of his protegés, Dwight Eisenhower, another gifted soldier who understood the necessity of diplomacy in coalition warfare. In Washington, the British Joint Staff Mission was led by Field Marshal Sir John Dill, who, having been chief of the imperial general staff from May 1940 to December 1941, was eventually removed by Churchill as the pair found only friction in those fraught times. His replacement, the more able soldier and strategist General Alan Brooke, also suffered under Churchill's wild ideas, late-night meetings, and constant barrage of demands for action. However, Marshall respected the sixty-year-old Dill, who forged easy relations with the Americans. In Washington, they found ways to make the Combined Chiefs of Staff work, and the intelligent, even-tempered, and gentlemanly Dill was close with Roosevelt. With Dill leading a staff of 3,000 soldiers and civil servants at the British Joint Staff Mission, this military machinery oversaw the coordination and compromises of war strategy.[8] Dill's death in November 1944 led to a great outpouring of grief from the Americans, to the extent that he was buried in Arlington National Cemetery.

Alliance warfare is exceedingly difficult, with conflicting national interests at play, as well as clashing personalities, service rivalries, resource constraints, and multiple actors to appease, from opposition politicians to probing journalists to an expectant public. The Axis powers were allies in name only, and the nations rarely coordinated their actions. In contrast, the great secret to the Anglo-American victory was their ability to solve problems, compromise when necessary, and find ways to coordinate in an agreed-upon long-term strategy. This successful cooperation first occurred while the US was neutral and Roosevelt inched the country towards supporting Britain and Canada with trade, munitions, and finance, and it continued as the British and Americans faced multi-front wars. For the US, with its strong isolationist instinct, it was vital to secure the defence of North America before taking the war to the Axis powers far from its shores. It was here, in hemispheric defence, that Canada had an outsized role. Naval patrols on the two coasts, but especially in the Atlantic, had been aided by some of the joint defence plans, first ABC-1 and then ABC-22. The US-Canadian alliance had been pragmatically built, one step at a time. The Dominion played a credible role early on, although now that the Americans were facing a two-front global war, Canada was consigned to the periphery.

When King lost his faithful adviser Undersecretary for External Affairs Oscar Skelton in January 1941, he was initially rudderless until he found a replacement in the thirty-seven-year-old Norman Robertson. The appointment of Robertson to the most senior position in the Department of External Affairs was a surprise to some, as King, who acted as his own minister of external affairs, was generally wary of young men. The Rhodes Scholar had none-theless proven himself a brilliant thinker and an effective commu-nicator with the prime minister, and he was an expert on the United States. Tall, gangly, and often seen in a rumpled suit, Robertson used witty and caustic commentary to guide King and the diplo-mats along the path of managing the crucial relationship with the US. Robertson was the right choice to head the department that was shifting its gaze from London to Washington, and he knew that Canada would have to work hard to retain the White House's interest in the Dominion. The new undersecretary argued that his countrymen "have tended to take it for granted" that Americans "will always regard Canadian interest as a close second to their own and appreciably ahead of those any third country," and yet he warned that the relationship had changed because of Britain's desperation to court the United States.[9]

Canada's legation in the American capital, first opened in 1927, was the mission abroad second in importance only to that in London. The four-storey mansion on Massachusetts Avenue was where wealthy Toronto lawyer Leighton McCarthy conducted business as Canada's minister to the US. Described by one journalist as "a handsome, stately, white-haired gentleman, whose warm Irish grin lightens a fairly ambassadorial dignity," Leighton, a former MP who was seventy-two years old in 1942, had known Roosevelt for years.[10] Having a president willing to pick up a phone and talk, and being invited to informal dinners at the White House, were benefits worth their weight in gold. Several fine civil servants from the Department of External Affairs rotated through Washington in the early years of the war, adding intellectual heft and focus to the legations' work, but as the British rushed to the "capital of the world," Canada needed its best there.

To meet the urgency of the moment, King and Robertson agreed to send Lester B. Pearson to work his magic. A long-time diplomat, former professor in history at the University of Toronto, and, since 1935, first secretary in the Canadian High Commission in London, "Mike" was graced with easy ways and an abundance of charm. Pearson had been especially effective in London, with the Anglophile Vincent Massey as high commissioner, taking the imperial edge off some of Massey's despatches and working well with the senior Canadian generals like McNaughton and Crerar. The boyish-faced and ever-smiling Pearson was a friend to most. One fellow diplomat remarked that he was "incapable of self-importance, ready in wit, and undaunted in the pursuit of his objectives and ideals."[11] Conversation came easy to him, with his command of history and politics, although he could also talk baseball and enjoyed trading hitting statistics from America's favourite pastime.

Minister McCarthy was not interested in the typical diplomatic gatherings and glad-handing in Washington, preferring to leave this to Pearson upon his arrival in the summer of 1942. Much work during the war—and ever since—happened at these parties, with a nudge given here and bits of information gleaned there, usually after libations had lubricated throats. Pearson's diary from his period in Washington was filled with the minutia and tediousness of these interactions, along with keen observations on how to navigate the halls of influence in Washington, with their army of politicians and lobbyists. In representing Canada, he was also savvy enough to supply information and facts to American journalists to promote the Dominion's interests wherever possible; however, vigilance was required in explaining Canada to the US, and in translating American foreign policy back to the cabinet in Ottawa.[12] Pearson summed up the challenge in March 1943 in a report that made its way to the prime minister. The Americans "often tend to consider us not as a foreign nation at all, but as one of themselves. . . . Because they take us for granted, they are perplexed when we show an impatience at being ignored and an irritation at being treated as less than an Independent State. Suspended, then, somewhat uneasily in the minds of so many

O.D. Skelton and Lester B. Pearson from the Department of External Affairs, both of whom were crucial in shaping Canada's foreign policy.

Americans between the position of British colony and American dependency, we are going to have a difficult time in the months ahead in maintaining our own position and standing on our own feet."[13] Just as Canada's senior commanders had to negotiate interactions with their American and British counterparts, its diplomats needed to engage in their own tricky dance.

———

Canadian diplomats jockeyed for influence in Washington, with all the other national agents and even with other Canucks. Prominent were those officials and buyers from C.D. Howe's Department of Munitions and Supply—which rose to 5,000 administrators and civil servants by April 1943. And leading the charge in the American capital were representatives from the Crown corporation

War Supplies Limited, who were there to sell Canadian war equipment and raw material. They secured millions of dollars in contracts to be placed in Canada.[14] To make the deals, they often overstepped their boundaries, sometimes by sweetening agreements with promises to provide arms and weapons to the Americans before the Canadian military, to the growing anger of their own country's generals. But Howe didn't care about nationalistic or inter-service competition; he simply wanted the many Canadian factories to keep producing so the enemy could be defeated.

The military realized that with the helter-skelter of Howe's trade experts, and with the Canadian diplomatic legation growing in stature, the armed forces needed to be better represented in the American capital. In June 1942, after more than a year of Canadian pressure on General Marshall to allow them to have a stronger military presence, the Americans relented. They did not want to open the door for other second-tier nations to be pestering the Big Two, but Canada could no longer be ignored. After discussions in Ottawa as to which of their best to put forward, Major-General Maurice Pope became chairman of the Canadian Joint Staff Mission. A soldier with uncommonly good diplomatic abilities, Pope came by his skill and subtlety naturally since his father had been Sir Joseph Pope, who had headed the Department of External Affairs when it was established in 1909. The son, Maurice, was a bilingual professional soldier who, having received the Military Cross for his bravery in battle during the Great War, had then stayed in the professional force during the lean interwar years. Pegged as an up-and-comer, he passed the Imperial Defence College course in Britain and was well known to many of the senior British and Canadian generals.

In the late 1930s, Pope was entrusted to oversee Canada's war plans, which focused on sending an expeditionary force overseas and on defending the coasts. He had also served on the PJBD, where he worked closely with senior American service personnel.[15] The general's presence in Washington was a signal that the Canadians were sending one of their elite, although the US never reciprocated by posting a soldier of Pope's stature to Ottawa. When the Canadian general arrived in the US in the steaming summer of 1942, the British watched his appointment with much interest, jealously guarding their bilateral relationship with the Americans. They attempted to bring Pope into their organization by sharing information, hoping he would respond in kind. Pope politely refused, aware of an earlier briefing note from civil servants warning that unless the Canadians acted separately from the British, the Americans would view them as mere colonials: "It would take decades to recover the ground that would thus be lost."[16] Pope would never have written such a windy and exaggerated declaration, but he understood the importance of Canada carving out its independence from the British.

Pope built on his favourable relationship with both the British and the Americans; and, like Pearson, he attended meetings, read secret reports, and met with the likes of General Marshall, who publicly called Pope's appointment a "happy augury" for future cooperation between Canada and the US.[17] One British report noted admiringly, "Pope keeps more closely in touch with current problems than probably any of the other Dominion service representatives."[18] Indeed, the general would write in his diary, "Much useful work . . . is possible by means of informal discussion. . . . Security is not absolute and what with a phrase here and a word there, together with what we are officially told, not only can the general picture of the moment be built up but also an intelligent forecast can be made of things that are to come."[19] But while effective cobbling together of information is often a key trait of diplomacy, listening, reporting, and occasionally intervening in strategic discussions is not the same as shaping those discussions. Canada understood that, despite its hundreds of thousands of soldiers, sailors, airmen, and others in uniform, it did not rank as a first-tier power.[20] On the home front, however, given their country's industrial might and agricultural contributions, Canadian diplomats and politicians felt that they should have more sway with the great powers. They would find that gaining influence in that arena was as difficult as making their way into the room where Anglo-American commanders made strategic military decisions.

———

Canada's place as a liminal nation—a Commonwealth country within the boundaries of North America—did not make inclusion on the Combined Boards any easier to achieve. These administrative bodies were established between the Americans and British to oversee wartime production. Run by bureaucrats and paper-pushing soldiers, the international coordinating agencies came to determine where the raw material was sent to be forged into the weapons of war, as well as where those weapons—tanks, aircraft, ships, and munitions—would be distributed. Shortages in a theatre of war could be traced back to the Combined Boards.

Canada's wartime output was significant and varied, ranging from shells to bombers and everything in between, along with food and mineral extraction. And yet when the British and Americans formed the Munitions Assignment Board in early 1942, Canada was denied a seat. In the field of armaments, the Americans produced about 61 percent of all Allied munitions, to Britain's 33 percent, with Canada in third place at 5 percent (excluding the Soviets). But Canada's sum had to be put into context since it was five times the combined output of all the other Allied powers.[21] The Canadians believed they deserved a seat on the munitions board, but the influential American Harry Hopkins, a close adviser to Roosevelt, refused to be swayed by any arguments, fearful of opening the board up to an unwieldy number of lesser powers.[22] The northern dominion did itself no favours in this regard. Major-General Pope used some of his capital to intervene and ensure that Canada was to have a voice at the board when Canadian production was under consideration. However, infighting among the departments in Ottawa—led by the powerful Minister Howe, who sought to minimize the board's decisions—left Canada unable to agree on what it wanted. Divided, it was conquered; and it remained on the sidelines.[23]

Despite this internecine warfare among the Canadians, diplomats at External Affairs, led by Norman Robertson, were pressuring King to let them push harder with the Americans in areas where Canada had shown leadership. Churchill and Roosevelt, along with Brooke and Marshall, were never going to allow King and his generals to wield influence in making critical military decisions, but Canada's industrial output demanded some recognition. Asserting the principle of functionalism—which states that representation should be based on contribution to a particular field or type of production—was a means for Canada to insist on sharing in some of the key work in international organizations. As Hume Wrong of External Affairs wrote of the principle that he was most

Canada's war production, minerals, and food were thought to be enough to allow the country's representatives to be involved in the Combined Boards. The Canadians were to be disappointed.

forceful in articulating, "each member of the grand alliance should have a voice. . . . proportionate to its contribution to the general war effort."[24] The middle powers—Canada, Australia, or Brazil—could have some authority if the principle was followed.

While King talked publicly about how the "high strategy of the war should be discussed by a small group in conditions of the most absolute secrecy"—a group that would include only voices from Britain and the United States—behind doors, the Canadians continued to press, protest, and talk up contacts in relation to the five main economic boards that coordinated the Allied war supplies, production, and economic activity.[25] Pearson and Pope did some heavy lifting, with the diplomat observing that in dealing with the British and Americans, "we could play both sides of the street, if we do so carefully and without trickery."[26] Canada continued to elbow its way onto the Combined Food Board, perturbed by the country's exclusion from this administrative body since Canada was an agrarian power. In this war of industrial wrath, food shortages were also an ever-present threat because of the relentless battle and the millions of men being conscripted into the armed forces who were therefore unavailable to plant the crops. Britain had already acknowledged that Canada's reaping of wheat and bountiful harvests "spell[ed] the difference between subsistence and starvation."[27]

The northern dominion assumed it would be invited to sit on the board, but was at first denied, again to its diplomats' surprise and its politicians' anger. Regrouping, the Canadians took the indirect approach, beginning a campaign where they forcefully reminded the great powers that they had sold or given away vast stores of wheat and other foodstuffs to allies around the world.[28] Slowly placing key representatives on the sub-agencies that fed information to the senior board, Canada eventually rose to full membership in late October 1943, a month after it received a seat on the Combined Production and Resources Board. "Canada's contribution to the war effort in the whole field of production and strength," wrote Churchill and Roosevelt, "is a source of admiration for us all."[29] The Dominion was a source of great strength to the Allied war effort, but there was no denying that Canada's late addition to a few of the more minor boards was also a source of exasperation for Ottawa.

Though Canada had only nominal success in joining the Combined Boards, its booming economy allowed it to become a lending nation. Trade with the US through the Hyde Park agreement rose from $275 million in 1942 to $301 million the next year, increasing still further to $314 million in 1944 before declining to $189 million in 1945.[30] This flourishing cross-border commerce led the Canadian government to have a surplus of American dollars at the end of the war, providing the country with great economic strength as it peered into the uncertainty of the postwar abyss. Canada's use of taxation to raise funds also added a new revenue stream for the state. In response to widespread anger over the predatory role of profiteers in the last war, government contracts were limited to a 10 percent profit, with all other returns taxed, although there were generous tax credits allowed for refitting plants or acquiring machinery. "No great fortunes can be accumulated out of wartime profits," proclaimed Finance Minister J.L. Ilsley.[31] Hundreds of millions of dollars were generated for the public coffers, including $466 million in 1945, and the potential divisiveness of industrial profiteering was smothered by government foresight and firm action.[32]

The state also sold war bonds, and multiple campaigns pushed these investments on Canadians, who bought them in the name of victory and—when they matured—of postwar prosperity. "The war seemed to be in everything we did," remembered Bob Bolster, a teenager whose life revolved around school, war films, and raising funds in the name of the soldiers overseas.[33] War loans and Victory Bonds secured $12.5 billion for the federal government, allowing Canada to pay for the war and provide a series of loans and gifts to Britain worth $3.468 billion, a huge sum considering that the entire war effort cost around $18 billion.[34] For the perennially poor Canada to be aiding Britain like this was utterly unthinkable before 1939, but officials at Whitehall noted that per capita the Dominion out-loaned the United States.

———

The Canadian legation became a full-fledged embassy on January 1, 1944, with McCarthy having been elevated to the rank of ambassador two months earlier. To further support the Dominion's interests in the US, the first Canadian Consulate General had been opened in New York in 1943 to stimulate trade and engage in low-key publicity of the Canadian war effort.[35] King's strategy of leaning into the US to assist Britain continued to pay dividends, especially as the US was dealing with other thorny allies, not the least being the Free French and the bloc of Latin American countries. The good neighbours to the north were not terribly pushy and paid their own way, enabling ambassador Leighton McCarthy to tell King that the American authorities "had given us pretty much all we had asked for."[36] That did not mean that there wasn't tension, or that the Canadians did not have to work hard—there was, and they did—but the victories outweighed the defeats.

By the summer of 1944, the aged McCarthy was absent from Washington much of the time, and Pearson was the true power. The forty-six-year-old diplomat became ambassador on January 1, 1945. Pearson continued to skilfully navigate Canadian interests, often charting a course on his own by using his common sense, personal connections, and light touch.[37] A velvet glove over an iron fist, Pearson preferred conciliation: but he also knew when to be tough and how to stand up to the bulldozing ways of the British or the friendly dismissiveness of the Americans. The ambassador would carry this well-honed approach forward into an astonishing political career that would see him rise to prime minister in 1963.

Major-General Maurice Pope also continued to represent Canada adeptly, overseeing a growing defence attaché group with able naval and RCAF members, although he was periodically drawn back to Canada to advise the government.[38] King needed Pope, with his good sense and deep knowledge of the inner workings of Washington, and from August 1944, the general served in a new position as military staff officer to the prime minister.[39] Journalists took note of Pope's influence, with the *Financial Post* writing that his "judgement is rated high by Mr. King."[40] Though King had no children, he had lost a nephew in the war at sea, and he and Pope occasionally talked about the war's strain on families. Like so many parents, Pope was one of those many Canadians who did his duty while worrying about loved ones. He had two sons serving in the infantry and artillery, and he was aware of the awful possibility that they might meet the same fate as that of his nephew, Major J.H.W.T. Pope, who was killed at the front.

———

The great genius of the Allied leadership was its ability to coordinate against the Axis powers, whose leaders largely fought separate wars. The Allies' foresight in propping up the Soviets in their death struggle against the Germans on the Eastern Front was also crucial to overall victory. It came with many costs, not the least being how it bound the democracies to a totalitarian mass murderer. Furthermore, Stalin's demands for a Second Front—in particular, the invasion of France—was a continual problem for the British and Americans, often dividing them, because they too were conflicted over when to invade Western Europe. But the disunion was never a chasm, and senior commanders like Dill and Marshall, backed by Churchill and Roosevelt, found consensus amid terrible strain. Canada was not a part of those conversations. Even though the young nation ached to act like an adult, Britain and the US preferred to keep it in a dependent position. However, the Dominion's surprising level of wartime wealth meant that it would have some influence during the fighting and in the war's aftermath, especially when this financial strength was combined with the vital role of its armed forces and wartime production. It was no easy path, but the Canadians tried to hew to their wartime strategy of avoiding disunity at home, fending off Britain's periodic moves to reclaim political control or speak on behalf of the dominions, and continuing to support the mother country by forging close ties with the United States.[41] That latter point was especially challenging because Canada had so little experience in standing with the Americans as equals. As Pearson wisely counselled early in 1944, "When we are dealing with such a powerful neighbour, we have to avoid the twin dangers of subservience and truculent touchiness."[42] It was never an easy balance to achieve, but Canada's representatives in Washington generally found that equilibrium, while acknowledging the country's limited role in the higher, strategic direction of the all-out effort against the fascists.

CHAPTER 13

THE COST OF ALLIANCE WARFARE

The Canadian Army in England was a "dagger pointed at the heart of Berlin," claimed Lieutenant-General A.G.L. McNaughton.[1] The army might have been a dagger, but it was more useful in 1940 as a shield. After the fall of France, two Canadian divisions were ready to defend Britain's coast from amphibious enemy attack, RCN warships had recently engaged the Germans off the French coast, and Canadian airmen were flying in defence of the British people. It was only the airmen in Bomber Command who were actively taking the war to the Nazis in occupied Europe, although this small force remained ineffective until more crews were trained as part of the British Commonwealth Air Training Plan and more bombers came off the assembly lines. Stalin, facing a continued German onslaught in 1942 as winter retreated, desperately called for an Anglo-American invasion to siphon off Hitler's forces. Every delay of this Second Front, as it came to be known, led the Soviet leader to think that the West was content to let the Communists and Nazis bleed each other white in battle, especially as 90 percent of the German Wehrmacht was fighting in the east.[2] He was not wrong. Churchill and Roosevelt preferred dead Germans and Russians to slain British and American soldiers. And yet the great fear in the West was that Stalin would seek a peace with Hitler.

Amid this growing pressure to show Stalin that the democracies were indeed pulling their weight, the British had established a strategy of raiding along the French coast to keep the Germans on their toes, to hone combined-arms operations, and to satisfy the Soviets. With the Canadian "dagger" aimed at the heart of Berlin left sheathed through 1940, 1941, and early 1942, the generals and senior politicians felt mounting pressure to see the army in action. A large raid against the French resort town of Dieppe was being planned for the summer of 1942, and the Canadian high command wanted in to strike a blow against the fascists as part of the Allied alliance.

———

In advance of this intensifying policy of raiding came the first invasion of Canadians into Britain. Canucks set foot on British soil in late 1939 with pride, excitement, and no little swagger. Like their fathers and uncles from 1914 to 1918, they brought with them a reputation as New World soldiers who had been hardened by the inhospitable land of snow and ice. The Canadians played up the stereotypes, with men offering freely that they were born in igloos, were known to raise wolves as pets, and were reared with a rifle in hand. American cowboy and Canadian Mountie stories had further strengthened the British notion of North American frontier society, even though several million Canadians lived in the major cities of Vancouver, Calgary, Winnipeg, Montreal, Ottawa, Toronto, and Halifax.[3] "Something in their bearing told the story, a combination of qualities, a naturalness and freedom of movement, a breeziness and alertness which suggested the new world," wrote Canadian high commissioner Vincent Massey of his countrymen's distinctiveness. "They resembled in many ways both Englishmen and Americans, but could not have been mistaken for either."[4]

"Somewhere in England" was the heading of many letters home, a phrase written for security reasons and, as infantry officer Burton Harper of New Brunswick remembered, because "it sounded very worldly, that we were on some fantastic mission."[5] Nearly half a million Canadians served in Britain during the war. For the most part, the Canucks liked the British, with whom they interacted on the streets, in the stores, and in the pubs. Many of the North Americans had roots in England, Ireland, and Scotland. They were also known for getting into trouble. The usual experience of young men with too much money, a zest for life, and a desire for female companionship led to all manner of crime and disciplinary issues. And no one wanted to die a virgin. A rise in prostitution and venereal disease caused moralists at home to worry about the fate of the Canadians, who were supposedly being preyed upon by those who were less innocent.[6]

Wild and boisterous, the Canadians had a reputation for living large and spending their accumulated pay in concentrated periods of mad revelry. At the same time, they often shared their ration stamps generously with the families with whom they were sometimes billeted or invited to stay, which allowed for the purchase of scarce food. Though kind to civilians, the Canadians engaged in healthy—and occasionally unhealthy—competition with the men of other military formations. The North Americans, for instance, were better paid than the British soldiers—$1.30 a day for a Canadian private versus about 50 cents for the British Tommy—and could do more with their money. One soldier, describing the efforts to win the favour of local women, noted, "naturally we sort of muscled in on their girls."[7] The German radio propagandist Lord Haw-Haw, whose broadcasts were meant to erode morale, were instead a source of amusement. Among his over-the-top claims was his description of the New World soldiers as lawless and dangerous layabouts who were a menace to the British and themselves: "The Canadians arriving in your midst will not be of much help in your war effort. Lock up your daughters and stay off the roads. Give these men a motorcycle and a bottle of whisky and they will kill themselves."[8]

In a legal sense, the Visiting Forces Act of 1933 guaranteed Canada control over its forces abroad, although in practice the Canadians were deeply entwined with the British in matters of doctrine, training, and organization. Some in the British high command, most notably General Bernard Montgomery, continued to view the Canadians through a colonial lens, but others were shown the errors of their ways. Fred Sherwood, who served in the Royal Canadian Naval Volunteer Reserve and rose to command a Royal Navy submarine during the war, recounted an incident on a training course. The Imperial officer was giving orders to a mixed group of officers from throughout the Commonwealth. "Fall out the Colonials," he ordered at the end. Some of the officers did. The Canadians continued to stand at attention. He gave the order again, to no effect. A third time, he raged, "Did you hear me?" The senior Canadian of the group sharply replied, "Yes, but we're not fucking Colonials!"[9]

The Canadian bluster was much curtailed as of January 1942, when the first Americans flooded into the British islands. The Yanks were even better paid than the Canucks and seemed even more rambunctious. "Over-paid, over-sexed, and over here," went the flippant remark in describing the Americans. Joe McGuire believed that he and his fellow Canadians "were on the wild side" in comparison to the British, but felt they were "not as wild as the Americans or the Australians! We seemed okay to the British when those guys were there."[10] Another Canuck, Ray Walker, was less sanguine about the Yanks, blaming them for high prices and bad behaviour: "They spoiled things for the rest of us . . . they're a bunch of bullshitters!"[11]

Despite the occasional clash of culture, the American GIs were welcomed by the British people and officials as something akin to saviours.[12] They would eventually number about two million, with another two million US air force personnel also serving. As more Americans arrived, the Canadians seemed to gravitate closer to the British, whom they met while carousing in the welcoming pubs, while sightseeing, and while strolling the streets, whether in the largest cities or the smallest villages. But there was no great clash between the Canadians and Americans, and they generally got along, sometimes banding together as North Americans in the Old World. That did not mean, however, that the Canadians sought to be Americans. J.K. Chapman, an RCAF navigator who enlisted early in the war, wrote in his memoirs, "We did not think of ourselves as second-class Americans. Indeed, we considered ourselves equal to or better than Americans and were inclined to pity them for having, mistakenly as we thought, declared their independence."[13] He wrote with unusual Canadian bravado, and yet in his statement he also revealed that Canadians were proud to be members of the British Commonwealth and saw themselves as different from the US.

Canadians did not have many formal interactions with Americans, mainly rubbing shoulders with them in the streets, in the bars, or in sports competitions. Baseball was popular among

Canadians and Americans watching a baseball game in Britain.

Canadians and Americans, and the British looked on, perplexed by the game, while the Canadians played hockey against one another, without too much threat from the British or the Americans. Many sporting rivalries were formed during the war, culminating in two high-profile football games between Canadians and Americans in early 1944. Their origin was in a pub, where the seeds to most good ideas were liberally watered. Major W. Denis Whitaker of the Royal Hamilton Light Infantry, who had played for the professional Hamilton Tigers, was talking to an American lieutenant who had recently received football equipment from the US. The Tea Bowl game was soon on, to be played at London's White City Stadium between the Canadian Army Mustangs and the Pirates of the Central Base Section of the US Army. The Canadian team was stacked with great players: several were Canadian Football League stars, including Whitaker, Captain George Hees of the Toronto Argonauts, Orville Burke of the Ottawa Rough Riders, and Jeff A. Nicklin of the Winnipeg Blue Bombers. The game, played on February 13, 1944, before a crowd of 30,000, saw the top military brass come out to watch their sides. National hubris was stoked in the stands, and on the field, in smash-mouth grid-iron football. The Mustangs took the win, with quarterback Orville Burke throwing a forty-yard pass to Whitaker to put them over the Pirates, and then a touchdown to Nicklin in the final seconds of the game for a 16–6 win.[14] The Canadians received a little silver teapot and bragging rights. Whitaker would serve as a lieutenant-colonel in the Normandy campaign; Hees as a brigade major, being wounded at the Walcheren Causeway, and later in life became a cabinet minister; and Lieutenant-Colonel Nicklin was killed in action as commanding officer of the 1st Canadian Parachute Battalion in Operation Varsity on March 24, 1945. The Americans, having suffered a blow to their pride, found better players and then thumped the Canadians in the second game before 50,000 spectators, leaving the series 1 to 1.

These games helped to stir good-natured competitions, but the North Americans understood and liked each other. The thousands of Americans in the Canadian Army were also a levelling influence, showing there were more similarities than differences between the Canucks and the Yanks. On August 19, 1942, the US State Department announced that 2,058 of the 16,000 Americans who had enlisted up to that point in the Canadian Army had returned to the American forces. Some 14,000 nonetheless decided to stay with their Canadian comrades, even though there was better pay in the US forces. The bonds of comradeship must have been the reason for Americans to make that decision, refusing to leave their mates. And those who were brought back to US units carried with them new knowledge of the Dominion. On August 19, 1942, Secretary of State Cordell Hull spoke of how these "young men who now returned to serve in the American forces will constitute a group of ambassadors of good-will to spread throughout the United States the story of Canada's great contribution to the common war effort."[15] Little did Hull know that, even as he spoke, the Canadians were engaged in bloody combat at Dieppe on the French coast in one of the most reckless and costly raids of the war.

———

In early 1942, Churchill was holding off Stalin with one hand and Roosevelt with the other. These tiring exertions provided insight into his quip that "There is only one thing worse than fighting with allies, and that is fighting without them!"[16] Britain's major allies urged an attack on the Germans through a cross-channel invasion of Northwestern Europe, but the British high command, particularly the thorny but brilliant chief of the imperial general staff, General Alan Brooke, warned that this would simply be suicide. The German defences were too strong; the Allies were short of landing craft, making it difficult to get enough infantrymen ashore; and naval and aerial firepower were insufficient to support the vulnerable invasion force should it manage to get onto land. The failure to win air supremacy meant that the Luftwaffe would tear apart the vulnerable supply craft that would be bringing essential supplies to the fighting forces stranded across the Channel. No, any invasion would be crushed in a devastating defeat. Even the Americans seemed to understand this, despite their aggression. One US proposal for a 1942 invasion, code-named "Sledgehammer," outlined the plan to send five divisions to France in case the Soviets were on the verge of collapse. The tens of thousands of soldiers, reported the planners, "should be considered a sacrifice for the common good."[17]

This type of horrible martyrdom was a compromise Churchill sought to avoid, although he was wary of looking weak, especially after the string of defeats to the Imperial forces around the world. He needed something to inspire the British people, to show the Americans he was not gun shy, and to pull weight with the Soviets. With his fertile mind looking for ways to keep Hitler guessing at where the Allies might attack, Churchill ordered a series of armed raids against occupied Europe. These actions would in no way lead to victory, but commando strikes would fire the imagination of the flagging public and would possibly draw in German reserves to defend the long coast. To lead these operations, Churchill sought a glamorous leader; he found him in Lord Mountbatten, who was appointed head of a new service branch, Combined Operations.

The handsome second cousin of Queen Elizabeth had been a mediocre naval commander. But Dickie, as he was known to friends, liked the offensive nature of raiding, delighting in the vision of striking in the dead of night, knocking the enemy back, and achieving a growing series of victories that might counter the litany of Allied defeats. Though his raids were never undertaken without a cost in resources or lives, Mountbatten built upon the success of earlier operations by British commandos. Seeking to make his mark, he wanted a big victory. The three services—the army, navy, and air force—had different goals and plans, and friction was soon evident. Even as Mountbatten was elevated to sit with the chiefs of staff committee, he had no forces to deploy in battle. He could plan grand schemes of violence, but he had no regiments, warships, or squadrons under his command. His Combined Operations headquarters also had only limited intelligence-gathering capabilities. In short, his raids required the consent and support of the other service arms, and while they were all on the same side, they were riven by fierce rivalries before, during, and after the war. A large-scale dash-and-destroy assault on Dieppe would also require soldiers; luckily for Mountbatten, the Canadian army commanders were yearning for a battle.

Lieutenant-General Harry Crerar wanted to prove himself as the temporary commander of First Canadian Army, which he was leading in the absence of General Andrew McNaughton, who was on leave due to fatigue and illness. Crerar had been the architect of the expanded Canadian Army as chief of the general staff in Ottawa, and now, having achieved an impressive series of victories from behind his desk at headquarters, he wished to lead that army into combat. At fifty-three-years-old, the five-foot-eight Crerar was trim and fit after a soldier's life, and he ached to make his own name in battle. The general lobbied the British to include the Canadians in the raid, using his connections with senior British officers like Brooke and Lord Mountbatten.[18] "It will be a tragic humiliation if American troops get into action on this side of the Atlantic before Canadians, who have been waiting in England for three years," he said, revealing another motivation.[19]

Mountbatten's Combined Operations headquarters planned the assault on the fortified port of Dieppe, which it knew would be a difficult target since garrisoned German forces were stationed there, but it was hoped that surprise and firepower would win the day. A bomber blitz, when combined with the huge guns of capital ships hurling shells ashore, might stun the enemy, who could be overrun in a straight-up-the-gut amphibious landing. The 2nd

Canadian Division, judged by General Montgomery as the best among the Canadian formations, trained aggressively from the early months of 1942. The division's soldiers would be augmented by British commandos and even 50 American Rangers. But this was to be very much Canada's day, with close to 5,000 of the 6,000 soldiers coming from Crerar's army.

The raid began to unravel almost from the beginning, with the other service chiefs skeptical of its value. Bomber Command was hitting the enemy through larger aerial sorties to overwhelm the German defences and to smash cities. Its air marshals were loath to redirect bomber resources to plaster the limited fortifications that lined the town of Dieppe. In contrast, Fighter Command, consisting of RAF and RCAF squadrons, was anxious for a decisive dogfight. The Germans had been using the tactic of patrolling on the defensive, with the goal of avoiding aerial battles unless they had decisive odds, and the frustrated Allied flyboys wanted a dust-up. They expected that the Dieppe raid would force the Hun to emerge from his lair. The conditions were far from ideal, though, and the 863 British, Canadian, and American fighter pilots would face severe tactical limitations because of the narrow window of time over enemy territory, as the Hurricanes and Spitfires had only about two hours of fuel, most of which would be burned off getting to and back from France. Nonetheless, the command believed that now was the chance to strike decisively against the Luftwaffe. It was the Royal Navy that was the most anxious about exposing their warships to land-based aircraft that might damage or sink them, a fate they had suffered in the Far East and in battles closer to home in Norway and Crete. Even as Mountbatten's Combined Operations embraced the raid, framing it as a dress rehearsal for the full-scale invasion of Europe to follow, Bomber Command all but removed its bombers from the planned fray and the navy reduced its commitment, refusing to put its largest warships in danger.

The Canadians began to get nervous about the operation, which was losing its muscular firepower assets. But when McNaughton returned from his illness, he did not push hard to test the raid's assumptions. For the sake of his soldiers, he should have. The most ludicrous notion was that the raid would be based on a surprise strike. Mountbatten's inexperienced staff had planned a five-pronged assault: first, British commandos and American Rangers would attack gun batteries on the far flanks while two small villages, Puys and Pourville, would be seized next to the main beach, with the Canadian amphibious landings going in at 5 a.m. When these strongpoints were taken, along with the all-important guns that overlooked the primary objective at Dieppe, the lead force of Canadian infantry and armoured units would be landed on the main beach half an hour later to deliver victory. It was an exceedingly complex schedule that included different objectives and synchronized times—and much that could go wrong. Poor intelligence assessments also missed the small chert rocks on the Dieppe beaches, which were treacherous to advance over and liable to get lodged in tank treads. Another intelligence failure was the lack of a proper appreciation of the German defences that had been strengthened for over two years, as well as enemy machine gun and artillery positions on the cliffs overlooking the beaches. Naval gunfire or bombers could not knock out these positions. Because they were impossible to neutralize, the staff officers increasingly downplayed them in various iterations of planning, and eventually simply hoped that the attackers would get off the beaches with limited casualties before the surprised defenders were brought to full alert.

The Dieppe operation nonetheless picked up its own momentum, especially with Dickie needing a win, the Canadians seeking action, and Churchill desperate to have something to show Stalin at a major Moscow conference slated for early August 1942. The opportunity to scoop up German documents and possibly an Enigma machine to break intelligence codes became another facet of the operation, grafted on to the already established plan. It involved a sizeable force of pinch raiders coming in behind the main Canadian thrust. That too was far-fetched, and even if the assault force somehow snatched the valuable encryption machine, the Germans would almost certainly realize its loss and change their signal codes.[20] A bad plan was becoming worse and worse.

When Operation Rutter was finally set for July 8, 1942, there were high hopes despite the obvious failure in planning, the naivete about achieving surprise, and the lack of sufficient resources to achieve the shock and awe required to smash the fortified enemy forces. But the complicated naval run-in to the French beaches was detected by a German air patrol that shot up the ships before flying off, while poor weather and choppy water made it difficult to disembark the first-wave soldiers into landing craft in a timely manner. With much going wrong from the start, and a well-reasoned fear that the German Luftwaffe would report the convoy, the raid was called off. Reports indicated that the Canadians were disappointed to return to Britain without having bloodied the enemy.[21]

After months of training and planning, the frustrated Canucks headed to the pubs, where they drank and speculated on reasons for the SNAFU (Situation Normal: All Fucked Up), a new American military acronym that was catching on. No attempt at secrecy was made, and soon word of the cancelled assault was spreading through British villages and towns—although the Germans in

Western Europe did not pick up on this chatter and speculation, and nor did the patrol aircraft properly identify the ships in the raid. Mountbatten was crestfallen over the aborted raid, but as he and his staff sifted through the entrails of the scrubbed operation, they kept circling an idea: what if the raid was remounted against the same place? With information leaking about the original site of Dieppe, the Germans would never suspect that the Allies would be so daring or reckless as to launch a second action against the identical site. It was an idea that could only have been fuelled by disappointment, vanity, and liberal doses of Scotch.

The operation was back on, now named Jubilee and set for August 19. However, there is no record of Mountbatten's order to mount the second raid—either it was not written down or it was destroyed—leading veterans and historians to engage in all manner of speculation and controversy over whether he had the support of other senior military leaders or if he had gone rogue. Conjecture aside, Mountbatten could not have conducted the raid without the other services, including Fighter Command and the Royal Navy. Furthermore, Churchill was clearly aware of Jubilee, speaking to Stalin about a forthcoming raid in early August when the two met in Moscow.[22] The British leader needed something, anything, to appease the Soviets, who he feared might make a separate peace with Hitler unless the Allies invaded Europe. A big operation was a bold wager in the great game of jousting over the Second Front.

The Canadians were informed of the reborn raid, and despite their inexperience, they began to worry. Writing less than a week before the raid, Crerar noted that "given an even break in luck and good navigation, the demonstration should prove successful."[23]

Complex military operations involving thousands of soldiers should not be based on blind luck, witless naivete, or casual arrogance.

———

On August 19, 1942, the multi-pronged operation fell on the Germans. On the far flanks, British commandos skulked forward before dawn, overcoming the defenders and knocking out several coastal artillery battery positions. Closer to the main Dieppe beach, on either side—Puys to the North and Pourville to the South—Canadian forces were to strike at 4:50 a.m. Delays due to the great distances landing craft had to travel led to uneven and uncoordinated landings. It did not matter. Puys was a death trap, with a narrow beach a mere 200 metres wide and a cove surrounded by high cliffs. Pourville allowed for a larger force to come ashore. The objectives for both sites were to knock out enemy artillery on the headlands that overlooked the main Dieppe beach, and then to drive inland. The blow had to be delivered with precision for the main attack to work, and the natural confusion and friction of moving the Royal Regiment of Canada to Puys and the South Saskatchewan Regiment and Queen's Own Cameron Highlanders of Canada to Pourville led to a late arrival as landing craft ran off course in the dark during their two-hour, 15-kilometre voyage to the beaches. Though the Germans had not caught wind of the Dieppe raid, they were ready to meet any assault when the tides allowed it. The garrison was on high alert.[24] Of course, they were. They did not have much else to do as a fortress formation except to practise to repel an invasion. Many Canadian survivors of Dieppe believed the enemy had been informed of the operation in advance: they had not, although they were prepared to throw back any Allied attack that was foolhardy enough to be launched against their dug-in positions.

The beach at Puys was soon a charnel house. "The Royals were shot down in heaps on the beach without knowing where the firing was coming from," shuddered one eyewitness.[25] Canadian journalist Ross Munro was on one of the landing craft that came in later to the battle, and he watched the catastrophe in the kill zone with growing terror as the Germans gunned down the exposed soldiers without mercy. He somehow survived and left on a landing craft. The experience, Munro wrote, "shocked you almost to insensibility."[26] The operation ended after three hours in a bloody shambles, with most of the force killed or captured.

At Pourville, the Highlanders and Sasks got off the beaches and drove inland. They made good initial strides, but soon the casualties rose as the defenders raked their advance with fire. While there were many individual acts of bravery—such as that of Lieutenant-Colonel Cecil Merritt, who led his dwindling Saskatchewan soldiers in battle and crossed a bridge several times in the face of enemy riflemen, for which he was awarded the Victoria Cross—the six hours ashore produced few tangible victories. Even worse, the Germans were gathering in strength as part of the counterattack, driving the survivors back to the beaches, where the ultimate flaw in the plan revealed itself. How were the two regiments to get back on their landing craft if they were engaged in a firefight? Only a sacrifice force left behind to hold off the enemy allowed some to escape.

Because of the delays and fighting on the flanks, the Germans were fully alert to the primary Canadian attack on the main beach that was planned to arrive a half hour after the other assaults.

What little chance the deeply flawed plan had of succeeding evaporated as defenders manned their posts, including hardened machine-gun positions and artillery pits atop the cliffs. The drive towards the objective by the Royal Hamilton Light Infantry and Essex Scottish was met with mortar, shell, rifle, and machine-gun fire even before their landing crafts touched down on the rocky beach that spanned 1.6 kilometres. The eight supporting destroyers' 4-inch guns did little to suppress the enemy fire. Churchill tanks from the Calgary Tank Regiment were also delayed and then had trouble finding purchase on the egg-sized chert rocks on the beach, some of which threw the tanks' tracks.[27] Scrambling forward, the infantry huddled at a low-lying sea wall, about half-way up the beach. Several attempts were made to charge forward from there, but these were driven back by a storm of steel, leading to withering losses. Despite the Armageddon of destruction, some of the Rileys—as the men from the Hamilton unit were known— fought their way through a casino that abutted the beach, advancing within the relative protection of the large building. They then engaged in close-quarter combat with the Germans in the streets of Dieppe.

Back on the beach, the Calgary tanks were largely impervious to bullets, and some of the Canadian infantry took cover around them as the troopers cooked off all their ammunition and hurled their last shells at the enemy. But it was a hopeless position, and even as the brave sailors on the landing crafts tried to return to the beach to pick up the doomed Canadians a little after 11 a.m., they were targets for enemy shells and mortar bombs. Private Ernest Ludkin of the Royal Hamilton Light Infantry was wounded but lucky to be evacuated, writing from a hospital after the battle that "the slaughter was terrific."[28]

Above the beaches, a massive series of dogfights raged throughout the day in the largest air battle of the entire war.[29] Focke-Wulf
Fw 190s and Messerschmitt Me 109s dived and climbed, firing
their guns and manoeuvring for position against RAF and RCAF
Spitfires, Hurricanes, and P-51 Mustangs. Tracer bullets and
explosions filled the sky, with the Germans having the advantage
of fighting on the defensive and the Allied airmen forced to tangle
with one eye on the enemy and the other on the dwindling fuel
gauge. All three of the Eagle squadrons—American pilots serving
in the RAF—also fought over Dieppe in Supermarine Spitfires.
During the day-long battle, the Americans added to their already
impressive totals by destroying several enemy aircraft, for the loss
of one pilot killed and one taken prisoner. In the end, ninety-nine
Allied fighters were shot down, about double the number lost by
the Luftwaffe in what one Canadian fighter pilot called, "a mad-
house in the air."[30]

Death raged above and below. Due to the confusion of broken
communication, Canadian reserve units were fed into the cauldron,
leading to the obliteration of Les Fusiliers Mont-Royal to no effect.
The pinch raid for the encryption machine was thankfully deemed
impossible, joining all the other failures that day. "The beach was
a deathtrap," recounted Lieutenant-Colonel Robert Labatt, commander of the Royal Hamilton Light Infantry, and the feverish
battle sputtered to an end around 2 p.m. as the Canadians ran
out of ammunition and the last of the shot-up landing craft pulled
away.[31] Only 2,211 Canadians returned to England, most of them
men who had never landed at Dieppe. Over nine hours, six of the
seven Canadian battalions sent into battle lost their commanding
officers. Another 1,946 Canadians were captured, at least 568 of
them wounded, and the final death toll was 907.[32]

Dieppe: a day of carnage and destruction.

The Canadian Army was mauled at Dieppe. Though official propaganda tried to claim it as a victory, the long casualty lists revealed the truth.[33] Crerar and McNaughton escaped censure by scapegoating the divisional commander, Major-General Hamilton Roberts, whose career was ruined. Higher up the chain of command, Mountbatten was delivered a heavy blow, a reversal met with no little satisfaction by the other service chiefs, who saw him a dangerous dilettante. The Royal Navy and Bomber Command went back to doing what they wanted to do: winning command of the sea and smashing German cities. Mountbatten and Crerar tried to establish a narrative that the lessons of Dieppe paved the way for the victory on D-Day two years later, but few direct teachings came out of this defeat that were not evident from other amphibious operations. However, the high-cost error of attacking a fortified port, the lack of bombers and naval gunfire support, and the masquerading of hopeful thinking as a plan all revealed gross failures that would be rectified by D-Day.[34] Furthermore, the spectre of the Dieppe defeat loomed over the staff officers who struggled with the plan to liberate Western Europe.

Canadian survivors talked about having been sold out by the British even as they took pride in having weathered a terrible storm on the beaches.[35] While victory has a thousand sires and defeat is an orphan, for the combat soldiers it was never clear who was to blame. Mountbatten's Combined Operations carried the most responsibility, although the Canadian high command too eagerly signed on to the raid without being a part of the planning, and then, when it was clear that the operation was taking on the stench of ad hockery and amateurishness, did not have the courage to pull out. This was colonial thinking at its worst. It revealed that McNaughton and Crerar had much to learn about how to deal with the British. The inter-service rivalries had likely doomed the raid too, revealing not only the challenge of alliance warfare for nations, but also for combat arms. In Ottawa, Dieppe would be— much like Hong Kong—a warning to King's cabinet that it needed to more closely watch its own generals.

Dieppe was also used to stir those on the home front to greater action in the pursuit of victory. Film and newspaper accounts revealed the stark cost of combat, and Canadians were staggered by the losses. But there was pride too. For instance, after American newsreels highlighted the role of the Rangers, making the raid seem like an American operation, near-riots erupted in Toronto movie theatres.[36] Americans had in fact played a more important role than Ottawa or Washington knew. While three of the Rangers died in the raid, including Lieutenant Edward Loustalot, a Louisiana native and the first American killed in action by German forces in ground combat in Europe, at least nine Americans serving with Canadian units would lie forever with their Canadian comrades at the Dieppe Canadian War Cemetery.

———

As seen through the lens of Canadian-Anglo-American relations, the most important aspect of Dieppe was that it allowed Churchill to show Stalin that his desired Second Front was no easy thing to achieve. The Soviet dictator shrugged at the butchery on the beaches since his forces suffered Dieppe-like destructions every day in the grinding warfare on the Eastern Front. The Allies absorbed the pointless carnage of the misguided operation and sent more aid to Russia while also intensifying the bomber war against Germany. More importantly, the British, led by Churchill and Brooke, waved the red flag of Dieppe to show the Americans why their reckless plan for a cross-channel invasion in 1942 would have meant an extinction-level event for the unlucky force committed to battle. The Americans came to see this and eased up their pressure on their allies to launch the ill-conceived invasion. In the realm of bilateral relations, King recorded in his diary a conversation with Roosevelt, who told him that Dieppe "made clear how terribly dangerous the whole business of invasion across the Channel was."[37] That may have been the most significant lesson of Dieppe, although the Canadians might be forgiven for feeling like pawns in this great power struggle.

CHAPTER 14

WEAPONIZING CULTURE

With the growing Allied losses and the titanic struggle on multiple fronts, culture became a state instrument for mobilizing Canadians to fully prosecute the war effort. Film, radio, comics, and other cultural products were created to tell Canadians, young and old, about the fighting forces overseas and the home front workers straining from the factory floor. The war also had the unintended consequence of stimulating the arts by creating opportunities for journalists and new artists at agencies like the Canadian Broadcasting Corporation (CBC) and the National Film Board (NFB). An important goal of Canadian cultural endeavours was to impress upon the Americans the Dominion's multi-faceted contributions to the war against the Axis powers. John Grierson, Canada's leader in the production of films and propaganda, believed that the deep penetration of the country's films into the United States had put forward "a most powerful platform before the American public, from which the Canadian effort can in due proportion and relationship be discussed."[1] And he was correct.

———

"The State or the United States," Canadian nationalists railed, pushing back against the dominance of American radio culture in the 1930s, a force that was overwhelming Canada and choking off its stories and identity. The country's fate, they warned, was annexation unless the federal government intervened against simple-minded and yet popular Yankee cultural products. Noted academic and man of letters Archibald MacMechan agreed that Canada faced "gradual assimilation, peaceful penetration, in a spiritual bondage—the subjection of the Canadian nation's mind and soul to the mind and soul of the United States."[2]

Building on Canada's success in the Great War, which fuelled state funding of the arts in a time of crisis, a burgeoning home-grown film industry produced features in the 1920s. While there was a burst of Canadian productions for the screen, the American Hollywood juggernaut that controlled distribution and theatres soon smothered the emerging industry. Radio was an easier and cheaper means of connecting Canadians, and it had been doing so since the first station in Montreal began broadcasting in May 1920. New stations soon followed, although their low wattage ensured that community news dominated, with local musicians singing in between advertisements for neighbourhood stores. However, as the wattage power increased to allow for greater broadcasting distance, Uncle Sam's commercial programs infiltrated across the border along the airwaves. Canadians embraced the invasion, content to laugh along with popular American comedy programs like *It Pays to Be Ignorant* and dramas such as *The Lone Ranger* or *The Shadow*. In the 1930s, about 80 percent of the radio programs available to Canadians came from the United States, bringing with them that country's news, culture, and history.[3] Federal and provincial authorities were ignorant, apathetic, or simply unconcerned about this cultural foray, and they put almost no funding into the arts in Canada, even when a whisper rose to a chorus as journalists and commissions warned that this neglect could only erode the emerging sense of what it meant to be Canadian. The exception to this indifference was the creation in 1932 of the Canadian Radio Broadcasting Commission, the precursor to the Canadian Broadcasting Corporation. "Fostering a national spirit and interpreting national citizenship" was the mission and mandate of the CRBC and, as of 1936, the CBC. The war would propel this nationalistic organization forward, with the goal of meeting the desire of Canadians to know more about the country's total war effort.

The 1930s had seen the Nazis produce a frenzied array of film and radio propaganda, productions that both amazed and troubled the Canadians who watched and listened as Hitler bent the German people's will to the state. Appreciating the power of such media, the King government established an information bureau even before Canada went to war, on September 9, 1939. Though King did not like the idea of coercing the electorate through propaganda, he believed that this bureau might help him and his cabinet colleagues craft persuasive messages to reach the 11.5 million citizens across the large country.

Just as industry, finance, and people were mobilized, so too was an increasingly expansive official propaganda arm of the state, which evolved into the Bureau of Public Information in December 1939. It sought to present messages stressing the importance of national unity and, as one report noted, of "sharing together in common experience, working and striving in great causes."[4] But in the initial culture barrage against the Nazis, the bureau proved to be all prose and no poetry, with its leaders and writers offering dull narratives laden with statistics. The civil servants who produced these missives seemed to think they were in the game of writing year-end official reports rather than capturing the spirit of the crusade that was emerging across the country. King acknowledged in April 1941 that the government needed to do a better job of telling this story, and that "the position of the United States now is such that factual information about Canada's part in the war would be welcomed."[5] Though writing in his typically obfuscating style, King clearly understood the importance of impressing upon Americans the extent of his country's expanding effort. The cabinet was slow to move, but in September 1942, after a drumbeat of complaints from journalists and opposition politicians that Canada was not doing enough to publicize its contributions to Allied victory, King and his ministers established the Wartime Information Board (WIB). The board soon engaged in an onslaught of cultural products to tell North Americans what the country was doing in the all-out battle for survival.

———

Under the dynamic leadership of John Grierson—a Scottish pioneer of the documentary film format who had been appointed the first commissioner of the NFB in October 1939—the WIB developed as a robust and successful state media body. While there were several WIB chairmen, the power lay with its general manager, Grierson. Short, wiry, and bursting with energy, Grierson—no one called him by his first name—hired cutting-edge filmmakers to helm the NFB-produced films that were intended to better highlight the Dominion's many military and industrial contributions to the Allied war effort and the defence of North America. Grierson argued that these were things that "Canadians need to know and think about, if they are going to do their best by Canada and by themselves."[6]

With the war prying open the government's coffers, Grierson was able to extract funding for his films. But he was also wary of the neutral American government's desire, before December 1941, to reject all propaganda, whether Axis or Allied. "While the voice of Canada must inevitably develop great importance in the United States at the present time," wrote Grierson early in the war, "it may be wise to determine with great care and foresight the nature of that voice."[7] Grierson nonetheless worked his contacts in the United States and achieved a considerable victory. The first NFB film in March 1940, *Canada at War*, was to be a joint production between the state agency and the popular American film series *The March of Time*. The film presented Canada's early war effort and was shown in the US, although it was caught in the crossfire of the battle between King and Ontario premier Mitchell Hepburn in the leadup to the March 1940 election. As part of his war of words against King, Hepburn used his provincial powers to censor *Canada at War*, refusing to allow it to be shown in Ontario theatres since he said it glorified King.[8] It did not, other than by showing him as Canada's prime minister leading the country. The Americans were more than a little confused over the banning of a film that drew attention to the 1st Canadian Division's role in going overseas to protect Britain, Canada's strengthening of fortifications along the North American coasts, wartime industry's churning out of armaments, and the country's robust voluntary enlistment system. Hepburn took fire from journalists who scathingly wrote

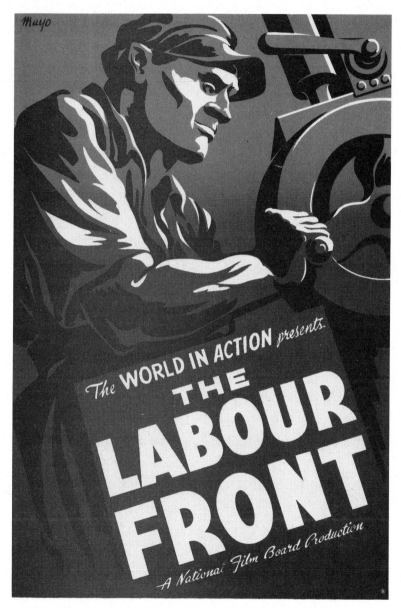

The *World in Action* poster. THE WORLD IN ACTION presents THE LABOUR FRONT. A National Film Board Production.

This NFB World in Action *poster highlights a Canadian film about the exertions of labour in support of the war effort.*

that he was hurting the war effort while claiming to defend it. He was also condemned by the American producer Louis de Rochemont for his backward and unhelpful actions since the film had also been made to show Americans that its northern neighbour was competently defending the hemisphere. Only twice had *The March of Time* been banned, noted de Rochemont: once by Hepburn and the other time by Hitler.

The dust-up, though embarrassing to Hepburn, was largely forgotten after King won the 1940 election, and the NFB continued to chart a course ahead. Two important series were birthed early in the war: *Canada Carries On* in 1940 and, the next year, *The World in Action*, with individual films based on ten- to twenty-five-minute shorts that were screened before longer features in the country's eight hundred theatres.[9] *The World in Action* was international in its scope—examining, for instance, the Allies' move to provide financial and food support for the Soviet Union and the necessity for democratic nations to fight the Axis powers. *The New York Times* wrote that the films in the series rose above nationalistic propaganda as "they interpret the facts squarely and by doing so have earned the respect of audiences who are struggling to understand more clearly the world in which they live."[10]

The *Canada Carries On* series focused on the national war effort, with films that often showcased the fighting arms. For example, *Breakthrough* (1944) centred on the Canadian infantry's fierce combat with the Germans, showing the North Americans as "another kind of army . . . a citizen's army of men and women, resolute and cheerful, an army whose discipline did not destroy its soul." Driven by crisp narration and enlivened by quick cuts along with interspersed footage and stirring music, the films in this series were of high quality. They rarely downplayed the Nazis' victories—with one of the first films, *The Front of Steel* in July 1940, presenting the Nazi blitzkrieg into Poland—but they often situated the Canadian martial ardour as emerging from a democratic nation that was engaged in a righteous fight. "Art is not a mirror," Grierson believed, "but a hammer. It is a weapon in our hands to see and say what is good and right and beautiful."[11]

At the NFB, Grierson won over his political masters, creating one of the largest documentary filmmaking studios in the world, with some 800 employees situated in offices in London, Washington, New York, and Ottawa. By late 1944, there were 3,112 prints of 761 films that were being shown throughout Canada to audiences numbering 465,000 a month. Even more Americans viewed the catalogue of films, with 1.5 million a month watching them in the last year of the war.[12] "Of all our wartime publicity activities in the United States," wrote Hugh Keenleyside of External Affairs, "the work of the Film Board under Grierson was at the time recognized as the most beneficially effective."[13]

———

"The Americans are managing by superb showmanship to make a great spectacle out of it," wrote Grierson, "and some Canadians, of course, imagine we ought to solve the information problem in similar fashion."[14] Under Grierson, who for a time led both the NFB and an energized WIB in a multi-front information war, the Canadians would try to match the Americans' talent for self-publicity and absorbing storytelling. A growing number of writers and civil servants gathered data from Canadian and external news sources to shape messaging around the war. They were aided in this by the release, in December 1941, of the first opinion polls that gauged domestic wartime attitudes. These polls, from the Canadian Institute of Public Opinion, offered unique insight into factors such as morale, trust in government, the prevalence of rumours, and what Canadians knew about the conflict.

Though Grierson was a filmmaker, he did not deny the communicative impact of radio, a technology that reached Canadians in their homes. The WIB fed the CBC with all manner of stories and information, although no program rivalled *Hockey Night in Canada* on Saturday, with Foster Hewitt providing the play-by-play—a broadcast that reached some 1.5 million listeners, or one in ten Canadians. Service personnel in Britain could also catch the hockey games as they were recorded on large phonographs and then transmitted by wireless to London, where they were rebroadcast on the BBC. After hearing one Stanley Cup game in April 1940, infantryman Arthur Wilkinson wrote home to his mother, noting, "It was grand to hear Foster Hewitt's voice and hear the crowd yell. It made me sort of homesick when I thought of Dad and you."[15] He did not survive the war to return to his parents.

The CBC also filed reports from England, with Marcel Ouimet, Peter Stursberg, and Matthew Halton producing some of the most influential journalism of their time. *We Have Been There* and *With the Troops in England* were programs broadcast from Britain about Canadians overseas, sharing the stories of these serving men and women with listeners in the Dominion and parts of the United States. The radio humanized the war, bringing voices and sounds of everyday life and combat to Canadians who huddled around the radio at news hour. "Tonight I heard my son," wrote one mother to the CBC. "Bless you."[16]

———

Canada's culture war was not supported and spread only by the state. While some critics had questioned the value of the arts in a time of shells, bombs, and bullets, many argued that with all Canadians required to "back the attack," as one of the aggressive phrases intoned, even poets, dramatists, and singers could find ways to aid the war effort. "If freedom is to endure, the arts must flourish," proclaimed one artist.[17] In a clash of ideas between democracy and fascism, creative works were an expression of liberty and freedom. Many painters and cartoonists turned their attention to graphic posters that urged Canadians to defeat the enemy, whether from the farms, factories, and mines, or in uniform.

As in the last war, official war artists were employed in the service of the state, with Charles Comfort, Jack Nichols, Carl Schaefer, Molly Lamb Bobak, and other luminaries serving in uniform, often attached to military units in the field to depict the war. They captured heroism and horror on canvas, and Aba Bayefsky, who sketched the death camps at the end of the war, wrote that "for the first time [he had] become aware of man's monstrous capacity for evil."[18] These artists left a powerful legacy, allowing future generations to imagine and reimagine the war effort by Canadians, and during the war several curated exhibitions were mounted in Italy, England, and North America to showcase their work to Anglo-American-Canadian audiences. These works did not shy away from depicting the trauma of war, be it the exhaustion of soldiers, the drowning of sailors, or the failure of the bomber crews to return from their nighttime sorties.

In a time where there was no shortage of threats, some societal leaders continued to warn against the American cultural menace. Low-brow and destructive cultural products that choked Canadian offerings needed to be turned back at the border, they insisted.

In the House of Commons on July 25, 1940, MP Tommy Church, a former populist Toronto mayor, argued that the American "gutter press"—his term for crime magazines and pulp fiction—was morally harming and should be censored.[19] While Canadians continued to cheerfully consume these spicy and sensationalistic stories instead of more timid domestic tracts, one unintended consequence of the war's impact on culture was the emergence of a homegrown comic book industry. Before the war, Canadian youth read American comic books—Disney stories or tales of The Batman—and even Canadians like Joe Shuster, whose first Superman comic book issue was published in 1938, were forced to go south to make their way. His caped crusader, per the comic's tagline, kept the world safe for "Truth, Justice and the American Way." But in the winter of 1940, the invasion of American comics northward was slowed as a result of paper and ink shortages, which were partially due to hydro-electric power being diverted to war industry.

Also because of the rationing of ink, the comics in the "Canadian Whites" series were printed in black and white, although bound with flashy coloured covers. The comic-book heroes included Johnny Canuck, who was often fist-fighting his way to victory over a muscular Hitler.[20] Brawny, courageous, and tough, but without superpowers, Johnny Canuck was an epitome, many liked to believe, of the gritty ordinary Canadians who had left their loved ones to strike at evil.[21] The name "Johnny Canuck" was in fact adopted by many Canadians overseas. Used as informal shorthand to differentiate the Canadians from the British "Tommy" and the American "Yank," it remained popular during and after the war.

—

One of the Canadian superheroes, Nelvana of the
Northern Lights, stops Hitler and his minions.

Despite the push behind a Canadian cultural offensive, the appeal of Hollywood films, which offered a steady diet of drama, comedy, and crime capers, was undiminished by the war. A few blockbuster films were set in Canada, including the 1941 production *The 49th Parallel*, in which Laurence Olivier played a French-Canadian trapper (with a dubious accent) who is to hunt down an enemy spy. The Nazi was transported by submarine, landing at Chaleur Bay, six kilometres west of New Carlisle, Quebec. Interestingly, only a year later, the Kriegsmarine imitated art when a German officer, Werner von Janowski, was dropped off by submarine in the summer of 1942. He was rapidly caught because of his accent, his use of old Canadian money, and the hyper-vigilance of a population on the lookout for spies.[22]

Aware of the power of the silver screen, the Department of National Defence took matters into its own hands to highlight the country's martial effort. *Corvette K-225* (1943) featured Randolph Scott commanding a Canadian warship, a role that took him far from his traditional westerns. The naval brass even allowed warships to be featured, giving them time off from their relentless convoy duty to add authenticity to the film. The production team shot in Halifax Harbour and along Canada's east coast from February to May 1943. The film depicts German U-boats wreaking havoc as they sink merchant vessels and warships, even machine-gunning survivors. (Here, the story draws upon the June 1918 commission of a war crime when a U-boat carried out similar immoral actions against the Canadian hospital ship *Llandovery Castle*). Scott plays the lieutenant-commander of HMCS *Donnacona* in a story centred around a series of convoy battles and the deadly cat-and-mouse game of fending off U-boat attacks. Camera crews even boarded ships, including HMCS *Kitchener*, to film during at least five convoy runs. Premiering on October 19, 1943, at the Central Theatre in Ottawa, *Corvette K-225* attracted a patriotic audience of service personnel and Ottawa's political elite. The film also played in the United States, and *The New York Times* reported positively on the "fidelity [of] the discomforts of an escort vessel's crew—the eternal tossing and rolling of the ship in a moderate sea; her plunging and gyrating in the grip of a North Atlantic gale, with tons of sea water pouring over her, battering and soaking every man."[23]

K-225 had built on the success of *Captains of the Clouds* (1942), which brought American star James Cagney to an Ottawa airbase to shoot the film in Technicolor. The idea was fielded by RCAF officers who wanted a way to dramatically showcase the British Commonwealth Air Training Plan. Uniformed officers inked a deal with Warner Brothers at the Waldorf Astoria Hotel in New York. While the first draft of the script was described as "tripe" by a senior RCAF officer, the plan went ahead with the full support of the air force, which would contribute yellow Harvard training aircraft. Experienced Canadian airmen—including Flight Lieutenant Owen Cathcart-Jones, who had already designed a board game, *Be an Airman*, to disseminate the RCAF's role to younger audiences—would act as technical advisers on *Captains of the Clouds*, with the air force putting on a hard press to aid the Hollywood filmmakers.[24]

The film's title came from a speech given by Canadian hero Air Marshal William "Billy" Bishop, the second-highest-ranking British Empire flying ace of the Great War. His evocative phrase "captains of the clouds" was appropriate for this film that followed several bush pilots who enlisted in the RCAF. These rough-and-tumble airmen flew dangerous missions across Canada in the interwar years, acquiring a tenacious reputation as resilient pilots who could master difficult flying conditions. It was a good role for the pugnacious Cagney, who as a Hollywood leading star was known for playing tough guys and gangsters, and in the film he and his misfit mates carry out a classic buzz dive through the graduation parade as Air Marshal Bishop is presenting wings to the graduating airmen. For several weeks in the summer of 1941, No. 2 Service Flight Training School at RCAF Station Uplands, south of Ottawa, became a huge Hollywood set. Real airmen

James Cagney, on the wing, shooting
Captains of the Clouds *at RCAF Station Uplands.*

mingled with the actors playing them. "It is most interesting to
hear RCAF men talking in Hollywood terms," wrote the unit
diarist. "People are no longer 'on duty.' They all seem to be 'on
the set' or 'on location.'"[25] Though much of the shooting was
at Uplands, select scenes were filmed across Canada. Additional
squadrons and aircraft were loaned for aerial dogfights and for
the climax of the movie, when a German Messerschmitt 109

(represented by a Hurricane painted with German colours and insignia) attacks a series of unarmed Hudson bombers flying to England. The desperate battle required grit and sacrifice, a message that the RCAF was only too happy to embrace as the ethos of its own aircrews, men who often faced an uneven fight against the skilled Luftwaffe fighters.

The premiere of *Captains* on February 21, 1942, was a good opportunity for the Canadian military to reinforce the strong alliance between Canada and the United States, and the RCAF ordered 195 members from its Central Band and Precision Drill Team to attend the screening in New York as part of the pageantry. The inaugural event at the 2,750-seat Strand Theater occurred in tandem with other openings across Canada, and in London, Melbourne, and Cairo. *The New Yorker* magazine good-naturedly sniped that the film was "about 45 percent superb Technicolor photography; stunt flying, 20 percent; detailed information on the training methods of the R.C.A.F, 15 percent; acting, 3 percent; technical effects, 2 percent; and of plot not a trace."[26] On the whole, however, reviews were generally positive—and to all parties' satisfaction, the film made money and raised the RCAF's profile.

———

Though the culture of Canadians in uniform drew upon a wider Allied panoply of songs and heroes, it was also uniquely reflective of the Dominion's history. Canadians had their own military customs, with many of the regiments reaching back to the mid-nineteenth century. Soldiers, sailors, and airmen sang ditties and rattled off obscenities unique to their service. A particularly ripe example was the song "North Atlantic Squadron," whose multiple verses, each more vulgar than the last, were not for the faint of heart. These songs, especially the dirty and raucous ones, insulated the society of soldiers, airmen, and sailors from that of civilians, while banding together those in uniform.

Just as the Americans had the United Service Organization to bring in Hollywood stars and famous comedians like Bob Hope, so too did the Canucks call upon several dozen entertainment troupes consisting of service personnel to relieve boredom, soothe nerves, and offer a much-needed laugh. Johnny Wayne and Frank Shuster, prewar comedians who came from Toronto's Jewish community and served in uniform, parlayed their Canadian war-based humour into tremendous success with *The Army Show*, which first played across Canada in training camps.[27] Presenting all manner of songs, skits, gags, and groaners while ridiculing rules, regulations, and discipline, Wayne and Shuster knew a sure-fire method of rousing a cheer and a roar of applause was to taunt officers in authority, to the delight of the rank and file. One *Edmonton Journal* review on July 15, 1943, noted the success of *The Army Show*, enthusing that its two stars "hope to be going overseas soon to show the people of Britain another side of Canada."[28] Wayne and Shuster did cross the Atlantic to conquer adoring crowds and to display a unique form of Canadian culture, in this endeavour joining other bands and theatre troupes already overseas. "What a wonderful escape from the tragedy of battles," wrote one Canadian soldier after enjoying the duo's comedic stylings.[29] The two jokers would return to Canada, where they took their show on the road for decades, ultimately reaching new North American audiences through television.[30]

Perhaps the most popular Canadian cultural icons overseas were cartoons published in *The Maple Leaf*, a service paper that had a publication for each theatre of war. Ottawa-born William "Bing" Coughlin, who trained at the Pennsylvania School of Art and served in the Sicily campaign, created Herbie, a sad-sack, chinless, and scared soldier. He had his intellectual genesis in Bruce Bairnsfather's anti-hero, Old Bill, from the last war, and Bill Maudlin's Willie and Joe, who were equally weary and anxious American GIs seeking to preserve their lives at the expense of heroics. Fearful of the enemy, Herbie and his mates were always getting into trouble and were simply trying to survive. Other cartoons resonated with the Canadian soldiers, bringing laughter or a knowing grimace, but it was Herbie who was much loved. After the war, one veteran wrote that Herbie "was proud to be Canadian. He didn't like being called 'British troops.' He was a Canadian. He came from Canada. His first name was Herbie, his second name Canadian. Pte. Herbie Canadian. That was important."[31]

———

"Canadian spoke here; English understood." So read the sign that Canadian airmen in North Africa had put up to remind their Royal Air Force comrades that they were different.[32] The country's cultural war aided in distinguishing Canadians from other English-speaking service personnel. That desire to highlight the difference was also waged through radio airwaves and on the silver screen, and ably supported by war posters, cartoons, stand-up comedians, and unique publications. The aim of most of these products and initiatives was to mobilize opinion and urge Canadians onwards in the total war against the fascists. Artistic output was also a means by which the Dominion emphasized the nation's contributions to the war, which were separate from those of Britain and the United States. As culture was weaponized, it stimulated new organizations, artists, and a novel appreciation of art. Leaving a profound legacy by transforming Canadian identity, the nation's wartime culture also served as a shield against not-so-benign advances of American popular culture. In the triangular relationship between Britain, Canada, and the US, culture helped to share North American values and perhaps even to bridge the divide. Britain's greatest fictional detective certainly thought so, at least in the 1944 Hollywood film *Sherlock Holmes and the Scarlet Claw*. In the wartime feature, the brilliant polymath in the deerstalker tells his assistant, Dr. Watson, and the film's many viewers, that Canada is the bridge that connects Britain and the United States. If culture was a means of communication and a shield, it was also a sword, carving out Canadian values and thrusting the Dominion's story throughout the Anglo-American sphere. As Grierson was to write of this cultural mission's success in penetrating across the border to reach American audiences, "No other country has acquired this integral place in the powerful propaganda machinery of the United States."[33]

CHAPTER 15

DEFENDING THE NORTH

"Army of occupation," went the cheeky phone greeting from American soldiers in the Canadian North. These men were among the thousands of US service personnel and civilians who were cutting a path through Canada's wilderness to build the Alaska Highway.[1] The salutation was no laughing matter in Ottawa, in that it was the cabinet's great worry that the Americans would enter the country by invitation through war-related projects or mutual defence—or would simply invade Canada if Japan or Germany captured a foothold on the coasts—and then would never leave. All wars have unintended consequences, and the death match against the Axis powers might, it was feared, inadvertently lead to Canada's unchecked drift into the arms of the United States through the loss of the North.

———

As Canadians and Americans struggled to defend North America, especially in the aftermath of the Japanese attacks in December 1941, one of the greatest challenges centred around the Alaska Highway. The initial iteration of the road—in fact, several roads stretching from Dawson Creek, BC, to Fairbanks, Alaska—was built by the US Army Corps of Engineers from March to late October 1942. Nothing short of an astonishing feat of engineering and labour, the highway was described by the Department of External Affairs as "an epic example of applied energy and skill."[2]

President Roosevelt had long desired an overland route into the northlands that would enable the US to draw out the full potential of the resources there. Though the Canadian government had previously shown very little interest in the project because of the enormous cost and the perceived lack of benefit, the war became the driver for moving it to action.[3] The country's Arctic terrain alone spanned over 36,000 islands and covered 1.4 million square kilometres, but the area had been almost entirely neglected by Canadians, who lived in largest numbers within a few hundred kilometres of the 49th parallel. Notwithstanding this absence of thought and action, there remained among many Canadians a nebulous pride in an imagined North. This icy landscape had often been presented in Canada's limited cultural products—particularly adventure films or the writings of Robert Service and Jack London— and it was often portrayed as a component of the country's identity. Of course, the northern terrain was seen very differently by the few thousand Canadians who made their lives there, most of whom were Indigenous people who would find their traditional lands forever changed by this new war.

Since 1937, Roosevelt had pressured King several times to support a highway that ran through Canadian territory to allow Alaska—not yet a state but an "organized territory"—to be supported in times of war and peace.[4] The Canadian prime minister demurred, seeing little value in sharing the enormous cost of building a road to connect southern Canada to Yukon, with its mere 5,000 residents.[5] Nonetheless, in the panic after Pearl Harbor, the

American section of the PJBD pushed hard for a road—known initially as the Alaska–Canada (ALCAN) Highway—to wind through the vast territory of the two countries. The project was formally recommended by the entire organization, and the president approved it without hesitation on February 11, 1942, willing to pay for its entire cost.[6] The Cabinet War Committee grudgingly agreed, although it was far more worried about the threat of the U-boats along the Atlantic coast. The ministers felt they could not reject the proposal in this time of great peril, even as the politicians had been warned for years about the spectre of allowing the Americans to lay down a road in Canada's North that might allow the US to gradually annex the underpopulated area. In one of many preliminary strategic studies, General E.C. Ashton, chief of the general staff in 1935, cautioned the cabinet that "the building of a north and south highway through B.C. provides a strong military inducement to the U.S.A. to ignore our neutral rights."[7] Now, however, because of the obligations of continental defence, the Canadians were unwilling to stand in the way of their allies.

———

The Americans were undeterred by the scope of the construction project, hurling thousands of soldiers and civilians at it from March 1942 onward as they engaged in the arduous, bug-infested work of cutting through old-growth forests, traversing ridges and rivers, and pushing up and down five mountain ranges. "It's miles and miles of nothing but miles and miles," recounted one African-American soldier who served in a segregated unit.[8] These were hard and demanding jobs, and they often fell to the Black soldiers who, having enlisted to fight the Nazis or Japanese were now called to face the Canadian wilderness. Another Black US soldier compared the tough work to convict labour. The bone-deep cold of winter was preferred by many to the swarming flies and waves of mosquitos that bled the soldiers in the summer, in spite of the supplied special hats, netting, and abundance of bug repellent.[9] In this war against nature, the pickaxe, the shovel, and the bulldozer were the weapons of necessity. Specially fitted blades were attached to bulldozers that gouged into the earth to wrench rocks and tree roots free in brute force assaults, while thousands of soldiers were deployed in back-breaking labour to level the ground and carve out the road. It was an unending battle against nature as mud suctioned boots off feet and streams washed away pontoon bridges.

Within six months, the teams laid down some 2,400 kilometres of rough dirt-and-gravel road, which would be expanded over the next year as parts of it collapsed during periods of thaw and freeze.[10] By 1943, US Army trucks were driving supplies northward, most of them going to forces stationed in Alaska to protect against the Japanese attack that never came. Along with the road came temporary housing, bridges, and even radio stations. While the road never proved to be a military necessity, with far more tonnage of goods being moved by air or by sea, it would play a formidable role in shaping the North.

Whitehorse grew from a small village to a large town with 10,000 inhabitants within a few short months in 1942, as this Yukon centre was forced to accommodate the invading army of civilian workers and soldiers. The streets were churned to a sea of sludge, and the skies were filled with aircraft landing, refuelling, and taking off again. This new hub of activity, noted one journalist, was the "focal point for commercial and military aircraft of two nations—fast fighters of many types, medium and large bombers,

Flying Fortresses—winging northward; centre of bush flying for a wide northern area; supply base for secret survey projects; and a headquarters for the greatest construction project the north country ever has seen—the building of the Alaska Highway."[11]

The limited number of hotels and boarding houses were overrun as men rented rooms by the hour, with many sleeping on the floor. The RCMP rushed to the now thriving yet unruly boomtown; however, its officers were a step behind the prostitutes and bootleggers who were already plying their trades. Swaggering American military police also patrolled aggressively, monitoring their soldiers and bringing a brooding alien presence to Whitehorse, where they seemed to harass civilians as often as their service compatriots. Insults were traded freely between the tough and independent residents and the discipline-enforcing military police. American soldiers were generally tolerated, but the military police acquired a mean reputation, with the member of Parliament for Yukon referring to them as the "Gestapo."[12]

For Northern Indigenous people, this mass influx amounted to yet another invasion from the south. Some of these local residents were employed in temporary labour, while others watched impotently as their traditional lands were despoiled. George Behn worked as a civilian guide for the military, later recounting that for "native people . . . it's something out of this world when you see all these Americans" splayed across the land.[13] The thousands of southerners who were flown in by aircraft brought with them a host of diseases. In the past, the trip northward had taken weeks, and sick workers were usually no longer infectious by the time they reached Indigenous communities. Now, mumps, meningitis, influenza, and other bacterial killers came with the soldiers and labourers. In 1942, for example, the Indigenous community of Teslin was confronted by eight waves of disease that infected almost everyone, with the population declining as the deaths outnumbered the births.[14] One observer from the south, worried about this new military presence, noted, "The influx of white people is having a very harmful effect upon the natives, and it is noticeable that the degree of this harm is in direct proportion to the closeness of the association that the natives have with the whites. The new era is here to stay and will continue to present many problems to the administration. One of these problems is how to soften the blow upon the natives and ameliorate conditions so as to prevent their complete devastation."[15] In the end, those in power had little concern for how to ease these disruptions to Northern and Indigenous ways of life, as the frenzy of war projects trumped all else.

———

The road construction was part of a slate of projects, and though the highway was undeniably an engineering marvel, a second major venture proved a gross failure. The American military wanted a secure oil pipeline to supply Alaska in case the Japanese navy cut off maritime supply routes. Oil was crucial to the war effort, and the German U-boat campaign along the east coast had raised concerns among Americans and Canadians about the possibility of the oil supply being kept from their markets. While the Japanese submarines were far less effective on the west coast, and the Canadian military believed it beyond the ability of the Japanese navy to engage in maritime interdiction in North American waters, in early 1942 there was heightened fear in the US. And so, to meet the goal of protecting fuel supply lines, the 1,000-kilometre-long CANOL (Canadian Oil) pipeline would be built, extending from the Imperial Oil facility at Norman Wells on the Mackenzie River in the Northwest Territories to a new refinery in Whitehorse, and from there, shorter pipelines would snake down to Skagway on the Pacific Coast. Despite Canadians viewing the pipeline with even more skepticism than the highway, Ottawa allowed their allies to pour immense amounts of money and resources into the ill-conceived project, bargaining for the option of buying the pipeline at the end of the war. But those who were in the know agreed with the astute Major-General Maurice Pope, who declared, "The Canol project as a defence measure has always seemed to be so far-fetched as to be absurd."[16]

The idea of the pipeline appealed to some dreamers, with *Maclean's* magazine writer Richard Finnie enthusing in one 1943 article, "It is one of the indisputably good things brought by the ill winds of war. Every well drilled, every foot of pipe laid, every mile of road built, every boat or barge launched, helps to crack open the North to enrich Canada and the United States." Though the costs were excessive, now was the time, Finnie declared, drawing upon a military metaphor as he likened the pipeline to a "spear at the heart of Japan."[17] With natural resources weaponized, Finnie was among the many who envisioned a richer and better-developed country emerging from these Northern projects after victory was achieved against the enemy. However, given the challenging movement of supplies and the difficult working conditions, the harsh reality of mass construction in the North put paid to romantic visions of spear-like pipelines. The oil flowed only sporadically, and by the time the pipeline was finally finished in 1944, the Japanese threat had receded.[18]

As the North was reshaped, King became increasingly anxious about Canada's claim of sovereignty and the menace of foreign penetration. "We ought to get the Americans out of further development there and keep control in our hands," he noted in his diary in February 1944.[19] But the pipeline was not worth grasping onto, and it was dismantled in 1945, having done little other than to cost a fortune—between about $130 million and a quarter of a billion dollars.[20] The failure of the pipeline, along with the abandoned kit and toxic waste that polluted the land and water throughout its long length, led to the project's condemnation in Washington as one of the most flagrant examples of wanton wartime spending. One Canadian journalist summed it up as "a junkyard monument to military stupidity."[21]

———

A third major Canadian–American cooperative initiative was the development of the Northwest Staging Route, a series of connected airfields and radio ranging stations that allowed for North American–manufactured aircraft to be flown from the south to the north and then across the Bering Sea to the Soviet Union. These airfields, distributed along the route from Edmonton, to Whitehorse, to Fairbanks, Alaska, were a lifeline across the sub-Arctic expanse, and the Alaska Highway's existence was sometimes justified by citing the highway's role in providing a stable land route to connect the communities that otherwise relied on aircraft. The "air road" took on new urgency after the Soviets became allies in June 1941.[22] The PJBD recommended that the airfields be further expanded, or new ones created, to assist the hard-pressed Soviets, who were only 90 kilometres away at the closest point between Siberia and Alaska.

THE WORLD IN *ACTION* PRESENTS

Our
NORTHERN
NEIGHBOUR
A NATIONAL FILM BOARD PRODUCTION

*"Our Northern Neighbour," reads this poster for an NFB film
extolling aid and good will to Canada's allies in the Soviet Union.*

The staging route, wrote journalist Charles Shaw in early
1942, "would give the United States the means of maintaining a
direct contact by plane with Alaska."[23] During the war, new air
routes were added and additional airfields built in Alberta and
British Columbia, including at Lethbridge, Calgary, Edmonton,
Grande Prairie, Fort St. John, Watson Lake, Beaton River, and Fort
Nelson.[24] The resulting North American air route of thirteen airports, eleven of which were on Canadian soil, was located safely
away from potential enemy fighters or unpredictable coastal
weather. The airports also had radio stations to coordinate and
direct the planes flying from south to north, refuelling areas to
ensure survival across the long route, and mechanics on hand to
fix aircraft that had the distressing tendency to suffer engine

failure in the harsh weather. "Alaska is as much a part of front-line defense in the West as are warship bases and troop concentrations on Vancouver Island and the British Columbia mainland," penned Shaw. "For a long time to come this undertaking may be looked upon as symbolic of the strengthening ties between the two great peaceful nations of the West who, in time of crisis, prepared to meet the enemy side by side."[25]

With the USSR having lost so many aircraft to the Germans in the opening phase of the war, Soviet resistance was based on replenishing supplies of fighters and bombers. In late September 1941, the expatriate Canadian millionaire press baron Lord Beaverbrook, Churchill's friend and one of his long-time political backers, met with Soviet foreign minister Vyacheslav Molotov and Stalin in Moscow to discuss Western aid. Minister of Aircraft Production Lord Beaverbrook was joined by Roosevelt's trusted envoy, W. Averell Harriman, and on October 1, 1941, a "first pro-tocol" was signed to supply the Soviet Union with 1,800 aircraft by the end of June 1942.[26] It was a significant allocation, especially since the Western powers needed every available fighter or bomber to support taking the war to Germany.[27]

Once the deal was inked, the challenge was to find a way to get these precious weapons to the Soviets. The Murmansk Run consisted of Allied supply convoys that, beginning in the summer of 1941, sailed through the cold and deadly Arctic Sea that was swarming with U-boats. Sailors understood that if their ship was sunk, they were all but certain to freeze to death, even if they made it to a lifeboat. Some forty-one Allied convoys steamed to the Russian ports of Murmansk and Archangel, delivering almost four million tons of supplies, munitions, weapons, and aircraft—about 23 percent of the total aid to the Soviets during the war.[28] Canadian merchant sailors and RCN warships followed along the dangerous route, usually via Iceland and Britain, and the Germans were desperate to cut the supply lines with their U-boats and shore-based aircraft. Surging forward from bases in occupied Norway, the U-boats and the Luftwaffe struck mercilessly and sank about 20 percent of all cargo.

The survivors suffered terribly in the ruthless weather conditions, and ice-encrusted ships were always in danger of capsizing. Sailors with bloodied and frozen hands used axes to smash the ice that seemed to grow on the ships like a crystal mould in a never-ending battle. The RCN contributed to about three quarters of the convoys and, against all odds, no warships were lost. Merchant seamen were not so lucky, and they would be among the many who were swallowed by the dark waters. Canadian sailor Alex Polowin, who served from age seventeen as an able-bodied seaman on HMCS *Huron*, a Tribal-class destroyer, recalled years later, "There was never a second that there weren't the fears of the enemy being there. It was a continuous thing. And the fear drained you of energy."[29]

There were also two air channels along which fighters and bombers were flown to Russia. The southern route ran from Florida to Brazil to Ascension Island in the Atlantic, and then on to Ghana, Egypt, Iraq, and finally Iran. It was a long transit of about 20,000 kilometres, requiring multiple stops and substantial fuel. The treacherous trip ensured that fewer than a thousand machines—mostly fighters—were delivered by this route. Because it was shorter, the Northwest Staging Route was used to fly thousands of fighters and light bombers manufactured in southern factories to airfields at Nome or Fairbanks, where Stalin's pilots waited to fly them to eastern Russia.[30] The Soviets asked for the

Bell P-39 Airacobra and the Bell P-63 Kingcobra, each of which proved its worth in aerial combat. Other Soviet favourites included the Douglas A-20 Havoc light bomber, the Mitchell B-24 bomber, and the Douglas C-47 Skytrain transport aircraft.[31] The Americans even developed Russian-language maintenance manuals and painted the machines in the Red Air Force's colours.

Making this great aerial route function required the work of thousands of Canadian and American ground crew, pilots, and support staff, operating out of multiple airfields.[32] The "Gateway to the North"—Alberta's provincial capital, Edmonton—became the most important and largest Canadian northern base, head-quartering North American airmen. The city's primary airport, Blatchford Field, was given almost $10 million by the Americans to upgrade buildings, lay down new runways, and construct hangars.[33] The aircraft that arrived from the south were often modified in the city of 100,000 to better withstand the relentless cold conditions of northern flying. Unsung heroes like the mechanics and long-distance-flying airmen kept this air bridge to the Soviets open, and despite the unpredictable—or predictably bad—weather conditions, close to 8,000 aircraft were delivered and only 133 lost.[34] It was a colossally successful program and another sign of the profitable alliance formed as Canada sought to cement what the Wartime Information Board described in one pro-Soviet film as a "lasting goodwill" with its fellow northern neighbour.[35] These aircraft were part of the staggering sum of North American contributions in support of the Soviet push against the Nazis, with the Americans alone providing $9.3 billion in aid, and Canada offering more than $167 million in war supplies and other essential goods.[36]

In Northern Ontario, fear of enemy agents sabotaging the crucial locks of the Saint Marys River at Sault Sainte Marie, which borders the US state Michigan, had necessitated early in the war that joint American and Canadian forces protect this essential inland water area. While the Americans were more anxious than the Canadians, especially about the unlikely scenario that bombers might be launched from German vessels off the coast, the Canucks again sought to meet the needs of their neighbours. The PJBD tackled this issue in January 1941, and came back to it several times after the Japanese offensives. Fighter aircraft were eventually deployed to the area, as well as radar stations, new housing facilities for garrison troops, and precious anti-aircraft guns. To view this as only an exercise in humouring the Americans would be to discount the complex nature of the negotiations, but such an enemy attack was never a deep concern for the Canadians, even though significant Dominion resources were put into the defence. This included 9,000 members of the Canadian Observer Corps, who were trained to watch the skies and ring the alarm should they see the Luftwaffe.[37] They never did. Willing to support their American allies, the Canadians nonetheless drew the line at having US Navy patrols in Hudson Bay, something Roosevelt pushed for but that the Canadians blocked through their representatives on the PJBD. They felt these patrols were both unnecessary and too detrimental a threat to sovereignty.

The North was a different matter, and Ottawa had not paid enough attention to American plans and deeds in that area. In March 1942, Hugh Keenleyside, senior diplomat, member of the PJBD, and keen observer of the North, observed of the Alaska Highway project, "I do not like the idea of Canada allowing the United States to construct a highway on Canadian territory (thereby acquiring a moral if not a legal right to its continued use, at will, in peace or war)."[38] King's cabinet was slow to realize it was too complacent in letting the Americans carry out the northern work without guardrails or even consultation with Canadian authorities. When pressed on this in the House of Commons, King defended the "joint defence projects" that he described as "of a purely wartime character." He felt the necessity of a common defence required that Americans be deployed on Canadian soil, and he likened the arrangement to RCAF squadrons "operating from Alaskan bases."[39] This quieted the opposition, although the remark was disingenuous as these situations were not the same at all. Escott Reid of External Affairs was more on the mark in April 1943, when he counselled that Canada had "not won from London complete freedom to make our own decisions on every issue— including that of peace and war—in order to become a colony of Washington."[40] While King did not like to be pushed in making decisions, he had to act, specifically when he was advised that a private American oil company was laying down a new pipeline that had not been discussed with Ottawa. King even noted, fearfully in his diary, "We were going to have a hard time after the war to prevent the US attempting control of some Canadian situations."[41]

In May 1943, having received ample warning from Canadian diplomats that the Americans were perhaps too comfortable in Canada's North, the cabinet appointed Brigadier H.W. Foster to work closely with the Americans. Before the attack on Pearl Harbor, Foster had been considered for a key diplomatic post to represent Canada in Japan, and now he was flying around the vast spaces of the North in a plane with a Canadian Red Ensign draped from the cockpit. To face the army of occupation, this army of one was given the title of special commissioner for defence projects

The poster reads:

THIS IS OUR STRENGTH

THE *New* NORTH

The doors of the Canadian north open on Asia and Europe. The Alaska Highway, new air fields, oil and mineral developments, make this area a strategic centre both for war needs and the future. Our northern flying routes link the continents together and make Canada a focal point in the new air age.

*"This Is Our Strength," claims this poster on the "New North"
by famed artist A.Y. Jackson. It notes that "The Alaska Highway,
new air fields, oil and mineral developments, make this area
a strategic centre both for war needs and the future."*

in the Northwest, and he was to observe and report on the American work. Some of the previously unfettered US action was reined in—with, for example, a few unnecessary road systems being blocked—and a firm agreement was reached, confirming that the US forces would leave Canada at the end of the war. Foster found ways to work with the Americans, who numbered over 45,000 in Canada by April 1943, including 12,000 in Prince Rupert, BC, the crucial west coast port that received the most supplies destined for Alaska.[42] The smooth operations were a combined result of Canadian judicious application of pressure and American willingness to be respectful visitors. Foster reassured the politicians and mandarins in Ottawa that "usually co-operative and happy relations prevail with all U.S. officials."[43] It didn't always look like that to outsiders. Vincent Massey, the ultra-imperialist Canadian high commissioner in Britain, nearly wailed that the Americans were moving on Canada "under cover of the needs of the war effort [and were] acting in the North-West as if they owned the country." The war, he believed, had left Canada too compliant in the name of unity of Allied purpose, and, he insisted, "the only threat to our independence comes from that quarter."[44] It came from other quarters, of course, primarily Germany and Japan, but an invasion of Canada was impossible for the Axis powers to carry out by the mid-point in the war. Hitler could not even orchestrate a successful attack on Britain in 1940, when he was at the height of his powers and Britain was at one of its weakest moments. However, in terms of a potential loss of Canadian independence, it was the US that was feared. Massey's comment revealed the difficult trade-offs required in war, as well as the stakes at play; in the view of the high commissioner in London, his friends in Ottawa had gone too far in accommodating the US.

The legacy of these Canadian and American military projects opened the north to the south, with Canada taking over the 1,954-kilometre portion of the road from Dawson Creek to the Alaska border in April 1946, and expanding it over the coming years. This was not welcomed by all, of course, and waterways in the region were contaminated by an untold amount of frightful pollution, coming from oil spills, broken-down equipment, and the clear-cutting of pristine forests. But few could deny that wartime construction and American occupation also brought prosperity and transformation along with disruption and change. A wave of wartime investment propelled Whitehorse forward: new buildings, an airbase, radio stations, and a hospital emerged, and in 1953 the city became the territory's capital.[45] As in other major shared Canadian–American garrisons, be they in Newfoundland or Iceland, there was no little vice to be found amid the wealth. Rarely did life in these centres return to the prewar status quo. King had other worries, remaining wary about the Northern defence projects as an extension of the traditional American threat to sovereignty. On a map, the road seemed to divide Canada. King believed the US encroachment was "one of the fingers of the hand which America is placing more or less over the whole of the Western Hemisphere."[46]

In the name of assisting their Soviet allies and defending the hemisphere, the Canadians made concessions to the Americans. But by the mid-point of the war, they concluded that they must be more vigilant and not give the US forces any reason to stay longer than necessary after the fascists were defeated. As part of asserting control over the newly opened North, King demanded that Canada shoulder most of the costs, though the fiscally cautious prime minister blanched at the price tag. The US was willing to share the expense, and was even perhaps a bit bemused by its neighbour's stance, but Ottawa swallowed the obligation of $123.5 million for twenty-eight airfields, fifty-six weather stations, and other buildings and structures.[47] The cabinet was insistent on paying for its share and ensuring that the Americans had no claim to Canada's North. The US indeed retreated, leaving behind the highway, structures, and airfields as a wartime legacy that eventually strengthened Canadian sovereignty over its terrain. In the North, as in other parts of the country, Canada came to realize that free-riding was out: this was the price of being a grown-up country.

CHAPTER 16

PROTECTING THE WEST COAST

"We're in this thing together," wrote American journalist Richard Harkness in assessing the Canadian and American defence of North America and the fight against the Axis powers at the end of 1942.[1] Together indeed, and especially in the battle for hemispheric security. While it was the British and the Americans who struggled to define the strategic direction of the war, with little input from Canada, it was Ottawa and Washington that were deeply entwined in ensuring that North America was safe from attack. The Japanese sneak attack that dragged the US into the war had led to most of the American warships being moved from the Atlantic to the Pacific, leaving the east coast vulnerable. Throughout 1942, Royal Navy and Royal Canadian Navy warships assisted the beleaguered Americans on that coast, another tangible way in which the Dominion supported its wounded neighbour. On the west coast, Canada would also do its part in defending its sovereign territory and standing with the United States, including fighting together in the strange Aleutian Island campaign.

———

The Americans finally staunched the bleeding in the Pacific with their critical victory in the battle at Midway Island, from June 4 to 7, 1942. Crypto-analysts had broken the Japanese codes to provide a glimpse into the enemy plans, allowing a strong American force to intercept the Imperial Japanese Navy at sea. Fought some 2,000 kilometres from Oahu, Hawaii, this was a near-run battle involving carriers, aircraft, and submarines. The American victory delivered a shattering blow as four of the six Japanese carriers were sunk. Though fighters and light bombers had again revealed their ability to kill capital ships, it would still be the ground-pounders, supported by their comrades in the other combat arms, who would, in the three years to come, have to attack the Japanese through a chain of 300 desolate islands.

As part of the offensive that led to the Battle of Midway, in June 1942 the Japanese had occupied Attu and Kiska, two of the northern Aleutian Islands. This archipelago of American islands, arcing 1,900 kilometres westward from Alaska, stretches out on the world map like a series of stepping stones seemingly leading to North America. The strike on Pearl Harbor had been a terrible shock, but an actual invasion and occupation of American mainland territory would be an unthinkable disaster that would require the pulling back of forces from other battle fronts to protect the homeland. The relative proximity of the Aleutians to Alaska had stirred American papers into all manner of dire warnings and pronouncements. One survey in August 1942 revealed that more Americans could find the Aleutians on a map than could locate Hawaii.[2]

If the Japanese were allowed to keep the windswept, fog-covered, barren volcanic Aleutians, and to further fortify them with supporting aircraft and warships, this could be a forward site from which to strike against North America. The threat was felt most keenly on the area of the Alaska mainland that was closest to the islands and that had been militarily neglected. Scrambling to adequately defend the Americans there, Washington diverted precious military resources to that isolated territory, pulling them away from the main theatres of battle in the Pacific, the Atlantic, the Mediterranean, and from forces preparing to invade Northwest Europe. War often makes for peculiar battlegrounds: from farmers' fields, to monsoon-swept jungles, to uninhabitable volcanic rocks surrounded by treacherous water.

In 1942, much of the Canadian military was either in Britain or focused on defending the North American east coast; however, given the joint plan to protect North America under ABC-22, the US asked for RCAF squadrons to shore up Alaska. In late February 1942, the PJBD had concluded that "the effective defence of Alaska is of paramount importance to the defence of the continent against attack from the West, since Alaska is the area most exposed to an attempt by the enemy to establish a foothold in North America."[3] As the forces in the northern territory were short on defensive armaments—particularly coastal and anti-aircraft guns—the local American commanders were seeking any support they could find. Even though the Canadians had strengthened their Pacific defences with new army and militia units, as well as warships and artillery pieces, the threat remained.

Fear flared to panic on June 20, 1942, when a Japanese submarine, *I-26*, shelled the lighthouse at Estevan Point on Vancouver Island. Two weeks earlier, the submarine had sunk the ill-fated *Coast Trader*, an American merchant vessel. It had little success in finding other prey, but a second submarine, *I-25*, sank the Canadian freighter *Fort Camosun*, with its cargo of lumber headed for England. A lighthouse was an odd target, given the many ships in the water, and the attack failed, with the submarine captain reporting, "It was evening when I shelled the area with about 17 shots."[4] The shooting was poor: most rounds landed too short, splashing in the water, or fell beyond the 38-metre-high structure. A brave lightkeeper, Mike Lally, climbed the tower stairs and turned off the light. He counted the shells that exploded nearby, leaving pigs in a nearby pen squealing in fright. The submarine fled the scene, having expended precious ammunition against a nearly useless target. Not surprisingly, the attack caused new waves of apprehension in BC. Rumours circulated that the long-awaited Japanese invasion would soon follow the mysterious attack. Defences were ordered to high alert, and for some of the most worried residents of the province, the incident justified the grim action of forcibly relocating Japanese Canadians and Japanese nationals. The unusual Japanese attack would later stoke the conspiratorial charge that somehow King had known in advance of the Japanese attack and let it happen to firm up support for an increasingly unlimited war effort, just as Roosevelt had supposedly done before Pearl Harbor to draw the US into the conflict. There is no evidence of conspiracy in either case. King did not need to do anything to convince British Columbians, who were willing to pay almost any price in the defence of the province. The Japanese vessel, *I-26*, left Canadian waters and hunted shipping in the Pacific, becoming one of the most devastatingly effective Japanese subs in the war until it met the fate of most Axis submarines and was sunk in November 1944.

———

While the Canadian high command had been wary of drawing limited resources away from the east coast to the west, King and his cabinet had insisted that the RCAF and the RCN aid the Americans in defending Alaska. Four squadrons were eventually sent to that most northern of fronts, and No. 111 Squadron mounted its first operations against Kiska in September 1942. Although the Japanese were well dug in and protected within the volcanic rock, ships bringing supplies were exposed in Kiska Harbor and bombed when the tricky weather was favourable. But the North American bombers faced brutal flying conditions as unpredictable winds and intense cold played havoc with engines. Airmen developed all manner of superstitious phrases, quips, warnings, and prayers to the wind gods. Canadian crews braved these conditions in their bombing attacks on Kiska, with No. 8 Squadron, RCAF, involved in these sorties. One Canadian airman, Pilot Officer George Woods, was awarded the American Air Force Cross for his role in these bombing operations.[5] Another RCAF officer, Squadron Leader K.A. Boomer, was flying an American P-40k equipped with additional fuel tanks to extend the range when he attacked and sank a Japanese Rufe seaplane. Boomer was awarded the US Air Medal and the Distinguished Flying Cross, and later fought in the war over Europe against Germany. The only RCAF member to be credited with victories against both the German and Japanese air force, he did not live to witness the war's end, being shot down and killed in 1944.[6]

"I want to see Canada continue to develop as a nation to be, in time, as our country certainly will, the greatest of nations of the British Commonwealth," King wrote in his diary at the end of 1942. While he abhorred the idea of sending Canadians into battle, he knew the cost that came with being a partner in the Allied war effort and especially understood his duty to protect North America.[7] To become a nation worthy of consideration,

Canada had to do its part. In September 1942, three anti-aircraft units—all in very short supply across the Dominion—were sent to Annette Island off Alaska's Panhandle.[8] RCN warships were also ordered to serve with the Americans around the same time, though they were sorely needed in the hard-pressing battle on the east coast. While this spread the Canadian military thin, King wanted to stand with the Americans in defending the long west coast of North America.[9]

With the Americans focused on several war fronts, US Army chief General George Marshall delayed sending troops to Alaska, mainly because his quarrelling Pacific commanders, General Douglas MacArthur and Admiral Chester Nimitz, were demanding more resources. To strengthen the northern front, on April 19, 1943, Lieutenant-General John DeWitt, commander of Western Defense Command and Fourth Army, met with Major-General George Pearkes, a Great War Victoria Cross recipient who was the senior Canadian general in Pacific Command. The American general requested Canadian ground forces participate in an invasion of Kiska, the rocky island about 35 kilometres long and varying in width from 3 to 10 kilometres. With an operation soon to be launched against Attu, the Kiska invasion was planned for late summer.

External Affairs recommended to the prime minister that Canada should contribute a force, "even if only of token proportions," to "make a thoroughly useful impression on the United States," building on the goodwill engendered by the dispatch of the RCAF squadrons to defend Alaska.[10] Serving shoulder to shoulder with the US would, Norman Robertson advised, signal to the American public and its leaders that Canadians were not passive about their North American defence obligations.[11] General

Pearkes was equally effusive, as was the chief of the general staff, Lieutenant-General Kenneth Stuart, who argued that the operation would give the Canadians combat experience.[12] One final argument made by Stuart was that it was important to use conscripted soldiers. Canadians had derided the conscripts drafted under the 1940 National Resources Mobilization Act as Zombies, accusing them of lacking the spirit required to serve beyond Canadian shores, though the limited scope of their postings was indicated in the terms of home-defence conscription.[13] Ordering them into this North American battle, wrote Stuart, would prove they were real soldiers and would "break down the hostile attitude with which such personnel were regarded by a large section of the Canadian public."[14] On May 31, the war cabinet authorized an infantry brigade of trained conscripts to fight in Kiska, although the order was given only after the ministers had General Pope in Washington ask Secretary of War Henry Stimson to formally request troops. He did so, allowing the cabinet, fearful of a Hong Kong–like debacle, to spin a potential disaster as an American-led and -requested operation.

An aspect of the cabinet's cautious appreciation was shaped by the costly battle on Attu. The Americans invaded the island on May 11, 1943, and the fighting was surprisingly nasty. Despite the strength of some 11,000 American GIs supported by aerial and naval warship bombardments, the Japanese garrison of fewer than 2,400 men fought hard and to the bitter end. The awful weather and rough terrain also caused hundreds of cases of exhaustion among the Americans. Slowly beaten back, the doomed Japanese garrison was finally crushed in late May, with most of the garrison starving and suffering from exposure. The ferocity of battle had been sobering to the Americans. The Japanese lost more than 2,350 dead, with only 24 taken prisoner, while the Americans suffered 549 killed, 2,350 wounded. The US was grimly aware of the resilient enemy's will to fight to the death.[15] The first battle on American soil was won; Kiska was expected to be captured only after a violent clash.

———

By June of 1943, the Canadian Army had increased its strength on the west coast to 34,316 soldiers. About 5,000 of them were ordered to take part in the Kiska campaign as part of Greenlight Force. Four Canadian units—the Canadian Fusiliers, Rocky Mountain Rangers, the Winnipeg Grenadiers, and the French-speaking Le Régiment de Hull—along with artillery and supporting units formed the Canadian army brigade group.[16] Brigadier Harry Foster, a respected overseas commander, was brought back to inject realistic training, and his officers began to instill gruelling physical drill to get the soldiers into battle shape. Some of the conscripts who did not want to serve outside Canada were coerced, but most went willingly or swallowed their objections.

With little time to integrate the Canadians into the American formations, Marines were brought in to hastily train the Canucks in Japanese tactics. To serve with the Yanks, the Canadians were equipped with American weapons like the 75mm pack howitzers instead of the 25-pounder artillery piece, or the 81mm mortar instead of the 3-inch mortar. However, training the Canadians effectively on the American M1 Garand rifle was deemed to be too difficult. The infantry remained armed with the Lee-Enfield rifle and Bren light machine gun. Distinctive American helmets and winter clothing were issued, although the Canadians donned their own battledress with national insignia. Foster tried to prepare the men for the coming battle, demanding firm discipline. When an American general asked him why the Canadians shaved daily even when undergoing difficult training, he replied, "I tell them I don't want them looking like a bunch of bloody Americans."[17]

Military intelligence estimated that there were about 11,000 Japanese defenders, but because of the US Navy blockade, the Japanese garrison had withered on the vine of the long supply chain.[18] Allied forces numbered some 32,000, with bombers carrying out a plan of destruction while warships fired their large-calibre guns off the southeast coast to draw enemy attention. Landing on August 15 and expecting a cross-fire of bullets and shells, the Americans and Canadians encountered only the crash of waves along the rocky beach. But with intelligence determining that the large Japanese garrison was at least four times the size of the one at Attu, the North Americans prepared to face a prolonged campaign.

Nerves were raw. Fog blanketed the island. Some of the landing craft took the anxious soldiers to the wrong beaches. However, thousands came ashore to an eery quiet. The enemy was holding his fire for some inexplicable reason. The first waves of GIs—including the First Special Service Force, a unique Canadian-American formation—raced inward, finding cover but frantically and frustratingly digging shallow slit trenches in the rocky terrain. Still there was no fire. Spreading out by companies, platoons, and sections, the Americans probed inland among the rocky terrain. Every crevasse could contain a booby trap, while snipers were believed to lurk in trees or among the volcanic rock.

The Canadians were ready to do battle. The commander of Le Régiment de Hull, Lieutenant-Colonel Dollard Ménard, who had

Canadian soldiers disembarking for battle at Kiska in August 1943.
Note the Canadians wearing American helmets.

fought bravely and been wounded at Dieppe, roared martially that his men sailed "without a kindly thought or intent towards the little yellow cut-throat 'sons of heaven.'"[19] On the second day of the invasion, the 16th, the bulk of Canadians came ashore in the northwest corner of the island in a thick fog. Again, there were no Japanese defenders, and the American engineers skedaddled away from the beach when the Canadian Fusiliers opened fire in the fog. A Canadian officer who felt that the Japanese were hidden and waiting to launch an attack noted in the brigade's war diary, "Ours will be the long hard job of digging them out."[20]

Throughout the island, there were no sustained firefights, ambushes, or living defenders. However, some trigger-happy Americans and Canadians, their nerves taut, randomly fired at the ghosts in the mist. Comrades were killed and maimed. "Everyone was shooting at each other," counted Peter Cottingham of the First Special Service Force.[21] One Canadian infantryman of the Fusiliers died when he was shot through the spine by an American machine-gun team blasting away at the spectres. Four other Canadians died by mines or in accidents, but not by enemy shells or small-arms fire.[22]

The Japanese had retreated from the island secretly at the end of July. The withdrawal had been intricately planned and carried out under the noses of the Americans, a mortification for the navy as the Japanese had slipped ships in and out of the blockade undetected. Despite the absence of an enemy garrison, it was not until the last week in August that Kiska was finally secured, after an exhaustive search through dugouts and fortified positions revealed only the remnants of abandoned kit and supplies. During the course of the Kiska campaign, with its anticlimactic end, the losses were light: 4 Canadians were killed; about 30 were wounded or fell severely ill. The Americans suffered 28 dead, most from friendly fire, and 70 sailors were killed when their ship struck a mine.[23]

In the aftermath of the massive build-up of resources and the Japanese retreat, the operation led to no little blaming of intelligence failures for the wasted allocation of men and materiel and the embarrassing vision of the Japanese slipping away in the fog. There were some positive outcomes, of course. The US armed forces had driven the Japanese from American soil, which had to happen at some point in the war. And in terms of continental defence, the Canadians had, for the first and only time in the war, served in a land battle with their American comrades on North American territory.

Prime Minister King felt the operation was a farce, writing in his diary long after the campaign that the "expedition should never have taken place." His assessment was made with a healthy dose of hindsight, although he would find a way to use the operation to his advantage.[24] Earlier, in May 1943, for instance, he penned that Canada's contribution "would psychologically have a good effect in the U.S., in Australia and in Canada as helping to balance the actions of American and Australians combined in the South West Pacific."[25] The bloodbath on Attu in May was also an indication that Kiska could have been a similar bitter confrontation. It was not, and it was fortunate that the North Americans did not have to annihilate a Japanese force fighting on the defensive. The number of casualties would have been ghastly. Furthermore, King employed the news from Kiska wisely, addressing the Canadian people over the radio on August 21. The prime minister enthused about the military cooperation between the two North American nations, Canada's support for the Pacific war, and Canadian soldiers' participation in driving back "the Japanese menace" from the United States.[26]

Quebec papers drew attention to the French-Canadian unit sent into battle, while journalists in English Canada took the opportunity to praise the Zombies who were now, it was said, serving their country. They also pointedly told them to continue to do so by voluntarily enlisting to fight against the Germans. British Columbians breathed easier as the Japanese were driven back. The *Winnipeg Free Press* went a step further, informing its readers that Kiska was the first in a series of operations to free the Hong Kong prisoners suffering in the camps, erroneously raising hopes among the many loved ones who worried about the soldiers suffering in cruel captivity in Japan.[27] There was no invasion to free the prisoners, and the Aleutians never became an active front. The Americans instead chose to attack Japan in a two-pronged

*An E.J. Hughes painting of Canadians climbing through snow
and wind at Barley Cove on Kiska. Hughes was an official
Canadian war artist sent to document the operation.*

advance along a broad axis, led by General Douglas MacArthur
and Admiral Chester Nimitz. Through a combination of sea battles,
amphibious island-hopping campaigns, submarine operations to
sever supply ship routes, and bombing missions to fire Japanese
positions with high explosives, the Americans steadily pushed
back the enemy perimeter to close in on the homeland islands.

———

By late 1943, most Canadian soldiers were removed from Kiska,
with the last troops departing in January 1944. It had been a
strange campaign—one derided as a fiasco for the friendly-fire

shootings and the massive build-up for an enemy who was not there. But while battle was not delivered, perhaps few soldiers lamented missing the chance to kill or be killed, and the operation had allowed Canadians and Americans to serve together. Important military lessons were shared and processed, in matters ranging from supply and transport to winter warfare to operational interoperability. Prime Minister King made this positive case in one of his addresses to Canadians, highlighting the importance of the Northwest Staging Route, which he argued had contributed to Soviet victory, the RCAF's missions with the Americans in Alaska, and Canada's "cooperation in the occupation of Kiska." The non-fight at Kiska revealed Canada's determination to "do her full part until the military power of Japan as well as the military power of Germany is finally destroyed."[28]

CHAPTER 17

CONTRIBUTING TO THE CAUSE

The year 1942 was a desperate time for the Allies. In North Africa, the see-saw battles were indecisive until late in the year, when General Bernard Montgomery's Eighth Army finally drove back the Afrika Korps—a force that was increasingly short of fuel, vehicles, and munitions because of progressively successful naval and air blockades in the Mediterranean. In Western Europe, the bombing campaign gathered in intensity, although it would not be until mid-1943 that more and larger four-engine bombers, carrying payloads of high explosives and incendiaries, began to inflict withering damage on the German war machine and people caught in the firestorms. The Eastern Front saw ongoing German advances and agonizing losses of Soviet forces and defenceless civilians as Nazi-indoctrinated death squads continued their vile mass murder of Russian communists, Jews, and innocents caught in their path, executing hundreds of thousands before turning to the industrialized slaughter of the Holocaust. While the war in the Pacific saw steady American martial success, it came at a high cost in lives, and the victories on remote islands remained far from the Japanese homeland. Over in the Atlantic, the Allies were suffering under the U-boat blitz, with hundreds of merchant ships sunk, each carrying precious war supplies, munitions, and weapons that had been built using astonishing amounts of minerals and labour in North America before being sent to the bottom of the ocean. By year's end, a crippling 7.2 million tons of Allied shipping had been destroyed by the Germans, most of it by the U-boats.[1] And more of the subs were being built and readied to go to sea. Few in the West could have predicted victory anytime soon; however, if it was to come, it would only be through the close coordination of the Allied forces to mobilize their fighting formations and strike strategically at the enemy. But where to attack?

———

In the Battle of the Atlantic, the RCN was stretched thin—equipped with too few corvettes and destroyers to adequately protect the convoys, and always asked to do too much. Even though the corvettes were sturdy warships that, in the words of Canadian seaman Frank Curry, were "able to withstand anything and remain afloat," they lacked the necessary weapons and radar to seek out the U-boats in battle.[2] Furthermore, unlike the Royal Navy warships, which, to be modernized, were removed from the North Atlantic Run, refitted in shipyards, and out of action for weeks, the RCN ships could not be spared from service. The convoys had to keep running and they needed their protectors. The Newfoundland Escort Force had been renamed the Mid-Ocean Escort Force in February 1942, and it consisted of fourteen escort groups with long-range destroyers and corvettes: five RN, five RCN, and four USN. But many of these escort groups, including RCN warships, were dragged off the convoy run to safeguard American shipping vessels being massacred along the east coast, as well as those going into the Caribbean to escort the oil tankers. Ongoing shortages of the swifter and better-armed destroyers left the worn-out corvette crews, who were never meant to take their small warships across the Atlantic, pushed to the breaking point.

Though the convoy work benefited from tactical and structural reforms, including the creation of more effective combat units that trained together to better fight the subs, the Americans and the British were increasingly aware that the RCN was overextended. Nearly half of the north Atlantic escorts were guarded by the Canadians.[3] At the same time, merchant ships protected by the RCN suffered the most casualties, largely because the warships had been relegated to shepherding the slow convoys that were the easiest U-boat victims. But the convoys could not be stopped or even slowed as Britain felt the pinch of the frayed supply chain, with its citizens facing fierce rationing and ongoing hardship. Smelling blood in the water, the U-boats pressed the attack, and the amount of Allied shipping sunk reached a punishing 800,000 tons in November.[4] The next month, when the Americans complained to the British that the Canadians were worn out and unfit for further sustained convoy duty, the RCN warships were temporarily pulled from the North Atlantic for refit and rest. The navy's high command felt the blow keenly. Viewing it as an inaccurate reflection of the Canadians' performance, admirals and captains argued correctly that the vast majority of merchant ships arrived safely through the screaming winter gales and lethal U-boat packs. The die, however, was cast. The navy brass was only slightly mollified by a Royal Navy report in early 1943 that conceded, "The Canadians have had to bear the brunt of the U-Boat attack in the North Atlantic for the last six months, that is to say, of about half of the German U-boats operating at sea."[5]

A Royal Canadian Navy depth charge attack on a submerged German U-boat. The sudden reversal in the Battle of the Atlantic in May 1943 changed the strategic equation of the war.

From this low point, the RCN bounced back. While the ill-equipped Canadian warships had still been pressed too hard for too long—with insufficient time to make sure all warships had proper weapons and, most importantly, more sensitive radar to better detect U-boats—as of April they were back on the ocean. Acknowledging the U-boat threat, some sixty VLR (Very Long Range) B-24 Liberator bombers were released from the Pacific to assist in the Atlantic, and they offered immediate assistance to the beleaguered ships below as they patrolled much of the area where the U-boats hunted their prey.[6] With the Royal Navy taking the lead, the combined forces destroyed forty-two U-boats in May 1943. These were unsustainable casualties, and in a remarkable reversal, Admiral Dönitz conceded defeat, ordering a retreat in late May. The Germans had lost the Battle of the Atlantic, as

*A B-24 Liberator flies high cover over a convoy. In its role of
driving the U-boats away from savaging the merchant ships
in convoys, airpower was increasingly critical to the supply line.*

Allied technology, tactics, and grit had tipped the balance. North
America would no longer be severely threatened by the U-boats,
which, though continuing to be a menace, were generally con-
fined to European waters.

While the RCN could not claim many U-boat kills, victory was
not measured in the high-profile destructions of the enemy but in
the number of merchant naval ships shepherded across the Atlantic,
with their crucial cargo of war supplies and weapons. Despite a
shortage of destroyers and frigates, the Canadians successfully
guided most of the merchant ships through the perilous sea. To
meet the threat and support Britain, the RCN grew to over 400

warships, making it the fourth largest navy in the world. Contributing significantly to the war of logistics, the fleet fulfilled the role of supplying Britain, keeping its people from starving, and transporting the arsenal required for the eventual liberation of Western Europe. The RCN warships—identified by a green maple leaf on their funnels—provided 48 percent of the convoy escorts in the North Atlantic, compared to 50 percent by the British and a paltry 2 percent by the Americans, as the US was focused on the Pacific campaign.[7] Together with their comrades in the Royal Navy, the Canadian sailors preserved the lifeline to Europe by preventing U-boat assaults on maritime trade. The strain had been awful—Rear-Admiral Leonard Murray characterized the escort forces as having "held the ring against the U-boats" through "sheer guts and will power."[8] In relentless battle, 1,990 RCN personnel were killed, along with another 1,628 Canadian and Newfoundland merchant mariners, but from September 1942 onward, 99.4 percent of the merchant ships reached their destination. And during the entire war, 25,343 merchant ships carrying 164,783,921 tons of cargo were escorted across the Atlantic.[9] In this overwhelmingly large figure were the foundations for defeating the Axis powers.

The steady work of the RCN was recognized by the Allies when, on April 30, 1943, Rear-Admiral Murray was appointed as commander-in-chief, Canadian Northwest Atlantic. Headquartered in Halifax, he held command over all shipping and airpower assets from the waters south of Nova Scotia to the ocean routes east of Newfoundland and north of 40 degrees latitude. While it was a small area in the global war, this did not diminish the feat of Murray serving as the only Canadian theatre commander of the war. His appointment was a sign of the Dominion's importance in defending the Northern continent, with American air and naval formations falling under Canadian command and North American officers working together in Halifax for the good of the war effort.[10]

———

With the Americans and British having agreed to delay the 1942 cross-channel invasion of France—an operation that could only have ended in a disaster many times the magnitude of Dieppe—attention was directed to North Africa. The architect of American strategy, General George Marshall, did not want to fight so far from Europe, viewing this front as a distraction on the periphery of German power. However, the British were already in place there, with General Bernard Montgomery and the Eighth Army coiled to strike. The little British general, loved by his troops as much as he was later loathed by the Americans, had won a series of battles through a cautious and methodical set-piece approach that combined heavy firepower and limited advances.[11] His victory at El Alamein on November 4, 1942, raised the spirits of the collective Commonwealth, making Monty a hero and providing a sorely needed win around which the British people could rally.

Having been put off from invading France, and as the president was demanding action for the army before the end of the year, the Americans conceded and prepared for Operation Torch, their first major land campaign outside the Pacific. Vichy France still controlled parts of North Africa, and the American commander, General Dwight Eisenhower, had to negotiate with the quislings. Diplomatic talks were crippled by the lingering French anger over the memory of the Royal Navy's attack on their navy at Oran in French Algeria in July 1940. The French refused to lay down their arms. And so, for several days, American soldiers storming ashore in a branched operation in November 1942 had to fight their way through French defenders. Eisenhower engaged in frantic discussions with Admiral Jean François Darlan, an odious Nazi sympathizer. While Eisenhower was condemned by American journalists for working with the French admiral, a truce was soon made, although not before 500 Americans became casualties and nearly 2,500 French were killed. Having first confronted de Gaulle's antics, and now Darlan's wicked intransigence, the Americans perhaps understood what good allies they had in the British, and especially the Canadians.

Darlan was removed as a divisive issue when a French patriot assassinated him on December 24, 1942, and by then the Americans were battling the hardened Afrika Korps. The Yanks were handled roughly in some bloody affairs, including in February 1943 at Kasserine Pass, where a much smaller German force smashed the inexperienced GIs. Eisenhower and his generals came to understand what almost every army in history learned the hard way: battle-tested troops will almost always overmatch those new to sites of combat and carnage.[12]

No Canadian units were involved in the ground war, but every second automotive vehicle in Monty's Eighth Army had come from the Dominion's production lines, attesting to Canada's industrial might.[13] That staggering fact has rarely made its way into the history books, even though it was crucial to Allied victory. Furthermore, as noted earlier, the RCN had denuded its already strained fleet by sending sixteen corvettes (and a British warship) to assist in the amphibious Torch landings, marking yet another instance of the RCN taking the hit for the Allied war effort. At the same time, RCAF squadrons served above the desert battles, while on the ground a few hundred Canadian officers and non-commissioned officers (NCOs) were attached to British regiments to gain invaluable leadership experience, which they took back to their men to better prepare them for coming operations. At least one Canadian, a sergeant in the Carleton and York Regiment, served with the Americans. Wounded and returned to England, he later wrote about his newfound respect, remarking, "I want to take back all I said about the American soldiers. I spoke of the ones in London, and but now I [want] to say that I met the ones in Africa, in fact I was attached to them for a while out there and believe me they are very good soldiers and people of the United States should be proud of their fighting troops. . . . my hat is off to them for their courage and fighting ability."[14]

After driving back the much smaller German forces in North Africa early in the year, the Allies wrangled over where to attack next. In January 1943, a prickly meeting between Roosevelt and Churchill took place at Casablanca. The key question was where to attack next. While the Soviets were demanding immediate action to siphon off German divisions from the east, the British were obstinate in refusing to launch the invasion of Western Europe before they were ready. They also had to hold off the Americans, who again fumed at supposed British timidness, especially as they watched the turning tide on the Eastern Front. Stalin's Red Army was in its endgame of finishing off the Axis forces besieged at Stalingrad through the stunning envelopment and destruction of a quarter million of Hitler's soldiers. Riding high on blunting the German advance into the Soviet Union, Stalin refused to attend the conference, but his envoys there all but accused the West, and the British in particular, of cowardice for their refusal to launch the invasion of Western Europe. Roosevelt, who consistently misjudged Stalin as a man with whom he could work, did not come to Churchill's rescue, preferring to keep his powder dry.

While Churchill accepted his bruises, the British staff officers came with plans, appreciations, and appraisals—having again out-prepared the Americans—and made it clear that any operation against fortress Europe in 1943 could not end in anything but annihilation. "We came, we listened, and we were conquered," one American officer complained.[15] Stalin, always willing to send countless numbers to their deaths to achieve his aims, sniffed at the reticence. But by refusing to attend the conference, he missed an opportunity to shape the conversation with his glowering presence and pointed observations. The erudite Churchill used the bilateral meeting wisely to work on the president, who eventually blanched at the mental image of thousands of Americans washing up on French shores. The invasion of Northwest Europe was postponed.

Even as the Western nations' alliance with Stalin was fraying, strategic compromises were agreed upon, including more Lend-Lease aid to the Soviets and a more frenetic strategic bombing campaign. However, with the invasion put off again, pressure had to be applied on the Axis powers through a continuation of the Mediterranean campaign. The next target was the German- and Italian-held island of Sicily, off the coast of mainland Italy. Fearful that the Soviet triumph at Stalingrad might lead Stalin to arrange a separate peace with Hitler as he had done in August 1939, Roosevelt also asserted a warlike call for the enemy's "unconditional surrender." No negotiated peace would be contemplated with the fascists, only full and complete victory.

—

The challenge of moving several hundred thousand soldiers, along with their trucks, tanks, artillery pieces, and all the supplies of war, demanded awe-inspiring and excruciatingly detailed planning. With an Anglo-American force already in North Africa—where victory in May 1943 led to some 250,000 Axis soldiers being made prisoners—the Allies were ready to strike Sicily. An amphibious assault against a fortified enemy might very well become a repeat of Dieppe, but the Canadians, somewhat surprisingly, wished to be a part of the operation. King's normally cautious cabinet had become more bullish, seeking a high-profile role for the army that had spent much of the war training in England, save for the disasters of Hong Kong, Dieppe, and a few minor expeditions. While Canadian commander General Andrew McNaughton was against splitting his army, believing that the comparatively small formation of five divisions and two armoured brigades would lose its impact if it was broken up, he was overruled by Defence Minister J.L. Ralston. The general was a fierce nationalist who had run into problems with Chief of the Imperial General Staff General Alan Brooke, who would increasingly undermine him, feeling he was unsuited for command and perhaps too insistent that the Canadians always fight together.[16] As he had also made an enemy of Ralston, McNaughton's days were numbered, even as the 1st Canadian Infantry Division and an armoured brigade were sent to Sicily to serve alongside six first-wave American and British divisions in the largest amphibious landing thus far in the war, on July 10, 1943.

Now that King's cabinet had sent Canadians into battle, the ministers did not want to miss the opportunity of sharing this news across the country. But because of legitimate security fears, the Allied theatre commander, General Dwight D. Eisenhower, refused to allow for the release of a communiqué. The cabinet stewed but accepted the need for confidentiality so as not to provide information to Berlin. However, when they saw a draft of the message that Eisenhower would deliver publicly shortly after the invasion, they were stunned to learn that it only made note of "Anglo-American" forces, leaving out the Canadians. King, who was always caught between pressing for influence and staying out of the way of the Big Two, rightly reacted poorly. Angry that the Dominion's soldiers were being grossly ignored, he insisted that the omission be rectified before the Canadian public was alerted to the historic landings.

The ever-important diplomat in Washington, Mike Pearson, raced about the city to meet his American counterparts and explain why it was crucial that Canada be mentioned in the announcement, especially given the perception among Allied forces that the Dominion's army was rusting in England. He also used all his contacts to arrange a phone call between King and Roosevelt. For the president, the Canadian complaint was a minor concern at best, perhaps brushed off with one of his favourite stock phrases, "what piffle," but the Ottawa cabinet ministers were fending off political accusations that they had unreasonably shackled the army, and this seemed to them like a matter of political life and death. The incident laid bare the challenges of coalition warfare.[17] The acceptable compromise was that General Eisenhower, as Allied commander of the operation, would include the Dominion in his announcement of the invasion and that King—who also longed to share the important news and rightly believed it was part of his duty as prime minister—could speak publicly and in more detail about Canadian participation in Operation Husky twenty-four hours after the landings. It seemed a fair compromise, and King was drafting his speech when the War Department in

Washington went rogue, breaking the agreement on the day of the invasion by stating that "British-United States-Canadian forces have launched an attack in Sicily." After some bewilderment in Ottawa, King went ahead and announced on CBC radio that "all Canada will be justifiably proud to know that units of the Canadian Army are a part of the allied force engaged in the attack."[18]

King felt that his intervention, especially the call to Roosevelt, had both paved the way for his country's recognition and saved himself from embarrassment. He went so far as to write in his diary—in a tone similar to literary hyperventilation—that had the announcement not mentioned Canada, his political career would likely have been over. King also carried a grudge against the British, who he believed had tried to minimize the Canadian involvement to raise their own profile with the Americans. London had, in fact, argued for Canada's inclusion, but this was lost in a welter of miscommunication. The incident was followed by two weeks of sharp and increasingly undiplomatic exchanges between King and Churchill, both of whom were frustrated by what had occurred. King even threatened to call an election over the issue.[19] "Was it any wonder that our people . . . were antagonized at the English," sniped King in his diary, "and were beginning to be more and more friendly with the Americans?"[20]

Far more important than the squabble over messaging was the largely uncontested landing on multiple beaches in southern Sicily on July 10 that kept the Canadian casualties initially very low. That would not last for long, as the Allies fought their way across the triangular-shaped island that spanned about 280 kilometres from north to south. Garrisoned by around 270,000 Axis troops, the rugged, dusty, and mountainous battleground favoured the defence. General Montgomery would direct the ground attack,

A hot, dusty, and determined Canadian in Sicily.

and he and his superior, General Harold Alexander, were mistrustful of the combat effectiveness of the Americans. After little initial resistance, spearhead British units charged northward up the main road along the eastern side of the island to Messina to cut off any retreating Germans. Dynamic, abrasive, and impossibly self-assured, General Montgomery was ever drawn to the limelight, and, believing the Axis forces to be on the verge of collapse, he took over a key road from General George Patton's United

States Seventh Army, which seemed to condemn the US formations to a sluggish advance.[21] With the Americans sidelined, the battle-hardened British soldiers in the Eighth Army would, he believed, plunge ahead along the main highway for a rapid victory that would add new glory to the Eighth Army. The untested Canadians would be positioned in the interior and not expected to do much fighting other than to guard the British left flank.

Wary of losing Sicily, as it would give the Allies another base from which their bombers could damage German war industry and oil refineries, Hitler flooded the island with paratroopers and other elite formations. South of Catania, about halfway up the island's east coast, Montgomery swallowed a defeat when the vaunted Eighth Army was stopped by vicious fighting. The aggressive General Patton, who would emerge as the US's best fighting general, also refused to play second fiddle to Monty and went hard-charging through the western part of the island. The Americans faced lighter opposition as they went the long way around, striking fast and with intensity. In this unplanned scenario, some of the toughest combat fell to the raw 1st Canadian Division, which clawed its way up the gut of the island through the Sicilian badlands.

Fighting with the Americans on the left flank—usually Major-General Terry Allen's 1st Infantry Division, the "Big Red One"— and the British on the right, the Canadians were wedged into battle. Under command of General Guy Simonds, the Canadians pressed forward, skilfully overcoming enemy resistance. They also engaged in infiltration tactics, moving around areas of resistance and often climbing through the rough terrain in darkness to surprise the defenders. "A special characteristic of the enemy manner of fighting," noted one 15th Panzergrenadier Division's report referring to the Canadians, "is that he does not attack over open ground, but attacks through areas that provide cover while diminishing the efficacy of the tanks."[22] The Germans, positioned on ridgelines, hilltops, and higher mountains, especially at Assoro and Leonforte, were overwhelmed by the Canadians, who manoeuvred around them or drove them from their prepared defences in feats of ingenuity and bravery. As a raw, untried unit, the Canadians were better than they had any right to be, impressing the British and Americans as well as the enemy forces.

Above the scorching battlefield, RCAF fighter and bomber squadrons harassed the enemy in five weeks of ground-strafing and bombing.[23] The Germans and Italians buckled under the onslaught as they retreated to the northeast part of the island to escape to mainland Italy. Sacrificial units were left to block the Anglo-American-Canadian advance, and after almost two weeks of rapid manoeuvring, the Allies found advances tougher to achieve as the enemy fought with new desperation. The Saskatchewan Light Infantry war diary noted, "The first flush of attack is over and now the division is settling into a hard grind."[24]

After many tough battles, the last Axis defenders surrendered on August 17 and the island was secured. Fascist Italy wobbled on the verge of collapse, with the loss of Sicily rousing new opposition to Mussolini's doomed regime. In defeat, enormous stores of German and Italian equipment were captured and 176,000 enemy soldiers were killed or sent to prisoner-of-war camps. However, it was not a complete victory, and Eisenhower's failure to use naval and air power to close the 3-kilometre water route from Sicily to the Italian mainland allowed 125,000 Axis soldiers to escape.[25] Allied formations would regroup and invade the mainland in early September, having lost almost 20,000 soldiers in

Sicily, including 2,310 Canadian casualties.[26] The Americans, the British, and the Canadians had stood together in a trial by fire.

———

King's obvious desperation to have it known that the Canadians were fighting in Sicily was equal parts correct and humiliating for the junior ally. Canada was reduced to begging for scraps from the high table. The Anglo-American high command could sniff that the Dominion's insistence, verging on whining, was unbecoming in a world of war, although much of the Canadian concern was also shaped by King's exclusion from strategic discussions, which he realized was ever more problematic. That reality was further crystalized at Quebec City in mid-August 1943, when Churchill, Roosevelt, and their staffs again came together to determine Allied grand strategy at the Château Frontenac. Even though the conference was held in Canada, one of the British observers felt that King was "not so much a participant in any of the discussions as a sort of genial host, whose task . . . was similar to that of the General Manager of the Château Frontenac."[27] This was a frank but accurate assessment of how little impact the Canadian leader had at the first Quebec conference, code-named "Quadrant." Stalin did not attend, although he had clout since his Red Army had savaged the Nazis twice in 1943—at Stalingrad in January, and then, in July, in the largest tank battle in human history at Kursk. These victories came at a terrible cost in Soviet lives; they also broke the back of the German Army in the east and ensured that the Russians would survive. Stalin's absence from the conference was a reminder that he was occupied with fighting the vast bulk of the enemy land forces—some 185 divisions of 5.5 million Axis soldiers—even as his army was supported by enormous quantities of Allied war supplies and a bombing campaign that was increasingly hurting Germany.

The first of two conferences at Quebec, Quadrant was crucial in giving Churchill and Roosevelt extended face time and allowing their staffs to wrangle and manoeuvre. The once supportive Roosevelt had denied King's request for inclusion in the meeting at the historic citadel—the same fortress that had turned back an American invasion in 1775—under the pretence that if Canada attended, the other dominions, or China and Brazil, would ask to be there.[28] There was a logic to this thinking, but it stung the Canadians. King did not want to risk being rebuked for pushing back, especially with the president upping the ante by declaring that he would refuse to travel to Quebec if Canada insisted on being included. It was one of the few times that Roosevelt bullied King, although the president did not see it that way. King retreated to the position of host, and his aides were reduced to looking through the keyhole to see what was happening in the room where decisions were made. And yet there was value in hosting the British and the Americans. King understood this, and he settled for being photographed and filmed with the great warlords. Optics were still an important prize for King.

Before Quadrant, at a May conference in Washington codenamed "Trident," the Americans were finally able to nail down an agreement with the British: the invasion of Europe would commence on May 1, 1944—though this was later moved to June 6, 1944. Further talks and planning continued at Quebec. The real work was done in England, as studies were conducted there on where to land, how to deceive the enemy to buy time for an

*The Big Two and the Canadian prime minister at the August 1943
Quebec Conference. In the middle sits King, with both
Churchill and him turned towards Roosevelt.*

exposed force in enemy-held territory, how many divisions would go ashore, how to protect them with air and naval firepower, and how they would be supplied. A shortage of landing craft to carry infantry, tank, and artillery ashore was a strange and perplexing weak link in the Allied operation that would involve thousands of warships, massive bomber strikes, and hundreds of thousands of soldiers.

Three months later, at Quebec, the British convinced the Americans that a thrust upwards through the Italian mainland would continue to exert pressure on Germany, suck in Axis divisions that might be deployed to shore up the Eastern or Western Fronts, and perhaps drive Italy from the war. Additional plans

357

were developed for more intense cooperation to build an atomic bomb, contribute more to the war against Japan in the Pacific, and provide ongoing support for China and the Soviet Union. The Canadians had already been involved in supplying uranium to the American atomic program (which will be covered later in the book), and this was another area in which the Dominion's minerals and raw resources fed into the multi-pronged victory campaign. But it did not buy them a voice at Quebec. As for King, he remained a friend to the president, facilitating his honorary doctorate from McGill University, while going out of his way to talk with Churchill to ease some of the jagged unhappiness over the Sicily announcement and its many miscommunications. The Western democracies continued to find ways to make their alliance work.

———

As host of the Quebec conference, King has always been viewed as master of ceremonies rather than a junior war leader. That he was playing the role of genial host likely did not register with many Canadians, who saw their prime minister hobnobbing with Churchill and Roosevelt and assumed he was an influential voice in grand strategy. He was not. Despite some personal triumphs for King, especially the deals he secured with the US on defence and industry, even his supporters lamented that he lacked the ability to motivate Canadians to great heights or deep sacrifice. That had to be left to others. King was not oblivious to his failings as an inspirational figure, but he was often cut to the quick by many Canadians' tendency to call Churchill and Roosevelt "our leaders."[29] He nonetheless continued to find ways to position Canada as a good ally, with the country's ground forces striving in battle, its bombers smashing the Axis powers' home fronts, and the navy keeping the essential sea lanes open to prepare for the liberation of Western Europe. But before that fraught invasion was launched, the Canadians would fight with their Anglo-American allies in Italy.

One of Canada's killed, Private Steve Slavik, a thirty-year-old of Czech origin who arrived in Canada in 1930. His headstone is engraved with these words, translated from his native tongue: "Born in a foreign land, in a foreign land he lay down his young life for democracy."

CHAPTER 18

FIGHTING TOGETHER IN ITALY

"The world has certainly been informed enough of the unguarded frontier, the long peace between our two nations. This is another step from the static to the active; from 'We will not interfere with each other' to 'We will do big things together.' The Force is an intensely dramatic embodiment of our common effort in a cause that commands the faith of all of us."[1] With these inspiring words, *Montreal Star* war correspondent Sholto Watt extolled the image of Canada and the United States striding forward together in the First Special Service Force, a unique joint American–Canadian unit. The Force, as it came to be known, was one of the "big things" that the two countries were doing in the war against the Nazis. In the summer of 1942, around 725 Canadian soldiers were sent to Fort William Henry Harrison outside of Helena, Montana, as part of an experiment. The Canucks joined American counterparts to train at the fort named for the US general who had fought against British North America in the War of 1812, an irony that was probably lost on most of the soldiers. The Canadians would serve alongside their new comrades in the Force, which was conceived as a specialist alpine unit that would raid in winter conditions. The size of a small brigade, this formation of three battalions of about 600 soldiers each had Canadians and Americans blended together.[2] The unit, which had almost been named the North American Force, became a symbol of the interconnected North American war effort.

———

Without knowing much about this new force or its deployment, other than that Lord Mountbatten—chief of Combined Operations and architect of the Dieppe raid—had orchestrated it to fight in special winter operations, the Canadian military and cabinet agreed to the proposal for a joint North American unit in June 1942.[3] At the foot of the Sawtooth Range of the Rocky Mountains, focused training and parachute jumps led to broken ankles and sprained backs, along with growing confidence and all-around hardening. When the snows fell, the soldiers were sent into the mountains to train for winter warfare, using skis to move rapidly, wearing camouflaged uniforms, and sniping targets. The Canadians and Americans came to know and respect one another too. Sergeant Bill Story recounted that the English language bound the men together, but "because the US presence is so pervasive in Canada with movies, radio, and so on, we knew more about the US than the Americans knew about us."[4] Friendships were soon made and a common understanding forged. The Americans learned that they should not joke about the royal family; the Canadians realized that their comrades from the South were riled by the catch-all term "Yanks." All the while, the American commander, Colonel Robert T. Frederick, worked the men relentlessly, aware that the Canadians came with distinct tactics, doctrine, and experience in weapon systems. While there were differences to overcome, Frederick, an inspiring and fearless leader who was wounded nine times in combat, told the Canadians and Americans who wore the Force's iconic unit patch—a deep red Indigenous spearhead that bore the words "USA" and "Canada" forming a white "T"—"We speak the same language, think much the same, have many similar customs, and are probably closer than the people of any other two nations."[5]

The Force was a unit in search of a role. Lord Mountbatten had conceived of it to fight in German-occupied Norway, where it was to destroy hydro-electric facilities. But the British scrubbed that operation in September 1942 when the Norwegian government-in-exile objected to it, fearful of the vengeance the Nazis would wreak on their people. This was also in the aftermath of the debacle at Dieppe, which had revealed that foolish planning based on unrealistic objectives and wishful thinking led only to humiliation and slaughter. King and his ministers were worried about the Canadians in the Force being lost in another fiasco, but Major-General Maurice Pope, from his position in Washington, offered sensible words of caution, advising that the US would not throw away the unit in a forlorn action. The cabinet agreed to let the Americans train and deploy the unit, describing the arrangement as a "token of intimate cooperation between the two countries."[6]

Lord Mountbatten was increasingly desperate to deploy his elite force, even suggesting that the winter warfare unit could be dropped into Russia to fight. How this would work—from ensuring supply and reinforcements to securing command and control within the Soviet army—had not been worked out, which was another sign of Mountbatten's fanciful approach to warfare. However, this operation would have been less traumatic to the unit than his other bizarre suggestion: that the Force float around the ocean in a hollowed-out glacier from which it would "emerge

A member of the First Special Service Force in winter warfare kit.

periodically and attack selected objectives."[7] No wonder the other chiefs of staff believed that Mountbatten was at times little more than a royal simpleton allowed at the big table because of his blue blood and fulsome friendship with Churchill.

Overtrained and bored, the Forcemen were ready for battle. The Canadian battalion had learned to use American weapons, such as the M-1 rifle and Thompson sub-machine gun, and all were anxiously awaiting the test of combat when the Force was finally ordered to take part in the Kiska landings in mid-August 1943. When the unit was deployed as a spearhead amphibious landing force—a far cry from the mountain warfare for which it had been trained—the Forcemen suffered no casualties, as the Japanese defenders fled the barren island. Journalists would have ached to tell the story as an emblem of Canadian–American military collaboration, but the unit was considered top secret, and no information slipped through the censors. That would change when the Force was soon hurled into battle in Italy.

———

Fresh from their victory in Sicily in August 1943, the Allies landed on the Italian mainland in early September. Montgomery's Eighth Army came ashore at Calabria on September 3 and faced little opposition. More fiercely contested was Lieutenant-General Mark Clark's invasion at Salerno, along the west coast near Naples, where the Germans stood firm along the high ground boxing in the shallow beachhead. From the heights, they poured devastating fire into the trapped American GIs and British infantrymen. Revealing the tenacious mindset of the defenders, one paratrooper wrote, "The Tommies will have to chew their way through us," a ferocious sentiment that was found in his diary after he was killed in battle.[8] Only the support of the navy's warships firing their crushing bombardments kept the Germans at bay, and the shelling eventually forced the enemy to retreat out of range. Redirected bombers also plastered the German entrenchments, with three RCAF squadrons assisting the hard-pressed Allied forces trapped in the beachhead.[9] Clark's Anglo-American divisions survived and commenced their slow advance northward along multiple routes, being harassed much of the way. The Germans fought on the best ground, laying ambushes and setting explosives to kill and maim. It was slow and painful fighting, but the Germans did it without their ally: Italy had waved the white flag in the face of the invasion and Mussolini was imprisoned. Though the Italians bungled the surrender and Il Duce was rescued by German special units, Hitler nonetheless lost access to hundreds of thousands of Italian soldiers who could have fought at his side or garrisoned the vast Mediterranean. His forces took control of much of the country and subjected its people to the brutal whip hand of the occupier.

Far from the fighting, the American senior commanders, especially General Marshall, remained angry with the British for pushing the Italian campaign further when they should have been assembling the enormous resources required for the invasion of Northwest Europe. It would, however, have been almost inconceivable for the Allies to hold back after their successful invasion of Sicily, peering into the Italian mainland as the Germans fortified it and somehow moving even part of the massive army back to England without losing ships to U-boat attacks. The advance up the Italian boot went ahead, although Marshall curtailed supplies to that theatre of war so that the build-up for operation Overlord—the invasion of Western Europe—could begin in earnest. None of that was known to the Allied soldiers as they struggled through the mountainous Italian terrain, fighting tooth and nail for survival, with the Americans driving up the west coast and the Anglo-Canadian forces up the east coast. Canada would eventually send a corps to Italy, consisting of two divisions and an armoured brigade, and it would bash its way forward by securing costly victories at Ortona in December 1943, breaking the Hitler Line in May 1944, and piercing the Gothic Line in August 1944.[10]

Although the North Americans rarely fought together in Italy, they began to do so when the Force arrived in Italy on November 17, 1943, to a congealing battle front. Ridges, rivers, and fortified passes lent themselves to ambushes and resulted in a nightmare struggle. The soft underbelly of Europe it was not, even though Churchill had famously characterized it as such to convince his American detractors of the value in striking at Hitler's crumbling empire in Italy. Having slowly retreated before the Allies, in late 1943 the Germans made their stand on the Winter Line, a series of concrete bunkers and field fortifications that used the high terrain to rain down deadly fire. Several mountains acted as anchors, with entrenched defenders on the peaks that provided the advantage of height and sight to make the invaders pay. One such position was Monte la Difensa, which British and American soldiers had tried to wrestle free from the Germans. Failing to take it, they were driven back with heavy losses. The unburied dead lay all along the rocky advance to the top.

The Force was ordered to assault this 960-metre mountain-top position in the last week of November, amid a steady deluge of cold rain. German snipers and machine-gunners watched all routes to the summit. Mines further blocked already inaccessible narrow gorges, and the Forcemen hunted for another route. The north face of the ancient volcano consisted of near-vertical cliffs and was largely unguarded since, with 70-degree inclines, it seemed an impossible route to the top. But that was where the Force would climb to attack the unprepared defenders.

Reconnaissance patrols scouted possible routes up the rock face to determine secure locations for ropes. Only small arms and ammunition could be carried. The goal was a rapid victory because the North Americans would be nearly helpless if caught in the open. On December 1, the British 46th and 56th Divisions launched their own assaults against surrounding positions, which drew attention away from the Forcemen's climb through and up the back door. As part of a multi-pronged distraction, a massive artillery bombardment from 925 guns pounded the enemy positions at Difensa and at Camino, a supporting strongpoint that had to fall to give the attackers any chance of holding the mountain.

An initial spearhead of 281 Forcemen began the extreme climb under cover of darkness in the late hours of December 1 and into the early hours of the 2nd. The slippery rocks were treacherous, although the sounds of grunting men exerting themselves were drowned out by the barrage. Muscles screamed as the soldiers pulled themselves up, climbing freehand while searching for crevices in the volcanic rock that was vibrating from the monstrous shellfire. The occasional goat path took some of the agony off bleeding fingertips; other spots required hand-over-hand climbing using ropes. Reinforcements were to follow. All lived in fear throughout the ascent that even a single alert sentry might catch the Force at its most exposed.

Having rested during daylight hours, the Canadians and Americans were in place before dawn on the 3rd. When the artillery bombardment finally moved off of the enemy positions, the first of the 400 German defenders from the 3rd Battalion of the 104th Panzergrenadier Regiment emerged from their protective dugouts. As the North Americans prepared to strike, the rustle of hundreds of men was heard by sentries and a challenge called out. It was met by small-arms fire. Shocked Germans scrambled to their defences and a fierce battle raged. As daylight broke, a heavy fog continued to obscure the rocky terrain that was pitted with countless crevices, slit trenches, and boulders where soldiers took cover.

Muzzle flashes were a deadly twinkling in the fog. Snipers, rifle-men, and machine-gunners fired wildly, while others threw grenades at anything that moved. Shells and mortar bombs landed amid the rocks, shattering them and sending splinters into the air as secondary weapons. Canadian Jack Callowhill, who had enlisted at age nineteen, was in the thick of combat before being knocked out by a bomb fragment. As he later recounted, you tried to survive in "your own little corner. You didn't know what the heck was going on."[11]

The fighting carried on throughout the cold morning on the 3rd, as the Forcemen slowly cleared enemy positions with bullet, bomb, and even bayonet. The panzergrenadiers were over-whelmed. Pockets of resistance were snuffed out and increasingly weary Germans gestured with white shirts to show their intention of laying down arms. But other defenders fought onward, and the Special Service Force reinforcements, carrying ammunition and medical supplies, were required to climb up through a shower of mortar bombs that were fired to interdict the route. The lieutenant-colonel of 1st Battalion, Thomas MacWilliam of Moncton, New Brunswick, led from the front, encouraging his men to drive the enemy back. He was killed on the 3rd when a shell detonated near his position. His wife had written to him that he was to be a proud father, news that he never received.

At one point, a small group of Germans tried to surrender with a white flag amid the cordite clouds and gut-punch blows of shells detonating on the volcanic rock. Captain William T. Rothlin, a twenty-five-year-old American graduate of the University of California, advanced to take the surrender and was shot dead. It was unclear if it was a trap or if other Germans simply saw an offi-cer in the open. Whatever the case, the Canadians and Americans slaughtered the vulnerable soldiers attempting to give up. Such was the savagery that emerged from the confusion of combat. John Dawson of 2nd Battalion remembered, "They were shooting at us and we were shooting at them." As enemy snipers picked off his comrades with head shots, he saw one close comrade take a bullet right through the helmet. "It was a hell of a thing to look at," wrote Dawson, ". . . his brains were running out, inside his helmet, and onto his face. That, to me, was la Difensa."[12]

The struggle continued as the Canadians and Americans methodically cleared the summit. Throughout the battle they suffered under enemy fire from positions on nearby hilltops, especially one on Monte La Remetanea. Howling wind and freezing rain added to the misery. Numb from the cold and the sensory assault, Forcemen held on during the gruelling day as the burst of adrenaline dissipated to bring hunger and enervation. But the battle was not over, and patrols and raiders continued to be sent against the Germans on Remetanea, resulting in intense struggles and the snatching of prisoners.

On the 5th, as the soldiers were at the breaking point after having captured the summit of Difensa in nasty fighting, the Force attacked Remetanea again in strength, with two of its three battalions. The grim clash of arms lasted into the 6th, and finally the Germans were on the verge of total defeat. On the 7th and 8th, the worn-down members of the Force surged forward in a final series of skirmishes and small-scale engagements to wipe out the remaining nests of resistance. The North Americans were finally relieved on the 9th, their battle won.

Lieutenant-General Mark Clark, commander of the Fifth Army, congratulated the unit for its spirited and dogged attack, observing that the success was a "tribute to fine leadership and a splendid reward for time spent in arduous training."[13] But the cost was high. The Force suffered 511 casualties, including 73 dead, 9 missing, 313 wounded, and 116 hospitalized for exhaustion (a condition that included battle stress and hypothermia).[14] About a quarter of the combat strength had been attrited, and no reinforcements were readily available. Both Canadian and American commanders in Italy were unwilling to send precious soldiers to the Force, which belonged to neither of them, but some reinforcements were finally found in training depots. Peter Cottingham, a Forceman from Manitoba, wrote of the battle, "The miracle was that any of us survived to tell about it."[15]

After months of warfare that favoured the defenders, the Americans launched a daring amphibious landing at Anzio, a seaside town on the west coast of Italy, some 60 kilometres south of Rome. Behind a devastating naval bombardment, British and American divisions came ashore on January 22, 1944. The Germans retreated in the face of the surprise assault, but the lead Allied formations moved too slowly off the beach, wasting time and allowing the enemy to recover. In the face of this criminally cautious advance, the Nazis hurled shells and strike forces against the beachhead, digging into the high ground around Anzio. The attackers' brilliant strategic manoeuvre was stymied by lifeless operational drive, and the American commanders on the ground seemed intent on snatching defeat from the jaws of victory.

The First Special Service Force was thrown into the maelstrom on February 1, facing trench warfare and curtains of shellfire. Opposite the Force were elements from the Hermann Göring

Panzer Division, a powerful armoured formation. The two sides traded blows in a series of raids. The Forcemen, faces blackened and weapons drawn, slunk out into the No Man's Land under the cover of darkness. Stealth was important, as was the use of other senses in the gloom. Experienced raiders were guided by the smell of enemy tobacco and body odour. When the Germans were found, raw aggression was unleashed in kill-or-be-killed brawls. "These night raids," recalled Sergeant John Dawson, were "very violent."[16] Grenades were thrown in close-quarters combat, and some stealth raiders used their knives to slit the throats of unsuspecting sentries. The Force was exerting its will on the Germans. Success came at a price, though, with one officer remarking, "We lost people every night during these raids."[17]

On February 8, 1944, Ojibway infantryman Tommy Prince, a skilled tracker and superb sniper, volunteered to lay a communication line forward to an abandoned farmhouse some 200 metres from a German position, where he would establish an observation post. For three days, he lurked in the dangerous forward zone, reporting back on enemy movement. When the wire was cut by a shell, Prince donned a peasant's cloak and wandered about, pretending to be a farmer. When he found the break, he fixed the line. Through his brave action, Allied artillery fire was directed onto the enemy positions to cause much destruction. He was awarded the Military Medal, and the citation read, in part, "Sergeant Prince's courage and utter disregard for personal safety were an inspiration to his fellows and a marked credit to his unit."[18] He was discharged in June 1945, having also been awarded the American Silver Star for a daring patrol he carried out against an enemy position. Prince was among the 4,300 Indigenous men and women who served Canada during the war. An unknown number of other

Indigenous men soldiered in the American forces, particularly those from bands or tribes that straddled the Canada–US border.

Continuing to fight on and off for two weeks, the Force defended on February 16 against a battalion-level German assault supported by tanks. The enemy was repelled in a fierce clash. During this period, the Canadian and American unit adopted the moniker of the "Devil's Brigade" for its uncompromising raiding against the enemy. One American journalist added to the mythology by writing that the "hard-striking spearhead of specialists . . . terrorized the Germans for 99 nights of blackfaced raiding."[19] It was even said, and certainly the Forcemen believed, that one captured soldier's diary recounted, "The black devils are all around us every time we come into the line and we never hear them come."[20] To stoke the fear, the North Americans had their arrowhead shoulder flashes imprinted on paper cards, which they would lay on the killed Germans or destroyed positions. The cards bore a cryptic message that read: "*Das dicke Ende Kommt noch!*" ("The worst is yet to come!")

Though the Force acquired a reputation for calculated mayhem, it was pulled from the line in late February, much reduced in strength. The unit was almost disbanded, being saved only after a lengthy scramble that led to the injection of new Canadian reinforcements and Americans from the US 4th Ranger Battalion, with the Canadians continuing to form about a third of the unit. *Montreal Star* journalist Sholto Watt, who travelled with the Force for some time, depicted it as an elite formation: "No parallel can be found for the U.S.-Canadian mixed force which has opened its fighting career in Italy with a series of brilliant victories."[21]

The long-awaited breakout from Anzio began at 6:30 a.m. on May 23, just as the Canadian Corps further to the east was

An April 1944 patrol party of the FSSF being briefed before slipping into No Man's Land to harass the enemy.

crashing through the heavily fortified Hitler Line. Fighting as an infantry regiment, the Force engaged in combined-arms combat with tank support. After an initial thrust broke through the Germans, supporting Sherman tanks came under heavy anti-tank fire, brewing up in flames as their fuel tanks exploded. Dark oily smoke infused with the gagging smell of charred flesh assaulted the senses. Over the course of a punishing day, it was attack and counterattack, with the German forces surging forward and the Allies pushing back. Five Tiger tanks, the largest and most frightening types of enemy armour, crashed into the position. "It was a terrible thing to be mixed up in," wrote one of the Forcemen. "It is hard to describe fully, the sights and sounds and the naked terror of such a battle."[22] Grinding warfare continued over the next week as the Americans slowly made gains in the advance on Rome. The first Allied soldiers to cross into the Eternal City at 4 p.m. on June 4 were members of the Force, a vanguard that was harassed by enemy mortar bombs and bullets. Even as the last of the Germans were pulling out in a fighting retreat, the Devil's Brigade was greeted by cheering Italians who thanked their liberators.

After the capture of Rome, fighting continued up the spine of Italy, even as the armies there were relegated further to a backwater theatre after the invasion of Northwest Europe. Historians have come to understand that these Allied forces were playing a crucial role in holding the enemy fast. Hitler kept an enormous garrison of fifty-five divisions in Italy and the surrounding area that could have been used to shore up other fronts. In April 1945, the Germans, 599,514 strong, faced 616,642 Allied soldiers in the Fifth and Eighth Armies, along with an additional million or so men and women in the long logistical tail that wound hundreds of kilometres south through Italy and into North Africa.[23] However, the Allies could better afford to keep their soldiers in southern Europe, for even a small number of these German defenders would have significantly stiffened resistance against the Red Army in the east and the Allied invasion in the west.[24] By the time victory finally came in Italy in May 1945, the Fifth Army had suffered 188,746 casualties while the Eighth Army had lost another 123,254, for a total of 312,000. The German losses were even higher at 434,646.[25] The Canadian Corps would continue to fight in Italy until early 1945, when it was removed to rejoin First Canadian Army in the final battles of Western Europe. Of the 92,757 Canadians who served in Italy, 5,399 were killed, 19,486 were wounded, and 1,004 were taken prisoner. Neither the Soviets nor the United States ever viewed the Italian theatre as a second front that could siphon off German strength—but they should have. By fixing the Germans here and forcing them to fight, the Anglo-American-Canadian armies weakened the Nazis' ability to hold the Eastern and Western Fronts in Northwest Europe.

——

The First Special Service Force had left Italy before the final victory, having been cut up and left badly in need of reinforcements. It got them—mostly Americans—and the Force landed in Southern France as part of an invasion in mid-August 1944. Additional battles were fought, but the unit was disbanded on December 5, 1944, near the village of Villeneuve-Loubet. The remaining Canadians were honoured with a parade by their American comrades and the unit passed into lore. "Out of the original 700 Canadians," remembered Staff Sergeant Thomas O'Brien, "there weren't very many of us left."[26] Though the Force never fulfilled its initially conceived commando role and the unit was eventually worn down in combat, the North Americans within it had symbolized the unity of the two countries and put into practice the hard business of fighting together against a common foe. "The international character of the Force has placed it in the position of representing the extent to which the United States and Canada cooperated in an undertaking," wrote Robert T. Frederick, who had commanded the unit and gone on to lead a division. "It is an exceptional example of complete integration of personnel of two armies into a single unit."[27]

CHAPTER 19

THE ALLIED AIR WAR

Oh! I have slipped the surly bonds of earth
And danced the skies on laughter-silvered wings;
Sunward I've climbed, and joined the tumbling mirth
Of sun-split clouds—and done a hundred things
You have not dreamed of—wheeled and soared and swung
High in the sunlit silence. Hov'ring there,
I've chased the shouting wind along, and flung
My eager craft through footless halls of air . . .

The Great War was fought by a generation that often expressed itself in song and poetry. The Second World War had its songs too, and sometimes the same ones that the soldiers' fathers and uncles had sung in the trenches, though war poetry was less common. And yet many men and women still put pen to paper to make meaning of their experience in uniform. One of the most famous English-language poems of the war came from a member of the Royal Canadian Air Force (RCAF), the American pilot John Gillespie Magee Jr. The gifted eighteen-year-old had turned down a scholarship to Yale University, choosing instead to enlist in Canada in October 1940. Magee, who wrote the verse above, completed his flight training as part of the British Commonwealth

Air Training Plan (BCATP), eventually serving overseas with No. 412 Squadron, RCAF. Flying the Mk Vb Spitfire from October 1941, he spent a year training and passing through instructional schools, and ultimately forayed into enemy territory on patrols. In November, an offensive operation over Western Europe saw Magee and three other RCAF Spitfire pilots tangle with the enemy. The Luftwaffe savaged the RCAF fighters, with three of the four aircraft shot down. The lone survivor was Magee.[1] His short active service ended soon after this on December 11, 1941, when he died in a mid-air collision over England. Flight Officer Magee was one of thousands of Americans who enlisted in the RCAF while the US was neutral, trained in the BCATP, and then served overseas in Canadian bomber and fighter squadrons.

Magee became the best known of the Americans to serve in the RCAF because of his sonnet "High Flight," which he penned a few months before his death. In addition to the sweeping words above, he finished the poem with:

> Up, up the long, delirious, burning blue
> I've topped the wind-swept heights with easy grace
> Where never lark, or even eagle flew—
> And, while with silent lifting mind I've trod
> The high untrespassed sanctity of space,
> Put out my hand and touched the face of God.

The sonnet was included in an exhibition of poems at the Library of Congress in February 1942, called "Faith and Freedom," and was republished in other anthologies. It likely reached more Americans as part of the Hollywood Victory Caravan, a celebrity tour that showcased Cary Grant, Bob Hope, and Laurel and

Hardy, and which included actress Merle Oberon reciting "High Flight."[2] The poem, which captures the exhilaration of flying—with machines breaking the bonds of gravity, soaring and slipping through the clouds, and chasing the enemy in the "burning blue"—remains popular with aviators and astronauts. The air war, "high in the sunlit silence," was both a wondrous area and a place of death. From the "untrespassed sanctity of space," the British Commonwealth and American airmen also took the hard way of war to those on the ground, both military and civilian.

———

In the early part of the war, Canada, with its puny prewar air force, had agreed to host the BCATP, a task that steadily expanded to an enormous undertaking that would involve the building of hundreds of bases, schools, airfields, and over 5,500 buildings to house trainees.[3] Tens of thousands of new airmen were attested into the RCAF and sent across the country, where they passed through a series of schools to learn their specialized trade. Though most were Canadian, the enlistees also included volunteers from other Commonwealth nations, airmen from conquered Western Europe, and Americans. The purchase or manufacture of several thousand training planes was a major industrial feat and a necessary investment in the training plan. All action was hurried along by desperation and an urgent concern that without a sufficient number of airmen the war might be lost. In late 1939, Prime Minister King had addressed the nation in a radio broadcast on the CBC, telling Canadians that hosting the BCATP would be a mission of "great magnitude" that would establish "Canada as one of the greatest air training centres of the world."[4]

Almost all flyers ached to become fighter pilots to emulate the heroes of the last war. The standards were high, however, and most of the hopefuls flowed into Bomber Command as gunners, navigators, and wireless operators. As the primary striking arm of the Allies, Bomber Command gathered in intensity from 1940 to 1943 as tens of thousands of airmen flew the increasingly sophisticated bombers, which grew from two-engine machines to four-engine behemoths capable of carrying several tons of high explosives and incendiaries. The army attacked around the periphery and the navy kept Britain in the war, but it was only the bombers that hurt the German people who supported the Nazi regime and the industry that supplied its armies.

Throughout the second half of 1940, classes of graduates emerged from the BCATP, although most were channelled back into the emerging schools to be instructors as the training program expanded across the country.[5] Another source of airmen were the young Americans seeking to serve in the air force or to work as trainers. They had been crossing the border since almost the start of the war, and those with aerial experience were snapped up to share their flying knowledge, although most sought to fly overseas in the war against the Nazis.

The RCAF was cautious about violating the American position of neutrality, even though the force was desperate for airmen. There could be no recruiting on US soil, and those Americans who crossed voluntarily into Canada to enlist had to be handled judiciously. Prime Minister King ordered that the armed forces "would have to be particularly scrupulous and careful about persons coming from the United States for purposes of serving in the present war."[6] However, as in other areas of collaboration between Canada and the US, this dilemma was often solved with

*A cartoon showing aircraft from the BCATP's hornet's
nest emerging to attack a retreating Adolf Hitler.*

a wink and a nod, and by many Americans fudging their country
of birth. The RCAF had higher standards than the army, usually
demanding high school education, and, like the navy, it had systemic barriers for racialized men, with Black, Asian, and Indigenous people almost always turned away.[7] Few Americans seem

to have been denied service, but of those accepted, not many were African American.

Within the North American brotherhood of flyers, tomfoolery and verbal jousting were the order of the day. Many of the American cadets proudly wore a badge emblazoned with "U.S.A." and the American eagle below their RCAF insignia. Canadian airman John Grimshaw, who enlisted at age eighteen, recounted the Canucks' friendly banter with their American friends and how "we Canadians delighted in calling [the eagle] an albatross."[8] Teasing aside, Douglas Harvey, a decorated Canadian pilot in the RCAF, observed that "thousands of American kids had come north to Canada to get their Wings in the RCAF. They added a new dimension to the force, their lifestyles a refreshing change from the more stolid Canadian approach."[9]

As a hero ace of the last war, Air Marshal Billy Bishop had returned to uniform in 1936, and in January 1940 he became director of recruiting. Bishop had many friends in the British, Canadian, and American aviation industry. The air marshal turned to a fellow flyer, New Yorker Clayton Knight, who had served with No. 206 Squadron, Royal Air Force over the Western Front, even though he always wore a distinctive American uniform. Sympathetic to the Allied cause, Knight drew upon his connections within the US flying community. So did Homer Smith, another Canadian Great War pilot and millionaire who was made an RCAF wing commander to assist in clandestine recruitment. Knight and Smith were a two-man show—known as the Clayton Knight Committee. Flying across the US, they spent lavishly and rounded up volunteers for the RCAF. The wealthy pilots projected the lavish life of the fighter pilot as they established a headquarters at the Waldorf Astoria Hotel in New York City, where they wined and dined potential recruits, and even provided loans for them to travel north.[10] In Canada, the RCAF senior brass was thrilled with the committee's success in enticing experienced aviators and strong recruits to cross the border, but they continually worried about being wrapped on the knuckles by Washington or, worse, formally censured. The US State Department, however, made little fuss over the committee's work, only communicating to their Canadian counterparts that American citizens should not be asked to swear allegiance to the King of Britain, Canada, and the Commonwealth. Furthermore, one Canadian diplomat was told on the sly that he might advise the committee to "get rid" of "incriminating correspondence in case their files were investigated by the FBI."[11] Aware of American sensibilities, King's cabinet passed an order in council stating that foreign nationals enlisting in the armed forces need not swear an oath, which likely suited the 300 American pilots who had enlisted by late November 1940.[12]

Knight and Smith launched new recruiting drives throughout 1941, though the entry of the US into the war in December soon ended their role. By January 30, 1942, there were 8,864 American nationals in the RCAF, although most of them enlisted by crossing the border on their own instead of being enticed into it at the Waldorf Astoria. Through the Clayton Knight Committee and other lesser known organizations, over 2,600 American volunteers—including 763 pilots—enlisted in the RCAF.[13]

The flow of airmen for the Canadian air force all but ended after the entry of the US into the war, and the North Americans worked together to allow Americans to return to their national fighting forces.[14] With the goal of making a smooth transition, one Department of National Defence headquarters order noted

"I'll be with you, boys"

Fly and Fight with the R·C·A·F

"Fly and Fight with the RCAF," says this poster as an airman looks to the skies. Several thousand of these airmen were American.

that "no delay will take place at the time of handing over American citizens."[15] A special train was commissioned that contained senior US and Canadian officers who travelled to some of the bases and schools to speak to American airmen about their options. The North Americans on the rail-line developed such close relationships that Brigadier Guy Henry of the US Army spoke of them "spreading friendship, good will, and mutual understanding throughout the entire breadth of Canada."[16] With the US offering higher pay, many airmen took the opportunity to return to their country's units, but, somewhat surprisingly, some 5,067 Americans remained in the RCAF, and at least 704 were killed in training accidents or combat.[17] Because of the bonds of camaraderie—forged by serving together in a tight-knit bomber—most US airmen who had trained in the BCATP continued to fly in their mixed-nationality crews as part of the RCAF. In the aftermath of Pearl Harbor, one Winnipeg paper interviewed Donald Gibbons, an American cadet in the BCATP who hailed from McDonald, Kansas, asking him if he would return to the US. "I think I'll stay," he responded, ". . . it's the same fight after all and we're in it together. Canada and the United States."[18]

———

It took time for the waves of North American airmen to cross the Atlantic, a period during which the Royal Air Force bombers struggled to find their purpose in the war effort. And yet the bombers were the only means by which to take the war to German-occupied Europe, with the goal of shattering production through widespread devastation. Despite predictions before the war that the bombers would always break through aerial defences to destroy cities and civilian morale, this was not the case. Two-engine machines like the Whitley or Manchester were not up to the task, as the ungainly aircraft, flying without any fighter support, were fodder for agile German fighters. Bomber crews nonetheless flew day and night as long as they could, braving wickedly cold temperatures and

THE ALLIED AIR WAR

mechanical failures, while always flying through the grinder of enemy defences that included, as the war progressed, high-powered searchlights and thousands of anti-aircraft guns. Confronted with nearly suicidal loss rates, the RAF pulled most of its bombers from their daylight death runs and assigned them to nighttime flying in May 1940. The death rate of crews dropped, but there were not enough aircraft and they did not carry sufficiently heavy bomb loads of high explosives to wreck cities. Just as the British people had revealed that they could withstand the Luftwaffe's punishment during the Blitz, German citizens showed the same resiliency. But the whirlwind of punishment would only grow.

The first RCAF bombers stood up in June 1941, with No. 405 Squadron flying twin-engine Wellingtons out of Driffield in Yorkshire. Other squadrons followed. The crews were rarely all-Canadian, with British, American, and other Commonwealth flyers joining together to become an isolated group of six or seven men that relied on one another to see it through. By the summer of 1941, RAF high command was forced to the difficult conclusion that the bombers would need significant tactical and technological improvements to deliver victory. Aerial photographs taken by the aircraft revealed surprising inaccuracy of aim. Faced with blackened cities, as well as wind, rain, and cloud cover, bombers not only missed the targeted factories or trainyards but often missed entire cities.[19] Slow improvements were made, and a crucial step forward was the introduction of larger bombers that could carry heavier payloads of explosives. In early 1942, the four-engine Handley Page Halifax and the Avro Lancaster became the workhorses of Bomber Command: robust in their ability to fly further into Germany and drop several tons of bombs, they could also absorb crippling damage and still get the crews home.

Air Marshal Sir Arthur Harris took the helm of Bomber Command in February 1942, during the depths of the Battle of the Atlantic, the defeats in North Africa, and the attritional, slow-moving battles in the Pacific. The career airman brought a new vitality to the strategic campaign. Unwaveringly confident in the power of the bombers to bring Germany to its knees, he was ably supported by his superior, Chief of the Air Staff Sir Charles Portal. "We have got to kill a lot of Boche before we win this war," said Harris, giving voice to what others—including his military and political superiors—had already worked towards.[20] The military objective was also fired by a desire for revenge on the part of the British people, who had seen 43,000 of their fellow civilians killed during the Blitz—with 20,000 more to follow in the coming years. Harris directed his airmen to smash German cities, disrupt the economy, kill those on the ground, and wear down the morale of survivors. Countless RAF reports reflected the reality that tactically striking tank or ball-bearing factories was nearly impossible given the war's limited technology, so Harris and others came to believe that carpet-bombing was the only way to hurt Hitler's war machine.

Even as the rising tide of the bomber war took the fight to enemy cities, German war production rose. It seemed a paradox, but in the face of an ongoing assault, Albert Speer, the German minister of wartime production, found ways to economize, modernize, and revolutionize production. Decentralizing industry by relocating it outside of cities saved many factories, with slave labourers from occupied territories assisting in the arduous work as hell rained down from above. As efficiencies were found, German war industry almost tripled from 1942 to 1944, before flatlining and then dropping off a cliff in the last year of the war due to the sustained

Allied bomber assault.[21] How much more the Führer's factories would have produced without the bombers obliterating and disrupting their operations is beyond calculation, although production was noticeably hurt by late 1943 as the aerial armadas struck repeatedly, causing shortages in steel, oil, coal, and other raw minerals. Furthermore, with tens of thousands and then hundreds of thousands of Germans killed or maimed, houses reduced to rubble, and food and medicine supplies disrupted, civilian morale was savaged as despair spread through the land.

Nazi propaganda urged the German people to fight onward, but pulling back resources from the fighting front was necessary to protect the cities. This had long been Stalin's aim in demanding a second front, and although he rarely acknowledged the value of the bombers, they forced the Germans to dilute their effective fighters and ground-based artillery in the east, especially the feared 88mm flak gun, which was also the German army's most effective anti-tank artillery gun. By war's end the numbers were staggering: to guard the cities, more than 900,000 German soldiers manned over 22,000 light and medium anti-aircraft guns, as well as 11,000 heavy 88mm guns.[22] To compare, the Nazis had only 12,000 anti-aircraft guns in all other theatres of war, from Italy to the Balkans, and from the Western Front to the Eastern Front.[23]

The aerial assaults came at a cost, which was borne most heavily by the aircrews who, night after night, in the parlance of the flyers, "got the chop" or went for a "burton."[24] Some of the gunners on the "kites" fought off the enemy fighters and periodically shot them down. Usually, the Messerschmitt Me 109s or Focke-Wulf Fw 190s were too fast for the Allied gunners as they raked an aircraft in fly-by shootings or lurked beneath the bombers before opening fire. The best course of action was evasion. Bruce Betcher,

A battered Hitler cowering in fear under Allied bombers.

an American from Minnesota, enlisted in the RCAF and flew as a pilot with several squadrons overseas. In late 1944, when he was on a bombing run over Berlin, a Junkers 88 night fighter emerged out of the gloom about 100 metres to the rear and off the starboard of his plane. Flight Lieutenant Betcher considered ordering his rear gunner to shoot at the Junkers, since it had not yet spotted their bomber, but he held his breath and stayed silent, and they escaped detection by drifting into the darkness. When questioned later by an intelligence officer at the base as to why he did not give the order, he replied, "Have you ever heard of the sheep chasing the wolves?"[25] The intelligence officer let the matter drop, and Betcher made it home with a Distinguished Flying Cross.

———

The RAF and RCAF were joined by the US Eighth Army Air Force (at the time known as VIII Bomber Command) in July 1942, when American crews first piloted six RAF Boston bombers. More intense missions began the next month, with B-17E Flying Fortresses battering marshalling yards in France. Seeking to bomb during the day in the name of greater accuracy, the Mighty Eighth learned the hard way, just as the RAF had, as its aircrews suffered heavy casualties. The B-17 Flying Fortress was a sturdy machine that bristled with heavy-calibre machine guns that were thought to be enough to defend against the enemy fighters. They could not. The Luftwaffe tore them apart with cannon fire, especially after they learned of the Fortress's weakness to head-on attacks. Even with these losses, the Americans would not be pushed off their plan for daytime bombing, which they believed was more accurate than the blind bashing approach of British and Canadian squadrons engaged in nighttime saturations. Again, they were wrong. Studies revealed that the American bombers, in their attempts to take out factories or buildings in precision strikes, were accurate only 2.2 percent of the time.[26] By day or night, the bomber was a sledge-hammer, never a scalpel.

Across the Atlantic, the BCATP was training thousands of airmen every month, and most of those who enlisted came from Canada. The politicians and air marshals had hoped that all the Canadians would be funnelled into the RCAF overseas, but the huge program required that many airmen remain in Canada as trainers, while new flyers were necessary to replenish the shredded RAF squadrons. As the bomber war intensified, tens of thousands of Canadian aviators would serve with the RAF. Minister of National Defence for Air Charles Power struggled to bring back many of the Canadians from the RAF to serve in the RCAF. The policy of Canadianization was not popular with the British, who found it disruptive and damaging to combat effectiveness. Nor did the veterans of the air war like it much. Breaking up bomber crews for nationalistic reasons did not seem like a good idea to airmen who lived in a world of chance and luck, and no one wanted to be separated from their buddies who had so far got them through the long hours in the air over enemy territory.

While 93,844 RCAF personnel served in other air forces—most of them in the RAF—RCAF squadrons continued to expand significantly, eventually totalling forty-eight overseas fighter, bomber, coastal, and other operational squadrons.[27] Throughout 1942, the RCAF air marshals and politicians pushed for the cre-ation of an all-Canadian bomber group, the equivalent of a sepa-rate army corps. Harris and other British air marshals resisted the effort, but the logic of numbers won out. The national bomber force No. 6 Group was formed on January 1, 1943. Describing the long campaign for an identifiable formation, one senior Canadian airman noted it took "patience, persistence, 95 percent diplomacy; the rest is tooth and claw."[28] Over time, there were fifteen front-line RCAF bomber squadrons, 87 percent of which were made up of Canadians by the end of 1944.[29] Based in the rolling Yorkshire hills in the north of England, No. 6 Group would become another symbol of Canada's visible assistance to the Allied war effort. Power told his British counterparts, "the ultimate Canadian objective . . . is really an independent air force in the same way as the U.S.A."[30]

The Lancasters and Halifaxes, along with the American B-17 Flying Fortresses and B-24 Liberators, could reach greater heights by 1943, usually coming in on their blacked-out objectives at 18,000 feet before dumping their payloads. They were also better able to find their targets with new navigational equipment and more accurate bomb sights that accounted for wind and speed. The Americans talked of bombing the enemy "'round-the-clock," day and night. RCAF Squadron Leader Walter Irwin, who had enlisted from Toronto when he was in his mid-twenties, recalled sharing an airfield with the Americans, "who flew in day light, whereas our attacks were always at night. We sometimes attacked the same target at night as they had struck in daylight, which must have been very unnerving for the Germans."[31]

On the ground, beneath the fall of the bombs, the German people lived in terror. The piercing sound of raid sirens and the hope of finding sanctuary in bomb-proof shelters became a daily reality for millions of military personnel and civilians, who would never forget the terrifying rush before the fall of bombs. But even these hardened shelters were not invulnerable. Some of the firestorms, like that at Hamburg in July 1943, created and stoked by 2,313 tons of high explosives and incendiaries, swept through the city, leaving a charred ruin where oxygen had been sucked from the shelters, suffocating or roasting alive the inhabitants. This was hell on earth. Four aerial attacks in close succession ended in 42,600 killed and 37,000 wounded.

"I had expected to die and I had accepted that fact," wrote RCAF airman Jack Singer, who had enlisted at age nineteen in June 1942 and survived thirty-one sorties and the war.[32] Many of his comrades did not make it home, as the airmen faced a war of long odds—odds that grew longer with each sortie that flew deeper into occupied Europe. Staff officers studied the survival rates of their crews with dismay, noting that by mid-1943 an airman had only a 17 percent chance of living through a thirty-operation tour, after which he would receive a rest of several months before going back for a second tour.[33] Even the infantry had a better chance of getting home. One survivor, Pilot Officer A.G. "Red" Sherwood, who flew forty sorties, remembered being on the verge of breaking because "the constant living in fear slowly but surely wore me down."[34]

———

In late 1943, the victories on the Eastern Front, the successful campaign in Sicily, and the slow-crawl up the Italian mainland, along with the surprise reversal of fortunes in the Battle of the Atlantic, saw the Allies turn the tide on the Axis powers. The weight of the machines in the bomber war was forcing the Nazi command to draw back crucial anti-aircraft resources from the front to protect against leaving cities as burned-out husks.[35] Alarmed by the gathering horror, the German high command also poured enormous resources into making aircraft to fend off the bombers, with this manufacturing stream topping 50 percent of all production in the Reich.[36] That German expenditure of resources alone justified the aerial campaign in the long war of attrition, even if some postwar philosophers, historians, and filmmakers would question its morality.

And yet the German people did not collapse under the strain. They were either too resilient or too trapped by the security state to rise up against their dictator. The Anglo-American senior air force staff and commanders wondered how to tip Germany into the abyss.[37] Berlin was believed to be the centre of gravity, and while it was far from the bases in England, a concentrated assault there might end the war. However, the German capital was also a veritable fortress of guns and weaving searchlights where concentrations of fighters lurked, waiting to be guided onto the stream of bombers by radar.

Though Berlin was plastered in a series of operations, at over 200 square kilometres it was so large that the bombers found it difficult to achieve much success other than in killing civilians. The Americans, realizing that their precious B-17s and B-24s were being wasted in the forlorn effort, cancelled their deep raid operations in October. With Air Marshal Harris at the helm, Bomber Command, consisting of RAF and RCAF squadrons, persisted against Berlin. The loss rate for No. 6 Group jumped to 6 percent per sortie in December and even higher in January, a debilitating attrition rate that could not be sustained. Survival probability rates plummeted to around 10 percent for a thirty-operation tour.[38] Those who made it back had been reduced to haggard, twitchy old men. The knock-out strike against Berlin had failed.

A Lancaster "bombed up" for a nighttime sortie against the enemy.

The cold weather of early 1944 resulted in a much-reduced pace for the bomber war, which provided time for a re-evaluation of the strategy. Plans for the invasion of Western Europe were being forged in England at SHAEF (Supreme Headquarters Allied

Expeditionary Force), with General Dwight Eisenhower in overall command. As part of the intricate invasion plans, the general and his staff demanded control over the bombers. Harris and his American counterpart, Carl Spaatz, objected, refusing to give up on the policy of precision bombing even though it had long since been revealed to be blind city smashing. Eisenhower won, as he should have, and as of March 1944 the bombers were directed towards German defences in the West to soften up fortifications along the Atlantic Wall, to slow the movement of defensive units, and, most importantly, to devastate critical infrastructure like bridges, roads, and rail lines.[39] When the invasion was launched in June 1944, the counterattacking German forces, especially their feared armoured units, would have to be slowed if the Allies were to have any success in holding the beaches.

The Allied air forces—with the Americans contributing the most—also won command of the air by destroying the Luftwaffe. Starting in February 1944, the RAF, RCAF, and especially American air forces flew against a series of targets in France. Since the bombers were wrecking infrastructure, the Luftwaffe was forced to respond: by early 1944, almost 70 percent of German fighters were defending the cities against the Allied bombers.[40] Drawn into battle against American P-51 Mustangs, P-47 Thunderbolts, and P-38 Lightnings, which were aided by RAF and RCAF Spitfires and Hurricanes, the Luftwaffe lost one third of its aircraft in February 1944. The next three months saw the destruction of almost the entire complement of pilots.[41] The long-range P-51s were particularly devastating, especially as their additional drop fuel tanks enabled them to fly up to seven hours. In a sense, the Mustang was a symbol of the Allied coalition, as the North American P-51 fighter was powered by a British Rolls Royce engine. The

Mustang pilots could search out their enemy and bring to bear their six .50 calibre M2 Browning machine guns, using them to regularly defeat the Focke-Wulf Fw 190s and Messerschmitt Me 109s. Allied bombers still went down in flames, but the thousands of aircraft coming out of American, British, and Canadian factories, and the many thousands of airmen being instructed in the BCATP and other training plans, made good the losses. Echoing the abrupt turn in the Battle of the Atlantic in May 1943, the Allies, with the Americans in the lead, broke the Luftwaffe as a fighting force, an essential act that paved the way for the invasion of Europe.

———

In the late summer of 1944, the Anglo, American, and Canadian bombers returned to their mission of pulverizing German cities. The RAF and RCAF flew together, hand in glove, with tens of thousands of Canadians serving in British squadrons and British-born in Canadian squadrons. Less well known is the story of the thousands of Americans who wore the RCAF uniform. Those US airmen in the fighters and bombers, alone and as part of aircrews, fought against the Axis powers, and they are among the 17,101 killed who served in the RCAF.[42]

The bombers carried the war to the Third Reich. As the survivors stood in their gutted cities, it was evident to all that Germany was being defeated. This collapse had been achieved by Canadian, American, and British aircrews fighting together and striking back, first when all looked bleak and victories were few, and from 1943 onward, in an unyielding battering. The bomber war alone did not deliver victory, but it helped to pave the way for the risky invasion in June 1944 that would determine the fate of the world.

CHAPTER 20

LIBERATION

"Dead soldiers floating in the water, others lying where they'd fallen on the beach, and clusters of wounded waiting for help. . . . I was hit with what war was about."[1] So wrote Gunner Wilson Bailey, remembering his sick feeling of coming onto Juno Beach in a landing craft and seeing his fellow Canadians dead in the water or writhing in agony on the blood-soaked battleground. This was D-Day, June 6, 1944, and it was a day of carnage.

The liberation of Western Europe from the Nazis would be long, difficult, and costly. For several years, the United States, Britain, Canada, the Free French, and other allies had been preparing for the invasion, but nothing could be done until command of both the sea and air was won. This goal had been achieved in two parts: with the defeat of the U-boats in the Battle of the Atlantic in May 1943 and with the destruction of Luftwaffe in early 1944. The peripheral land campaigns in North Africa, Sicily, and mainland Italy had also chiselled away at enemy strength and, more importantly, had pressured Hitler to commit precious military resources and divisions to defending those theatres of war. This strategic policy of attrition had assisted the Soviet Red Army in the east, even as Stalin's forces had borne the heaviest burden against the German army. The tough Russian soldiers had driven back the invaders throughout 1943. In the centre, the Allied bombers smashed cities and infrastructure, unleashing Armageddon on the Nazi war machine that was run by its compliant and coerced citizens until, finally, the production of war materiel flatlined and dropped into oblivion.

On the North American home front, a massive volume of war supplies and weapons had been manufactured in the US's "Arsenal of Democracy," with substantial contributions also coming from its northern neighbour, the so-named "Aerodrome of Democracy" that was also a powerful forge of weapons. Safe from direct attack after the worrisome early years in the war, this base of operations allowed for the build-up and strike-back of Allied armed forces against occupied Western Europe. But Canada's participation was not limited to supplying airmen, munitions, armoured vehicles, food, and minerals. Its fighting forces would be hurled into battle, especially First Canadian Army, which would stand with its British and American counterparts on D-Day, after which these formations would, together, fight through Northwest Europe to liberate the oppressed.

———

Planners in England had long struggled with the monumental task of invading Europe. The multinational army was under the command of US General Dwight Eisenhower, a battle-tested warrior who had secured victories in North Africa and Sicily. Canadian overseas journalist L.S.B. Shapiro described the general in glowing terms, noting, "Never before has an American carried the full and unreserved confidence of British forces; never before has an American, so plainly an Anglophile, retained the complete faith of his own people. Eisenhower is more than a symbol of unity; he is its most ruthless practitioner."[2] Friendly, congenial, and aware that one of his primary roles as supreme commander was to keep the international alliance intact, Eisenhower carried the immense burden of being entrusted with the lives of several million Allied soldiers.

The "Great Crusade," as Eisenhower referred to the coming invasion, would see over 150,000 soldiers attack on the first day of battle, supported by thousands of fighters and bombers to clear the enemy from the skies, and a naval armada of 6,900 warships and vessels to protect and carry in the waves of infantry, engineers, artillery, and armoured formations. While there had been much planning before 1944, the staggeringly complex operation had become more focused with General Eisenhower's appointment as commander early in the year. However, despite the mass of men, resources, and firepower available to the Allied armies, the planners feared that the German defenders might destroy the landing force with relentless armoured counterattacks. The amateurism of the past was replaced by a hard-nosed realism. At only 30 kilometres, the route from Dover to Calais was the shortest distance from Britain to France, and this limited span would allow the Allied fighters and bombers maximum time over the coastal battlefield after crossing. Hitler's high command could also read a map, and it had stacked the best German divisions at Calais. An elaborate Allied deception plan consisting of turned agents, phantom armies, and even bomber strikes against fortifications in the north reinforced in Hitler's mind that Calais would be the epicentre of battle.[3] It was not.

The Allies instead prepared to come ashore in the Normandy region, with six divisions amphibiously landed along five beaches in Operation Overlord. Three airborne divisions would drop into the battle space to sow confusion and act as an outer ring of protection in the first critical days of combat by breaking up enemy counterstrikes along an 80-kilometre front. Canada's 3rd Infantry Division was tasked with storming the heavily defended Juno Beach; on either side were British divisions—the 3rd and 50th. The two lead American divisions—the 1st and 29th—were to strike through Omaha Beach, while the 4th Division was to break the German lines at Utah Beach. In this history-making operation, the Canadians were selected to stand with the British and the Americans.

Operation Neptune was the naval counterpart to Overlord, and 126 Royal Canadian Navy warships supported the enormous armada. Before June 1944, RCN destroyers had been engaged in sweeping patrols against the Kriegsmarine, and several running battles had been waged along the French coast.[4] In North America, the RCN took over the lion's share of escort duties across the Atlantic, with its fleet eventually growing to over 400 warships. But as the planners prepared for the invasion, they worried that just a few enemy destroyers or U-boats skulking within the armada would slaughter the thousands of vulnerable soldiers in unarmed landing craft even before they reached the beaches. And so there were rigorous naval operations against the German fleet in the months before the battle, driving the enemy out of the area.

The final checks were made in early June while the invasion force was sequestered in controlled camps and onboard ships to prevent the leakage of information. And then disaster seemed to loom. At Eisenhower's headquarters, meteorologists gave warning of a terrible storm that might sweep through the English Channel on June 5, disrupting the entire operation. Some officers advised that the plan should be delayed until the next available window to be timed with favourable tides several weeks away. To launch the operation in the storm would spell disaster, and unless it was called off the Germans would likely catch wind of it. Eisenhower wrestled with the options, but, showing his grit, he pushed the invasion only to the next day, and took to praying to the weather gods. They answered with calmer metrological conditions. The operation was on, with D-Day set for June 6.

The 3rd Canadian Division, under the command of Major-General Rod Keller, readied itself for the dire combat to come. Soldiers wrote last letters to loved ones and made pacts with comrades to share word of their death with next of kin. RCN warships prowled at the ready, many of them in support of the Canadian landing on Juno Beach, but sixteen Bangor-class RCN minesweepers were assigned to the American sector, where they completed the vital job of clearing mines from the approaches to Omaha and Utah beaches.[5] Briefings to the flotilla warned that it could expect heavy casualties but that the minesweepers must not waver.[6] This was an all-out effort, and the Allies would have only one shot at victory.

———

In Ottawa, Prime Minister King had spent most of the war focused on carefully balancing the divergent interests within his country, to the point that he often retreated from any decisions about Allied grand strategy or even the deployment of the armed forces. In one revealing display of King's thinking, when Ralston asked him to intervene with Churchill so that the Canadians could be a part of the North Africa invasion in Operation Torch, he recoiled, writing that such action "goes the whole length of placing me in the position, as head of the Canadian Government, of settling the strategy so far as Canadian troops are concerned."[7] Peculiar statements were known to emerge from King's mouth in times of distress, but such thinking allowed the British and the Americans to continue to push the Canucks to the periphery or to use them where they wanted. For example, King's cabinet had not been consulted on General Eisenhower's appointment as supreme commander. More surprisingly, Canadian politicians had no idea when D-Day would occur. Aides rushed to wake King early on June 6 to inform him of the invasion.[8]

In the battle-royale to liberate France, the Canadians would fight under British command, with General Bernard Montgomery leading these forces. The cocksure general was much loved by the Canadian soldiers, although he tended to command them with little regard for Canada's status as a separate nation. Perhaps if King and his cabinet had shown more interest in preserving the autonomy of the country's army commanders, the relationship overseas between Canadian and British generals might have been different; that said, Monty had made a career of doing what he believed was right and of paying little heed to political sensibilities. Insufferable as he was at times, the hero of El Alamein had a good eye for talent, and he was impressed with the Canadians in Sicily—especially with their commander, Lieutenant-General Guy Simonds. Dismissive of nationalistic feelings, he did not like Canadian Army commander General Harry Crerar, calling him "very prosy and stodgy," and sniffing that "he is very definitely not a commander."[9] A rocky time was in store for the two Canadian generals, but it would be Simonds, as II Corps commander, who would be the first to lead on the battlefield. The Canadian–British colonial relationship died hard.

The 18,500-strong 3rd Canadian Division began its run-in to Juno Beach in darkness during the early hours of June 6, with nine companies from five infantry regiments spearheading the assault, supported by elements of two tank regiments. Leaving behind the vast armada of warships, who were ready to inflict thundering firepower against the prepared Axis defences, the forces going ashore endured a desolate, cold voyage as the box-like landing craft pushed through the water and waves, moving about 1,500 first-wave soldiers towards their destiny. The infantry kept their head down, staring into the sloshing water and vomit that washed over their boots, whispering silent prayers, and swearing they were not meant to be sailors.

In the Channel, RCN destroyers with their 4.7-inch guns prepared to launch the supporting barrage. The first guns barked death

A landing craft transporting Canadians to Juno Beach on D-Day.

around 5:30 a.m. as shells were hurled over the 2,000 landing craft making their way to the beaches.[10] Above the battlefield, fighters patrolled to create an air umbrella, although rarely did the Luftwaffe chance a suicidal run into the hornet's nest. The German high command remained unaware of the looming battle, and many of the senior generals were away from their posts. Somewhat incredibly, intelligence had failed to pick up signs of the invasion. However, there had been an ongoing debate about how to meet an Allied force, and while some of the best armoured units were stationed at Calais, there remained a central reserve that could be thrown into battle once it was determined where the primary blow would fall. In fact, many in the German high command welcomed the long-awaited assault from England because they felt it could be defeated, which would then allow some of the reserves tied down in the west to be moved to block the Red Army's advance in the east.[11]

On Juno Beach, the German 716th Infantry Division was hammered by naval shellfire, although most of the 2-metre-thick concrete bunkers were unscathed and the guns within them remained operational. Hitting low-profile positions that housed machine guns and light artillery was too much to ask of the naval gunners, and as the landing craft moved towards the beaches, bullets rang off the steel siding in rhythmic beating that warned the Canadian infantrymen of what awaited them on the beach. Coming ashore between about 7:50 and 8:10 a.m., the vanguard of the force ran into the churning gunfire.[12] As some of the landing craft opened their doors, the enemy machine-gunners raked the inviting target, tearing apart the soldiers before they had a chance to charge forward on to the sand.

Despite the butchery, the dozens of machine guns could not zero in on all the landing craft along the 10-kilometre-stretch of coastline, and as the first waves hit, the infantry drove forward across the kill zone. Coming late to the battle, but serving a crucial role in supporting the sandpounders, were M4A3 Sherman tanks that "swam" into shore equipped with floatable devices. The mortar bombs, high explosive shells, and sniper and machine-gun bullets dulled the senses of those in the space of violence. Most found the courage to advance on the enemy, aware that only the already dead and maimed, and those soon to join them, would be left on the beach. When nineteen-year-old Private William Curran of the Royal Winnipeg Rifles hit solid ground, the sound deafened him and the terror caught in his throat as he moved past the slain and those dying. "It was like a bad, bad dream," he would later write. "You see something terrible in front of you and you think that you will wake up. . . . I did not think I would make it home."[13] He did, even though many of his comrades did not.

Success came down to sacrifice, as some infantrymen charged forward to draw fire, usually with their lives, while others raced ahead. Slowly the assault force breeched the concrete barriers and barbed wire extending in some places to a depth of 10 metres. Within two hours, most of the lead units broke through the beach defences that were now shrouded in dark clouds of cordite. Follow-on forces arrived to support the drive. The Canadians spent the day clearing out buildings and structures behind the forward defensive system, eventually advancing 11 kilometres inland and achieving the deepest Allied movement of the day. The Canadian survivors—359 were killed and 715 wounded on that fateful day—were bolstered with secondary formations, including flail tanks with chains that beat the ground to explode mines.[14] But even in victory, the infantry had no idea whether they would be facing a major armoured counterattack, or if the Americans and British had made it ashore.

———

On the left flank of the Canadians, the 3rd British Division had fought its way through the enemy lines, and the Tommies revealed tremendous resilience in standing fast against the 21st Panzer Division heaving itself against the beachhead. The enemy was stopped short by mauling defensive fire and the panzers retreated to Caen, a major urban centre only a dozen kilometres away that at one time had housed 55,000 people. This would be the hard shoulder of the Germans' defensive line to contain the British and Canadian forces pushing off from the beaches.

Further to the south, on the Canadians' right flank, the British 50th Division—a veteran unit of the desert war in North Africa that had also survived the retreat from Dunkirk—came blasting ashore on Gold Beach. Sherman tanks that landed directly on the beach supported the infantry, and together they surged into the interior within a few hours. It was a similar story on Utah Beach, where the 4th American Division overcame light resistance to force their way inland. However, the 1st Division ran into a buzz saw on Omaha Beach. The 352nd German Division burrowed deep into the surrounding high ground, raking the Americans coming off the dunes with fire. The swimming tanks sank in rough water, leaving the American GIs even more exposed. Soon the waterline was strewn with bodies and the beach was a charnel house. After several grim hours amid a dark cloud of oily smoke and apocalyptic scenes of horror, those Americans caught in the crossfire drew upon nearly unbelievable nerve to stalk their way forward and break the line. Supporting units of the 29th Division added weight to the task of mopping up the dugouts and fortifications, one punishing yard at a time. At the cost of some 2,000 casualties, the beach and surrounding area were in American hands by day's end.

Canadian newspapers reported on the invasion on June 7, with one paper claiming it was "the day of reckoning—and also of liberation—for the millions of oppressed people of Europe."[15] That Canada was playing a part and was given its own beach to capture thrilled many. With the country in such a lead role, the report cautioned, "Our people at home must be prepared for news of heavy casualties."[16] And indeed, that was the case. There were 4,414 Allied deaths on that day: 2,501 of them were American and almost 400 were Canadian.[17]

As the Allied divisions pressed inward from the coast, they met up with the paratrooper formations, including 1st Canadian Parachute Battalion, that had landed among the surprised defenders. The next day, the lead units of the 150,000 soldiers in France advanced to create space for follow-on forces, even though the beachheads were crowded and many of the important anti-tank regiments were caught up in the chaos.[18] None of the soldiers at the front and few of the generals in the rear knew of what to expect in the coming clash. However, those young men who formed the Allied thrust knew they would soon be fighting on the defensive against enemy counterattacks. Even if Hitler and his high command remained uncertain as to whether the Normandy landings were a mere feint or the primary assault, German commanders on the ground were more aggressive, and immediately several of the best panzer divisions were moving to Caen to contain the Canadian and British breakout and drive its forces back into the Channel. To the south, the Americans faced a different obstacle—the bocage. In this terrain, tightly packed hedges from generations of farming created a grid system within which the defenders were well concealed and where they had the advantage of open fields of fire. The Allied forces had won the first day of the battle, but the coming week would determine if they could survive.

———

"There is no substitute for a battle," believed Lieutenant Burton Harper, a New Brunswicker who fought through Normandy with a British infantry regiment. "No amount of training can substitute for battle."[19] The lead Canadian units, north of Caen, were advancing to contact. The British were battling the 21st Panzer Division, while the 12th SS Panzer Division had rushed to Caen and was preparing to hurl the Canadians back into the Channel. On the left of the divisional push off the beaches, the North Nova Scotia Highlanders and the Sherbrooke Fusilier tank regiment were to seize the airfield at Carpiquet, on the outskirts of Caen, which would give Allied fighters a good site from which to operate and reduce their fuel consumption.

In the early afternoon, the infantry and troopers in their Sherman tanks were mauled by a larger force of 12th SS Panzer Division Hitlerjugend that attacked overland, backed by some fifty tanks.[20] As an elite formation, the 12th SS consisted of Hitler Youth who had been indoctrinated in the vile Nazi ideology. These mostly underage soldiers were ferocious, uncompromising, and known for taking few prisoners. One of the senior commanders,

Colonel Kurt Meyer, a veteran of the Eastern Front who was destined to lead the division, ordered his soldiers to gobble up the "little fish," declaring, "We'll throw them back into the sea."[21]

The overextended Canadians were caught in the French villages of Authie and Buron, where they were blitzed by German Mark IV and Mark V Panther tanks. The Fusiliers lost twenty-one Shermans, although seventeen enemy tanks were destroyed.[22] Both sides suffered several hundred killed and wounded, and dozens of Canadian prisoners were captured here and in other battles along the front. In the next week, at least 156 Canadian prisoners would become the victims of war crimes. Executed behind the lines by the Nazis, their bodies were buried in shallow graves.[23] When the Canadians later learned of this, they promised vengeance, but now they were simply trying to survive the enemy onslaught.

Further away from Caen, the 7th Canadian Infantry Brigade dug in around the villages of Norrey, Putot, and Bretteville and waited for the coming battle. They could see the fury of combat on the left flank, although the 12th SS did not attack here until late on June 8. With time to prepare, the Canadians created all-around defences bristling with artillery, anti-tank guns, Sherman tanks, and machine-gun positions. When the Hitlerjugend fell on them in the early hours of the 8th, they held their ground. Fighting for their lives, small teams of infantry armed with PIAT (Projector, Infantry, Anti-Tank) weapons faced down the main battle tanks. Six Panthers were left in smoking ruins along with dozens of dead attackers.[24] The battle ended on the 9th, having been crucial in preventing the Hitler Youth from reaching the beach and gutting the Allied lines of communication. The Canadians lost 2,831 killed and wounded in the first week of battle, but the Nazi soldiers found that the little fish had big teeth.[25]

———

The creation of artificial ports, known as Mulberries, assisted in the mass movement of materiel, with each of the Allied divisions consuming at least 500 tons of supplies a day, and much more if engaged in combat. But with every advance into the enemy lines, the logistical tail lengthened. The legion of trucks, all of them consuming precious fuel, had to go farther each day as they carried ammunition, food, and everything else the armies needed to press the Germans back. However, the Allies were almost never targeted by the now-ravaged Luftwaffe, whereas Allied bombers, fighter-bombers, and fighters harassed any troops or soft-skinned vehicles not under cover, able to slow the forming up of attacking units. And later in July and August, fighter-bombers like the Typhoon, armed with 500-pound bombs, became more effective against strongpoints, especially as a system of communication was cemented to allow ground forces to call in supporting aerial fire or bombs.[26]

To the south, the Americans struggled to break out from their hemmed-in beachheads. While it was important to drive forward so that reinforcing divisions could come ashore, the US forces were also tasked with seizing the ports to allow for the vital delivery of supplies, especially artillery shells, to ease the shortages that were plaguing Eisenhower's armies. First Cherbourg had to fall, and then the Brittany ports at Brest, Lorient, and St. Nazaire. Again, this war of red tooth and claw, of carnage and combat, relied on the flow of logistics. But a swift victory was not possible, with the bocage country proving far more difficult to fight through than intelligence reports had predicted, as the normally overwhelming American firepower was diminished within the segmented battle-field. The First United States Army under the command of General

Omar Bradley, a veteran of the North Africa and Sicily campaigns, moved incrementally as the Germans fought an effective delaying action around Cherbourg. By the time the port finally fell on June 27, the harbour had been demolished to the point that it would take a month of intense rebuilding before the first ships could unload their precious supplies.

The enemy also locked into Caen, effectively blocking the British and Canadian advance there. General Eisenhower watched worriedly as Montgomery, commanding 21st Army Group in Normandy—two armies consisting of British, Canadian, Polish, Belgian, and other forces—and General Bradley, commanding US First Army and, later, 12th Army Group, moved too cautiously for his liking. The supreme commander knew his armies were in a race to prevent the German counterattacking formations from arriving in strength. The Allies had twenty-one divisions in Normandy at this point, but the Germans had moved eighteen divisions there and had the advantage of fighting on the defensive.

To strike forward beyond the beaches, Montgomery planned Operation Epsom for June 18 to break the enemy lines. A freak storm that raged through the Channel delayed the offensive until the 25th, and also damaged the artificial harbours. With much of the Allied air support grounded, the enemy rushed anti-tank guns to the British front, leaving the infantry and armoured units, once they finally attacked, unable to make much progress in the crawl southward to Falaise. Though the Germans continued to hold Caen, Epsom and some of the battles to follow dragged the best armoured formations into the front opposite the British and Canadians, a diversion that would bear fruit in July when the Americans were finally able to break out against the much weaker forces opposite them.

In the meantime, the 3rd Canadian Division was becoming severely worn down and cut up in the long struggle. Its soldiers suffered from exhaustion, the "Normandy glide" (a mild form of dysentery), and the hardship of living on unappetizing rations. There were few respites. The tired Canadians launched an attack on July 4 to snatch Carpiquet airfield to the west of Caen. The airfield was surrounded by a series of fortified hangars and bunkers, as well as 88mm anti-tank guns and hull-down tanks that were partially buried so that only the barrels and turret were showing. Intelligence photographs revealed that the 12th SS soldiers were ready for the advance that would go in over 2 kilometres of flat ground. It had to be a shock and awe operation. Four Canadian battalions supported by the weight of 760 British and Canadian artillery pieces crashed forward at 5 a.m.[27] Advancing behind a creeping barrage and across the cratered battlefield, the Canadians passed through black smoke and cordite that polluted the air. The attacking force could not be stopped, even as an enemy counter-barrage of shells and mortar bombs took its toll. Though hundreds of the Hitler Youth were captured and killed, they often fought to the last round. "They look like babies," remarked one Canadian corporal, "but they die like mad bastards."[28]

The fortress of Caen continued to rebuff Montgomery's forces, and by July 7 he had had enough. Bombers were sent against the city, dropping some 2,570 tons of high explosives. The Germans were soon pressed back by two British Divisions—the 3rd and 59th—attacking from north to south, and by the Canadian 3rd Division rushing from west to east into the city. The North Americans tore through their nemesis, the 12th SS, savaging them with a shell-heavy bombardment that allowed the infantry and armour to drive forward over the farmers' fields outside the city before engaging in urban warfare amid the wreckage. "In the reeking shambles of their city, the place looked like the end of the world," reported one CBC journalist from Caen. But amid the destruction, the Canadians were greeted by French men, women, and children.[29] On July 10, the Germans retreated across the Orne River. The cost of liberation was high. Since July 4, the Canadians had lost 330 killed and 864 wounded, although, with the capture of Carpiquet and Caen, fighter aircraft now had more space to make their bases in France, and British troops to the south were freed to advance.[30] But there would be no immediate breakthroughs to restore mobility to the battlefield, only a series of violent and costly engagements to wear down the German defenders.

A Canadian mortar team taking the fight to the Germans.

———

The Nazis had been chewed up around Caen, and yet five weeks into the raging campaign, Hitler remained focused on Calais, where he expected another major Allied invasion to fall. He was also looking to the east, where a fresh Soviet offensive on June 22 had ripped a hole through the Wehrmacht and was now drawing in reinforcements like a sucking chest wound. The Soviets had perfected the art of operational warfare—using large formations like a series of army corps to engage the enemy while other armoured units slashed through or around them. As evidence of the frenzied fighting, the Germans suffered about 450,000 casualties, more than in the entire Normandy campaign.[31] Stalin's forces lost even more soldiers, but with more manpower and larger armies they could afford them in the grim war of attrition.

While the Germans in Normandy had lost much of their ability to strategically counterattack, they nonetheless remained brutally effective at the tactical level, where soldiers killed soldiers. Dug in on the best terrain, and with machine guns, mortars, panzers, and artillery situated to create kill zones, they left Montgomery's forces with little room to manoeuvre. The only way to make the hard yards was by following artillery-driven, heavy-metal warfare that smashed through the prepared defences, a tactic that was also hoped to manage the number of Allied casualties, unlike the totalitarian Soviets who spent their soldiers' lives freely.

The Anglo-Canadian offensive Operation Goodwood rolled forward guns blazing on July 18, with the goal of reaching Falaise. But even as over a thousand bombers hammered the enemy lines, the armoured assault ran into the stacked defences of the Germans' best divisions, including anti-tank batteries of 88mm guns and 55-ton Tiger tanks. The British Shermans were shredded by shellfire. Goodwood had only limited gains, and some 320 armoured vehicles were left as blackened metal corpses. It was no better on the Canadian front.

On July 11, the newly established II Canadian Corps, under command of Lieutenant-General Guy Simonds, was ready for battle, although it consisted of only the exhausted 3rd Canadian Division and the newly arrived 2nd Canadian Division. The forty-one-year-old Simonds was well respected by the British, especially General Montgomery, who appraised him as the best Canadian general because of his success in Sicily. He was also cold, determined, and too willing to take casualties. Simonds remained the Canadian battlefield commander because Crerar was in England waiting for more space to open up in France to allow for additional units to cross the Channel. Montgomery was only too happy to keep him there and away from active command.[32]

In the battles south of Caen, the Canadians made only minimal gains. They also took heavy losses, and this phase of battle ended on July 25 at Verrières Ridge, where they were stopped cold. One German officer described the Canadian frontal attack up the ridge with little fire support as a "most unreal sight," noting it was "sheer butchery."[33] The arrival of First Canadian Army headquarters under General Crerar around this time coincided with giving the fighting formations time to pause, regroup, and lick their wounds. The Anglo-Canadian advances were slow in the face of enemy strength, but they achieved the strategic victory of drawing the best units to their front. Montgomery's 21st Army Group was opposed by 14 divisions and 600 tanks, while the Americans faced a paltry 9 divisions and 110 tanks.[34]

On July 25, the Americans finally launched their long-awaited offensive, Operation Cobra. The withered defenders were again pounded by bombers and concentrated artillery fire, and after an initial slow start, General Bradley's US First Army broke through the enemy lines. On July 31, the logistical deadlock was eased when the Americans secured Avranches, a crucial town through which several roads ran. The Germans had no time to regroup as they were hounded in defeat by General George Patton's Third Army, which he whipped forward from early August, enveloping static positions to be snuffed out later.

In the face of this looming disaster, Field Marshal Günther von Kluge begged Hitler to allow his armies to retreat to more secure positions. But with the Eastern Front collapsing, the dictator saw any ground given in the west as a defeat: he unwisely ordered that some of the key panzer divisions be moved from the Anglo-Canadian front to counterattack the Americans. Studying his maps, Hitler envisioned a six-division strike that would cut through Patton's army. It was a delusion and, even worse, Allied codebreakers had intercepted and revealed the manoeuvre. Massed Allied air power—with the USAAF, RAF, and RCAF squadrons flying together—harassed the exposed forces along the lines of communication as they closed with the Americans. "It was like a scene from Dante's Inferno," recalled one pilot. "The whole area was filled with tanks and what was probably the trucks of their supply echelon—soft skinned vehicles which stood no chance against our cannon."[35] When the Germans finally met the Americans in battle on August 7, the alerted GIs lashed the lead formations, ultimately blunting the offensive at Mortain. In the smouldering ruins, the Nazis were mortally wounded. The enemy was also now trapped in a collapsing battlefield, with the Americans striking northward and Monty's 21st Army Group coming in over the top, driving eastward to doubly envelop Kluge's two armies.

As part of the northern envelopment of the enemy, First Canadian Army under command of General Harry Crerar launched an offensive on August 8. The goal was to connect with American forces and close the Falaise pocket in which the Germans appeared increasingly trapped. Operation Totalize was based on a massed armoured strike through several dozen small towns and villages, most of them stubbornly occupied by defenders. Advancing on a relatively narrow front, an aerial bombardment was planned to pave the way for a force of tanks and armoured personnel carriers. General Simonds—who Crerar allowed to plan the operation—ordered that there would be "no holding back."[36] The drive on the enemy would continue notwithstanding heavy expected casualties. In the initial attack, the worst losses were caused by a group of American B-17s that dropped their bombs short in the confusion of battle. Some 350 Canadian and Polish soldiers were killed or wounded, and the thrust's momentum was delivered a severe jolt. While surveying the destruction, the enraged Canadian divisional commander, Rod Keller, demanded a revolver from a nearby soldier, declaring, "I'm going to shoot the first goddam American I see."[37]

These appalling errors happen in the friction of battle, and the horrified British, Polish, and Canadians soon found their footing, moving forward again. The enemy was initially steamrolled, although the Germans fought with tenacity, including the Canadians' nemesis, the 12th SS, which sometimes battled to the last bullet and boy. The Hitler Youth would be annihilated as a formation in the coming two weeks. Long-range artillery clashes and shorter melees of small-arms combat continued for several days and the first phase ended on August 11, after the gobbling up of 13 kilometres.[38]

The Allied forces were slowly closing the escape exit for the two German armies that only began to retreat from the Falaise trap on the 15th. A double envelopment of the enemy seemed to signal defeat, but a squabble between Montgomery and Bradley squandered the win. Patton's formations were galloping along to the south of the German armies, seeking to shut the escape route, while the Canadian, British, and Polish units were trying to complete the encirclement from the north to snap the door shut on the 100,000 soldiers in the disintegrating pocket. Above the battlefield, Allied air power cut up anything that moved along the roads, adding to the graveyard of burned-out trucks and riddled corpses that lay like a great swath as the Axis retreat degenerated into a rout.[39] Amid a haze of black smoke, burning woods, and dust stirred into the air to create unworldly swirling clouds, the panicked enemy ran for their lives. Canadian infantryman John Neff, serving in a Sherman tank, wrote in his diary about the horror all around him, lamenting, "I have never seen such a mess of burned and blasted flesh."[40] But Montgomery was slow to grasp the need to tighten the noose around the Germans' necks, and he reserved substantial forces for a future drive into northern France and Belgium. Equally disastrous, Bradley ordered Patton to stop his advance at Argentan for fear of being overextended and, it would appear, for the purpose of embarrassing his hated rival, Montgomery.[41] Unable to dampen the jealousies, General Eisenhower watched this war between his generals and chafed over their misreading of the battlefield, aware that the situation demanded boldness of action as the enemy was at his most vulnerable.

Canadian infantryman and a burning Sherman tank in St. Lambert,
France, during the fierce battle to close the Falaise Gap in August 1944.

At Chambois on August 19, Canadian and American forces
finally met up and closed the exit on the trapped Germans. Enemy
units continued to dribble through the porous line over the next
couple of days, but Hitler's legions had suffered a tremendous
defeat. In the pocket were close to 8,000 destroyed or abandoned
tanks, trucks, and field guns, along with up to 10,000 dead soldiers.[42] About 50,000 others were made prisoners. This was the
end of the battle for France, and many thought that Berlin would
soon sue for peace.

———

"Every show we survive I learn more," wrote one Canadian officer
at the end of the long battle in Normandy.[43] During the seventy-
seven days of combat, the Allies had made it ashore and survived

the enemy's counterattacks before methodically advancing through the fortified terrain. But the Germans had the advantage of fighting on the defensive, which they did with consummate skill and steadfast courage. The Allies suffered few calamitous reversals, although the push forward into prepared positions was always a slow and costly grind. Some of the staff officers and journalists far to the rear complained about the deadlock in June and early July, but it was simply a result of tough fighting akin to the trench warfare in the Great War, where no breakthrough could occur before the enemy was worn down in battle. While about 40,000 German soldiers escaped the disaster at Falaise to fight on in the north, the Wehrmacht suffered some 400,000 casualties during the entire campaign (with about half of these captured), compared to the Allies' 206,000 losses.[44]

The Americans, the British, and the Canadians led the assault through Normandy, with Canadian warships, aircraft, and ground units standing by their allies. There were 18,444 Canadian casualties, almost all of which fell on the infantry and armour. Two Canadian infantry divisions (and one armoured division and an armoured brigade) fought in Normandy: and the 3rd and 2nd Divisions served in more "intense combat days" than any other British division.[45] Though the Canadians were never the equal of the British or the Americans in terms of size, importance, or impact, they played an outsized part in freeing the French. They would continue to advance against the enemy in the coming months, contributing to the Allied mission to destroy Hitler's forces and end the terrible war.

CHAPTER 21

DEFEATING THE NAZIS

"I believe that the toughest fighting is now over," wrote General Harry Crerar, commander of First Canadian Army. "Indeed, if we were not at war with a government of fanatics, an unconditional surrender would have taken place a week or so ago."[1] With these words, penned after the victory in Normandy, the general echoed many in the Allied high command who felt the end was near. But while the Germans were routed and Paris liberated, the soldiers in the Wehrmacht refused to fold, even though defeat seemed inevitable. Many were driven by a belief in protecting their homeland, around which Allied forces were converging; by a fear of their officers; and perhaps by an awareness that the horror that the Third Reich had inflicted on the world would not lead to its foot soldiers receiving gentle treatment from the victors. And so the German army fled northward from France. It had received little strategic direction other than to hold out for the supposed miracle of wonder weapons being developed by Hitler's scientists—rocket-propelled jets and other fantastic machines—that might turn the war against the invaders. Canadian forces would continue to march on the enemy, being unexpectedly called upon to deliver victory on key battlefields, and especially to open up the crucial Belgian port city of Antwerp for the Allied forces to deliver the final death blow to the Nazis.

———

After the victory in Normandy, General Dwight Eisenhower faced a dilemma of where to attack next with his army of 49 divisions and over 2.1 million soldiers. Though they outnumbered the Germans by at least two to one in the west, they were spread out over hundreds of kilometres and constrained from unleashing the full power of the large force because of a scarcity of war supplies.[2] Dire shortages of shells, fuel, and almost everything else resulted from the long logistical lines stretching back to the Normandy area. Trucks were driven continuously to and from the beachheads, leading Lieutenant Donald Pearce of the North Nova Scotia Regiment to describe the drivers as the "unsung heroes" that "never make the newspapers but who are very much of the essence of modern war."[3] Larger and closer ports needed to be captured up the French coast to assist with the logistical famine, which was made all the worse because the Allied bombers had smashed the railways to slow German counterattacking forces before the invasion. Equally bedeviling to the high command was the new question of whether to assault on a wide front into the industrial heartland of the Ruhr and farther south into the Saar region, or whether the Allied forces should leap forward with a narrower stab into the heart of Germany.

British field marshal Bernard Montgomery, who had been accused of being sluggish and too safe in the fighting in Normandy, came up with a daring operation that would be known as Market Garden.[4] With misplaced confidence, Montgomery proposed that the Allies thrust northeast across the Rhine River, forcing the Germans to fall back in confusion and, he promised, ending the war in 1944. This plan focused a spearhead along a narrow front, although it would also leave the advancing force exposed to counterattack. Unlike Montgomery's safe, firepower-heavy setpiece battles in Normandy, Market Garden was a linked assault requiring the capture of three successive major bridges in the Netherlands, around Arnhem and Nijmegen. British and American airborne divisions would drop in and hold the positions long enough for a concentrated armoured lunge to burst forward, cross the bridges one after another, and finally break through the enemy lines. In this drive of almost 100 kilometres, everything would have to go right or it would all go wrong.

Eisenhower and his staff worried about the plan, which could be blunted at any of the chokepoint bridges and required enormous resources. In fact, the dedication of weapons and forces to this sector would effectively starve other Allied armies, particularly the hard-charging General George Patton, who faced weaker resistance in the Saar region. Chain-smoking and sleep-deprived, Eisenhower was anxious about the risky manoeuvre, but he believed that, for the sake of the coalition, he had to allow Montgomery to roll the dice. The American general authorized the operation on the condition that Montgomery would formulate a way to open Antwerp, the inland port with 50 kilometres of docks and the capacity to move 100,000 tons of materiel a day. Though the city had been captured on September 4, the long approach to it through the Scheldt estuary remained in German hands. Europe's largest port was unusable to the Allies, who were increasingly feeling the pinch of the long supply lines.

Field Marshal Montgomery focused intensely on Market Garden, characteristically ignoring Eisenhower's order to capture Antwerp. With his eyes on the prize, Montgomery almost indifferently instructed General Harry Crerar's First Canadian Army to drive northward to liberate several French ports and cities along the Channel. Only after this would they be sent to open up Antwerp, and as most resources were going to Market Garden, he ordered a low priority for ammunition allocation to accomplish the task.[5] Although Montgomery had little faith in Crerar, he gave the Canadians a critical operation, albeit one far from the main action. The ports of Le Havre, Dieppe, Boulogne, and Calais, defended by garrisons of many thousands of Germans and bristling with high-calibre guns, were not without value of course, and they could move in much needed supplies. But even if they were all captured undamaged, they would collectively be less useful than Antwerp for relieving the logistical challenge. Hard battles to open up ports were all very far from the glory of Montgomery's ambitious plunge into Germany and the ongoing celebrations in Paris. Committed to playing the role assigned to him, Crerar also sought to prove himself. He ordered a series of operations against these Atlantic fortress positions from the landward side along what became known as the Long Left Flank.

Striking in early September, the Canadians moved fast to the assault, hoping to catch the Germans on the back foot. Dieppe fell to the 2nd Canadian Division on September 1 without a fight, and the troops marched through the town's streets as liberators to the tune of "The Maple Leaf Forever," Canada's unofficial national anthem. Some visited the graves of comrades who had fallen in the disastrous raid some twenty-one months earlier. Jack Wishart served with the 2nd Anti-Tank Regiment in the liberation of the

French and later the Dutch. Recalling the sight of the French people jumping about, waving flags and cheering on the Canucks, he noted that "in those few moments our sacrifices were not in vain."[6]

Major-General Dan Spry's 3rd Division had the more difficult task of capturing Boulogne, some 150 kilometres further up the coast. As a veteran of the Italian campaign, the thirty-one-year-old Spry was battle hardened and well suited to command, replacing the injured Keller, who had been mediocre at best in Normandy. General Spry ordered an artillery bombardment of the enemy garrison to start on September 5. Wasps—Universal Carriers fitted with a flamethrower—spewed napalm-like liquid fire that added to the terror of the trapped German garrison troops. After almost two weeks of this hell, made worse by bombers unleashing their high explosive payloads on the fort's defences, the Canadian infantry swarmed forward on the 17th.[7] The obscuring dust clouds laced by eruptions of flame and tracer bullets created a hellscape in which fighting raged until the last of the brave German defenders surrendered on the 22nd. Almost 10,000 were in the bag and hundreds of uncounted slain lay amid the ruins, their body parts strewn amid discarded equipment. The siege cost 634 Canadians killed and wounded.[8] By mid-October, the ports at both Dieppe and Boulogne were receiving merchant ships to feed the Allied armies advancing far inland.

The shortages of gas and shells, along with everything else the vast armies needed to fight, became even more critical after the failure of Market Garden. The plan had collapsed under the weight of its complexity, and the invaders had been thrashed by rapid German counterattacks. The thunder run through the three bridges by General Brian Horrocks's XXX Corps—consisting of some 20,000 vehicles—slowly ground to a crawl, and the operation finally failed because of enemy strikes against the vulnerable air-borne troops, made easier because two crack panzer divisions had moved into the area to recover from the clash in Normandy. The British and Polish formations were mauled as they clung to the furthest bridge at Arnhem, and the Allies were guillotined in what was said to have been "a bridge too far."[9]

By September 25, the battle was over, Monty's reputation was in tatters, and Eisenhower was in a fury. Anxious to recover from the setback, Eisenhower looked forlornly at Antwerp, which was still unusable because the Germans held the terrain leading to it from the sea. "If we can only get to using Antwerp," Eisenhower lamented to his mentor, Chief of Staff General George Marshall, "it will have the effect of a blood transfusion."[10] While the pugnacious Montgomery would never admit to it, he had gone all-in on the knock-out and had neglected the Canadians, who had much of the Allied victory depending on their success. However, the defeat in Market Garden could be remediated if the Allies could open the pipeline of war supplies from North America and Britain to the now stalled armies in Northwest Europe.

———

The large Belgian city of Antwerp, located 80 kilometres from the sea, was defended by the German Fifteenth Army at Walcheren Island, South Beveland peninsula, and the Breskens Pocket in the Scheldt area. All three positions had to fall before the great port city could receive merchant ships. The Canucks had come ashore on D-Day and held the beachhead with impressive defensive fighting abilities, even though the slow crawl to capture Caen and to push southward had been marred by some reversals. With the

Canadians' victories along the coast in freeing the Channel ports going largely unrecognized, Crerar's legions were now ordered to the Scheldt to engage in combat of the wettest, muddiest, and most wicked kind.

With increasingly depleted forces, the Canadians faced a monumental challenge as the October weather reduced the Dutch terrain to a sea of mud. The three interconnected battlefields were held in strength. Each of the distinct areas had to be attacked in unison by the three shot-up Canadian divisions, along with supporting British and Polish forces and an American division. General Crerar was denied his big battle because he was hospitalized in Britain with dysentery, so the task of commanding the assault—despite shortages of shells, soldiers, and artillery—fell to General Guy Simonds. Planning a multi-pronged operation, Simonds ordered the 2nd Division to drive into Walcheren Island, which lay astride the most westward entrance to the Scheldt estuary, with the 3rd Division to the south facing the flooded Breskens Pocket—an area of German resistance bounded by the Leopold Canal to the west and south and the North Sea to the northwest. The 4th Canadian Armoured Division was to attack to the east, driving northward where its mobility could be best deployed against the enemy. In the boggy fields, the defenders had all the advantages as the waterlogged farmland, riven with dykes, was held by the 14,000-strong 64th German Division. The divisional headquarters issued an order on October 7 that the defence of the Scheldt was "decisive for the further conduct of the war." If it fell to the Allies, its loss "might deliver a deathblow."[11]

The 3rd Canadian Division attacked on October 6, surging across the Leopold Canal behind a heavy artillery bombardment of 327 guns.[12] An initial Canadian foray into the 15- by 35-kilometre battlefield by several battalions of the 7th Canadian Infantry Brigade was soon stopped as the Germans threw their weight of reinforcements against the line. The Canadians went to ground in the mud. Under the shriek of shells and mortars, and in the face of repeated enemy attacks, they held on. Private Bill Hollett of the Lincoln and Welland Regiment wrote to his father on October 23 that he had spent nearly two weeks under fire, telling him, "the papers can't begin to describe it and I can't either."[13] Three days later, he was killed.

The Canadian attack sucked the Germans into the fight, drawing them away from the back door for an audacious amphibious assault by the 9th Canadian Infantry Brigade.[14] Coming ashore at the northeast edge of Breskens on October 9 in tracked amphibious troop carriers known as Buffalos, the Canadians drove into the enemy's innards. The reclaimed farmland was divided into an enormous checkerboard cut by high dykes that formed a key feature in the battlescape. "We scramble over them, or drive on top of them," wrote one Canadian infantrymen; "they are bad to fight over, but merciful to hide behind."[15] Rain reduced the fields to a sea of oozing mud. Dead animals and men added to the apocalyptic vision and the gut-wrenching stench. "Our troops are continuing their push through a never-never land," reported a CBC journalist. "It's a sombre, bizarre scene in this godforsaken part of the world."[16] This was an infantryman's war, often limited to a few hundred metres in each misty, waterlogged, and desolate direction.

Despite the diabolical conditions, the 64th Division was beaten back, its defensive pocket collapsing by mid-month.[17] While tanks were all but useless, air support proved its worth in the sodden battlefield. The Canadians were able to call in Typhoons that, with their rockets and bombs, utterly demoralized the Germans, who had no response to the dominating air power.[18] After being systematically defeated in engagements large and small, the 64th Division surrendered on November 3. The exhausted 3rd Canadian Division, which had been supported by the 52nd British Division since October 18, suffered over 2,000 casualties, including 545 killed and missing.[19] Though the strain and exhaustion weighed heavily, Captain Hal MacDonald of the North Shore (New Brunswick) Regiment wrote to his wife, "What we're fighting for is always clear in our minds."[20]

———

Antwerp had fallen to the British on September 4, but the enemy still had control of the estuary through a powerful garrison on Walcheren island, preventing any use of the port. The 2nd Canadian Division was tasked with getting onto the island to destroy the German guns. In early October, the division marched northward from Antwerp, steadily chewing its way through defenders who fought with almost fanatical intensity to block them from reaching the connecting artery to Walcheren on the eastern side of the island.[21] The effects of this raw violence could not be shrugged off or subsumed forever. Hundreds of Canadians broke down from battle stress, with one in every four non-fatal casualties in Normandy being attributed to mental fatigue and invisible injuries.[22] "It's not the physical hardships of this war that are going to leave their mark on us," wrote Lance-Bombardier Bert Field in a letter home that revealed his "sick desperation." Instead, it was "that continual battle that goes on inside each one of us."[23]

The Canadians were, however, still fighting in this campaign of concurrent battles, and when the 2nd Division finally marched its way to Walcheren's entrance, the lead units blanched in the face of a 1,200-metre-long causeway leading to the island. It was heavily guarded and any attempt to cross it would likely result in heavy casualties. But Simonds felt he had no choice but to order the 2nd Division to overcome the position. To assist them, Simonds's fertile mind had turned to the bombers. With Walcheren below sea level, if the air force dropped its high explosives on the dykes that held back the sea, the island would be flooded, thus trapping the Wehrmacht in its many strongpoints or slowing its ability to counterattack. These garrisons could be picked off one by one. A good military plan it was, although one that would salt the land for years. Dutch leaders pleaded with the general not to destroy their homeland.[24] Having studied the unpleasant situation, Simonds pushed ahead with his strategy and eventually won over the air marshals, Eisenhower, and Churchill. The extremely risky mission would, he said, save Allied soldiers' lives. On October 3, some 247 Lancasters blew apart the western dyke, which led to widespread submerging of fertile farmland. Simonds's plans were often too complex, failing to account for the friction of combat or expecting too much of those at the front end, but he was Canada's most aggressive, innovative, and ruthless general of the war.

Drawing the short match, the 2nd Division were ordered to cross the long causeway on the east side of the submerged island.[25] Fought over several days starting on October 31, the result was a terrible slaughter, although the attack drew some German reserves that waded through the flooded terrain. On the other side of the island, British commandos came ashore and snuffed out the demoralized Germans, and on November 8, the final defences fell to the Allied forces.

I British Corps, also under the command of First Canadian Army, was on the right flank, battering its way through German defences south of the Maas. In one of the few battles in Northwest Europe where Canadians and Americans fought side by side, the 4th Canadian Armoured Division was with the US 104th (Timberwolf) Division.[26] This was the American division's first action in Europe and its GIs fought bravely, even if, like most units new to combat, it took higher casualties than the British and Canadian formations next to it in the line.[27]

With the Scheldt cleared, Antwerp accepted the first convoys of merchant vessels bringing war supplies on November 28. A celebration marked the arrival of the first ship, complete with military bands, national anthems, and representatives from Eisenhower and Montgomery's headquarters. An open Antwerp would ensure the Allies' ability to keep driving the Nazis back. But even though First Canadian Army had delivered a monumental prize, no one had invited the Canucks to the ceremony.

The invisible army had suffered 6,367 Canadian casualties in the beastly conditions, and British soldiers attached to it lost an almost equal number.[28] Thousands of Germans were killed, 24,000 captured, and the mission accomplished. After long neglecting the Canadians, Montgomery finally paid the appropriate attention, lauding their long and hard fight. "It has been a fine performance," he declared, "and one that could have been carried out only by first class troops."[29] This was the Canadian Army's most consequential victory of the entire war.

———

At home, King and his cabinet were aware of the Canadian victories and the lengthening casualty lists. From early October onward, after the losses in Normandy and the clearing of the Channel ports, the staggering number of soldiers' deaths and woundings were accompanied by growing reports that the Canadian Army was running out of reinforcements for hollowed-out front-line infantry units. King panicked, railed, and demanded briefings from his chief of staff, Lieutenant-General Ken Stuart. How could there be shortages given that tens of thousands of trained soldiers were in England and Canada? In a series of cabinet discussions and in meetings with the high command, the prime minister frantically underscored earlier military promises that the huge expansion of the armed forces would never make conscription necessary. He received the equivalent of a shoulder shrug.

Minister of National Defence Colonel J.L. Ralston, who was deeply sympathetic to the fighting man, went overseas to see for himself, talking to service personnel of all ranks to determine the extent of the bloodletting and the gaps in the ranks. He returned in mid-October and told King that the reinforcement problem was worse than reported. Infantrymen had suffered three out of every four casualties in Normandy, and there were not enough trained ground-pounders in the system.[30] The army had miscalculated loss rates for units in combat, basing casualty estimates on Italy and other less intense theatres of war.[31] Now conscription was necessary, Ralston advised, imploring King to follow through on the mandate given to him by Canadians in the April 1942 plebiscite that released the government from its promise of never bringing in a draft for overseas service. King had promised "Not necessarily conscription, but conscription if necessary," but with the war seemingly all but over, King believed that conscription

Minister of National Defence J.L. Ralston meets a Canadian soldier during his trip overseas in October 1944. He returned to the Canadian cabinet and insisted that Prime Minister King enact conscription.

would tear the country apart as English Canada turned on the opposition in Quebec. "My first duty is to Canada," wrote King early in the war, and his ultimate strategy was to "keep our country united."[32] That may have been true, but it also meant that he was willing to turn his back on the desperate soldiers overseas in battle with the fascists.

As King searched for a solution to the dilemma, his unsettled mind came to believe that a military conspiracy was afoot, and one that had entangled Ralston. While the long-serving prime minister preferred coalition building, compromise, and even concessions in times of crisis, he also knew when to fight. Having negotiated fruitlessly with Ralston for two weeks, and realizing that the cabinet was on the verge of being ripped apart by mass resignations, King fired Ralston on November 1 (after coldly producing the minister's letter of resignation submitted to him in the aftermath of the plebiscite, two and a half years earlier).[33] The other cabinet ministers were shocked at Ralston's political death, although they largely toed the line. The crisis was not over, however, as the army still needed trained infantrymen.

Prime Minister King turned to General Andrew McNaughton as his new minister of national defence. The inspiring face of the Canadian Army in the first four years of the war, McNaughton tried to rally Canadians to enlist in greater numbers, appealing especially to the home-defence conscripts. But despite his fame and exhortations, the conscripts refused, and in public speeches the minister was booed and derided. Most Canadians remained committed to the war—working in home front industry, accepting shortages and rationing, and already having voluntarily enlisted by the hundreds of thousands—but forcing young men to serve against their will was too much for many, even those bent on destroying the Nazis.

However, this middle ground was fast disappearing. By the third week in November, English-Canadian Liberal members of Parliament were on the verge of revolt over King's refusal to bring in conscription. King's lengthy run as prime minister seemed to have finally come to an end. But then the consummate survivor reversed himself, ordering some 16,000 NRMA (National Resource Mobilization Act) conscript soldiers to be sent overseas, much to the astonishment of political commentators and the Progressive Conservatives, who were licking their chops at the prospect of returning to power. King did not necessarily win every political battle, but he won all the necessary ones in his long and remarkable career.

The second conscription debate was not as divisive as the plebiscite in April 1942, and while it dragged on for over a month, it did not directly single out Quebec as had been the case during the Great War, although some firebrands, muckrakers, and intemperate journalists caused damage. About 13,000 NRMA soldiers were eventually sent overseas to shore up the fighting forces, and they were drawn from communities across the country. Those who eventually served in Western Europe did so credibly, replenishing the wasted infantry regiments that had limped out of the front lines after the Scheldt victory.[34]

———

With Antwerp open, the Allies' supply nightmare was solved and the Germans now faced certain defeat. In the east, the Red Army had made a meatgrinder advance through Hitler's forces, while the Anglo-American-Canadian bombers continued to smash infrastructure in Germany and occupied Europe, severely diminishing the enemy's ability to produce weapons and move them to the shrinking fighting fronts. Even as soldiers and flak guns had been pulled back to defend the cities—with 25,000 artillery and anti-aircraft guns being situated in urban areas—they were unable to shield terrified civilians against the waves of bombers.[35] Nearly everything was reduced to rubble, including the great landmarks of centuries-old churches and universities. With food and oil in short supply over the cold winter of 1945, the Third Reich was on the verge of collapse. For the people in the ruins, who spent most nights huddled in bomb shelters praying for deliverance, the terror and trauma were overwhelming. Little sympathy was found in Britain, Russia, or North America. After the war, when the corpse counters had finished their grim work, 593,000 German civilians were tabulated as having been killed in the bombing campaign, and even more were wounded.[36] And yet, in early 1945, still the German people fought on.

A now healthy General Crerar prepared First Canadian Army for a new offensive through the Rhineland in early February 1945. The Allies had, by this time, survived Hitler's last-gasp operation known as the Battle of the Bulge. On December 16, the delusional Führer ordered a desperate armoured assault through the snow in the Ardennes Forest, hoping to split the Allies and then thrust forward to capture Antwerp. Cutting off the supplies from the port would, he believed, force a negotiated peace. The panzers were short of fuel from the start, although heavy clouds and snowfall greatly reduced the ability of Allied fighters and bombers to intervene. The Allies were surprised by the counterstrike, with the Americans additionally weakened by their own shortages of soldiers as their eighty-nine divisions had only a trickle of reinforcement reserves, but the American soldiers fought well, refusing to break. The enemy offensive was blunted rapidly, and Patton's Third Army was particularly effective in moving with haste to hammer the now overextended forces that suffered over 80,000 casualties and used up their precious resources of fuel and armour.[37] The Nazis' gamble had failed.

As the Allies prepared for a new offensive in February, they were aware of the race to liberate the oppressed before starvation wiped out the Dutch people. A cold winter added to the misery of the emaciated wraiths in the Netherlands who were plagued with food shortages and widespread malnutrition. First Canadian Army and the US Ninth Army were to spearhead a pincer movement towards the Rhine River. Their goal was to envelop the defenders in a forward zone before the Allies commenced a deeper drive into the heart of Germany. Crerar had missed most of the key campaigns in 1944 because of illness, although Montgomery, with his lingering mistrust in the Canadian's lack of command experience, also desired to keep him from leading at the front. Now Crerar had his chance. The Battle of the Rhineland in early February 1945 would follow the Anglo-Canadian approach to combat, with a firepower-heavy, frontal assault; in fact, one observer sniped humorously of the Canucks, "if 'fuck' and 'frontal' were removed from the military vocabulary, the Canadian army would have been both speechless and unable to attack."[38]

Thirteen divisions, 1,200 guns, and 3,400 tanks were under Crerar's command. With a total strength of over 470,000 troops, this was the largest formation ever commanded by a Canadian, and it included Belgian, Dutch, Polish, British, American, and Canadian units. "The Canadian Army thus becomes the most ingenious collection of nationalities since the French Foreign Legion," wrote one journalist. "Canadian troops certainly do not possess a voting majority in their own army."[39] At zero hour on the chilly morning of February 8, Canadian and British soldiers made the initial juggernaut assault. The Allies anticipated rolling over the much weaker German forces, but that plan was thwarted when the ground, which needed to be frozen to support the weight of armoured vehicles and trucks, thawed in the days before the guns barked the start of the campaign.

Behind crushing artillery support, the British and Canadian infantry and armour advanced through the porridge-like mud in

Operation Veritable, but as they had little room to manoeuvre, the outgunned and outnumbered Germans were able to maximize their firepower. While the defenders could not stop the offensive, resolute fighters made the attackers pay for every inch of ground. Enemy mortar bombardments and frantic counterattacks ran up the Allied casualties. These assaults sometimes staggered the exposed infantry and drove them back; however, the experienced Anglo-Canadian force was increasingly able to anticipate these shock tactics.[40] As one front-line Canadian remarked, "It is always easier to kill a rat out of his hole than in it."[41]

Within three days, the trench system was broken, although the double pincer movement was slow in forming up because, to the south, the US Ninth Army faced a nearly impassable lake as the Germans opened the dams over the Roer River. The American operation was delayed, allowing the enemy to shift several panzer divisions to block Crerar's army.[42] Facing a stiffening front, four British and two Canadian divisions struck on February 15, but the weather again assailed the Allies. Along parts of the front, highly motivated paratroopers defended effectively, fighting with desperation, ferocity, and what one Canadian described as "fanatical resistance."[43]

When the Americans finally launched their offensive on February 21, they encountered a much-weakened German force. As in Normandy, the Canadians and British had drawn some of the best enemy divisions against themselves, paving the way for the Americans to cross the Roer on February 23 and then break out two days later as they galloped to the Rhine. This deep progress, in turn, forced the enemy to pull back on the Anglo-Canadian sector. Never did the Allies fight in isolation on this front. The land

*The Canadian cartoonist Bing, who created the much-loved Herbie
character, depicts the friendly rivalry between US and Canadian soldiers.
The American MPs (military police) are dismayed that the Canadians
have stolen the tires off their jeep, as indicated by the "Merci beaucoup"
sign in the windshield. The tag-line "This Hands-Across-the-Border
Stuff Can Go Too Far!" is also a joke about the easy exchange of trade
goods in North America with the wartime erasure of the border.*

forces supported one another, and air power made life miserable for the retreating Germans.

———

The Canadians continued to serve in the drive on Germany, but their part in the Rhineland battle largely ended on March 10. They had lost 379 officers and 4,925 other ranks in about four weeks, and Eisenhower was to write to Crerar about the Canadians' success that "speaks volumes for your skill and the valor of your soldiers, that you carried it through to a successful conclusion."[44] Though victorious, the assault was also bloody, and it gutted many units. Since September, General Crerar had been seeking to reunite the two Canadian corps so that they could better use resources and be a larger, more identifiable force in the Allied battles in Northwestern Europe.[45] While Crerar's existing army already had many more international soldiers than Canadians, the arrival of I Canadian Corps from Italy in early April finally reunited most of the land forces in First Canadian Army. The Canadians never fought separately from the British, but Crerar's army would lead in the final liberation of the Dutch people, an act for which they would be recognized as independent of the British and Americans.

After more than four years of occupation, the 4.5 million Dutch who had not been liberated in October were suffering terribly. The German occupiers had robbed the country blind, stealing two thirds of all cars and buses, dismantling factories to ship them away, and weaponizing food to starve the population into submission.[46] The Gestapo and the Dutch internal police, filled with quislings and collaborators, hunted members of the resistance, torturing and murdering those they caught. Some 120,000 Dutch

Canadians liberating the Dutch in 1945.

Jews had been rounded up for the death camps, and a quarter million Dutch men were conscripted to work as slave labour.[47] Occupation under the fascists was a time of unending misery, degradation, and terror.

"I saw a tank in the distance, with one soldier's head above it, and the blood drained out of my body, and I thought: 'Here comes liberation.'"[48] So wrote a Dutch civilian from The Hague, recalling the arrival of the Canadians in April 1945. Cries were mixed with cheers in a guttural release that attested to their salvation.

As the weather warmed, the Canadian liberators brought food, colour, and life while the Nazi regime thrashed about in its final death throes. And yet diehards continued to resist. First Canadian Army's battle losses from March 12 to the end of the war numbered 5,515 Canadian and 533 British casualties.[49]

The Canadians and British also overran Bergen-Belsen, a German concentration camp in Lower Saxony, where the stench and sight of more than 13,000 decomposing corpses in mass, open graves assaulted the senses. Allied soldiers encountered other death camps in which the Nazi regime had carried out the Final Solution of genocide against Jews and those branded as undesirables. Corporal Roy Lane, who served in two armoured regiments, was rocked by Belsen, noting, "This is why we were there: to put an end to Hitler's evil agenda of exterminating Jews, uncooperative Germans, Europeans and others of unpopular racial origins."[50] For the Allies who had lost so much since D-Day, these unimaginable sights were a sign that their struggle had been a just one.

———

The Canadians did not win the war on their own, although they were a small if undeniably valuable part of the Allied ground forces. By the time they served in the Scheldt offensive, Crerar's army was fighting at a high level of combat effectiveness. Despite Montgomery's misgivings of Crerar, the Canadian general had performed well, though the battles he commanded were largely safe ones that relied on the Allied advantage in firepower. The final campaigns in 1945, where Canadians, British, and Americans served together, revealed how far the North Americans had come in just five years—from focusing on hemispheric defence to taking the war to the Nazis in their homeland. Often the Dominion's contribution was lost amid the larger Anglo-American efforts, or was simply lumped in with them, but the soldiers who were there, serving shoulder to shoulder, came to recognize the Canadian role in the defeat of the Nazis.

Dave McIntosh flew as a navigator with the RCAF's No. 418 Squadron. The Canadian spent time with other Allied airmen in the mess, drinking, singing, and telling stories, before heading out into the darkness in search of enemy aircraft. Among his international comrades in arms, he was frequently mistaken for being British or American. However, after one conversation with a fellow airman, lubricated with ample beverages, it dawned on the Yank that McIntosh and his fellow Canuck airmen were different. "Why you bastards," he said, "you're not American at all."[51]

CHAPTER 22

WAR AGAINST JAPAN

"The Canadian commitment must be determined in the light of such factors, amongst others, as Canada's place as a Pacific nation, her membership in the Commonwealth, and her close friendship and common interest with the United States, as well as her interest in completing the destruction of the Axis by the overthrow of Japan."[1] This February 1944 memorandum revealed the cabinet's struggle to determine the country's commitment to the Pacific war. Even before the D-Day landings, Britain had pressured Canada to support its soldiers in battle in Southeast Asia, as London was anxious to regain lost colonies to restore the empire. King had been compliant in matters of grand strategy, but he refused to be coerced into standing with Britain in this far-flung fight. The veteran politician always did best by biding his time before he found an issue over which to strike. Such an issue had come in late January 1944, when Lord Halifax, the tall, aloof, and cadaverous British ambassador to the United States, spoke in Toronto about a united Imperial foreign policy. Churchill had shipped Halifax off to the US after he had advocated for peace with Hitler in May 1940, and now the aged ambassador enthused about the how the dominions and Britain would be stronger if they presented a united front against the influence of Russia, China, and the United States.

King spent much of the war seeking a middle ground between imperialists and nationalists within his country, and between supporting Britain and giving the US what was necessary to make that happen. He would not be pushed into linking Canada's foreign policy to Britain's. This was the third rail for King, something he had fought against for over two decades in politics. And so the Canadian saw Halifax's public speech, which had not been shared in advance with his government, as a conspiratorial attack on what King called "national sovereignty."[2] Furthermore, after Halifax's words galvanized many imperially minded Canadians to demand additional aid for Britain—a key aim of the Progressive Conservative Party—King considered declaring an election over the issue. He came to his senses, however, realizing that, with the war in Europe still undecided, dropping the writ would be a disruptive commotion for the electorate, although he paid close attention to his government's formal response to London in early February. In that document, the cabinet reinforced Canada's right to choose its military commitments. The country's strategy in the Pacific would be to fight against Japan as it had been engaged in that war since the battle at Hong Kong, but to refuse to stand by the British in reclaiming its former colonies. The response was also guided by Canada's "close friendship and common interest with the United States."[3] King twisted the blade, refusing to be pushed by the Imperials into a renewed London-led strategy.

———

Having been excluded by the British and the Americans from setting Allied grand strategy in the war against the European fascists, even as Canada's military forces fought on the oceans, in the air, and in multiple land campaigns, King and his cabinet sought more control over the Dominion's role, contribution, and influence in the war against Japan. Canada's leadership was also aware that the country's impact would be small in scale and of little consequence in the final victory. Since 1942, the Americans had methodically advanced in the Pacific, and the Japanese threat to North America had long since been eliminated. In a sign of desperation, they had floated thousands of incendiary balloons across the ocean with the goal of causing forest fires in the western hemisphere. These Fu-Go 10-metre-diameter hydrogen balloons were next to useless, although the 9,300 intercontinental weapons had caused some concern among military planners when it was thought they might be armed with biological agents.[4] They never were, and the high-altitude balloons caused neither significant fear nor fires. In contrast, at this stage in the war, the American bombers that were smashing and burning Japanese cities needed little help from the British or the Canadians to drive Japan to its knees. Bombers versus balloons was a stark indication of the imbalance in the war in the Pacific.

Before the manpower crisis that led to conscription was fully revealed in October 1944, King and his ministers had been convinced by the Canadian military high command to commit a moderate force to the Pacific. The generals offered an overstrength infantry division of 25,000 soldiers, aware that anything larger would likely spook the cabinet. To prepare for fighting the Japanese, the army was aided by several dozen officers who acted as "observers" in the Pacific campaign. Attached to American, British, and New Zealand forces as of February 1944, they were to study and acclimatize to the new style of fighting and then bring those lessons to units training for battle.[5] The minister of national defence,

A.G.L. McNaughton, observed that a motivating factor for equip-
ping the division with American weapons was that the "obvious
necessity for the future to co-ordinate the defence of North
America."[6] The RCAF and the RCN initially had far more ambitious goals for their units in the Pacific, because the air war with
Germany had been decisively won and the RCN's senior brass
wanted a more glamorous role than North Atlantic convoy duty
to better situate itself in the postwar period as a naval power.[7] The
military commanders were backed by the Department of External Affairs, which urged that Canada should commit military
resources to the Pacific; standing with the United States, it was
hoped, would give the country greater influence when the powerful Americans remade the postwar world.

King's perspective on Canada's relationship with Britain might
have been expressed as "cooperation when necessary, but not
necessarily cooperation all the time." And yet the prime minister
was much more accommodating with the Americans. He strained
against London in seeking his country's independence; however,
he had a much more difficult time with the Americans. It might
be said that this was all new for Canada, and it often required that
King screw his courage to the sticking place to occasionally say
no to the White House. Normally wary of committing armed forces
to further battle, King nonetheless accepted the military and diplomatic advice that the three Canadian services should be present
in the final clash with Japan. However, as the war in Europe lurched
towards victory, the cabinet cut back the RCAF and RCN forces
and limited action to the northern Pacific, refusing to let Canadians serve with the British in Southeast Asia. Believing, among
other things, that the fighting in that theatre was too close to what
he called "Imperial wars," King feared the public perception of

Canada as assisting Britain in reclaiming its empire.[8] While he was a great supporter of the British connection to Canada, he also confided to his diary, "Instinctively I revolt at anyone from the Old Country exercising even outwardly any semblance of control over Canada."[9]

The US did not need the help of Canada or Britain in the final assault against Japan, but it agreed to take on their forces for the sake of the established alliance. American planning moved ahead. The invasion would be awful. Strategists worried that any strike on the enemy homeland would be through and over the bodies of Japanese civilians conscripted to fight to the death. The Americans did not relish the thought of sending in the Marines and infantrymen to machine-gun and bayonet their way forward through a sea of women and children armed with sharpened sticks and rudimentary bombs. As the Japanese had a long history of refusing to surrender, it was predicted that hundreds of thousands of American soldiers would be killed or wounded. But far more Japanese would be slaughtered. The hope was that a new superweapon might prevent the need for the invasion, a prolonged bombing campaign, or the cordoning off of the waters by US submarines, leading to the slow starvation of the Japanese people.

———

"In event of any serious difficulty the Canadians will side with the US," said Secretary of War Henry Stimson in a December 30, 1944, briefing to President Roosevelt.[10] Stimson was referring to the ongoing strife between British and American authorities over the production of an atomic bomb. Britain and the US had an opportunity to act together early in the war by sharing the enormously complex scientific work of creating an atomic weapon, but the British had spurned the Yanks. By the summer of 1942, the Americans were going it alone, creating a massive program of soldiers and scientists known as the Manhattan Project, with Canada having a small part to play in the weaponization of the atom.

"This war is one of brains and scientific ingenuity rather than one of man power, mass infantry and massacre," wrote Frederick Banting, the decorated Great War doctor and the co-discoverer of insulin therapy, a treatment that saved millions of diabetics from a wasting death.[11] Banting believed in the power of science to defeat the fascists, and research and innovation indeed played a key role in the war, although it went hand-in-hand with the fighting forces that would have to get mud on their boots and blood on their bayonets. As one of the world's greatest medical innovators, Banting could be forgiven for his belief that science would end the war, and in that pursuit he devoted much energy to the development of biological weapons before his death in an air crash on February 21, 1941. He was also well aware that in the field of atomic research, several scientific breakthroughs had been made in the late nineteenth century, with the discovery of radioactivity, the electron, and radium. Scientists soon after developed theories of splitting the atom to unleash awesome energy, even as science fiction writers mused about the breathtaking potential. Weaponizing the atom would, as British physicist Frederick Soddy noted in 1904, provide the means to "destroy the earth."[12]

Canada's natural and mineral resources had contributed to Allied victory, with the country's aluminum, nickel, lead, and steel being transformed into the weapons that fought the fascists. Early in the conflict, and with much secrecy, Howe's Department of Munitions and Supply had secured majority control over Eldorado

Gold Mines Limited. The mines at Great Bear Lake in Canada's North West Territory produced many things, although it was not gold that the government needed, but uranium.[13] Only two countries within the Allied sphere of influence produced uranium—Congo and Canada—and this natural resource once again allowed Canada to strengthen its influence with the United States.

The National Research Council (NRC) encouraged and conducted state-funded science in Canada, and the agency's director, Chalmers Jack (C.J.) Mackenzie, was a great proponent of the atomic program. Mackenzie ensured suitable funding for nuclear physicist George Laurence, a leader in the field who almost succeeded in forging the first human-made nuclear chain reaction. The British took note, and in 1942 they moved their research and development program, code-named "Tube Alloys," to Canada to avoid bombing attacks, to be closer to resources, and to effect a partnership with the Americans. The program's relocation to the Montreal laboratory created an Anglo-Canadian centre of some of the countries' best minds, even though they failed to convince the US to share information. As the Americans surged ahead with the Manhattan Project, there was a dawning understanding that the country that controlled the atom bomb might rule the world.[14]

"It is an opportunity Canada as a nation cannot afford to turn down," declared Mackenzie, advising the cabinet to continue to assist the Manhattan Project.[15] He hoped that Canada's supply of uranium, which was crucial to the future atomic bombs, would secure some advantage for the country. While the US was concerned about its supply of the critical mineral, it was not going to share any of its decision making about the development of the atomic bomb or its use in the war. The gruff and determined

General Leslie Groves, who was charged with creating the staggeringly intricate infrastructure for the atomic program (and who had previously overseen the construction of the Pentagon), came to Canada to ensure that the US's ally to the north was indeed unwavering. Groves was the type of man to kick down a door before he knocked. Sweeping into Ottawa, the general met with Howe and was instantly impressed by the minister's spartan office and his no-nonsense style that matched his own.[16] That Howe had been born in the US and graduated from MIT also calmed Groves. He left without having to resort to measures such as demanding that the president intervene or, as urged by some aides, forcing the Canadians to yield all their uranium supplies through pressure or threats.

The Canadians again stood by their allies, and it was their uranium that was weaponized in the atomic bombs used against the Japanese in 1945. Canada's atomic work in 1944 would take place at Chalk River, the Ontario site where scientists built a nuclear reactor that generated plutonium from uranium. The country's sale of almost all its nuclear material to the US infuriated the British, who thought the Canadians should have sold only to them.[17] While Ottawa was to be disappointed as the Manhattan Project was too big and too shrouded in secrecy to allow the Canadians to exert any real influence, King's government would parlay its control of rare minerals and top-notch government-funded scientists to secure postwar inclusion in atomic control committees. This was not a terribly disappointing result for Ottawa, as no one there had expected that the Americans would open the door to the atomic program, and it ensured that Canada would be a part of the postwar atomic discussions.

Never able to become a substantial partner in the Manhattan Project, King and his cabinet often felt stuck in the middle between its irate British and American allies, even as the country was acknowledged as important for its supply of uranium. This was a natural resource that Canada had in abundance, and its exploitation during the war left the country well positioned in the Cold War to use its hydro-electricity, rare minerals, and oil fields to enrich the country and prove its worth in the alliance with the United States.[18] During the war, however, it was American scientists and soldiers who would succeed in the revolutionary breakthrough that utterly changed the path of history. The atom bomb was a weapon, King understood after one briefing, that "could mean the destruction of civilization."[19]

———

As the Americans were closing in on the Japanese home islands, one RCN cruiser, HMCS *Uganda*, was serving in the Pacific. *Uganda* was one of the most up-to-date warships in the Canadian navy. A Fiji-class light cruiser displacing over 8,000 tons and 169 metres long, it was equipped with modern fire control arrangements and with heavy guns to pound enemy ships or shore positions. In mid-April 1945, *Uganda* took part in the massed assault against airfields on Kyushu and a group of islands between Okinawa and Formosa, called Sakishima Gunto. As part of the 4th Cruiser Squadron of the British Pacific Force, which included four carriers, the Canadians were tasked with protecting the carriers from Japanese air attack. The Japanese air force often resorted to kamikaze attacks in which pilots crashed their planes armed with high explosive bombs into the Allied warships below. *Uganda*'s

HMCS Uganda *in the Pacific.*

anti-aircraft guns peppered the skies as both the British and the Canadians adapted to this new way of fighting.[20] A month later, on May 13, *Uganda* directly bombarded Sukama airstrip to deny the airfield to the Japanese as part of the larger campaign for Okinawa.

Even as Japan was in the throes of total defeat, its forces continued to fight onward, with cultural norms demanding a struggle to the death to ensure honour. Canada's 6th Canadian Division was raised for the coming ground war in the Pacific. Under the command of Major-General Bert Hoffmeister, a veteran of Italy and Northwest Europe, the infantry were kitted with American equipment except for their uniforms. The experienced Hoffmeister instigated new intensive training, advocated for a distinct badge to foster a unique identity, and even met with Army Chief of Staff George Marshall. Despite this preparation, the division never had a chance to serve in the Pacific because the war ended before its deployment.[21] How the Canadians and Americans engaged in joint land warfare operations would have added a new saga to the story of North American relations.

HMCS *Uganda* continued to fight, although its service would be marred by a perplexing incident among its crew. With the Canadian government insisting that all service personnel in the Pacific be volunteers, *Uganda*'s officers were forced to ask the ship to vote on whether or not to continue service. Perhaps not surprisingly, the crew, unhappy with the heat, strain, and danger, voted to go home. While one wonders how many Allied soldiers, sailors, and airmen would likely have followed suit had they been given the same choice, this unconventional process of voting was incomprehensible to the British and Americans experiencing similar hardship. *Uganda*'s officers were horrified and pleaded with the crew to reverse their decision, but the sailors were having none of it. At the end of July, Canada's cruiser slunk away, its officers deeply humiliated and the warship's good work blotted out as the RCN was excluded from the Allied fleet that steamed to Tokyo at the war's end.

Other Canadians served in the Pacific, especially with British forces, even though they were little acknowledged by either contemporaries or historians. At least 400 Canadians were part of No. 1 Special Wireless Group of the Royal Canadian Corps of Signals, a vanguard unit in Australia that was monitoring Japanese intelligence. There were also about 150 Chinese Canadians serving as part of Force 136, a branch of the British Special Operations Executive that fought behind Japanese lines, sabotaging vulnerable positions and assisting the British and Chinese. Above the vast and mixed terrains in which the land forces clashed in battle, the RCAF's 435 and 436 Squadrons flew in Burma, dropping supplies,

A Douglas Dakota from 435 Squadron, RCAF, which supplied
British forces in Burma and on other fronts in Southeast Asia.

coping with wretchedly unpredictable weather that included mon-
soons, and always dealing with the threat of Japanese fighters and
anti-aircraft fire. Atholl Sutherland Brown, an RCAF pilot in the
Burma theatre, spoke for many of his comrades, both in the air
and on the ground, when he wrote that "their efforts and sacrifices
were unrecognized and largely forgotten in the panorama of the
war."[22] Including C Force's troops in Hong Kong, about 10,000
Canadians served in national units in the Pacific.

In the total war that demanded a balancing of resource allocation and military commitments, Canada focused on nearly every
front except the Pacific. Even there, however, it provided, or planned
to provide, some naval, air, and land forces to stand by its allies.

In the higher Canadian strategic direction of the war, King's cabinet's aim was to refuse to submit to the British desire for Canada to join in the fight for its empire, and instead to stride forward with the Americans in the final battle against Japan. This was a sign of how far Canada had come during the course of the war in becoming a North American nation.

———

President Roosevelt did not live to the see the victory that he had orchestrated. Sickly from congenital heart failure, the president had given his all—and the war had taken it. Roosevelt's death on April 12, 1945, at age sixty-three was nonetheless a shock to those nations unified in the war against the fascists, even as it was not surprising to those who had worked intimately with him, especially after the exertions of his unprecedented successful campaign for a fourth term as president in 1944. The president's normally sharp powers of observation were dulled, he trembled, and he had trouble following conversations. But Roosevelt had embodied the American war effort and had inspired countless millions with his talk of inalienable freedoms and liberation from oppression. Some despaired that his death would be a hobbling blow to the Allied crusade, even though journalists and politicians were at pains to note that the worldwide war effort was powered by much more than one great leader. "His spirit lives in the people he served," wrote Toronto's *Globe and Mail*. "The war will proceed to victory and the way will open to lasting peace."[23]

The by now deranged and drug-addled Hitler, hiding deep in his bunker under Berlin's Reich Chancellery as the Soviets closed in on the outskirts of the demolished city, believed that he was divinely protected. Roosevelt's death appeared to be the first of many Allied reversals that would allow his Nazi regime to survive and then turn the tide against the Allies with the introduction of wonder weapons like the jet fighter. It was a chimera. Only days later, the Red Army was advancing through rubble-filled Berlin in relentless combat, and within two weeks of Roosevelt's death, Hitler fired a bullet into his brain. The Nazi Thousand Year Reich had collapsed after just thirteen years. On the Italian front, as German forces surrendered, the lesser fascist Mussolini was summarily executed on April 28, 1945: in open contempt, Italian partisans hung the once proud dictator by his feet. They well understood that the war Mussolini had waged and the misery he had brought to the Italian people deserved nothing less than summary death.

Canadians lamented Roosevelt's passing from the world stage. The president had been much loved in the Dominion, with many having taken to seeing him as the leader of the North American war effort. After attending Roosevelt's funeral at Hyde Park, King had reflected upon their relationship as he returned to his lonely home that was rarely enlivened by laughter or the comfort of friends. He experienced the weight of Roosevelt's death, and he "knelt down and thanked God for the great friend he had given me in the President."[24] King might have thought then about a chummy note from Roosevelt in November 1941, when the president hoped his friend also felt "that it is a grand and glorious thing for Canada and the United States to have the team of Mackenzie and Roosevelt at the helm at times like these." While the president allowed that "probably both nations could get along without us," their personal friendship had "brought some proven benefits for both nations."[25] That was an understatement: two different leaders, whose agendas were not so harmonious and who were instead at each other's throats, would have shaped a much more fragmented and ineffective North American war effort.

King had lost many close advisers and friends in his life, but he continued to soldier on, even though he barely knew the new president, Harry Truman. Neither did anyone else outside the United States. Thrust into the Oval Office, the sixty-one-year-old vice president from Missouri was unprepared for the monumental task. Roosevelt had included him in almost no discussions about higher strategy, so he was immediately briefed on war plans and the Manhattan Project. "I feel like I have been struck by a bolt of lightning," said the new president.[26] Sickened by the weighty responsibility in front of him, Truman surprised many as he rose out of the vice-presidential shadows to guide the country firmly forward.

Japan should have long since given up, but Roosevelt's demand for unconditional surrender was too much to accept as the act of laying down arms might endanger their godlike emperor. The Japanese resolved to fight onward, even as bomber attacks burned their cities to the ground, US submarines choked the island of incoming resources by sinking merchant ships, and the vast naval armada carrying invading soldiers closed in on their protective outer islands. Many months and possibly years of brutal fighting were predicted by American staff officers. It would be a horror show. But Truman's advisers also briefed him that the US had a new miracle weapon that harnessed the power of the atom, an advance that might force the enemy's surrender and prevent a long, drawn-out slaughter of American soldiers and Japanese civilians. The president learned that the Manhattan Project had grown to employ more than 150,000 people and had cost more than $2 billion. The astonishingly complicated nature of the scientific work had been matched by an enormity of resources and American inventive drive. Everything about the weapon remained experimental. Before the first test explosion, scientists were not sure what to expect. Some even worried that splitting the atom might ignite the planet's atmosphere and end life on earth. But work proceeded. Two bombs—Little Boy and Fat Man—were prepared for use against Japan, to be dropped by modified B-29 Superfortress bombers.

———

"I wish we were fighting against Germans," remarked one marine on Guadalcanal after the ruthless victory over Japan was finally secured on February 9, 1943. "They are human beings, like us. . . . But the Japanese are like animals."[27] The racially charged war in the Pacific led to the perpetration of unimaginable cruelty and war crimes by both sides. After the half year of defeats following Pearl Harbor, American forces had steadily advanced on the Japanese homeland, moving closer in a series of "island-hopping" campaigns. Since 1944, however, American warships and submarines had slowly been strangling Japan of oil and essential raw materials, and in November 1944, B-29 bombers based in the Marianas began their attack on the Japanese home islands. The cities of predominately wooden structures were more susceptible to fire-bombing than European ones, and soon the urban areas were blackened with ash.[28] The capture of Iwo Jima in March 1945, at the loss of 27,000 American casualties, furnished the Allies with airfields, allowing for more fighter escorts of the bombers and eroding what was left of the gutted Japanese defences. On June 21, 1945, Okinawa fell to the Americans after three months of intense combat that cost another 12,000 Americans killed, although over 200,000 Japanese soldiers and civilians were either killed or committed mass suicide. Those grim statistics were a foreboding of the Japanese willingness to fight to the death or end their own lives to escape the humiliation of capture.[29]

In the hope of forcing the Japanese to surrender, atomic bombs were let loose on Hiroshima on August 6 and on Nagasaki on the 9th, shocking the world and finally convincing Japanese emperor Hirohito that it was futile to fight onward. The apocalyptic mushroom-shaped fireball of dust and debris erupted upwards with the bomb's detonations, following a flash of light brighter than the sun. At least 80,000 people were killed instantly in Hiroshima and perhaps 40,000 in Nagasaki, with tens of thousands of others left to die in agony from radiation sickness and ghastly burns. To put these numbers in perspective, while the atomic bombs were a new depravity in a war that had unleashed an unending stream of nightmares, it is believed that at least 333,000 Japanese people died in conventional bombing attacks, including about 100,000 on March 9 and 10, 1945, in a firestorm in Tokyo that consumed entire neighbourhoods.[30]

Keeping his promise to the Western Allies, Stalin had declared war on Japan on August 8, three months after the triumph in Europe. This ended any remaining Japanese hope of a negotiated end to the conflict. Japan's unconditional surrender came into effect on August 15, 1945, with American, British, Canadian, and other Allied representatives meeting on USS *Missouri* to sign the formal surrender document on September 2. The United States and its city-destroying atomic bombs had revealed to the world— and especially the Soviet Union—that the US would stride forward into the uncertain postwar years as the dominant global economic and military power.

The Allied prisoners of war who suffered in the fetid Japanese camps wept with joy at the use of the atomic bombs that saved their lives. These emaciated and sick men had been pushed close to death by prolonged mistreatment, malnutrition, and beatings from their cruel Japanese overlords. Even as the Americans were closing in on the home islands, the guards taunted the prisoners, threatening that, when the invasion came, they would never live to see freedom. All would be executed.

"I have literally grown up in a prison camp," wrote Kenneth Cambon, a young rifleman who had enlisted at age eighteen in the Royal Rifles of Canada and was captured at Christmas 1941 with the fall of Hong Kong. "Most of all my experience has been on the more unpleasant side of life . . . starvation, sickness, cruelty, robbery, torture, depravity . . . all overshadowed by death."[31] Riven by disease and aged beyond their years by violence, physical hardship, and wilful neglect, most of the prisoners were also scarred by permanent disabilities and fading eyesight as a result of the systematic starvation. Invisible trauma plagued all of them too. Percy Wilmot had been wounded in the Battle of Hong Kong, and then suffered terrible damage to his health in the camps. The Americans who liberated him and so many others treated their starving and abused comrades with great sympathy. Food and care were offered in liberal doses. Wilmot wrote to his son, "the Americans are very good to us . . . and I shall never forget their kindness."[32]

———

Canada played only a bit part in the American war in the Pacific. Yet this theatre of combat allowed the Dominion to exert greater autonomy over its military forces while at the same time more closely aligning itself with the United States. The Americans did not need Canadian or British support in the endgame with Japan, but Canada chose to stand in measured ways by its North American partner, both to serve as a good ally and to position itself in the uncertain postwar world. The twisted fascist ideologies had been destroyed, with Italy falling first, the Nazis holding out until May 1945, and the Japanese succumbing under the atomic clouds in August of that year. But even as fascism was utterly defeated, Soviet-style totalitarianism communism was on the rise, and it would soon divide the world. The war's legacies lived on and would inform the new world that emerged out of the destruction of the old.

CHAPTER 23

THE LEGACIES OF WAR

"In the years to come, this monument shall stand as a symbol of that friendship which has been sealed by the blood of our heroic sons." So declared the US secretary of war, Dwight F. Davis, at the raising of a memorial in Arlington National Cemetery on November 11, 1927. That stone marker honoured Americans serving in the Canadian Expeditionary Force during the Great War, at least 35,612 of whom, though having been born in the US, were counted as having donned the King's uniform. Another 20,000 likely served who were not calculated in the survey.[1] After the Second World War, Canada ensured that the fallen among the 30,000 Americans serving with Canadian forces were also commemorated by the memorial, signalling a continuum of respect and bearing witness to the collective sacrifice of the two nations.[2] Records showed that the Canadian Army had 18,848 American citizens who marched with it; another 9,000 American volunteers were in the RCAF, most of them in Bomber Command. At least 797 American airmen were fatalities and 107 Americans died while serving in the army. These slain Americans had all attested that they were "born in the USA," and more certainly enlisted who, in an attempt to slip through the barrier of neutrality laws, did not identify themselves by their country of birth.[3]

*The Cross of Sacrifice at Arlington cemetery honours fallen
Americans who served in the Canadian armed forces.*

There are no known statistics for the number of Canadians
who served in the US armed forces, but one of the many was
Sergeant Charles A. MacGillivary. Born in Charlottetown, Prince
Edward Island, MacGillivary served with the US 71st Infantry
Regiment of the 44th Division and was fighting on New Year's
Day 1945 when he advanced on a German machine gun.[4] The
twenty-seven-year-old knocked it out and, later in the day, took
part in destroying three more machine-gun positions before he
was wounded in battle—with his left arm torn off by small-arms
fire. "Through his indomitable fighting spirit, great initiative,
and utter disregard for personal safety," noted his citation for
the Medal of Honor, he had led his men in a great trial of combat.
MacGillivary received the highest American award at the White
House in the fall of 1945. These comrades in arms—Americans

in the Canadian forces and Canadians in the American forces—were but one of many living legacies that emerged from the close relationship between the North Americans in the crucible of the Second World War.

———

Canada and the United States had been good allies: united in the defence of democracy, they had been willing to serve together in the fight against the Axis powers. Proven time and time again to be reliable in a period of unremitting strain, the Canadians controlled their fears against being assimilated by the US, while contributing more than Washington believed possible. From Prime Minister King on down, the Canadians pushed only lightly against the Americans, save for a few issues on which they reacted with vigour. Except during a few desperate moments in the naval war, the country's military autonomy was faithfully maintained at the operational level. So, too, was Canadian sovereignty vigilantly upheld; although even in these touchy areas, the Canadians were able to bend and compromise, especially in joint defence projects that required the Americans to be stationed in the North.

While the United States' colossal wartime contributions to victory have never been in doubt, Canada's have been largely ignored by most international historians. And yet by safeguarding North America together, the cooperative nations created a secure base of operation that allowed for war-winning industrial mobilization and financial support to be funnelled into the hard-fought struggle. As the long war of attrition progressed, the US and Britain came to recognize Canada's industrial might. By 1945, Canada had status as the world's fourth leading industrial power, and its economic strength made it one of the greatest creditor nations, second only to the US. Canada was not another country at Washington's trough; it was invited inside the house to eat with the American family. Why? Because the Americans needed the Canadians. First, to cooperate in defending North America. Second, to collaborate in maximizing wartime industrial production. Third, once the continent was protected and weapons were shipped to allies like Britain and the Soviet Union, to unite in sending North American fighting formations into the many campaigns against the Axis powers. Though it is important not to overemphasize the impact of Canada's armed forces, they were active in multiple theatres, and by war's end the country had the world's fourth largest navy, a hard-hitting army, and a robust air force.

Fascism was defeated, but it came at a terrible cost. Six million Jews were annihilated in the Holocaust, and an estimated 60 million people were killed during the war. The Soviet Union bore the worst losses, with the German armed forces killing massive numbers of soldiers and civilians. At least 27 million Soviets died in the struggle, and Germany lost 6.9 million dead. Most of the Soviet dead were civilians, caught in the maw of war and deliberately targeted in wicked acts; most of the German dead were combatants, despite the sustained bombing campaign against the cities. Those countries that were turned into battlefields saw the greatest losses to civilians—desperate victims who had nowhere to run as the clashing armies and pitiless bombs rained down. Fifteen million Chinese are thought to have been killed by the Japanese—through direct assault, famine, or disease—in their relentless war on occupied soil.[5] The aggressive Axis powers of Italy and Japan, which wreaked ruin on so many, suffered fewer losses than many of their victims: some 500,000 Italians were slain, and the Japanese lost an estimated 2 million. The United States and Britain had 418,500 and 449,000 killed, almost all of them military personnel, although 60,000 British people died in bomber and rocket attacks.[6] That a major land war was not fought on British or North American soil saved infrastructure and lives, while also allowing for the full application of people and industry in prosecuting the war beyond British, American, or Canadian borders.

Of the almost 1.1 million Canadians in uniform, 45,000 were killed and 55,000 wounded.[7] Those who served understood the cost in this war of necessity. Chaplain Laurence Wilmot wrote of the weary and battered Canadian soldiers in Italy discussing after one battle the need to "deliver humanity from the Nazi scourge."[8] In the fight against evil, any price had to be borne by this generation to achieve victory. As Canada was a country of only 11.5 million, its 45,000 dead marked a heavier loss, per capita, than that suffered by the US, where the citizenry were 131 million and the war dead 418,500. While it is crude to make such comparisons, and every death diminished these two nations, it is simply important to note that Canada's service on multiple fronts and in the defence of North America came at a heavy price for the large country with its small population.

——

On the day Canada declared war on Nazi Germany, the country's premier public servant under King, O.D. Skelton, had observed that many unpredictable legacies would arise from unintended consequences: "What social revolutions, what changes of boundaries, what new alignments of powers, what new dictators, what new memories of hate and hopes of revenge, who can say?"[9] Skelton did not live to see the world remade or to witness Canada move with and respond to these monumental shifts in geopolitics or across society. The Canadian economy had been supercharged by the crisis, propelling it out of the mire of the Depression. Food, minerals, and munitions had been the sinews of the country's war effort, with hydro-electric power, aluminium, and wheat becoming especially important to the US. As the fourth largest Allied producer, Canada manufactured $9 billion worth of material, although its economy was deeply linked to that of the US.[10] The great worry among Canadians as victory loomed was that the country would slip back into economic hardship.[11] In all aspects of Canadian lives, the state had intervened in the name of winning the war. Now, urged on by its expanded and influential civil service, it would guide the transition towards peace.

The treatment of Canadian veterans would be crucial in this passage towards prosperity. Government departments and programs were established to assist those moving to "civvy street," with the Veterans Charter in Canada, like the GI Bill in the US, offering loans, training, and educational opportunities for ex-service personnel to start families, buy houses, and open businesses. In Canada, some 54,000 veterans went to university in the first five years after coming home, and almost double that number were retrained for new occupations.[12] Many were hired in the civil service, which swelled from 46,000 public employees in 1939 to 115,000 in 1945.[13]

The Canadian population grew from 11.3 million in 1939 to over 12 million in 1945, and there was also a boom of babies in the decade after the war, with 1 million born between 1945 and 1947, and more to follow.[14] The new baby bonus subsidy from

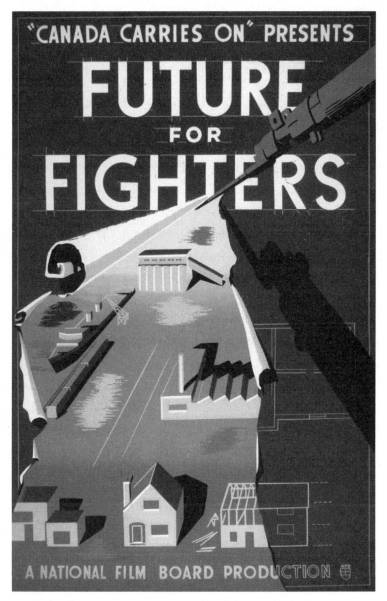

A National Film Board production, Future for Fighters, *which explores the postwar integration of veterans into Canadian society.*

the federal government provided a sliding scale of around $7 per child, per month, which was a substantial sum that raised many out of poverty. This progressive act was followed by other social security programs intended to aid Canadians, it was said, from the cradle to the grave. King, the cabinet, and his civil servants had led the country through the war years; they were even more successful, innovative, and daring in the war's aftermath.

A frenzy of wartime production had resulted in new factories, learned expertise, the greater harnessing of electricity, and the creation of more efficient road and rail lines. Dozens of new air-fields established by the British Commonwealth Air Training Plan—as well as the thousands of trained pilots, mechanics, and air traffic controllers—would form the infrastructure for a postwar air connectedness. With the transition from war to peace, industry switched to manufacturing civilian goods, again aided by the state in the form of tax incentives and other types of assistance that enabled the switch from guns and munitions to household goods and commercial commodities. New and expanded war industries that produced steel, synthetic rubber, aluminum, and hydro-electricity would now power civilian economies. Many factories shifted from armoured vehicles to stylish cars, with sales of civilian vehicles exploding in the immediate postwar years. All the while, the wartime industrial process continued to be integrated with the US, supplying everything needed by cash-flush Canadians who were building new homes and lives in the suburbs.[15]

———

"Canada has emerged in every sense of the word into a world power," crowed Prime Minister King in a September 1944 diary entry.[16] He could rightly be proud of overseeing an enormous war effort against the fascists, and this had also transformed the nation, but Canada was not a global power. Nonetheless, the war forged a new country and there were high hopes for Canada at the inaugural United Nations conference in San Francisco, held from April to June 1945. Canadian service personnel, wrote journalist Lionel Shapiro, "had been fighting for a new world, a better world."[17] Now its politicians had to deliver it.

The United States had moved from isolation to internationalism, and in 1945, as a superpower, it was imbued with a sense of responsibility for its allies. President Roosevelt had accepted this mantle, inspiring people around the world through words and deeds, even as his vision was cut short by death. Having liberated Western Europe, America would now find that its wealth, trade, and production were fundamental to rebuilding it. In this new world order, the White House also worked to hinder attempts by Britain to re-exert control over its colonial empire. Roosevelt's proclamation of the Four Freedoms had provided a bright dream for oppressed people, spurring them to demand independence from their European rulers. The unspooling of empires would redraw the maps of colonialism; it would also provoke trauma, rebellion, and civil war in most emerging countries.

On the financial front, the Americans brought together countries in the summer of 1944 at Bretton Woods, New Hampshire. Delivering Roosevelt's remarks to the conference delegates, Treasury Secretary Henry Morgenthau Jr. told them, "Commerce is the lifeblood of a free society."[18] American willpower and treasure established and bankrolled the International Monetary Fund, the World Bank, and the General Agreement on Tariffs and Trade. These mechanisms of financial support stabilized economies and strengthened confidence in postwar trade. The United Nations' discussions in San Francisco were another concrete sign of American leadership. As much of the world came together to produce a rules-based system out of the ruins of war, some expected Canada to stride forward, as it had done during the war. They were to be disappointed. King, an elder statesman who appeared too elderly, made little impact. After a brushed-aside speech filled with self-serving platitudes and cringy banalities, King left the UN meetings, returning to Canada to campaign in the federal election that few expected him to win. The new middle powers, as they were called—a group that Canada had led during the war—were now steered by the Australians, who were vocal against the United States, Britain, and the Soviet Union, the great powers that would shape the postwar international structure. Though France tried to exert influence, it was steadily blocked by Britain. Churchill's thinking had been revealed months earlier in a letter denouncing De Gaulle's inclusion in the Yalta conference, where he remarked, "It is not French blood that is being shed to any extent in any quarter of the globe. . . . Canada has more right to be considered the 'Fourth Power.'"[19] Given this inclination on the part of Britain, Canada might have pushed harder for influence. But King was more concerned with keeping his powder dry to preserve his more consequential role of continuing to build bridges and smooth relations between Britain and the United States.

The defeat of the fascists opened the way for the Western democracies to reconstruct their ravaged economies and repair their riven societies, even as these nations' uneasy alliance with the Kremlin was in its death throes. Prior to Germany's defeat, Stalin had imposed his will on Churchill and Roosevelt, forcing them to agree that the expanded Soviet sphere of influence would include Poland along with the other doomed states that were occupied by the Red Army. "This war is not as in the past," argued Stalin with his typical severe frankness. "Whoever occupies a territory also imposes his own social system."[20] The West could do nothing to oppose Stalin, even as Churchill blanched at the nations sacrificed to communism in Eastern Europe. Roosevelt's inspiring words in the Atlantic Charter would be an unattainable vision for those caught behind the Soviet Iron Curtain that soon separated the east from the west.

Friendly wartime Uncle Joe no more, the Soviet dictator also worked to undermine the unsteady democracies of Western Europe and their war-weary people, who had rightly lost faith in much of their leadership as they stood in the rubble of their burned-out cities, faced food shortages, and grieved the legions of dead. German civil society had been broken down by the bomber strikes and by the Red Army as it swept westward, raping, murdering, and driving millions of Germans before them. Almost all European nations—the victors and the vanquished—were mired in despair. The depths of starvation and cruelty were nearly unimaginable for the Canadians and Americans enjoying the prosperity of the early postwar years.

By witnessing this suffering, the Allied leaders came to understand that the Soviets were inflaming communist revolution in many of the destabilized Western countries like Greece, Italy, Czechoslovakia, and even France. Stalin also had a spy network devoted to gathering intelligence on technological advances, particularly the atomic bomb. "Hiroshima has shaken the whole world," said the Soviet dictator. "The balance has been destroyed."[21] Only the secret to the atom would restore the prewar equilibrium. He set out to steal it.

———

In June 1942, Moscow had established an embassy in Ottawa, which was staffed by soldiers, diplomats, and agents that spied on Canadians—particularly on their supply of uranium for the Manhattan Project. Clandestine attempts were also made to flip scientists who would share or sell secrets. On the fringe of this cloak-and-dagger work was a low-level cipher clerk in the embassy, Igor Gouzenko. He had come to the capital with his pregnant wife and their child, and he was stunned by the comparative opulence of Canada that was untouched by violence. Near the end of the war, when Gouzenko was recalled to the Soviet Union, he agonized over the prospect of going home, aware that the secret police frequently interrogated, abused, and even executed those who returned from abroad for fear they would bring back the disease of capitalism to infect the communist body.

Facing a bleak future, on the night of September 5, 1945, the twenty-six-year-old Gouzenko stole from the embassy more than 100 secret documents that detailed a robust spy network in Canada, Britain, and the United States. After initially being denied refuge by the Canadian authorities, Gouzenko despaired he would be caught by the Russians and "disappeared." Following a fraught period of hiding from Soviet agents, Gouzenko finally made his mission known, and he and his family were brought into protective custody.[22] Upon learning of the spy rings in the West, King overcame his natural inclination to duck and hide, but not before musing on how the problem could go away if the Russian committed suicide. Ottawa soon recognized the importance of the revelation contained in the documents, and knew that those in power had to inform Canada's allies about the spies that were working within their borders.

The aged and experienced King had narrowly won the June 1945 election, stunning his doubters and critics who had believed that the electorate would vote for change since the Liberals had been in power since 1935. The party had indeed grown long in the tooth, having weathered its fair share of controversies and hard realities, from the decision to send soldiers to Hong Kong, to conscription, to Canadians' grief over the country's wartime dead. If King's victory had been a surprise, Churchill's defeat in Britain's July 5 election had been shocking. But Churchill was a hard man to kill off: he was soon shaping the narrative of the war as the author of best-selling histories, as a respected statesman beating the war drum against communism, and again as prime minister from October 1951. Whereas Churchill had been venerated as the right leader during the war but was deemed unfit for the challenges of rebuilding Britain after victory in 1945, his overshadowed counterpart, King, was entrusted with Canada's postwar growth. The consummate survivor, the seventy-two-year-old Canadian won the election, largely because of the success of forward-thinking Liberal social programs that eased the nation's transition from war to peace.

With the Gouzenko Affair coming on the heels of his political victory, King warmed to the idea of using the exposure of the Russian spy ring as a means of reinserting himself into the conversation between Washington and London. He travelled to both capitals—a quite extraordinary exertion for the aged leader—to hand deliver the news about Stalin's covert actions. "How strange it is," King wrote in his diary in October 1945, "that I should find myself at the very centre of this problem, through Canada possessing uranium, having contributed to the production of the bomb."[23]

Gouzenko was hidden and sheltered, and he later became a celebrity of sorts. Frequently interviewed for his opinion on the Soviet Union, he published several best-selling books and made a habit of obscuring his identity by putting a paper bag over his head, claiming it helped him hide from unseen Soviet assassins. The communist spies revealed by his documents, including twenty-two Canadians who were charged, were rounded up in a coordinated multi-country sting in February 1946. Journalists went wild over the disclosure of espionage, with *The Globe and Mail* announcing that "the atom secret" had been lost to the Soviets.[24] The mania over communist stooges heightened internal security concerns in Canada and the United States, which would metastasize into the Red Scare frenzy pushed by Senator Joseph McCarthy in the coming years. Spurred on by what was happening in the US, the Royal Canadian Mounted Police vigorously investigated suspected Canadians, focusing on members of the civil service and armed forces who it believed were compromised. Most egregiously, this new "insecurity state" targeted gay men and women.[25] With same-sex relations illegal under Canadian law until 1969, it was thought that "homosexuals," as they were then labelled, were more vulnerable to blackmail. And so, from the early 1950s onward, thousands of Canadians were hounded from their jobs, their reputations destroyed and their lives scarred forever, because of their association with communist organizations or because of their sexuality.

Back in the early years of the Cold War—the name George Orwell gave to this period in October 1945—Stalin worked to actively undermine the democracies. The Soviet occupation of

Eastern Europe, the Berlin Blockade, and the 1948 coup in Czecho-slovakia were all aggressive acts. Korea was cleaved in two, with a communist north and a Western client-state south, while Germany was also divided into a communist east and a proto-democratic west. General Eisenhower had proclaimed to the Germans, "We come as conquerors, but not as oppressors."[26] Indeed, the peace process was magnanimous, allowing for the reconstruction of a devastated West Germany and its inclusion in the alliance against communism. To the shock of some Canadian veterans, the former enemies joined the Western military alliance in 1955, as part of the forward defence against the Soviet armed forces. A divided Korea became a battleground in 1950. War raged between the communist north, backed by the Soviets and Chinese, and the south, which was aided by a Western coalition led by the United States. Some 30,000 Canadians fought in that war, on the ground, at sea, and in the air, serving with Americans, British, and other allied nations in driving back the communists. At a heavy price in civilian and military lives, the Western alliance triumphed.[27] In the deepening Cold War, Canada chose its side; neutrality was not an option. Canadians would stand against communism, just as they had fought against fascism.

———

The wartime necessity of supporting Britain had driven Canada into the US sphere of influence. Defending North America had required military cooperation and, occasionally, interoperability of armed forces along the borders and the coasts. Defence production had entangled many sectors of the two economies, creating interconnections that were impossible to sever at war's end. Dean

Acheson, undersecretary of the US Department of State, wrote that the "magnitude and success of our wartime economic relations with Canada" would lead to a relationship of "utmost importance in the postwar period."[28] But it was a potentially troubled union for the smaller, less wealthy, and weaker country. The severe consequences of a misstep with the US focused the mind of Canada's guiding class. Forced to grow up during the war in the absence of Britain's close support, and often working in opposition to Whitehall's unwise attempts to dominate the dominions, King and his circle of advisers moved forward on multiple fronts to engage, placate, and carve out a future with the superpower to the south.

Despite the potential riches to be gained from future trade or economic entwinement with the US, the Liberals under King tried to slow or reverse some of the war-related reintegration. Just as it had refused Lend-Lease, Canada elected not to draw upon America's Marshall Plan, which in 1948 offered funds to Britain and Western Europe, with some $13 billion made available in recovery programs to stabilize the tottering democracies. But as it had done during the war, the US helped its northern neighbour, this time by allowing European nations to use Marshall aid money to purchase Canadian goods. This was a vital boost to trade and to Canada's economy.

Unfortunately, North American goods and funds were not enough to restore Britain, and the formerly powerful nation limped into the postwar years much reduced because of its disintegrating empire and its staggering debt. Assistance was needed. No longer great, Britain had been reduced to calling upon Canada for a major loan, which would be, in the words of economist John Maynard Keynes, a "financial Dunkirk" to rescue the island kingdom.[29] Harbouring a lingering bitterness over how London had sometimes treated Canadians with condescension, some of the ministers were not feeling generous. But for political, sentimental, and strategic reasons, King got his way with the cabinet, arguing that a broken and broke Britain was a potential disaster that would ultimately lead to the likelihood of Canada being annexed by the United States.[30] Even as Canada embraced its inevitable North American destiny, King still hoped that the British magnet would pull his country back from the forceful draw of the titan to the south. Britain borrowed $3.75 billion from the Americans, along with another $1.25 billion from the Canadians, which was about 10 percent of the northern country's GNP.[31] The Americans took note and were also grateful for the $2 billion in loans and credits that Canada offered to Western European countries. Despite this astonishing level of generosity, Canada's economy grew during the uncertain period of postwar reconstruction, rising from $11.8 billion in 1945 to $18.4 billion in 1950.[32] The war had changed Canada and had created the conditions for its citizens to enjoy a peace grounded in prosperity.

Notwithstanding the greater wealth to be found in closer North American ties, King's was the way of gradual course corrections. When the independence of India and its bloodstained partition in 1947 ended the British Empire, Canada helped define the uncertain relationship between downtrodden Britain and the new countries of India, Pakistan, and Ceylon that emerged through the decolonization process.[33] Since 1942, Australia had felt abandoned by Britain as the Japanese threat surged, and it had forged strong military alliances with the United States.[34] Canada had also followed that route, agreeing to a near erasure of the border to enable the movement of goods. However, when the Americans offered another favourable trade deal in 1948, King fretted that this might lead to too much entanglement given the close integration of the nations' economies during the war years. Always more alchemist than chemist, King followed his gut, which told him to back away. This decision was confirmed when he turned to a medium who channelled an old friend. President Roosevelt's spirit warned King to be wary of unnamed American agents plotting to subjugate Canada through the subtle ensnarement of commerce.[35] King killed the deal. He continued to fight for Canada, but he had run his race by November 1948, when he wearily handed the crown to his successor, Louis St. Laurent.

Given his long political reign, no other Canadian was more responsible for the country's evolution into an influential nation than William Lyon Mackenzie King. Though he was never loved by Canadians, King's legacies are legion. He sought the advice of ministers, civil servants, journalists, and entities from the spirit world, but it was King who often interpreted the swirling currents of opinion among the Canadian public, and who was especially attuned to the delicate balance between linguistic, regional, and class demands. "Only he and God (and sometimes he had his doubts about God) knew how things should be handled," noted one adviser.[36] King steered the country forward with little glamour, being wary of unleashing passions among a people who were easily divided. That the prime minister was a table rapper who looked for guidance from the departed was titillating to Canadians when this detail was revealed shortly after his death on July 22, 1950. It also rapidly reduced the dour and uninteresting King to a clownish figure. He survived in the Canadian memory for decades as a political punchline: a dreary and indecisive man who was overshadowed by others and often paralyzed by caution. Instead of acknowledging him as a flawed human being, warts and all, most history books showcased only his warts. For a time, King was condemned for having sold out Canada to the US. This was a grossly unfair charge that revealed a failure on the part of his critics to understand the limited choices he faced in 1940 as he sought to support Britain. What was true, however, was that he was frequently reduced to the role of supplicant in his dealings with Churchill and Roosevelt. He could have fought harder in the political or strategic gladiatorial arenas. "The strong glove over the velvet hand," sneered Pearson, "has nothing to commend it."[37]

And yet obscured beneath this barrage of easy caricature and rascally mockery was King's canny political manoeuvring, his skilful orchestration of the war effort that did not alienate French Canada, and his postwar leadership in guiding the country into a period of unprecedented prosperity. The success of his strategy in dealing with the US revealed him to be a statesman of the first order. Indeed, to his critics one might respond that King was the longest-serving prime minister in the British Empire and Commonwealth, and that political leaders do not hold power for 7,829 days by being simpering weaklings or repulsive jesters to voters. One of his great strengths was in hiding his strength, leaving the "king of contradictions" as the most complex political figure in Canadian history.

———

In the postwar years, Canada sought to carve out its own independent foreign policy, even if that action positioned the country firmly within the American-led Western alliance system. Canada's strategy was based on a willingness to take on global responsibilities, and a key tenet was that the country's leaders had to be mindful of national unity and ensure that Britain and the US did not come into conflict.[38] Ottawa dreaded the day it might be called upon to choose a side. This was a balancing act, as it had been during the war. But now the gravitational pull of the American superpower made maintaining equilibrium even more treacherous. As Pearson was to write in 1948, Canada's Department of External Affairs was not "a tail to the American State Department."[39] Nor were the country's armed forces to be a mere appendage to the American military. To head off conflict, the Permanent Joint Board on Defence (PJBD) continued in its advisory role, with the "permanent" aspect remaining true to its founders' intention to negotiate security issues.

The North Americans continued to concentrate on hemispheric defence. Andrew McNaughton, the respected Canadian nationalist and veteran of two world wars, was appointed to the PJBD. As the Soviets were an Arctic nation, the Americans viewed the northern frontier as vulnerable. General Carl Spaatz, chief of the US Army Air Forces, observed in February 1947 that strategic air power left North America exposed, remarking, "We are, in fact, wide open at the top."[40] Canada's military was more sanguine in assessing the communist threat, noting that the Russians were solidifying their occupation of Eastern Europe and were little interested in the vast Arctic. However, faced with the war on the west coast and the building of the Alaska Highway, the air staging route, and the northern pipeline, Ottawa had been obligated to think more strategically about the North. "It is of great importance that Canada should carefully safeguard her sovereignty in the Arctic at all points and at all times," warned one military appreciation, "lest the acceptance of an initial infringement of her sovereignty invalidate her entire claim and open the way to the intrusion of foreign interests of a nature which might create an ultimate threat to national security."[41] The good allies of the Second World War continued their positive relationship in the early years of the Cold War. North American collaborative military talks and joint committees put plans into place for Arctic testing stations, military manoeuvres, a radar shield, and a common air

Operation Musk Ox was a 1946 Canadian Army operation in the Arctic that spanned eighty-one days. Winter warfare tactics were tested, along with the use of snowmobiles. The RCAF provided airdrops of supplies, and several American observers were present.

defence system. Though funding for projects in the North was, from the late 1940s onward, limited and episodic in comparison to the attention and spending devoted to defending against the greater danger of communism in Europe, the North was a new joint Canadian and American front where issues of command and resource allocation had to be monitored.[42] With a keen interest in security, Canadian authorities paid their way and managed US expectations to avoid being reduced to bowing to or beseeching the decision makers in Washington.

In the Cold War, Canada chose its side: it would stand with the West. Never neutral when the chips were down, the Dominion also charted its own path forward. The Canadian people were stridently anti-communist, as revealed in public opinion polls.[43] The high-profile Gouzenko Affair rattled Canadians, who, being fearful of the communist threat, were eager to forge closer ties with the Americans. The war had smashed many old stereotypes about the United States, but the military, diplomatic, and civilian leadership remained anxious for Canada to avoid being reduced to an American vassal state. They sought collective security beyond North America, partially to balance against US dominance in the hemisphere.[44] In 1949, Canada was a founding member and key player in creating the North Atlantic Treaty Organization (NATO) to protect Western Europe from communist aggression. More than 110,000 Canadians had died in the battles against the Kaiser's armies in the Great War and in the fight against fascism, and it was Canadians who had played vital roles in driving back occupiers and in returning freedom to the oppressed. That was not to be forgotten. The Dominion had earned its place in the alliance with blood. In 1951, Canada honoured its NATO commitment,

sending 10,000 military personnel to Europe and eventually forming an infantry brigade group, an air division of twelve squadrons,
and dozens of warships to stand forcibly against "totalitarian
communist aggression," as Louis St. Laurent labelled the Soviet
threat in 1948.[45] The fascists had been destroyed in the war only
to be replaced by the spectre of communism, and Canada would
respond with martial might to keep the peace. It is a defence and
security obligation that continues to this day.

——

If the war shaped Canada's outlook beyond its shores, so too
did it remake the country at home. "Newfyjohn lives on in the
memory of thousands of corvette sailors as a warm and outgoing
place," recounted one Canadian veteran, "the home of hospitable
and friendly people."[46] Most of the Canadians were gone from
Newfoundland within a few months of the end of the war, and
even the US's ninety-nine-year leases were cut short. Fort Pepperrell
was shuttered in 1961 and the base at Stephenville closed in 1966,
although the last contingent of US military personnel did not leave
until 1997. However, the separate dominion had become a part
of Canada long before that, when Newfoundlanders voted to
join as the tenth province on March 31, 1949. The ties of friendship, prosperity, and security established during the war had done
much to strengthen the argument for confederation. At the same
time, Newfoundland had also been a point of contention between
the US and Canada, and King's government had been adamant
that the island be included within Canada's sphere of influence
and forward defence.

The year that Newfoundland entered into Canada, an injustice was rectified when Japanese Canadians were given the right to vote on April 1, 1949, and allowed to return to British Columbia. Major-General Maurice Pope wrote after the war that Japanese Canadians were no menace and that they were "expelled from their homes at a time when Canadians were priding themselves that they were fighting for freedom," adding, "Fear is a poor counsellor, and groundless fear even worse."[47] Pope was correct, and yet fear there was. Racism was also a factor that drove the assault on civil liberties. A significant and misunderstood issue was how Canada had tethered itself to the US in the name of securing a unified hemispheric defence and responded to the perceived threat to the west coast in early 1942. When President Roosevelt caved to pressure to remove Japanese Americans from the coast after Pearl Harbor, Canada marched in lockstep.

For decades, the Japanese-American and Japanese-Canadian communities remained silent about their trauma. In the late 1970s, however, a new generation rediscovered this historic abuse and these communities mobilized for redress. They studied the archives for concrete evidence, gathered oral testimonies, and unearthed the long-buried history. Slowly winning journalistic and then political support, champions of the issue demanded redress to right the past. An official apology came first in Washington, where, on August 10, 1988, the US Senate announced a compensation package for Japanese Americans that included $20,000 for each individual imprisoned, some $1.25 billion in total. Having dragged out negotiations for years, the Canadians followed suit once the Americans acted. Within a month, Prime Minister Brian Mulroney rose in the House of Commons to apologize for the forced removal of Japanese Canadians from the coast and to offer $21,000 to each person who had been affected, for a total of some $400 million.[48] These official apologies were necessary acts of recognition, even if the recompense was too low when one considers what these Canadians suffered—the loss of freedom, the dispossession of property and land, and the deep shame of being branded as disloyal within their own country.

A war of such magnitude and fury left deep scars. Despite the legacy of harm to Japanese Canadians, Canada had fought on the side of good. Given the intense social panic in the months after Pearl Harbor, the weakness of Canada's west coast defences, the pressure from the Americans to conform to their actions, the evidence of Japanese communications that seemed to portend terrorist action in advance of an invasion, and the inherent racism against Asians in North America, it would have taken great courage and future foresight for King's cabinet to have responded differently to the perceived threat by Japanese Canadians and Japanese nationals in BC. This is not to excuse their actions, but to make sense of them within the context of the time. The state-driven relocation of Canadians remains a warning to future generations about the strength of passions unleashed in times of war, when a potent mix of fear, anger, desire for security, and racial animosity can easily drive actions against vulnerable communities.

———

"When we went overseas, for the first time in our lives we felt that we represented Canada," reflected Second World War signaller Norman Penner.[49] While this was a sentiment that many of the

Great War generation shared, the stimulation of a Canadian sense of identity was cumulative, with the world wars as events that wrought transformation. That the country's identity was fundamentally altered is best captured by the creation of Canadian citizenship. In January 1947, Prime Minister King received the first certificate, although the driving force had been Paul Martin, minister of national health and welfare, who had visited the Canadian cemetery at Dieppe and had been deeply moved by the sacrifice represented there. He wanted it known to future generations that those who died in the fight against Hitler, the Nazis, and other fascists were Canadians and not just British subjects.[50]

The war also created new cultural agencies, new funding, and a new urgency to tell Canada's story. John Grierson had overseen the Wartime Information Board, a sword to carve out a Canadian identity, and the National Film Board, a shield to protect it from being overwhelmed by the Americans. An artist, a maverick, and a firebrand, Grierson had benefited from the crisis-driven expansive allocation of funds, though he was less well suited for peacetime bureaucracy. He left the country in the aftershocks of the Gouzenko Affair, when his loyalty was called into question, even as he remained a leader in the field of documentary filmmaking. The war had forged a new Canadian culture distinct from Britain's, but one that was in danger of being enveloped by the United States. Could Canada stand against American hegemony? The CBC and the NFB had found their mission during the war by mobilizing ideas, presenting Canadian stories, and offering those in the Dominion alternatives to the inundation of American news, publicity, and propaganda. They continue their work to this day.

In the summer of 1949, Vincent Massey and several prominent commissioners were appointed by the St. Laurent government to study arts and culture. They crossed the country, listening and meeting with hundreds of cultural groups that urged state support in these spheres. Although not much could be done about the economic supremacy of the United States, a behemoth that wielded 70 percent of all capital investment in Canada, perhaps a cultural bulwark could be established to develop what it meant to be Canadian.[51] The Massey Commission's report in 1951 asserted that state funding for the arts was in the "national interest" and that it would profoundly impact how Canadians saw themselves. This was the origin of a charged arts and culture movement in the country, and its legacy included the establishment of new institutions like the Canada Council for the Arts and the National Library of Canada, better funding for the National Gallery of Canada and the Public Archives of Canada, dedicated finances for universities, the conservation of historical sites, and a heightened awareness of the need to shape and shield Canadian identity in the face of an American cultural blitzkrieg.[52] The stimulation of culture, arts, and history is one of the positive, if unintended, legacies of war.

———

The Second World War forever altered Canada's relationship to Britain and the United States. Canada was launched forward into a prosperous period of economic growth, even as it balanced its new security commitments in North America and the world, and within the Cold War. As it had during the war, in matters of culture, trade, defence, and diplomacy, Canada carved out its own future, working with the Americans at times and constraining them at others—protecting itself while remaining a good ally. The past would inform the future, with the Second World War redefining the history of the northern continent.

CONCLUSION

"Never to be in the way, and yet never out of it," was the philosophy of Major-General Maurice Pope in dealing with the British and Americans.[1] The Dominion's strategic actions throughout the war were predicated on assisting Britain in the fight against the Axis powers and on pursuing its own national interests as a junior if important ally in the Anglo-American coalition. At the same time, this delicate balancing act could not be achieved without a close alliance with the United States. Canada sought to position itself between its closest allies, anxious to support where possible, while also struggling to stand on its own.

The defence of North America was an undeniable primary concern for Canada. To fully aid Britain, North America had to be fortified. The crisis demanded that Canada work closely with the United States, a cooperation resulting in entangled defence, industry, and trade that before the war would have been unthinkable. And yet the desperation wrought by the early enemy victories required such a commitment. How Canada and the US achieved this unity, especially in matters of joint security, was a marvel of compromise and conciliation. The North Americans rarely shouted past each other; instead, they had to talk, listen, and solve innumerable challenges.

On the home front, the size of Canada's industrial output was staggering for a prewar nation that was undeveloped and sickly from the lingering agony of the Depression—though, again, such giant strides forward could not have been achieved without the backing of the Americans. Canada's armed forces also served effectively with the US to defend the Atlantic and Pacific coasts in the desperate battles against the German and Japanese submarines. As concerns were aired, especially in the North, about sovereignty in relation to *Pax Americana*, the Canadians gave and got, fretted and worried, but almost always stepped up to meet their obligations to the US. The protection of Alaska and the Kiska campaign were examples of joint contributions on the west coast. First Special Service Force was a unique unit that brought shared glory through combat, while larger Canadian and American national formations fought together in Sicily, on the Italian mainland, and then in Northwest Europe. North Americans defended one another at sea, and they took the fight to Germany in the bomber war. They bled, battled, and ultimately prevailed in the European land war, and First Canadian Army was a part of the great liberation of the oppressed who suffered terribly under the cruel Nazis.

Canada's grand strategy evolved during the war. This was no "mission creep," as the modern military lexicon would label it, but rather a simple reality of the changing nature of the worldwide war. King's desire in 1939 and 1940 for Canada to make a limited contribution—one that would include a small expeditionary force, the production of munitions, and the training of airmen—was blown to bits by the German victories of 1940. In the aftermath of this traumatic moment, everything changed for Canada, and King understood that to stand by Britain his country would have to lean into the US. He accordingly orchestrated deals to protect North America and super-charge the Allied war economies. The prime minister succeeded in many areas, but he found it a constant struggle for his country to have a voice, especially by early 1942 when the Anglo-American coalition was forged and its military and political leaders were debating grand strategy. Canada had few means by which to insert itself in those crucial discussions, but King, the master of biding his time, waited, watched, and paced around the exterior. What could the country have done under different leadership? It might have gone scorched earth by retreating to its borders and even curtailing trade in an act of national blackmail. That seems unthinkable, but more erratic events have occurred between nations in times of high stress. If Canada had withheld its broad and deep aid or even reduced its commitment, the alliance of democracies would have suffered, at the very least from the loss of crucial resources needed for fighting the Axis powers. King's careful statecraft instead guided him cautiously forward, even as he worried about his country being drawn into the Imperial war effort or the American sphere of influence. King and his cabinet could have done more—pushed harder to be at the table where the higher direction of the war effort was debated— but they had little experience in how to do this. And yet Canada did not waver in its support for Britain, even though King was forced to turn his country ever increasingly towards the US. In this war of utter necessity, where victory was required at any cost, Canada was sometimes in the middle, sometimes pushed aside; it assisted and was recognized; it gave and was ignored; and yet its more than a million service personnel strode forward into battle, backed by the workers in the factories, the miners deep in the earth, the farmers in the fields, and all who contributed to the all-out war.

Shortly after taking office in 1945, President Harry Truman had been apprised by the State Department that "Canada has developed during the war years into a nation of importance. . . . The strength of the overseas armies was particularly remarkable." The countries' shared border, the need for a joint defence of North America, and the northern nation's ability to "stand on its own feet, paying it own way" made Canada a dependable ally for the US during the Cold War.[2] The briefing should have added that Canada's wartime industry made massive contributions to victory, that its food saved millions, that its aluminum was essential to aircraft production, that its hydro-electricity powered America's northern industries, and that its scientific knowledge and uranium were funnelled into the atomic weapons. This war marked one of the few times in the history of North American relations when the US needed Canada. The Dominion, in turn, had to learn to act as a full-fledged nation; it had to be an ally, if a junior one. Cooperation and coordination secured North America, unleashing the full potential of wartime economies and creating a safe realm from which to send land, sea, and air combat forces overseas. Defending the northern continent also took work, and the US remained grateful to Canada, treating it better than almost any other nation because it was more important than almost any other nation.

After victory in 1945, the Canadian armed forces served the nation's interests by being involved in NATO, NORAD, and peacekeeping operations, and by continuing to act as a supportive ally, although the long and dark shadow of American economic and cultural dominance became a preoccupation and worry for many Canadians in the late 1960s. While Canadians were right to be concerned that their prosperity came with the negative side effect of American industrial might crushing many home-grown industries, the 1965 Autopact—which allowed for the free flow of automobiles between the two nations and created hundreds of thousands of good jobs—seemed the opposite of a plot to snuff out the country's economic survival.[3] Nonetheless, sovereignty was no easy thing to manage for Canadians, who found that the will was easier than the way. The 1960s was a period of gathering anti-American sentiment in Canada as a sense of nationalism stimulated through culture, politics, and intellectual discussion was further stoked by nightly television broadcasts that showed the racial injustice in the US and its losing war in Vietnam.[4] Even as the two nations continued to be linked by robust trade, conjoined economies, and natural resources that had to be managed— with rivers, water, and pollution respecting no boundaries—their Second World War alliance faded from memory. In Canada, in particular, because of insufficient commemoration through symbolic acts and physical memorials, the war lost its importance, being replaced by other narratives, legends, and pressing matters.[5] If history is not preserved, taught, and told, it will eventually wither away, as this monumental story of cooperation in the fight against fascism did in the 1960s.

———

The Good Allies offers a history of Canada's exertions during and after the Second World War—in the fields of warfighting, politics, diplomacy, trade, finance, industry, culture, and memory construction. The story of how the country navigated these sectors more than eighty years ago is still relevant in the Canada of today. Policy-makers who grapple with the challenges of security and sovereignty, of a rampant and dominant American culture, and of the subtle appeal of easy wealth through trade will find lessons here. While the war issues don't always map perfectly onto the reality of the new century, perhaps there is comfort for contemporary strategists and politicians in knowing that it was no easier for Canadians to navigate these challenges from 1939 to 1945. But they did so, and successfully. Present-day Canadians are reminded through this history that although the Canadians of the war years supported the Americans at every turn, they also impressed upon their friends, at times forcefully, that they needed their neighbours to the North. The transactional nature of the relationship must be heeded, as well as the mindful application of pressure, goodwill, and compromise. But allyship goes both ways. Canada was a strong military power that paid its way, and that can not be minimalized: the Canadians of the war years were by no means free riders. Since the late twentieth century, Canada has often been accused of such passivity in the realms of defence and security, being particularly maligned for the neglect of its armed forces. It needs to step up or at least show its allies why this accusation is wrong.

For Canada and the US, their union during the Second World War was not an alliance of wartime convenience. In this historic moment, Canada irrevocably turned away from Britain, profoundly diminishing its reliance on Commonwealth defence, culture, diplomacy, and trade, even if many English Canadians continued to view the Old Country with much fondness, refusing to relinquish their shared history. Untethered, Canada was forced to stride forward with high expectations and great uncertainty. As for the Americans, they accepted the need for the North American alliance. Though the US was undoubtedly a superpower, it had defeated the fascist threat only to face a new communist menace. The isolationists were beaten back and the internationalists emerged, aware that to remake and lead the new world order in America's interests, the US needed allies. Just across the northern border was one of its closest and one of its best. Even though Canada and other alliance partners have not always lived up to the high expectations of the White House, the US knows it is stronger with allies than without them.[6] That is a lesson for the next president who sits in the Oval Office—and those to follow—as he or she seeks to mobilize the West to confront new threats in the unstable and contentious early twenty-first century, a period of rising powers, bad actors, and mad dictators.

Lord Palmerston observed caustically in the nineteenth century that Britain had no permanent friends, only permanent interests. It is to the credit of Canada and the United States that they have maintained a permanent friendship—notwithstanding disagreements and differences—and have worked to serve permanent shared interests in the defence of the northern hemisphere. The origins of that enduring pact are to be found in the Second World War, an enormous calamity that demanded that Canada find a way to secure its homeland and work with the US so it could more fully aid Britain. Navigating between history and geography, heart and head, Canadians were forced to grow up, be good allies, and discover what it meant to be North American.

ENDNOTES

INTRODUCTION

1   J.W. Pickersgill, "Mackenzie King's Political Attitudes and Political Policies: A Personal Impression," John English and J.O. Stubbs (eds.), *Mackenzie King: Widening the Debate* (MacMillan of Canada, 1977) 18.

2   Eliot Cohen, *Conquered into Liberty: Two Centuries of Battles along the Great Warpath that made the American Way of War* (New York: Free Press, 2011).

3   Stetson Conn, Rose C. Engelman, and Byron Fairchild (eds.), *Guarding the United States and Its Outposts* (Washington: Office of the Chief of Military History, 1964) 4.

4   The King diaries are preserved at the Library and Archives Canada (LAC). They have been digitized and are available online as part of the LAC's search engine; they will be cited in this book as King diary. This entry is from 8 November 1935.

5   L.B. Pearson, *Mike: The Memoirs of the Right Honourable Lester B. Pearson, volume 1: 1897–1948* (Toronto: University of Toronto Press, 1972) 226.

6   J.L. Granatstein, *How Britain's Weakness Forced Canada into the Arms of the United States* (Toronto: University of Toronto Press, 1989), J.L. Granatstein, *Canada's War: The Politics of the Mackenzie King Government 1939–1945* (Toronto: Oxford University Press, 1975); C.P. Stacey, *Arms, Men and Governments: The War Policies of Canada, 1939-1945* (Ottawa: Queen's Printer, 1970); J.L. Granatstein and Norman Hillmer, *For Better or for Worse: Canada and the United States into the Twenty-First Century* (Toronto: Thomson Nelson, 2007).

7   J.W. Pickersgill, *Seeing Canada Whole: A Memoir* (Markham: Fitzhenry and Whiteside, 1994) 217.

8   George P. Auld, "The British War Debt: Retrospect and Prospect," *Foreign Affairs* 16.4 (1938) 640–50; Kori Schake, *Safe Passage: The Transition from British to American Hegemony* (Cambridge: Harvard University Press, 2017) 256.

9   For the cost and legacy of the Great War, David Reynolds, *The Long Shadow: The Legacies of the Great War in the Twentieth Century* (New York: W.W. Norton, 2014).

10   Maurice Pope, *Soldiers and Politicians: The Memoirs of Lt.-Gen. Maurice A. Pope* (Toronto: University of Toronto Press, 1962) 165.

11   *House of Commons Debates*, 25 January 1937; C.P. Stacey, *Six Years of War: The Army in Canada, Britain and the Pacific* (Ottawa: Edmond Cloutier, 1957) 14.

12   Hundreds of books have been published on most aspects of the Canadian, including this author's two volume history: Tim Cook, *The Necessary War: Canadians Fighting the Second World War, 1939–1943* (Toronto: Allen Lane, 2014) and *Fight to the Finish: Canadians Fighting the Second World War, 1943–1945* (Toronto: Allen Lane, 2015).

13   There is a robust literature on Canadian and American relations over two centuries, although the relationship during the Second World War remains untold in a full-scale book. For some of the best writing and analysis, see Granatstein and Hillmer, *For Better or for Worse*; Robert Bothwell, *Your Country, My Country: A Unified History of the United States and Canada* (New York: Oxford University Press, 2015); John Herd Thompson and Stephen J. Randall, *Canada and the United States: Ambivalent Allies*, 4th edition (Montreal: McGill-Queen's University Press, 2008); Stephen Azzi, *Reconcilable Differences: A History of Canada-US Relations* (Toronto: Oxford University Press, 2015); J.L. Granatstein, *Yankee Go Home? Canadians and Anti-Americanism* (Toronto: HarperCollins, 1996).

14   Library Archives Canada (LAC), Record Group 25 (RG 25), v. 5749, file 52(C), pt. 1, Pope to Jenkins, 4 April 1944.

15   Michael Beschloss, *Presidents of War* (New York: Broadway Books, 2019) 394.

16   Frederick W. Gibson and Barbara Robertson (eds.), *Ottawa at War: The Grant Dexter Memoranda, 1939–1945* (Winnipeg: The Manitoba Records Society, 1994) 242.

17   J.L. Granatstein, *A Man of Influence: Norman A. Robertson and Canadian Statecraft, 1929–1968* (Ottawa: Deneau Publishers, 1981) 120.

18   Chris Dickon, *Americans at War in Foreign Forces: A History, 1914/1945* (Jefferson: McFarland and Company, 2014) 160.

19   Fred Gaffen, *Cross-Border Warriors: Canadians in American Forces, Americans in Canadian Forces* (Toronto: Dundurn Press, 1995) 87.

20   J.K. Chapman, *River Boy at War* (New Brunswick: Goose Lane, 1985) 13.

CHAPTER 1: RISE OF THE FASCISTS

1   A copy of the speech can be found in LAC, O.D. Skelton papers, v. 5, file 6, "Reciprocity in Defense," 18 August 1938. On the speech's significance, see Michel Fortmann and David Haglund, "Canada and the Issue of Homeland

Security: Does the 'Kingston Dispensation' Still Hold?" *Canadian Military Journal* (Spring 2002) 17–22.

2 Robert H. Whealey, *Hitler and Spain: The Nazi Role in the Spanish Civil War, 1936–1939* (Lexington: The University Press of Kentucky, 1989).

3 Ian M. Drummond and Norman Hillmer, *Negotiating Freer Trade: The United Kingdom, the United States, Canada, and the Trade Agreements of 1938* (Waterloo: Wilfrid Laurier University Press, 1989).

4 C.P. Stacey, *Mackenzie King and the Atlantic Triangle* (Toronto: Macmillan of Canada, 1976) 49.

5 Digital Archives of Franklin Roosevelt Library, Private Secretary's file, series 3, box 25, Robins to Roosevelt, 28 December 1934; Ibid., Armour to Phillips, 25 October 1935.

6 Douglas B. Craig, *Fireside Politics: Radio and Political Culture in the United States 1920–1940* (Baltimore: Johns Hopkins University Press, 2000).

7 Quote from King diary, 17 September 1932; on King's cautious approach to national finance, see Blair Neatby, *William Lyon Mackenzie King: The Prism of Unity: 1932–1939, volume III* (Toronto: University of Toronto Press, 1976).

8 King diary, 29 June 1937; Maureen Hoogenraad, "Mackenzie King in Berlin," *The Archivist* 20.3 (1994) 20.

9 On the diary, see Chris Dummitt book, *Unbuttoned: A History of Mackenzie King's Secret Life* (Montreal: McGill-Queen's University Press, 2017).

10 On conscription, see J.L. Granatstein and J.M. Hitsman, *Broken Promises: A History of Conscription in Canada* (Toronto: Oxford University Press, 1977).

11 King diary, 13 September 1938; and see J.L. Granatstein and Robert Bothwell, "'A Self-Evident National Duty': Canadian Foreign Policy, 1935–1939," *Journal of Imperial and Commonwealth History*, 3 (1975) 222.

12 King Diary, 23 March 1939; see an earlier and similar observation, King diary, 9–10 September 1936.

13 Norman Hillmer, "O.D. Skelton and the North American Mind," *International Journal* 60.1 (Winter 2004–2005) 93.

14 Norman Hillmer, "Defence and Ideology: The Anglo-Canadian Military 'Alliance' in the Nineteen Thirties," *International Journal*, 33.3 (Summer 1978) 588–612; C.P. Stacey, *Six Years of War: The Army in Canada, Britain, and the Pacific* (Ottawa: HMSO, 1966), 34; C.P. Stacey, *Arms, Men, and Governments: The War Policies of Canada, 1939–1945* (Ottawa: HMSO, 1970) 106.

15 J.L. Granatstein, *Canada's War: The Politics of the Mackenzie King government, 1939–1945* (Toronto: Oxford University Press, 1975) 57.

16 Chris Dickon, *Americans at War in Foreign Forces* (Jefferson, North Carolina: McFarland and Company, 2014) 137.

17 Stephen J. Harris, *Canadian Brass: The Making of a Professional Army, 1860–1939* (Toronto: University of Toronto Press, 1988) and R.A. Preston, *The Defence of the Undefended Border: Planning for War in North America, 1867–1939* (Montreal: McGill-Queen's University Press, 1977) 217.

18 Christopher M. Bell, "Thinking the Unthinkable: British and American Naval Strategies for an Anglo-American War, 1918–1931," *The International History Review* 19.4 (1997) 789–808.

19 W.A.B. Douglas, *The Creation of a National Air Force: The Official History of the Royal Canadian Air Force* (Ottawa: Department of National Defence, 1986) 128–29; for other warnings, see LAC, RG 24, v. 2692, file HQS 5199-A, "The Maintenance of Canadian Neutrality on event of war between Japan and the U.S.A.," 10 March 1933.

20 Galen Roger Perras, *Franklin Roosevelt and the Origins of the Canadian-American Security Alliance, 1933–1945* (Westport: Praeger, 1998) 35–36; A.R.M. Lower, "The Defence of the West Coast," *Canadian Defence Quarterly* 16 (October 1938), 32-38; King diary, 1 December 1936 and 5 March 1937.

21 For these ties see Doug Delaney, *The Imperial Army Project: Britain and the Land Forces of the Dominions and India, 1902-1945* (Oxford: Oxford University Press, 2017).

22 LAC, RG 24, v. 20319, 951.013 (D20), Crerar Secret memo to the Minister, 15 March 1938.

23 LAC, RG 24, v. 20319, 951.013 (D20), Crerar to CGS, 13 March 1938.

24 King diary, 23 March 1939.

25 DHH, 112.3M22009 (D27), "Observations on Canada's Defence Policy," 14 October 1937.

26 Galen Roger Perras, *Stepping Stones to Nowhere: The Aleutian Islands, Alaska, and American Military Strategy, 1867-1945* (Vancouver: UBC Press, 2003) 37-38.

27 DHH, 112.3M2009 (D22), Ashton to Mackenzie, "Conversations held in Washington, DC on the 19th and 20th January, 1938."

28 "Warm Appreciation Here of Roosevelt's Assurance Canada would be Guarded," *The Ottawa Citizen*, 18 August 1938, 4.

29 King diary, 18–20 August 1938; W.L. Mackenzie King, *Canada at Britain's Side* (London: Macmillan, 1941) 170; and Norman Hillmer, *O.D. Skelton: A Portrait of Canadian Ambition* (Toronto: University of Toronto Press, 2015) 285–87.

30 Quotation from Roger Frank Swanson, *Canadian-American Summit Diplomacy, 1923-1973: Selected Speeches and Documents* (Toronto: McClelland & Stewart, 1975) 48–50.

31 House of Commons, 25 January 1937; Stacey, *Six Years of War*, 14.

32 King diary, 24 November 1936; King diary, 11 January 1938.

33 Roger Sarty, "Mr. King and the Armed Forces: Rearmament and Mobilization, 1937-1939," *The Maritime Defence of Canada* (Toronto: The Canadian Institute of Strategic Studies, 1996) 112; C.P. Stacey, *Historical Documents of Canada, Volume V: The Arts of War and Peace, 1914–1945* (Toronto: Macmillan of Canada, 1972) 523.

34 Escott Reid, *Radical Mandarin: The Memoirs of Escott Reid* (Toronto: University of Toronto Press, 1989) 111.

35 W.L. Mackenzie King, "Canada's Defence Policy," *Canadian Defence Quarterly* 15 (October 1937–July 1938) 135; House of Commons Debates, 16 May 1938, 3179; King diary, 14 November 1938.

36 King diary, 27 September 1938.

37 King diary, 27 January 1939.

38 Neville Sloane, "Chamberlain, Appeasement and the Role of the British Dominions," *London Journal of Canadian Studies* 23 (2007–2008) 74–75.

39 Warren F. Kimball, *The Juggler: Franklin Roosevelt as Wartime Statesman* (Princeton: Princeton University Press, 1991) 7.

40 Digital Archives of Franklin Roosevelt Library, Private Secretary's file, series 3, box 25, Roosevelt to King, 11 October 1938; for King as appeaser, see Roy MacLaren, *Mackenzie King in the Age of the Dictators* (Montreal: McGill-Queen's University Press, 2019).

41 Gerhard Weinberg, *Visions of Victory: The Hopes of Eight World War II Leaders* (Cambridge: Cambridge University Press, 2005) 8–9.

42 Pearson, *Mike*, volume 1, 125.

43 C.P. Stacey, *A Very Double Life: The Private World of Mackenzie King* (Toronto: Macmillan of Canada, 1976) 190–91.

CHAPTER 2: FACING THE NAZIS WITHOUT THE US

1 King diary, 26 August 1936.

2 King diary, 28 September 1938.

3 Stacey, *Arms, Men and Governments*, 7.

4 For the assault on his lack of service, see King's painful speech in the *House of Commons Debates*, 20 April 1920; Kirk Hallahan, "W. L. Mackenzie King: Rockefeller's 'other' public relations counsellor in Colorado," *Public Relations Review*, 29(4), 2003, 401–414.

5 Francis M. Carroll, "The First Shot was the Last Straw: The Sinking of the T.S.S. *Athenia* in September 1939 and British Naval Policy in the Second World War," *Diplomacy and Statecraft* 20.3 (2009) 403–13.

6 King diary, 4 September 1939.

7 Presidential Speeches, Miller Center, September 3, 1939: September 3, 1939: Fireside Chat 14: On the European War | Miller Center.

8 King diary, 3 September 1939.

9 "In the United States," *The Windsor Star*, 5 September 1939, 4.

10 "Neutrality Up Again," *Calgary Herald*, 18 September 1939, 4.

11 Michael Fullilove, *Rendezvous with Destiny: How Franklin D. Roosevelt and Five Extraordinary Men Took America into the War and into the World* (New York: The Penguin Press, 2013) 5.

12 Steven Casey, *Cautious Crusade: Franklin D. Roosevelt, American Public Opinion and the War Against Nazi Germany* (Oxford: Oxford University Press, 2001) 20–28.

13 For an overview, Robert A. Devine, *The Reluctant Belligerent: American Entry into World War II* (New York: Knopf, 1979).

14 Carol R. Byerly, "War Losses (USA)," in *1914–1918—Online International Encyclopedia of the First World War.*

15 Debi and Irwin Unger, *George Marshall* (New York: Harper Collins, 2014) 88.

16 David M. Kennedy, *The American People in World War II: Freedom from Fear* (Oxford University Press, 2003) 2.

17 King diary, 5 September 1939

18 See Frederick B. Pike, *FDR's Good Neighbor Policy: Sixty Years of Generally Gentle Chaos* (Austin: University of Texas Press, 1995).

19 Lita-Rose Betcherman, *Ernest Lapointe: Mackenzie King's Great Quebec Lieutenant* (Toronto: University of Toronto Press, 2002) 280–81.

20 *House of Commons Debates*, 9 September 1939, 60 & 63.

21 *House of Commons Debates*, 8 September 1939, 34.

22 On guiding Canada into the war, see King's diary, 1–10 September 1939; Tim Cook, *Warlords: Borden, Mackenzie King, and Canada's World Wars* (Toronto: Allen Lane, 2012) 208–213.

23 Stacey, *Six Years of War*, 53.

24 Hal Lawrence, *A Bloody War: One Man's Memories of the Canadian Navy, 1939–45* (Toronto: Macmillan, 1979) 27.

25 Dominion Secretary to Secretary of State for External Affairs, 26 September 1939 in David Murray (ed.), Documents on Canadian External Relations (*DCER)* volume 7 (Ottawa: Queen's Printer, 1974) 549–51.

26 F.J. Hatch, *Aerodrome of Democracy: Canada and the British Commonwealth Air Training Plan, 1939–1945* (Ottawa: Department of National Defence, 1983) 16–17.

27 Paul Marsden, "The Costs of No Commitments: Canadian Economic Planning for War," in Norman Hillmer, et al. (eds.), *A Country of Limitations: Canada and the World in 1939* (Ottawa: Canadian Committee for the History of the Second World War, 1996) 199–216.

28 King diary, 17 October 1939.

29 J.W. Pickersgill, et al, *The Mackenzie King Record,* volume 1 (Toronto: University of Toronto Press, 1960) 43.

30 Andrew Stewart, "The 1939 British and Canadian 'Empire Air Training Scheme' Negotiations," *Round Table* XCIII (2004) 739–54; Granatstein, *Canada's War,* 57.

31 See Hatch, *Aerodrome of Democracy.*

32 Department of National Defence for Air, Ottawa Air Training Conference, *Report of the Conference* (Ottawa: King's Printer, 1942) 13.

33 Granatstein, *A Man of Influence,* 110.

34 LAC, MG 27, III-B-5, Ian Mackenzie papers, v. 29, X-6, "Appreciation of the defence problems confronting Canada," 5 September 1936; "Sino-Japanese Dispute," 24 February 1933, in Alex Inglis (ed.) *DCER* vol. 5, 377.

35 LAC, King Papers, Memoranda and Notes, v. 228, O.D. Skelton, "Canadian War Policy," 24 August 1939. On Skelton's influence, see Norman Hillmer, *O.D. Skelton: A Portrait of Canadian Ambition* (Toronto: University of Toronto, 2015).

36 LAC, Harry Crerar papers, v. 10, D211, Liaison with Military Attache.

37 John T. Saywell, *Just Call Me Mitch: The Life of Mitchell F. Hepburn* (Toronto: University of Toronto Press, 1991) 434.

38 Reid, *Radical Mandarin,* 3.

39 W.L.M. King "Canada at Britain's Side," in W.L.M. King, *Canada at Britain's Side* (Toronto: Macmillan, 1941) 1.

CHAPTER 3: A CATACLYSM

1 King diary, 23–24 April 1940.

2 "Roosevelt and King Hold Meeting But Nature of Talk Kept Secret," *The Gazette* (Montreal), 24 April 1940, 1.

3 King diary, 23–24 April 1940. For a public statement, see *House of Commons Debates,* 12 November 1940. The president had been briefed by Hull; see Digital Archives of Franklin Roosevelt Library, Private Secretary's file, series 3, box 25, Hull to Roosevelt, 23 April 1940.

4   For the failure of the French army, see Robert Doughty, *The Seeds of Disaster: The Development of French Army Doctrine, 1919–1939* (Hamden: Archon Books, 1985).

5   W.J.R. Gardner (ed.), *The Evacuation from Dunkirk: Operation Dynamo, 26 May–4 June 1940* (London: Routledge, 2000).

6   King diary, 10 June 1939.

7   Frederick W. Gibson and Barbara Robertson (eds.), *Ottawa at War: The Grant Dexter Memoranda, 1939-1945* (Winnipeg: The Manitoba Record Society, 1994) 70.

8   Perras, *Roosevelt and the Canadian-American Security Alliance*, 55.

9   Gilbert Norman Tucker, *The Naval Service of Canada*, volume II (Ottawa: King's Printer, 1952) 25–26; Fraser McKee, *The Armed Yachts of Canada* (Erin: Boston Mills Press, 1983).

10 Henry Hemming, *Agents of Influence: A British Campaign, a Canadian Spy, and the Secret Plot to Bring America into World War II* (New York: Public Affairs, 2019) 3.

11 King diary, 19–20 May 1940.

12 King diary, 24 May 1940.

13 Christopher Bell, *Churchill and Sea Power* (Oxford: Oxford University Press, 2012) 197.

14 King diary, 16 June 1940.

15 Hugh Keenleyside, *Memoirs of Hugh L. Keenleyside: On the Bridge of Time*, volume II (Toronto: McClelland & Stewart, 1982) 100-103; Gary Evans, *John Grierson and the National Film Board: The Politics of Wartime Propaganda* (Toronto: University of Toronto Press, 1984) 84–85.

16 Blair Fraser, "Canada in Washington," *Maclean's* (15 February 1945) online.

17 LAC, Department of External Affairs, RG 25, A2, v. 774, file 353, "The Present Outlook," 30 April 1940.

18 Martin Gilbert, *Churchill and America* (London: Free Press, 2005) 201.

19 Reid, *Radical Mandarin*, 138.

20 Keenleyside, *Memoirs of Hugh L. Keenleyside*, 36.

21 LAC, W.L.M. King papers, C-282902, Keenleyside to King, Report of Discussions with President Roosevelt, 23 May 1940; King diary, 26 May 1940; Fred E. Pollock, "Roosevelt, the Ogdensburg Agreement, and the British Fleet: All Done with Mirrors," *Diplomatic History* 3 (Summer 1981) 203–219.

22 Digital Archives of Franklin Roosevelt Library, Private Secretary's file, series 3, box 25, King to Roosevelt, 23 April 1937.

23 Robert Jackson, *Before the Storm: The Story of Bomber Command, 1939–1942* (London: Cassell & Co., 2001 [original 1972]) 117.

24 King diary, 30 May 1940; Stacey, *Arms, Men and Governments*, 331.

25 "Churchill's Exhortation," *The Globe and Mail*, 5 June 1940, 6.

26 J.R. Leutze, *Bargaining for Supremacy: Anglo-American Naval Collaboration, 1937–1941* (Chapel Hill: University of North Carolina Press, 1977) 73–75.

27 "What France Has Lost," *Toronto Daily Star*, 19 August 1940, 6.

28 King diary, 16 June 1940.

29 Pickersgill, *Seeing Canada Whole*, 197.

30 Daniel Byers, "Mobilising Canada: The National Resources Mobilization Act, the Department of National Defence, and Compulsory Military Service in Canada, 1940–1945," *Journal of the Canadian Historical Association* 7.1 (1996) 175–203; *House of Commons Debates*, 24 March 1942, 1565.

31 Keenleyside, *Memoirs of Hugh L. Keenleyside*, 46.

32 Joyce Hibbert, *Fragments of War: Stories from Survivors of World War II* (Toronto: Dundurn Press, 1985) 70.

33 *House of Commons Debates*, 20 June 1940, 944.

34 John Saywell, *Just Call me Mitch: The Life of Mitchell F. Hepburn* (Toronto: University of Toronto Press, 1991) 451.

35 Saywell, *Just Call me Mitch*, 452.

36 "Canada and U.S. Now Faced by Need for Joint Defense," *The Financial Post*, 15 June 1940, 9.

37 LAC, King papers, v. 286, file Church to Colquhoun, A Programme of Immediate Canadian Action Drawn Up by a Group of Twenty Canadians, July 17–18, 1940.

38 Michael S. Neiberg, *When France Fell: The Vichy Crisis and the Fate of the Anglo-American Alliance* (Harvard University Press, 2021) 1.

39 Beschloss, *Presidents of War*, 372.

40 Unger, *George Marshall*, 93; Dalleck, *Franklin Roosevelt and American Foreign Policy*, 223–24.

41 Fullilove, *Rendezvous with Destiny*, 65.

42 Bruce Hutchinson, "Canada and US Policy," *Maclean's*, 15 August 1940.

43 Granatstein and Hillmer, *For Better or For Worse*, 143–44.

CHAPTER 4: COMING TOGETHER

1 C.P. Stacey and Barbara Wilson, *The Half-Million: The Canadians in Britain, 1939–1946* (Toronto: University of Toronto Press, 1987) 11.

2 Hector Mackenzie, '"Arsenal of the British Empire"? British Orders for Munitions Production in Canada, 1936–39," *Journal of Imperial and Commonwealth History* XXXI (2003) 46–73.

3 J.L. Granatstein, "Arming the Nation: Canada's Industrial War Effort,

1939–1945," (Ottawa: paper prepared for the Canadian Council of Chief Executives, 2005) 4. Republished in J.L. Granatstein, *Canada at War: Conscription, Diplomacy, and Politics* (Toronto: University of Toronto Press, 2020) 277–87.

4 Stacey, *Arms, Men and Governments*, 36.

5 *House of Commons Debates*, 20 November 1940, 259–61.

6 Canada, Royal Commission on Dominion-Provincial Relations, *Report of the Royal Commission on Dominion-Provincial Relations, volume I* (Ottawa: King's Printer, 1940) 179.

7 On Howe, see Robert Bothwell and William Kilbourn, *C. D. Howe: A Biography* (Toronto: McClelland & Stewart, 1979) 128–79.

8 *House of Commons Debates*, 20 November 1940, 259–61.

9 Jeremy Stuart, "Captains of Industry Crewing the Ship of State: Dollar-a-Year Men and Industrial Mobilization in WWII Canada, 1939–1942" (Master's thesis: University of Calgary, 2013).

10 Robert Bothwell, "'Who's Paying for Anything these Days?' War Production in Canada, 1939–1945," in N.F. Dreisziger (ed.), *Mobilization for Total War* (Wilfrid Laurier University Press, 1981) 62.

11 *House of Commons Debates*, 14 June 1940.

12 "The Integration of War Industry in Canada and the United States," 27 December 1940, in David R. Murray (ed.), *Documents on Canadian External Affairs*, vol. 8 (Ottawa: Supply and Services Canada, 1976) 283.

13 Beverly Baxter, "What Price Neutrality?" *Maclean's*, 15 June 1940.

14 Warren F. Kimball, *Churchill and Roosevelt, volume 1: The Complete Correspondence* (Princeton University Press, 1984) 37–39.

15 Terry Reardon, *Winston Churchill and Mackenzie King* (Toronto: Dundurn, 2012) 122.

16 David Bashow, *All the Fine Young Eagles: In the Cockpit with Canada's Second World War Fighter Pilots* (Toronto: Stoddart, 1997).

17 Arthur Donahue, *Tally Ho! Yankee in a Spitfire* (New York: Macmillan, 1941) 9.

18 Mark A. Stoler, *Allies in War: Britain and America Against the Axis Powers, 1940–1945* (London: Hodder Arnold, 2007) 14.

19 Winston Churchill, *The Second World War: Their Finest Hour* (Boston: Houghton Mifflin, 1949) 198.

20 King diary, 19 July 1940.

21 King diary, 29 July 1937.

22 "Dominion Secretary to Secretary of State for External Affairs," 24 June 1940, DCER, vol. 8, 99–100; Churchill, *The Second World War: Their Finest Hour*, 145–46.

23 Stanley Dziuban, *Military Relations Between the United States and Canada, 1939–1945* (Washington: Official Chief of Military History, 1959) 15–16.

24 "Report of Conversations in Washington," n.d. July 1940, *DCER*, vol. 8, 160.

25 Bruce Hutchinson, "Uncle Sam's Ottawa Ace," *Maclean's*, 1 August 1940.

26 LAC, RG 2, 7c, v. 2, CWC minutes, 26 July 1940.

27 Pickersgill, *The Mackenzie King Record*, v.1, 130–31; and for a more detailed examination, see J.L. Granatstein, "Mackenzie King and Canada at Ogdensburg, August 1940," in Joel J. Sokolsky and Joseph T. Jockel (eds.), *Fifty Years of Canada–United States Defense Cooperation: The Road from Ogdensburg* (Lewiston: The Edwin Mellen Press, 1992) 9–30.

28 "In Defence of North America," *Toronto Daily Star*, 19 August 1940, 6.

29 Thompson and Randall, *Canada and the United States*, 153.

30 Pollock, "Roosevelt, the Ogdensburg Agreement, and the British Fleet," 203–19.

31 King diary, 22 August 1940.

32 David Mackenzie, *Inside the Atlantic Triangle: Canada and the Entrance of Newfoundland into Confederation, 1939-1949* (Toronto: University of Toronto Press, 1986) 44; and see Digital Archives of Franklin Roosevelt Library, Private Secretary's file, series 3, box 25, King to Roosevelt, 7 September 1940.

33 *House of Commons Debates*, 12 November 1940, 54–58.

34 Prime Minister of Great Britain to Prime Minister, 22 August 1940, *DCER*, vol. 8, 142.

35 For this worry, see D.C. Watt, *Succeeding John Bull: American in Britain's Place, 1900–1975* (Cambridge: Cambridge University Press, 1984).

36 "'Axis Powers Not Going to Win'—Roosevelt," *Victoria Daily Times*, 30 December 1940, 3.

CHAPTER 5: DESPERATION ON THE FINANCIAL FRONT

1 Bruce Hutchinson, "What the U.S. Election Means to Canada," *Maclean's*, 15 December 1940.

2 James MacGregor Burns, *Roosevelt: The Lion and the Fox, 1882–1940* (New York: Harcourt, 1956) 449.

3 "What the U.S.A. Thinks," *Life*, 29 July 1940, 20.

4 Garry J. Clifford and Samuel R. Spencer, *The First Peacetime Draft* (Lawrence: University Press of Kansas, 1986) 214, 221.

5 R.L. DiNardo, "The Dysfunctional Coalition: The Axis Powers and the Eastern Front in World War II," *The Journal of Military History* 60.4 (1996) 711–30.

6 Churchill, *The Second World War: Their Finest Hour*, 398; and see Steven High, *Base Colonies in the Western Hemisphere, 1940–1967* (Toronto: Palgrave-Macmillan, 2009).

ENDNOTES

7   "Memorandum by Dominions Secretary," 31 August 1940, *DCER*, vol. 8, 14445.

8   Conn et al., *Guarding the United States and Its Outposts*, 9.

9   For the poll, see Joseph P. Lash, *Roosevelt and Churchill: The Partnership that Saved the West* (New York: W.W. Norton, 1976) 213; David Reynolds, *From Munich to Pearl Harbor: Roosevelt's America and the Origins of the Second World War* (Chicago: Ivan R. Dee, 2001) 85–87.

10 John W. Jeffries, *A Third Term for FDR: The Election of 1940* (Kansas: University Press of Kansas, 2017).

11 "Press Acclaims U.S. Result," *The Leader-Post*, 7 November 1940, 4.

12 "He Invites World Trust," *The Leader-Post*, 7 November 1940, 4.

13 King diary, 5 November 1940.

14 Granatstein and Hillmer, *For Better or For Worse*, 127.

15 J.L. Granatstein, "King and His Cabinet: The War Years," in John English and J.O. Stubbs (eds.), *Mackenzie King: Widening the Debate* (Toronto: Macmillan, 1977) 175.

16 Dziuban, *Military Relations Between the United States and Canada*, 92.

17 *House of Commons Debates*, 12 November 1940, 53.

18 Directorate of History and Heritage (DHH), file 112.3M2 (D496), CGS Appreciation of Military Situation, February 1941.

19 King diary, 31 December 1941.

20 LAC, Harry Crerar papers, v. 1, Crerar to McNaughton, 9 September 1940; Canadian War Committee Minutes, 29 July 1941.

21 William Rayner, *Canada on the Doorstep: 1939* (Toronto: Dundurn, 2011) 188.

22 Dickon, *Americans at War in Foreign Forces*, 150–51.

23 LAC, RG 24, v. 18569, file 133.009 (D131), Americans in Canada's Armed Forces, WWII.

24 Gaffen, *Cross-Border Warriors*, 61.

25 Warren F. Kimball, "Lend-Lease and the Open Door: The Temptation of British Opulence, 1937-1942," *Political Science Quarterly* 86 (1971) 232–59.

26 Gibson and Robertson (eds.), *Ottawa at War*, 132.

27 R.D. Cuff and J.L. Granatstein, "The Hyde Park Declaration, 1941: Origins and Significance," in R.D. Cuff and J.L. Granatstein, *Ties that Bind: Canadian-American Relations in Wartime from the Great War to the Cold War*, second edition (Toronto: A.M. Hakkert, 1977) 73.

28 Perras, *Stepping Stones to Nowhere*, 49; Maurice Matloff and Edwin M. Snell, *Strategic Planning for Coalition Warfare, 1941–42* (Washington: Department of the Army, 1953) 16.

29 The classic study is Warren F. Kimball, *The Most Unsordid Act: Lend-Lease, 1939–1941* (Baltimore: Johns Hopkins University Press, 1969).

30 H. Duncan Hall, *North American Supply* (London: Longmans, 1955) 160.

31 George C. Herring, *From Colony to Superpower: U.S. Foreign Relations Since 1776* (Oxford: Oxford University Press, 2008) 525.

32 LAC, King papers, Recent Trends in Economic Relations between Canada and the United States, 287996-288005; Granatstein, *A Man of Influence*, 114.

33 King diary, 13 March 1941.

34 Stacey, *Historical Documents of Canada, Volume V: The Arts of War and Peace, 1914–1945*, 651-52.

35 Digital Archives of Franklin Roosevelt Library, Private Secretary's file, series 3, box 25, Canada 1941, King to Roosevelt, 24 April 1941.

36 *House of Commons Debates*, 28 April 1941, 2286–89.

37 *House of Commons Debates*, 28 April 1941, 2289.

CHAPTER 6: WAR PRODUCTION FOR THE WORLD

1 For Americans in the CEF, see Richard Holt, *Filling the Ranks: Manpower in the Canadian Expeditionary Force, 1914–1918* (Montreal: McGill-Queen's University Press, 2017).

2 Dickon, *Americans at War in Foreign Forces*, 171.

3 "90% of U.S. Voters Would Fight if Canada is Invaded," *New York Times*, 19 May 1942, 2.

4 Stoler, *Allies in War*, 31.

5 Aloysius Balawyder, "Canada in the Uneasy War Alliance," in Aloysius Balawyder (ed.), *Canadian Soviet Relations, 1939-1980* (Oakville: Mosaic Press, 1981) 1–14.

6 R. Warren James, *Wartime Economic Co-operation: A Study of Relations Between Canada and the United States* (Toronto: Ryerson Press, 1949) 69, 76.

7 Matthew J. Bellamy, *Profiting the Crown: Canada's Polymer Corporation, 1942-1990* (Montreal and Kingston: McGill-Queen's University Press, 2005); Pierrick Labbé, "L'arsenal canadien: Les politiques canadiennes et la fabrication de munitions au Canada Durant la Deuxième Guerre mondiale" (PhD: University of Ottawa, 2012); J. de N. Kennedy, *History of the Department of Munitions and Supply: Canada in the Second World War: Production Branches and Crown Companies* (Ottawa: HMSO, 1950).

8 *The Industrial Front* (Ottawa: King's Printer, 1944) 6.

9 J.L. Granatstein, "Arming the Nation: Canada's Industrial War Effort, 1939–1945," (Ottawa: paper prepared for the Canadian Council of Chief Executives, 2005) 8.

10 Ruth Roach Pierson, *"They're Still Women After All": The Second World War and Canadian Womanhood* (Toronto: McClelland & Stewart, 1986).

ENDNOTES

11 Granatstein, "Arming the Nation: Canada's Industrial War Effort," 8; J.L. Granatstein, *Mackenzie King: His Life and World* (Toronto: New York, 1977) 149; Stacey, *Arms, Men and Governments*, 51.

12 Barbara Dickson, *Bomb Girls: Trading Aprons for Ammo* (Toronto: Dundurn, 2015) 105.

13 P.C. 1003 (17 February 1944).

14 Matthew Evenden, *Allied Power: Mobilizing Hydro-electricity during Canada's Second World War* (Toronto: University of Toronto Press, 2015) 4.

15 *House of Commons Debates*, 26 January 1942, 37.

16 Matthew Evenden, "Aluminum's Permanent Revolution" in Simo Laakkonen, Richard Tucker, and Timo Vuorisalo (eds.), *The Long Shadows: A Global Environmental History of The Second World War* (Corvallis: Oregon State University Press, 2017) 197–216; Duncan C. Campbell, *Global Mission: The Story of Alcan* (Montreal: Alcan, 1985) 251.

17 James, *Wartime Economic Co-operation*, 102.

18 John Macfarlane, "Agents of Control or Chaos? A Strike at Arvida Helps Clarify Canadian Policy on Using Troops against Workers during the Second World War," *The Canadian Historical Review* 86.4 (December 2005) 619–40.

19 DHH, 314.009 (D244), "Guarding Vulnerable Points."

20 Evenden, *Allied Power*, 37.

21 Michel Hennessy, "The Industrial Front: The Scale and Scope of Canadian Industrial Mobilization during the Second World War," in Bernd Horn (ed.), *Forging A Nation: Perspectives on the Canadian Military Experience* (St. Catharines: Vanwell, 2002) 151. Stats drawn from LAC, RG 28, R2-R8, v. 862, report, "Canada's Industrial War Effort."

22 Jessica Van Horessen, *A Town Called Asbestos: Environmental Contamination, Health, and Resilience in a Resource Community* (Vancouver: UBC Press, 2016) 7; *The Industrial Front* (Ottawa: King's Printer, 1944) 208.

23 James, *Wartime Economic Co-operation*, 140.

24 For the challenge, see James Pritchard, *A Bridge of Ships: Canadian Shipbuilding during the Second World War* (Montreal-Kingston: McGill-Queens University Press, 2011).

25 *The Industrial Front* (Ottawa: King's Printer, 1944) 162.

26 Kennedy, *History of the Department of Munitions and Supply*, 505.

27 *House of Commons Debates*, 11 March 1941.

28 Matthew Moore, "The Kiss of Death Bestowed with Gratitude: The Postwar Treatment of Canada's Second World War Merchant Navy, Redress, and the Negotiation of Veteran Identity" (Masters thesis: Carleton University, 2016).

29 LAC, RG 28, R2-R8, v. 862, report, "Canada's Industrial War Effort."

30 *The Canada Yearbook 1946* (Ottawa: HMSO, 1946) 202–203.

31 Lizzie Collingham, *The Taste of War: World War Two and the Battle for Food* (Toronto: Allen Lane, 2011) 1–4.

32 Gibson and Robertson (eds.), *Ottawa at War*, 67.

33 Robert Bothwell, "A Curious Lack of Proportion: Canadian Business and the War," in Sidney Aster (ed.), *The Second World War as a National Experience* (Ottawa: The Canadian Committee for the History of the Second World War, 1981) 29.

34 James, *Wartime Economic Co-operation*, 59.

35 Granatstein, "Arming the Nation," 9–10; *The Industrial Front* (Ottawa: King's Printer, 1944) 26.

36 *The Industrial Front* (Ottawa: King's Printer, 1944) 29; Stacey, *Historical Documents of Canada, Volume V: The Arts of War and Peace, 1914–1945*, 647.

37 Kennedy, *History of the Department of Munitions and Supply*, viii.

38 Crystal Sissons, *Queen of the Hurricanes: The Fearless Elsie MacGill* (Toronto: Second Story Press, 2014) 55.

39 *The Industrial Front* (Ottawa: King's Printer, 1944) 142; Stacey, *Historical Documents of Canada, Volume V: The Arts of War and Peace, 1914–1945*, 647.

40 Stacey, *Six Years of War*, 36.

41 *The Industrial Front* (Ottawa: King's Printer, 1944) 44, 48.

42 Kennedy, *History of the Department of Munitions and Supply*, 47.

43 S. McKee Rosen, *The Combined Boards of the Second World War* (New York: Columbia University Press, 1951) 232-3; H. Duncan Hall, *North American Supply* (London: Longmans, 1955) 3.

44 Bothwell, "A Curious Lack of Proportion," 33.

45 Graham Broad, "'Not Competent to Produce Tanks': The Ram and Tank Production in Canada, 1939–1945," *Canadian Military History* 11.1 (2002) 35.

46 Clive M. Law, *Making Tracks: Tank Production in Canada* (Ottawa: Service Publications, 2001) 13.

47 *The Industrial Front* (Ottawa: King's Printer, 1944) 60; Law, *Making Tracks*, 22; Hall, *North American Supply*, 223.

48 Richard Overy, *Why the Allies Won* (New York: W.W. Norton, 1995) 202.

49 Law, *Making Tracks*, 55.

50 See Clive M. Law, *Drive to Victory: A Pictorial History of Canadian Army Vehicles* (Ottawa: Service Publications, 2016).

51 See Charles K. Hyde, *Arsenal of Democracy: The American Automobile Industry in World War II* (Detroit: Wayne State University Press, 2013).

52 Stacey, *Historical Documents of Canada, Volume V: The Arts of War and Peace, 1914–1945*, 244.

ENDNOTES

53 All statistics in Kennedy, *History of the Department of Munitions and Supply.*

54 Beschloss, *Presidents of War*, 393.

55 Kennedy, *The American People in World War II*, xii. For slight discrepancies in figures, see Overy, *Why the Allies Won*, 192.

56 "Canada—A Valiant Ally," *Pittsburgh Sun-Telegraph* (Pennsylvania), 26 August 1943, 18.

57 Law, *Making Tracks*, introduction; Kennedy, *History of the Department of Munitions and Supply*, 76, 100.

58 H. Duncan Hall and C.C. Wrigley, *Studies of Overseas Supply* (London: HMSO, 1956) 46–52.

59 William R. Young, "Mobilizing English Canada for War: The Bureau of Public Information, The Wartime Information Board and a View of the National during the Second World War," in Sidney Aster (ed.), *The Second World War as a National Experience* (Ottawa: The Canadian Committee for the History of the Second World War, 1981) 198.

60 Lawrence R. Aronsen, "From World War to Limited War: Canadian-American Industrial Mobilization for Defence," *Revue International d'histoire militaire* 51 (1982) 211.

61 Kenneth R. Wilson, "Grand Alliance," *Maclean's*, 1 February 1942.

CHAPTER 7: A MULTI-FRONT WAR

1 Dalleck, *Franklin Roosevelt and American Foreign Policy*, 309.

2 Richard A. Harrison, "A Neutralization Plan for the Pacific: Roosevelt and Anglo-American Cooperation, 1934–1937," *Pacific Historical Review* 57.1 (1988) 47–72; and Michael A. Barnhart, *Japan Prepares for Total War: The Search for Economic Security, 1919–1941* (Ithaca: Cornell University Press, 1987).

3 Granatstein, *A Man of Influence*, 98.

4 Mark Skinner Watson, *The United States Army in World War II: The War Department: Chief of Staff: Prewar Plans and Operations* (Washington: Department of the Army, 1950) 397.

5 Memorandum from Chief of the General Staff, 3 April 1941, *DCER*, vol. 8, 190.

6 C.P. Stacey, "The Canadian-American Permanent Joint Board on Defence, 1940–1945," *International Journal* 9.2 (1954) 112.

7 Keenleyside, *Memoirs of Hugh L. Keenleyside*, 55.

8 Memorandum from Chiefs of Staff to Ministers of National Defence, 22 April 1941, *DCER*, vol. 8, 195; Douglas, *Creation of a National Air Force*, 383.

9 LAC, RG 24, v. 20319, 951.013 (D16) Permanent Joint Board on Defence, First Report.

10 Stacey, "The Canadian–American Permanent Joint Board on Defence, 1940–1945," 118.

11 Biggar to Mr. Mayor, 3 May 1941, in *DCER*, vol. 8, 205; DHH, 112.11 (D1A), C.G.S. Memo re: Basic Plan No. 2, 22 April 1941. For a full discussion, see Richard Goette, *Sovereignty and Command in Canada-US Continental Air Defence, 1940–57* (Vancouver: UBC Press, 2018) 71–85.

12 Franklin Roosevelt Library, file Canada: Permanent Joint Board on Defence, Roosevelt to LaGuardia, 16 May 1941.

13 Thompson and Randall, *Canada and the United States*, 166.

14 Dziuban, *United States Army in World War II*, 109.

15 Stacey, *Arms, Men and Governments*, 348; Richard Goette, "The Acid Test of Sovereignty: Canada, the United States, and the Command and Control of Combined Forces for Continental Defence, 1940–1945," in Abe Roof and Christine Leppard (eds.), *New Perspectives on Canada in the Second World War* (Calgary: University of Calgary Papers in Military and Strategic Studies, 2012) 29.

16 For a Canadian appreciation, see DHH 314.0009 (D17), Canadian Joint Staff, Washington, A.B.C.-22 and the Canada-United States Permanent Joint Board on Defence, 10 August 1942.

17 James, *Wartime Economic Co-operation*, 9.

18 Kimball, *Forged in War*, 22.

19 Warren F. Kimball (ed.), *Churchill and Roosevelt: The Complete Correspondence*, 3 volumes (Princeton: Princeton University Press, 1984).

20 Conn et al., *Guarding the United States and Its Outposts*, 13.

21 W.A.B. Douglas, "Alliance Warfare 1939–1945: Canada's Maritime Forces," in *Revue Internationale d'Histoire Militaire* 51 (1982) 166; Samuel Elliot Morrison, *History of the United States Naval Operations in World War II, Volume II* (Boston: Little, Brown and Company, 1947) 69.

22 King diary, 6 August 1941. Also see Gibson and Robertson (eds.), *Ottawa at War*, 193.

23 King diary, 12 August 1941.

24 Herring, *From Colony to Superpower*, 531.

25 Takuma Melber, *Pearl Harbor: Japan's Attack and America's Entry into World War II* (Medford, MA: Polity Press, 2021).

26 Charles Eade, *The War Speeches of the Rt Hon. Winston S. Churchill*, volume 2 (London: Cassell, 1952) 151, 202.

27 Dalleck, *Franklin Roosevelt and American Foreign Policy*, 192; Brendan Simms and Charlie Laderman, *Hitler's American Gamble: Pearl Harbor and the German March to Global War* (London: Basic Books, 2021) 361.

ENDNOTES

28 Stacey, *Canada and the Age of Conflict*, 321–22.

29 J.L. Granatstein and Norman Hillmer, *First Drafts: Eyewitness Accounts from Canada's Past* (Toronto: Thomas Allen Publishers, 2002) 267.

30 Stacey, *Six Years of War*, 438.

31 Kent Fedorowich, "'Cocked Hats and Swords and Small, Little Garrisons': Britain, Canada and the Fall of Hong Kong, 1941," *Modern Asian Studies* 37.1 (February 2003) 111–57; Terry Copp, "The Decision to Reinforce Hong Kong: September 1941," *Canadian Military History* 20.2 (Spring 2011) 11.

32 On the failure of intelligence, see Timothy Wilford, *Canada's Road to the Pacific War: Intelligence, Strategy, and the Far East Crisis* (Vancouver: UBC Press, 2011); Stacey, *Six Years of War*, 442.

33 Georges 'Blacky' Verreault, *Diary of a Prisoner of War in Japan, 1941–1945* (Rimouski: Vero, 1996) 40.

34 On the battle, see Carl Vincent, *No Reason Why: The Canadian Hong Kong Tragedy—an Examination* (Stittsville: Canada's Wings, 1981) and Brereton Greenhous, *"C" Force to Hong Kong: A Canadian Catastrophe, 1941–1945* (Toronto: Dundurn, 1997).

35 "War Comes to North America," *The Globe and Mail*, 8 December 1941, 6.

36 King diary, 11 December 1941.

CHAPTER 8: DOMESTIC VICTIMS OF HEMISPHERIC DEFENCE

1 Marc Milner, *Canada's Navy: The First Century* (Toronto: University of Toronto Press, 2010) 99.

2 R.T. Elson, "Canada and U.S. to Work Hand in Glove in War," *The Winnipeg Tribune*, 8 December 1941, 8.

3 LAC, RG 2, file D-19-2, Unity of Command on the Pacific Coast, 10 December 1941; LAC, RG 24, v. 5209, file HQS 15-73-4 Part 1, "Notes for Meeting Canadian Section, Permanent Joint Board on Defence," 3 January 1941; Galen Roger Perras, "Who Will Defend British Columbia? Unity of Command on the West Coast, 1934-1942," *Pacific Northwest Quarterly* 88 (Spring 1997) 59–69.

4 LAC, RG 25, v. 5758, file 71 (s), "Recent Trends in the United States-Canada Relations," 27 December 1941.

5 Charles Bishop, "Cabinet Taking Up New Aspect of Pacific War," *The Ottawa Citizen*, 16 February 1942, 1.

6 Douglas, et al., *The Creation of a National Air Force*, 408–409.

7 Granatstein and Hillmer, *First Drafts*, 270.

8 BC Archives, GR 1222, v. 153, copied and held at DHH, Position of the Japanese in British Columbia, 24 September 1940.

9 J.L. Black, *Canada in the Soviet Mirror: Ideology and Perception in Soviet Foreign Affairs, 1917–1991* (Ottawa: Carleton University Press) 123.

10 Reg Whitaker, "Official Repression of Communism during World War II," *Labour/Le Travail* 17 (1986) 135–68.

11 Granatstein, *A Man of Influence*, 85–87.

12 Lita-Rose Betcherman, *The Swastika and the Maple Leaf: Fascist Movements in Canada in the Thirties* (Toronto: Fitzhenry & Whiteside, 1975); Stephen Azzi, *Reconcilable Differences: A History of Canada-US Relations* (Don Mills: Oxford University Press, 2015) 129.

13 See Suzanne Evans, *The Taste of Longing: Ethel Mulvany and her Starving Prisoners of War Cookbook* (Toronto: Between the Lines, 2020).

14 Galen Roger Perras, "Aleutian Allusions: Mackenzie King's Diary and the Invasion of Kiska in 1943," *Canadian Military History* 16.1 (2007) 7.

15 On the fear, real and imagined, see Bradley St. Croix, "The Omnipresent Threat: Fifth Columnists' Impact on the Battle of Hong Kong, December 1941," *Close Encounters in War Journal* 1, 1–18.

16 Stacey, *Six Years of War*, 169.

17 DHH, 112.3M2 (D232), "Appreciation Re Air Landing Troops," 24 January 1942.

18 King diary, 11 December 1941.

19 LAC, King Papers, v. 321, King to Bezeau, 21 April 1942.

20 King diary, 3 June 1942; also see another warning around this time that Canada must defend itself to stave off American dominance, LAC, King papers, v. 350, Wrong to King, 7 April 1942. For prewar concern, Roger Sarty, "Entirely in the Hands of the Friendly Neighbour: The Canadian Armed Forces and the Defence of the Pacific Coast, 1919–1939," *The Maritime Defence of Canada* (Toronto: Canadian Institute of Strategic Studies, 1996).

21 Stoler, *Allies in War*, 28.

22 LAC, J.L. Ralston Papers, MG 27, III B11, v. 37, "An Appreciation of the Military World Situation with Particular Regard to its Effect on Canada," 4 August 1942; LAC, Maurice Pope papers, v. 1, diary, 1 June 1942.

23 Douglas, et al., *The Creation of a National Air Force*, 411.

24 LAC, King papers, v. 319, file 3369, PJBD meeting, 25–26 February 1942; Dziuban, *Military Relations*, 239-40.

25 Kerry Ragnar Steeves, "The Pacific Coast Militia Rangers, 1942–1945," (MA Thesis: University of British Columbia, 1990).

26 LAC, RG 24, v. 11764, file PC010-9-1, Operational Plan of RC to Implement Joint Canadian-United States Basic Defence Plan, 1940.

27 G.N. Tucker, *Naval Service of Canada: Official History* (Ottawa: King's Printer, 1952) 363–64.

28 Thomas Buell, *Master of Seapower: A Biography of Fleet Admiral Ernest J. King* (Boston: Little and Brown, 1980) 299.

29 W.A.B. Douglas, et al., *No Higher Purpose: The Official Operational History of the Royal Canadian Navy in the Second World War, 1939–1943* (St. Catharines: Vanwell, 2002) 339.

30 Dave McIntosh, *Hell on Earth: Aging Faster, Dying Sooner, Canadian Prisoners of the Japanese During World War II* (Toronto: McGraw-Hill Ryerson, 1997) 104; J.L. Granatstein and Gregory A. Johnson, "The Evacuation of the Japanese Canadians, 1942," in Norman Hillmer (eds.), *On Guard for Thee: War, Ethnicity and the Canadian State, 1939–1945* (Ottawa: Canadian Committee for the History of the Second World War, 1988) 103–106.

31 Patricia E. Roy, J.L. Granatstein, Masako Iino, and Hiroko Takamura, *Mutual Hostages: Canadians and Japanese during the Second World War* (Toronto: University of Toronto Press, 1990) 54–55.

32 "How to Treat Enemy Aliens," *The Daily Independent* (Illinois), 12 December 1941, 2.

33 For Italians and Germans, see John E. Schmitz, *Enemies Among Us: The Relocation, Internment, and Repatriation of German, Italian and Japanese Americans during the Second World War* (Lincoln: University of Nebraska Press, 2021).

34 Beschloss, *Presidents of War*, 397–98.

35 R.T. Elson, "Study U.S. Treatment of Japs," *The Vancouver Daily Province*, 8 January 1942, 1, 6.

36 LAC, King papers, D58190-94, Declaration of Existence of a State of War Between Canada and Japan, 8 December 1941.

37 Thompson and Randall, *Canada and the United States*, 173; Roy, Granatstein, Iino, and Takamura, *Mutual Hostages*, 36.

38 Roger Daniels, *Prisoners Without Trial: Japanese Americans in World War II* (New York: Hill and Wang, 1993) 57.

39 See Stephanie Hinnershitz, *Japanese American Incarceration: The Camps and Coerced Labor During World War II* (Philadelphia: University of Pennsylvania Press, 2021).

40 Lyle Dick, "Sergeant Masumi Mitsui and the Japanese Canadian War Memorial: Intersections of National, Cultural, and Personal Memory," *The Canadian Historical Review* 91.3 (September 2010) 435–63.

41 Opentextbc.ca; Canadian History, 6.17, Japanese Canadians in the Second World War. Also see the online exhibition, "Writing Wrongs: Japanese Canadian Protest Letters of the 1940s," Nikkei: National Museum and Cultural Centre (nikkeiplace.org).

42 Roy Miki and Cassandra Kobayashi, *Justice in our Time: The Japanese Canadian Redress Settlement* (Vancouver: Talonbooks, 1991) 37.

43 Roy Ito, *We Went to War: The Story of the Japanese Canadians who served during the First and Second World Wars* (Stittsville: Canada's Wings, 1984).

44 Masayo Umezawa Duus, *Unlikely Liberators: The Men of the 100th and 442nd* (University of Hawaii Press, 2006) 156.

45 Robert Asahina, *Just Americans: How Japanese Americans Won a War at Home and Abroad* (New York: Gotham Books, 2006) 13.

46 King's diary, 19 to 24 February 1942; Beschloss, *Presidents of War*, 397.

47 "B.C. Opinions Vary on Plan," *The Vancouver Daily Province*, 17 March 1945, 6.

48 Gordon Robertson, *Memoirs of a Very Civil Servant: Mackenzie King to Pierre Trudeau* (Toronto: University of Toronto Press, 2000) 41; Richard J. Needham, "One Man's Opinion," *Calgary Herald*, 25 September 1945, 4.

49 CWM, online exhibition, War Against Japan, Canada at War Against Japan, 1941–1945 (warmuseum.ca)

50 Miki and Kobayashi, *Justice in our Time*, 49.

CHAPTER 9: TREADING CAREFULLY WITH THE AMERICANS

1 Granatstein, *A Man of Influence*, 118.

2 Dawn Alexandrea Berry, "Cryolite, the Canadian Aluminium Industry and the American Occupation of Greenland during the Second World War," *The Polar Journal* 2.2 (2012) 219–35; Aluminum Company of Canada to Department of External Affairs, 9 April 1940, in David Murray (ed.), *Documents on Canadian External Affairs*, vol. 7, 947.

3 Maurice A. Pope, *Soldier and Politician: Memoirs* (Toronto: University of Toronto Press, 1962) 144–45.

4 King diary, 8 May 1940.

5 "Extract from Memorandum from Under-Secretary of State for External Affairs to Prime Minister," *DCER*, vol. 7, 966.

6 Douglas, et al., *No Higher Purpose*, 131; "Illustrative Material," *Documents on Canadian External Affairs*, vol. 8, 71.

7 "Memorandum from Under-Secretary for External Affairs to Prime Minister, 10 April 1940," *DCER*, vol. 7, 948.

8 Conn, et al., *Guarding the United States and Its Outposts*, 458.

ENDNOTES

9 Egill Bjarnason, *How Iceland Changed the World: The Big History of a Small Island* (New York: Penguin, 2021) 136.

10 Winston S. Churchill, *The Second World War: The Grand Alliance* (Boston: Houghton Mifflin Company, 1950) 138.

11 "Secretary of State for External Affairs to High Commissioner in Great Britain," *DCER*, vol. 7, 769; *House of Commons Debates*, 18 June 1940.

12 LAC, RG 24, v. 15024, War Diary, Cameron Highlanders of Ottawa, 7 July 1940.

13 Steven J. Bright, "Z Force on the Ground: The Canadian Deployment to Iceland, 1940–41," *Canadian Military History* 31.1 (2022) 20.

14 "Iceland: A Hard Life," *Time* (13 January 1941) 23.

15 For a detailed historical report, see DHH, "Z" Force in Iceland, Report No. 33, Army Headquarters, 16 December 1939, digitized on Directorate of History and Heritage website, ahq033.pdf (canada.ca).

16 L.K. Bertram, *The Viking Immigrants: Icelandic North Americans* (Toronto: University of Toronto Press, 2020) 124–30.

17 Lawrence, *A Bloody War*, 75; also see Jeffrey A. Keshen, *Saints, Sinners, and Soldiers: Canada's Second World War* (Vancouver: UBC Press, 2004) 238–39.

18 Michael T. Corgan, "Franklin D. Roosevelt and the American Occupation of Iceland," *Naval War College Review* 45.4 (Autumn 1992) 36–37.

19 Douglas, *The Creation of a National Air Force*, 581–610.

20 Elliot Roosevelt (ed.), *F.D.R.: His Personal Letters*, volume III (New York: Duell, Sloan and Pearce, 1947) 73.

21 King diary, 5 July 1940; Stacey, *Six Years of War*, 83–86, 178–82.

22 Éric Amyot, *Le Québec entre Pétain et de Gaulle—Vichy, la France Libre et les Canadiens Français, 1940–1945* (Fides: Saint-Laurent, 1999).

23 Robert B. Bryce, *Canada and the Cost of World War II: The International Operations of Canada's Department of Finance, 1939–1947* (Montreal: McGill-Queen's University Press, 2005) 65–66; C.P. Stacey, *Canada and the Age of Conflict: A History of Canadian External Affairs* (Toronto: Macmillan of Canada, 1981) 300–301.

24 "Canadian Acting Consul in St. Pierre and Miquelon to Secretary of State for External Affairs, 25 December 1941," *DCER*, vol. 9, 1648–1650.

25 Pearson, *Mike*, volume 1, 200. For the best account, see Martin Auger, "A Tempest in a Teapot: Canadian Military Planning and the St. Pierre and Miquelon Affair, 1940–1942," *Acadiensis: Journal of the History of the Atlantic Region* 33 (2003) 47–72.

26 For King's observations, see his diary entry for 26 December 1941.

27 Pickersgill, *Seeing Canada Whole*, 215.

28 King diary, 25 December 1941.

29 Andrew Roberts, *Masters and Commanders: The Military Geniuses Who Led the West to Victory in WW2* (Toronto: Penguin Books, 2009) 449.

30 On Churchill's speech, see Reardon, *Winston Churchill and Mackenzie King*, 177.

CHAPTER 10: FORTRESS NEWFOUNDLAND

1 *House of Commons Debates*, 8 September 1939; Peter Neary, "The History of Newfoundland and Labrador during the Second World War," Dispatches, Canadian War Museum, online. The History of Newfoundland and Labrador during the Second World War I Dispatches I Learn I Canadian War Museum. For the best book on Newfoundland and the war, see Peter Neary, *Newfoundland in the North Atlantic World, 1929–1949* (Kingston: McGill-Queen's University Press, 1988).

2 James K. Hiller and Mike O'Brien, "Newfoundland," *1914–1918-online. International Encyclopedia of the First World War.*

3 Tim Cook, *Lifesavers and Body Snatchers: Medical Care and the Struggle for Survival in the Great War* (Toronto: Allen Lane, 2022) 426–27.

4 See G.W.L. Nicholson, *More Fighting Newfoundlanders: A History of Newfoundland's Fighting Forces in the Second World War* (St John's: Government of Newfoundland, 1969).

5 Christopher A. Sharpe and A.J. Shawyer, "Building a Wartime Landscape," in Steven High (ed.), *Occupied St John's: A Social History of a City at War, 1939–1945* (Montreal: McGill-Queen's University Press, 2010) 42; and "Letter from Prime Minister to Commissioner of Defence," *Evening Telegram* (St. John's) 27 March 1941.

6 Robert Kavanagh, "W Force: The Canadian Army and the Defence of Newfoundland in the Second World War," (MA thesis: Memorial University of Newfoundland, 1995).

7 Douglas, *The Creation of a National Air Force*, 387, 484–85.

8 Gilbert N. Tucker, *The Naval Service of Canada: Its Official History* (Ottawa: King's Printer, 1952) 203, 531.

9 MacKenzie, *Inside the Atlantic Triangle*, 31.

10 "Barter with Britain," *New York Times*, 8 September 1940.

11 Conn, et al., *Guarding the United States and Its Outposts*, 377.

12 Bill McNeil, *Voices of a War Remembered: An Oral History of Canadians in World War II* (Toronto: Doubleday, 1991) 34.

13 See Melvin Baker and Peter Neary, "Governor Sir Humphrey Walwyn on the United States Bases in Newfoundland, 15 October 1945," *Newfoundland and Labrador Studies* 36.2 (2022) 292–94.

14 Darrell Hillier, *North Atlantic Crossroads: The Royal Air Force Ferry Command Gander Unit, 1940–1946* (Mount Pearl Atlantic Crossroads Press, 2021).

15 See Carl Christie, *Ocean Bridge: The History of RAF Ferry Command* (Toronto: University of Toronto Press, 1995) and Dziuban, *Military Relations between the United States and Canada, 1939–1945,* 181–91.

16 Douglas, et al., *No Higher Purpose,* 133.

17 King diary, 7 November 1940.

18 LAC, RG 24, v. 2687, file HQS 5199 pt 9, Chief of Staff Committee, Brief Appreciation of the Situation as of 24th February 1941.

19 Douglas, et al., *No Higher Purpose,* 129.

20 Lawrence, *A Bloody War,* 111.

21 Richard Goette, "Britain and the Delay in Closing the Mid-Atlantic 'Air Gap' during the Battle of the Atlantic," *The Northern Mariner* XV.4 (October 2005) 19–41.

22 Winston Churchill, *The Second World War: The Grand Alliance* (Boston: Houghton Mifflin Company, 1950) 122. On Churchill's calculation, see Christopher M. Bell, "The View from the Top: Winston Churchill, British Grand Strategy, and the Battle of the Atlantic," in Marcus Faulkner and Christopher M. Bell (eds.), *Decision in the Atlantic: The Allies and the Longest Campaign of the Second World War* (Kentucky: Brecourt, 2019) 20–45.

23 Tucker, *The Naval Service of Canada,* volume II, 187.

24 LAC, RG 24, v. 3892, NSS 1033-6-1, pt. 1, Nfld. Convoy Escort Force, Notes for the Minister of National Defence, 1 July 1941.

25 Paul Collins, "'First Line of Defence': The Establishment and Development of St John's, Newfoundland as the Royal Canadian Navy's Premier Escort Base in the Second World War," *Northern Mariner* 16.3 (2006) 15–32.

26 On technology, see David Zimmerman, *The Great Naval Battle of Ottawa* (Toronto: University of Toronto Press, 1989).

27 Marc Milner, *North Atlantic Run: The Royal Canadian Navy and the Battle for the Convoys* (Toronto: University of Toronto Press, 1985) 64.

28 LAC, RG 25, v. 2903, file 2341-40C, Future Communications between Canada and the USA on Defence Matters, 27 July 1941; Stacey, Arms, *Men and Governments,* 313.

29 LAC, RG 24, v. 5177, file S. 15-1-350, pt. 1, Heakes to AOC EAC, 23 September 1941; Douglas, et al, *No Higher Purpose,* 595.

30 Richard Goette, "The Command and Control of Canadian and American Maritime Air Power in the Northwest Atlantic, 1941–1943," *Canadian Military History* 26.2 (2017) 10.

31 LAC, RG 24, v. 5177, file S. 15-1-350, pt. 1, hand written note, CAS to Power, 3 November 1941.

32 DHH, 181.002 (D156), "Notes on Convoy Organization Western North Atlantic," 20 March 1942; Stacey, *Arms, Men, and Governments*, 360–67.

33 High (ed.), *Occupied St John's*, 9.

34 Lisa Banister (ed.), *Equal to the Challenge* (Ottawa: Queen's Printer, 2001) 177; Tucker, *The Naval Service of Canada*, 322.

35 Sharpe and Shawyer, "Building a Wartime Landscape," in High (ed.), *Occupied St John's*, 22; DHH 314.009 (D17) pt. 2, file 2-1-1, Pope to Henry, 7 April 1944.

36 John N. Cardolis, *A Friendly Invasion: The American Military in Newfoundland 1940 to 1990* (St. John's: Breakwater Press, 1990).

37 Donald E. Graves, *In Peril on the Sea: The Royal Canadian Navy and the Battle of the Atlantic* (Toronto: Robin Brass Studio, 2003) 121.

38 Wade Werner, "Boom in Newfoundland," *Salt Lake Telegram* (Utah), 4 August 1941, 4.

39 Peter Neary, "'A Grave Problem Which Needs Immediate Attention': An American Report on Venereal Disease and Other Health Problems in Newfoundland, 1942," *Newfoundland Studies* 15.1 (1999) 79–103.

40 Steven High, "Rethinking the Friendly Invasion" in High (ed.), *Occupied St John's*, 175.

41 Paul Collins, "Canada's Plan to Torch St. John's During the Second World War: Upper-Canadian Arrogance or Tabloid Journalism?," *Newfoundland Studies* 24.2 (2009) [viewed online] paragraph 6.

42 LAC, RG 24, v. 11927, MS 1400-4, Vol. 1, "Instructions Issued to Certain Colonial Dependencies On 'Scorched Earth Policy.'"

43 Leslie Roberts, "Canada and the War at Sea," in Stephen Leacock and Leslie Roberts, *Canada's War at Sea* (Montreal: Alvah M. Beatty, 1944) 22.

CHAPTER 11: U-BOATS IN NORTH AMERICAN WATERS

1 Hillmer and Granatstein, *For Better or For Worse*, 150.

2 Bernard Edwards, *Attack and Sink!: The Battle for Convoy SC 42* (Wimborne Minster: New Guild, 1995).

3 Douglas, et al., *No Higher Purpose*, 255.

4 Frank Curry, *War at Sea: A Canadian Seaman on the North Atlantic* (Toronto: Lugus, 1990) 59.

5 Marc Milner, *Canada's Navy: The First Century* (Toronto: University of Toronto Press, 1999) 102.

6 Marc Milner, *The Battle of the Atlantic* (St. Catharines: Vanwell, 2003) 83.

7 For the campaign, see Michael Gannon, *Operation Drumbeat: The Dramatic True Story of Germany's First U-Boat Attacks Along the American Coast in World War II* (New York: Harper & Row, 1990).

8 Michael Hadley and W.A.B. Douglas, "U-boat Operations," Canadian Encyclopedia, online.

9 Lawrence, *A Bloody War,* 111.

10 Conn, et al., *Guarding the United States and Its Outposts,* 431, Table 5; Marc Milner, "The Atlantic War, 1939–1945: The Case for a New Paradigm," in Marcus Faulkner and Christopher M. Bell (eds.), *Decision in the Atlantic: The Allies and the Longest Campaign of the Second World War* (Kentucky: Brecourt, 2019) 13.

11 Dan Van der Vat, *The Atlantic Campaign: World War II's Great Struggle at Sea* (New York: Harper and Row, 1988) 236.

12 DHH, 193.009 (D6), Chiefs of Staff Committee to the Ministers, 30 April 1942.

13 Robert Fisher, "We'll Get Our Own': Canada and the Oil Shipping Crisis of 1942," *The Northern Mariner* 3.2 (1993) 35.

14 Curry, *War at Sea,* 63.

15 Douglas, et al., *No Higher Purpose,* 412.

16 Lawrence, *A Bloody War,* 98–103.

17 *House of Commons Debates,* 27 January 1942, 75.

18 Neville Thompson, *The Third Man: Churchill, Roosevelt, Mackenzie King, and the Untold Friendships that Won WWII* (Toronto: Sutherland House, 2021) 177.

19 On the plebiscite, see J.L. Granatstein and J.M. Hitsman, *Broken Promises: A History of Conscription in Canada* (Toronto: Oxford University Press, 1977).

20 Yves Tremblay, *Volontaires: Des Québécois en guerre, 1939–1945* (Montréal: Athéna, 2007) 17.

21 LAC, King papers, MG 26, series J1, v. 332, 284204-5; and Thompson, *The Third Man,* 219–20.

22 Milner, *Canada's Navy,* 104.

23 Michael Hadley, *U-Boats Against Canada: German Submarines in Canadian Waters* (Montreal: McGill-Queen's University Press, 1985) 104.

24 Shawn Cafferky, "A Useful Lot, These Canadian Ships: The Royal Canadian Navy and Operation Torch, 1942–1943," *The Northern Mariner* 3.4 (October 1993) 1–17.

25 For the best account, see Roger Sarty, *War in the St. Lawrence: The Forgotten U-boat Battles* (Toronto: Allen Lane, 2012).

26 Douglas How, *Night of the Caribou* (Hantsport: Lancelot Press, 1988) 276–79.

27 Brian Dubreuil, "Battle of the St. Lawrence," Canadian Encyclopedia, online.

28 Marc Milner, *The U-boat Hunters: The Royal Canadian Navy and the offensive against Germany's Submarines* (Toronto: University of Toronto Press, 1994) 17.

CHAPTER 12: SOVEREIGNTY AND STRATEGY

1   King diary, 17 May 1945.

2   LAC, Escott Reid papers, v. 13, file US and Canada, "The United States and Canada: Domination, Cooperation, Absorption," 12 January 1942.

3   Stacey, *Historical Documents of Canada, Volume V: The Arts of War and Peace, 1914–1945,* 609.

4   R.D. Cuff and J.L. Granatstein, "Getting on with the Americans: Canadian Perceptions of the United States, 1939–1945," in R.D. Cuff and J.L. Granatstein (eds.), *Ties that Bind* (Toronto: Samuel Steven Hakkert, 1977) 104–105.

5   Michael Stevenson, *Canada's Greatest Wartime Muddle: National Selective Service and the Mobilization of Human Resources during World War II* (Montreal-Kingston: McGill-Queens University Press, 2001).

6   King diary, 27 July 1941.

7   Hall, *North American Supply,* 60.

8   See Alex Danchev, *Very Special Relationship: Field Marshal Sir John Dill and the Anglo-American Alliance, 1941–1944* (London: Brassey's Defence Publishers, 1986).

9   Granatstein and Hillmer, *For Better or For Worse,* 148.

10 Blair Fraser, "Canada in Washington," *Maclean's* (15 February 1945) online.

11 C.P. Stacey, *A Date with History: Memoirs of a Canadian Historian* (Ottawa: Deneau, 1983) 73; Charles Ritchie, *The Siren Years: A Canadian Diplomat Abroad, 1937–1945* (Toronto: Macmillan of Canada, 1974) xi.

12 Robert Bothwell and John English, "The View from Inside Out: Canadian Diplomats and Their Public," *International Journal* (Winter 1983–84) 47–67; and Pearson, *Memoirs,* volume 1, 206–11.

13 LAC, King papers, v. 350, "Certain Developments in Canada–United States Relations," Pearson to McCarthy, 18 March 1943.

14 Kennedy, *History of the Department of Munitions and Supply,* viii.

15 Doug Delaney, "'A Word Here and a Phrase There': Major General Maurice A. Pope and the Canadian Joint Staff Mission, Washington, 1942–1944," in Greg Kennedy (ed.), *Defense Engagement since 1900: Global Lessons in Soft Power* (Kansas: University Press of Kansas, 2020) 125–26.

16 "The Proposed Establishment of a Canadian Military Mission in Washington," 18 June 1941, *DCER,* vol. 8, 232.

17 "Joint Canadian Staff Set Up in Washington," *The Ottawa Citizen*, 4 July 1942, 8. For Pope on his own role, see DHH 314.0009 (D17), Canadian Joint Staff, Washington, A.B.C.-22 and the Canada-United States Permanent Joint Board on Defence, 10 August 1942 and LAC, RG 24, v. 5184, Extracts from Minutes of Meeting of Cabinet War Committee, 11 March 1942.

18 J.L. Granatstein, *The Generals: The Canadian Army's Senior Commanders in the Second World War* (Toronto: Stoddart, 1993) 214.

19 LAC, Maurice Pope papers, v. 1, Pope's diary, 31 March 1943.

20 This was also Pope's sensible appreciation. See LAC, A.G.L. McNaughton papers, v. 199, file PA6-9F-5, Pope to McNaughton, 11 June 1943.

21 S. McKee Rosen, *The Combined Boards of the Second World War* (New York: Columbia University Press, 1951) 232–33.

22 Pope's diary, 30 June 1942; LAC, King papers, "Munitions Assignment Board," 29 May 1942, C243554.

23 Maurice Pope, *Soldiers and Politicians: Memoirs* (Toronto: University of Toronto Press, 1962) 201; Pope diary, 21 August 1942; Gibson and Robertson (eds.), *Ottawa at War*, 314 and 408.

24 Stacey, *Canada and the Age of Conflict*, 333; J.L. Granatstein, "Hume Wrong's Road to the Functional Principle," in Keith Neilson and Roy A. Prete (eds.), *Coalition Warfare: An Uneasy Accord* (Waterloo: Wilfrid Laurier Press, 1983).

25 For King's views, *House of Commons Debates*, 9 July 1943.

26 Pearson, *Memoirs*, volume 1, 211.

27 G.E. Britnell and V.C. Fowke, *Canadian Agriculture in War and Peace, 1935–1950* (Stanford: Stanford University Press, 1962) 104.

28 Black, *Canada in the Soviet Mirror*, 133.

29 James, *Wartime Economic Cooperation*, 338.

30 James, *Wartime Economic Co-operation*, 35.

31 J.L. Granatstein, *The Best Little Army in the World: The Canadians in Northwest Europe, 1944–1945* (Toronto: Patrick Crean, 2015) 52.

32 Granatstein, "Arming the Nation," 8.

33 McNeil, *Voices of a War Remembered*, 130.

34 Stacey, *Canada and the Age of Conflict*, 358; Granatstein, *Canada's War*, 312–15.

35 Keenleyside, *Memoirs of Hugh L. Keenleyside*, 110.

36 King diary, 22 March 1943.

37 For insight into Pearson's time in Washington, see the film, *Diplomat at War, 1941–1945* (1973).

38 See Bill Rawling, *Victor Brodeur: officier de la marine canadienne, 1909–1946* (Outremont: Athéna Éditions, 2008).

39 For a deeper exploration of Pope in Washington, see Claude Leblanc, "Maurice A. Pope: A Study in Military Leadership" (Ph.D. dissertation: Royal Military College of Canada, 2016).

40 "King's Extra Ear," *The Financial Post*, 10 March 1945, 6.

41 King diary, 18 March 1942.

42 John English, *Shadow of Heaven: The Life of Lester Pearson, volume 1: 1897–1948* (Toronto: Lester & Orpen Dennys, 1989) 259.

CHAPTER 13: THE COST OF ALLIANCE WARFARE

1 George Ignatieff, "A.G.L. McNaughton: A Soldier in Diplomacy," *International Journal* 22.3 (Summer 1967) 404.

2 Stoller, *Allies in War*, 39.

3 Tim Cook, "Immortalizing the Canadian Soldier: Lord Beaverbrook, the Canadian War Records Office in the First World War," Briton Busch (ed.), *Canada and the Great War: Western Front Association papers* (Montreal: McGill-Queen's University Press, 2003) 46–65.

4 *The Canadians at War, 1939/45*, volume II (Reader's Digest, 1969) 537.

5 CWM Oral History, 31D1 HARPER, Burton Harper.

6 LAC, RG 24, v. 12613, file 11, "Analysis of the VD Problem in the Canadian Army Overseas," 1945.

7 LAC, RG 24, v. 12318, file Censor/4/1, CMHQ file 4.

8 Jonathan Vance, *Maple Leaf Empire: Canada, Britain, and Two World Wars* (Don Mills: Oxford University Press, 2012) 177.

9 Mack Lynch, et al., (eds.), *Salty Dips:* volume 1 (Ottawa: Naval Officer's Association of Canada, 1983) 15.

10 Willilam Horrocks, *In Their Own Words* (Ottawa: Rideau Veterans Home Residents Council, 1993) 149.

11 Christopher Somerville, *Our War: How the British Commonwealth Fought the Second World War* (London: Weidenfeld and Nicholson, 2020) 240.

12 See David Reynolds, *Rich Relations: The American Occupation of Britain, 1942–1945* (New York: Random House, 1995).

13 J.K. Chapman, *River Boy at War* (New Brunswick: Goose Lane, 1985) 13.

14 C.P. Stacey and Barbara Wilson, *The Half Million: The Canadians in Britain, 1939–1946* (Toronto: University of Toronto Press, 1987) 89–90.

15 "2,058 Transferred to American Forces," *New York Times*, 20 August 1942, 3; Dickon, *Americans at War in Foreign Forces*, 194.

16 Stoller, *Allies in War*, 41.

17 Kimball, *Forged in War*, 142.

18 Paul Dickson, *A Thoroughly Canadian General: A Biography of General H.D.G. Crerar* (Toronto: University of Toronto Press, 2007) 201.

19 Granatstein, *Canada's Army*, 209.

20 For the pinch raid, see David O'Keefe, *One Day in August: The Untold Story Behind Canada's Tragedy at Dieppe* (Toronto: Knopf Canada, 2013). O'Keefe's book enhances our understanding of the operation, but then improperly situates the raid as a driving force, which it was not. In effect, he has the tail (the pinch raid) wagging the dog (the full-scale assault). This is wrong.

21 Ross Munro, *Gauntlet to Overlord* (Toronto: Macmillan, 1945) 305–306.

22 For the deepest dive into the raid and conspiracies, see Brian Villa, *Unauthorized Action: Mountbatten and the Dieppe Raid* (Toronto: Oxford University Press, 1989); for Churchill and the raid, see Winston Churchill, *The Second World War: The Hinge of Fate*, volume IV (London: Cassell, 1951) 444.

23 LAC, RG 24, v. 10765, file D126, Crerar to McNaughton, 11 August 1942.

24 T. Murray Hunter, *Canada at Dieppe* (Ottawa: Canadian War Museum Historical Publication No. 17, 1982) 16.

25 DHH, CMHQ Report 89, 4, available online.

26 Munro, *Gauntlet to Overlord*, 325–28.

27 Hugh Henry, "The Calgary Tanks at Dieppe," *Canadian Military History* 4.1 (Spring 1995) 61–74.

28 Audrey and Paul Grescoe, *The Book of War Letters* (Toronto: Macfarlane, Walter and Rose, 2003) 243–44.

29 Ross Mahoney, "'The support afforded by the air force was faultless': The Royal Air Force and the Raid on Dieppe, 19 August 1942," *Canadian Military History* 21.4 (Autumn 2012) 17–32. For the official report, see RG 24, v. 10870, 232c2 (D5), Report by the Air Force Commander on the Combined Operation Against Dieppe, August 19th, 1942.

30 Rod Mickleburgh, *Rare Courage: Veterans of the Second World War Remember* (Toronto: McClelland & Stewart, 2005) 52.

31 Brereton Greenhous, *Dieppe, Dieppe* (Montreal: Art Global, 1992) 108.

32 For casualties, see Stacey, *The Canadian Army, 1939–1945*, 80.

33 On selling the mission, see Timothy Balzer, "'In Case the Raid Is Unsuccessful . . .' Selling Dieppe to Canadians," *The Canadian Historical Review* 87.3 (2006) 409–30.

34 For some lessons, see Cook, *The Necessary War*, 283–85; and for its debilitating impact on the constructed memory of the war in Canada, see Cook, *The Fight for History*, 229–36.

35 LAC, RG24, v. 12319, file 4/Censor/4/8, Field Censor (Home) Report, 20 August–3 September 1942.

36 William Young, "Building Citizenship: English Canada and Propaganda during the Second World War," *Journal of Canadian Studies* 16. 3&4 (1981) 122.

37 King diary, 21 August 1942.

CHAPTER 14: WEAPONIZING CULTURE

1 LAC, RG 53, v. 1, Grierson to Robertson, 1 September 1942.

2 J.L. Granatstein, *Yankee Go Home: Canadians and Anti-Americanism* (Toronto: HarperCollins, 1997) 77.

3 Jonathan Vance, *A History of Canadian Culture* (Don Mills: Oxford University Press, 2009) 354.

4 William R. Young, "Mobilizing English Canada for War: The Bureau of Public Information, The Wartime Information Board and a View of the National during the Second World War," in Sidney Aster (ed.), *The Second World War as a National Experience* (Ottawa: The Canadian Committee for the History of the Second World War, 1981) 196.

5 "Maclean's Editorial," *Maclean's*, 1 May 1941.

6 John Grierson, "A Film Policy for Canada," *Canadian Affairs* 1.11 (15 June 1944) 4, 13.

7 Gary Evans, *John Grierson and the National Film Board: The Politics of Wartime Propaganda* (Toronto: University of Toronto Press, 1984) 59.

8 See Saywell, *Just Call me Mitch*, 441–42.

9 William Goetz, "The Canadian Wartime Documentary: 'Canada Carries on' and 'The World in Action,'" *Cinema Journal* 16 (1977) 59–80.

10 Evans, *John Grierson and the National Film Board*, 169.

11 James H. Marsh, "John Grierson," *The Canadian Encyclopedia*, online.

12 Evans, *John Grierson and the National Film Board*, 162.

13 Keenleyside, *Memoirs of Hugh L. Keenleyside*, 103.

14 Evans, *John Grierson and the National Film Board*, 94.

15 Alta R. Wilkinson (ed.), *Ottawa to Caen: Letters from Arthur Campbell Wilkinson* (Tower Books, 1947) 17.

16 A.E. Powley, *Broadcast from the Front: Canadian Radio Overseas in the Second World War* (Toronto: Hakkert, 1975) 8.

17 Vance, *A History of Canadian Culture*, 311.

18 Laura Brandon, *Art or Memorial? The Forgotten History of Canada's War Art* (Calgary: University of Calgary Press, 2006) 56.

19 *House of Commons Debates*, 25 July 1940, 1928–1929. The long history of this deep worry is analysed in Mary Vipond, "Canadian Nationalism and the

Plight of Canadian Magazines in the 1920s," *The Canadian Historical Review* 58 (March 1977) 43–63.

20 John Bell and Michel Viau, "Canadian Golden Age of Comics, 1941–1946." Collections Canada, https://www.collectionscanada.gc.ca/comics/027002-8300-e.html.

21 Ryan Edwardson, "The Many Lives of Captain Canuck: Nationalism, Culture, and the Creation of a Canadian Comic Book Superhero," *The Journal of Popular Culture* 37.2 (2003) 187.

22 Dean Beeby, *Cargo of Lies: The True Story of a Nazi Double Agent in Canada* (Toronto: University of Toronto Press, 1996).

23 Bosley Crowther, "Corvette K-225," *The New York Times*, 21 October 1943.

24 All information drawn from Hugh A. Halliday, "Airman on set," *The Legion*, 7 September 2017, accessed online.

25 Halliday, "Airman on set," no page, online.

26 "The Current Cinema," *The New Yorker* (21 February 1942) 49.

27 "Gag Lines on Officers Bring Army Show Laughs," *The Globe and Mail*, 31 July 1943, 4.

28 "Army Show Enchants City," *The Edmonton Journal*, 15 July 1943, 9.

29 W. Ray Stephens, *The Canadian Entertainers of World War II* (Oakville: Mosaic Press, 1993) 46.

30 Reginald C. Stuart, "Borders and Brows: Mass Culture and National Identity in North America since 1900," in Michael D. Behiels and Reginald C. Stuart (eds.), *Transnationalism: Canada-United States History into the 21st Century* (Montreal: McGill-Queen's University Press, 2010) 53–54.

31 *The Canadians at War, 1939/45*, volume II (Reader's Digest, 1969) 423.

32 *The Canadians at War, 1939/45*, volume II (Reader's Digest, 1969) 538.

33 LAC, RG 53, v. 1, Grierson to Robertson, 1 September 1942.

CHAPTER 15: DEFENDING THE NORTH

1 For the phrase, see Ken S. Coates and William R. Morrison, "The Army of Occupation": Americans in the Canadian Northwest During World War II" in P. Whitney Lackenbauer (ed.), *Canadian Arctic Sovereignty and Security*: Historical Perspectives Occasional Paper no. 4 (2011).

2 Hugh Keenleyside and Gerald S. Brown, *Canada and the United States: Some Aspects of their Historical Relations* (New York: Alfred A. Knopf, 1952) 369.

3 BC Archives, GR 122, box 138, copied by DHH, Pattullo to Mackenzie King, B.C.–Yukon—Alaska Highway, 9 May 1938.

4 King diary, 5 March 1937; LAC, O.D. Skelton papers, v. 27, file 9, memorandum, February 1937.

5 P. Whitney Lackenbauer, "Race, Gender, and International 'Relations': African Americans and Aboriginal People on the Margins in Canada's North, 1942–1948," in Laura Madokoro, et al. (eds.), *Dominion of Race: Rethinking Canada's International History* (Vancouver: UBC Press, 2017) 116.

6 M.V. Bezeau, "The Realities of Strategic Planning: The Decision to Build the Alaska Highway," in Kenneth Coates (ed.), *The Alaska Highway: Papers of the 40th Anniversary Symposium* (Vancouver: University of British Columbia Press, 1985).

7 Ashton to Skelton, 24 August 1939, in *DCER* vol. 5, 265. For other insights, see H.L. Keenleyside, "The Canadian U.S. Permanent Joint Board on Defence, 1940–1945," *Behind the Scenes* 16.1 (Winter 1960–61) 51–75.

8 Lael Morgan, "Mile and Miles: Remembering Black Troops Who Built the Alcan Highway," in Bob Hesketh (ed.), *The Northern Wartime Projects* (Edmonton: Canadian Circumpolar Institute, 1996) 150.

9 Matthew F. Delmont, *Half American: The Epic Story of African Americans Fighting World War II at Home and Abroad* (New York: Viking, 2022) 119.

10 DHH, 314.009 (D17), Progress Report, Canada–United States Joint Projects, 31 August 1943.

11 Jack Paterson, "Back Door to Alaska," *Maclean's*, 1 September 1942.

12 Coats and Morrison, "The Army of Occupation," 67.

13 George Behn, Local Civilian Guide for Military https://royalbcmuseum.bc.ca/exhibits/living-landscapes/prnr/alaska/george_behn.htm

14 Shelagh D. Grant, *Sovereignty or Security?: Government Policy in the Canadian North, 1936–1950* (Vancouver: UBC, Press, 1988) 89.

15 Ken S. Coates, *Best Left as Indians: Native–White Relations in the Yukon Territory, 1840–1973* (Montreal: McGill-Queen's University Press 1991) 102.

16 Pope, *Soldiers and Politicians*, 219.

17 Richard Finnie, "CanolBlitz," *Maclean's* (15 August 1943) 42.

18 DHH, 314.009 (D17), United States Defence Projects and Installations in Canada, 12 January 1944.

19 King diary, 17 February 1944.

20 John David Hamilton, *Arctic Revolution: Social Change in the Northwest Territories, 1935–1994* (Toronto: Dundurn Press, 1994) 54; Kenneth S. Coates "Canol Pipeline," *The Canadian Encyclopedia* (online).

21 Leslie Roberts, *The Mackenzie* (New York: Rinehart, 1949) 239.

22 *House of Commons Debates*, 28 February 1944; J.A. Wilson, "Northwest Passage by Air," *Canadian Geographical Journal* 26.3 (March 1943) 107–115.

23 Charles L. Shaw, "Bomber Road," *Maclean's*, 1 January 1942.

24 DHH, 314.009 (D17), Progress Report, Canada–United States Joint Projects,
    31 August 1943.

25 Charles L. Shaw, "Bomber Road," *Maclean's*, 1 January 1942.

26 Robert W. Coakley and Richard M. Leighton, *Global Logistics and Strategy*
    (Washington: Office of the Chief of Military History, 1955) 101–102; Stoler,
    Allies in War, 31.

27 Hubert Van Tuyll, *Feeding the Bear: American Aid to the Soviet Union, 1941–
    1944* (New York: Praeger, 1989); Alexander Hill, "British Lend Lease Aid and
    the Soviet War Effort, June 1941–June 1942," *The Journal of Military History*
    71.3 (2007) 773–808.

28 Paul Kemp, *Convoy: Drama in Arctic Waters* (London: Arms and Armour,
    1993) 235.

29 Maura Forrest, "A Canadian veteran remembers the terrible Murmansk Run,"
    Barents Observer, 18 May 2015, accessed online.

30 Conn, et al., *Guarding the United States and Its Outposts*, 269–70.

31 Blake W. Smith "The Northwest Route to Alaska," in Alexander B. Dolitsky
    (ed.), *Allies in Wartime: The Alaska–Siberia Airway During World War II*
    (Alaska: Alaska-Siberia Research Center, 2007) 2.

32 DHH, H.A.S. 5199-W-1 F.D. 20, 8 July 1942.

33 Steven Boddington and Sean Moir, "The Friendly Invasion: The American
    Presence in Edmonton," in K.W. Tingley (ed.), *For King and Country:
    Alberta in the Second World War* (Edmonton: Provincial Museum of Alberta,
    1995) 182.

34 Stan B. Cohen, *The Forgotten War: A Pictorial History of World War II in
    Alaska and Northwestern Canada, Volume 1* (Missoula: Pictorial Histories
    Publishing, 1981) 44–46; Wesley Frank Craven and James Lea Cate, *The Army
    Air Forces in World War II*, volume 7 (Washington: Office of Air Force
    History, 1983) 152–72.

35 Young, "Mobilizing English Canada for War," 198.

36 Aloysius Balawyder, "Canada in the Uneasy War Alliance," in Aloysius
    Balawyder (ed.), *Canadian–Soviet Relations, 1939–1980* (Oakville: Mosaic
    Press, 1981) 1–14.

37 Dziuban, *Military Relations between the United States and Canada, 1939–
    1945*, 196–97.

38 Keenleyside Memorandum, 3 March 1942, in *DCER*, vol. 9, 1183.

39 *House of Commons Debates*, 1 February 1943, 20.

40 LAC, Escott Reid papers, v. 6, file 10, "Some Problems in the Relations
    between Canada and the United States," 16 April 1943.

41 King diary, 29 March 1943; Clyde Sanger, *Malcolm MacDonald: Bringing an End to Empire* (Montreal: McGill University Press, 1995) 237–39.

42 DHH, 314.009 (D375), Memorandum for the Under Secretary, 19 April 1943.

43 LAC, RG 36/7, v. 3, file 1, pt. 2a, Foster to Cabinet War Committee, 31 July 1944.

44 Vincent Massey, *What's Past Is Prologue: The Memoirs of the Right Honourable Vincent Massey* (London: Macmillan, 1963) 371.

45 Pierre Berton, *The Mysterious North* (Toronto: McClelland & Stewart, 1956) 99.

46 King diary, 21 March 1942.

47 Elizabeth Brebner, "Sovereignty and the North: Canadian–American Cooperation, 1939–45," in Bob Hesketh (ed.), *The Northern Wartime Projects* (Edmonton: Canadian Circumpolar Institute, 1996) 56; LAC, RG 25, 1989–90/029, box 34, file 52-c(s), p2, Withdrawal of United States Forces from Canada, 18 April 1946.

CHAPTER 16: PROTECTING THE WEST COAST

1 Richard L. Harkness, "Pearl Harbor to Now," *Maclean's*, 1 November 1942.

2 Perras, *Stepping Stones to Nowhere*, 97.

3 Joint Canadian–United States Basic Defense Plan No. 2 (Short Title ABC–22), 28 July 1941, in *DCER*, vol. 8, 249–61; John F. Hilliker (ed.), *Documents on Canadian External Relations*, vol. 9 (Ottawa: Department of External Affairs, 1980) 1180.

4 Michael Whitby, "The Quiet Coast: Canadian Naval Operations in Defence of British Columbia, 1941–1942," in Peter T. Haydon and Ann L. Griffiths (eds), *Canada's Pacific Naval Presence: Purposeful or Peripheral* (Centre for Foreign Policy Studies Dalhousie University, 2000) 77.

5 Erin O'Toole, "Filling in the Family Story Behind an Empty Medal Box," *The National Post*, 5 January 2021.

6 Douglas, et al., *The Creation of a National Air Force*, 417.

7 King diary, 30 December 1942; Granatstein and Bothwell, "A Self-Evident National Duty," 224–25.

8 Norman Dawber, Royal Canadian Air Force, https://www.thememoryproject.com/stories/106:norman-dawber/

9 King diary, 30 May 1943; David Zimmerman, *Maritime Command Pacific: The Royal Canadian Navy's West Coast Fleet in the Early Cold War* (Vancouver: UBC Press, 2015) 10–11.

10 "Memorandum from Under-Secretary of State for External Affairs to Prime Minister, 27 May 1943," *DCER*, vol. 9, 1171.

11 LAC, King Papers, v. 348, file 3770, Robertson to King, 27 May 1943.

12 LAC, RG24, v. 2919, file HQS 9055(1), Stuart to Ralston, 26 May 1943.

13 See Daniel Byers, *Zombie Army: The Canadian Army and Conscription in the Second World War* (Vancouver: UBC Press, 2016).

14 Directorate of History and Heritage (DHH), Captain G.W.L. Nicholson, "The Canadian Participation in the Kiska Operation," December 1943, part I, 9.

15 Conn, et al., *Guarding the United States and Its Outposts*, 294–95.

16 Stacey, *Six Years of War*, 174–75.

17 Galen Roger Perras, "When We Got There, The Cupboard Was Bare": Le Regiment de Hull and Kiska, 1943," *Canadian Military History* 24.2 (2015) 80; Tony Foster, *Meeting of Generals* (Toronto: Methuen, 1986) 273.

18 DHH, Captain G.W.L. Nicholson, "The Canadian Participation in the Kiska Operation," December 1943, part I, 3.

19 Perras, "When We Got There," 78.

20 LAC, RG 24, v. 14165, file 1,030, 13th Canadian Brigade HQ diary, 9 August 1943.

21 Mickleburg, *Rare Courage*, 68.

22 DHH, Captain G.W.L. Nicholson, "The Canadian Participation in the Kiska Operation, December 1943," part II, 34.

23 Perras, "When We Got There," 82; DHH, Captain G.W.L. Nicholson, "The Canadian Participation in the Kiska Operation," December 1943," part II, 49.

24 King diary, 26 October 1944.

25 King diary, 27 May 1943.

26 LAC, King Papers, v. 361, file 3853, "Memorandum re participation of Canadian forces in operations in Alaskan and Aleutian areas," August 1943.

27 "Kiska Is Grenadiers' First Step on Road to Hong Kong," *Winnipeg Free Press*, 23 August 1943.

28 "King Gives Names of Units to Kiska," *The Gazette* (Montreal), 23 August 1943, 1 and 20.

CHAPTER 17: CONTRIBUTING TO THE CAUSE

1 Milner, *Battle of the Atlantic*, 85.

2 Bill McNeil, *Voices of a War Remembered: An Oral History of Canadians in World War II* (Toronto: Doubleday, 1991) 291.

3 Roger Sarty, "Rear-Admiral L.W. Murray and the Battle of the Atlantic," in Lieutenant-Colonel Bernd Horn and Stephen Harris (eds.), *Warrior Chiefs: Perspectives on Senior Canadian Military Leaders* (Toronto: Dundurn Press, 2001) 183–84.

4 Kennedy, *The American People in World War II*, 147.

5 Milner, *Canada's Navy*, 118.

6   Christopher M. Bell, "Air Power and the Battle of the Atlantic: Very Long
    Range Aircraft and the Closing of the 'Air Gap,'" *The Journal of Military
    History* 79.3 (July 2015) 671–719.

7   Douglas, et al., *Creation of a National Air Force*, 546.

8   Sarty, "Rear-Admiral L.W. Murray and the Battle of the Atlantic," 186.

9   Clay Blair, *Hitler's U-boat War: The Hunted, 1942–1945* (New York: Random
    House, 1998) 707; Cook, *Fight to the Finish*, 195–96.

10 Douglas, Sarty, and Whitby, *No Higher Purpose*, chapter 11.

11 On the British way of war, Stephen Hart, *Montgomery and "Colossal Cracks":
    The 21st Army Group in Northwest Europe, 1944–45* (Westport, CT: Praeger
    Publishers, 2000).

12 On the American learning curve in battle, see Peter R. Mansoor, *The GI
    Offensive in Europe: The Triumph of American Infantry Divisions, 1941–1945*
    (Kansas: University of Kansas Press, 1999).

13 Kennedy, *History of the Department of Munitions and Supply*, 100.

14 RG 24, v. 12321, CMHQ file 4/Censor Reps/1/2, Field Censors (Home)
    reports, 6–20 September 1943.

15 Mark A. Stoler, *Allies and Adversaries: The Joint Chiefs of Staff, the Grand
    Alliance, and the U.S. Strategy in World War II* (Chapel Hill: University of
    North Carolina Press, 2000) 103.

16 For a sympathetic portrayal of McNaughton, see John Rickard, *The Politics of
    Command: Lieutenant-General Andrew McNaughton and the Canadian Army
    1939–1943* (St. Catharines: Vanwell, 2010).

17 Pearson, *Mike*, 241–42.

18 LAC, King papers, MG 26 J1, v. 346, C7041, 298,501–298,503.

19 For the affair, see Brandey Barton, "Public Opinion and National Prestige: The
    Politics of Canadian Army Participation to the Invasion of Sicily, 1942–1943,
    Canadian Military History 15.2 (2006) 23–34.

20 King diary, 8 July 1943.

21 Rick Atkinson, *The Day of Battle: The War in Sicily and Italy, 1943–1944*
    (New York: Henry Holt and Company, 2007) 123–24.

22 Lee Windsor, "The Eyes of All Fixed on Sicily: Canada's Unexpected Victory,
    1943," *Canadian Military History* 22.3 (Summer 2013) 17.

23 See Alexander Fitzgerald-Black, *Eagles over Husky: The Allied Forces in the
    Sicilian Campaign, 14 May to 17 August 1943* (Helion, 2018).

24 LAC, RG 24, v. 15246, Saskatchewan Light Infantry war diary, 23 July 1943.

25 Robert Citino, *The Wehrmacht Retreats: Fighting a Lost War, 1943* (University
    Press of Kansas, 2012) 195; Ian Gooderson, *A Hard Way to Make War: The
    Italian Campaign in the Second World War* (London: Conway, 2008) 100.

26 Cook, *The Necessary War*, 372–74.

27 Lord Moran, *Churchill: Taken from the Diaries of Lord Moran* (Boston, 1966) 117.

28 Stacey, *Historical Documents of Canada, Volume V: The Arts of War and Peace, 1914–1945*, 608.

29 C.P. Stacey, *Mackenzie King and the Atlantic Triangle* (Toronto: Macmillan of Canada, 1976) 54.

CHAPTER 18: FIGHTING TOGETHER IN ITALY

1 Sholto Watt, "Crack Mixed Force is Gradually Becoming American," *The Montreal Star*, 9 April 1944.

2 *The Canadians at War, 1939/45*, volume II (Reader's Digest, 1969) 374.

3 DHH, AHS Report No. 5, The 1st Canadian Special Service Battalion, 2–3.

4 Joseph A. Springer, *The Black Devil Brigade: The True Story of The First Special Service Force in World War II* (Pacifica: Pacifica Military History, 2001) 18.

5 James A. Wood, *We Move Only Forward: Canada, the United States and the First Special Service Force, 1942–1944* (St. Catharines: Vanwell, 2006) 32.

6 LAC, RG 2, B-2, v. 24, Minutes of the War Cabinet Committee, 28 October 1942.

7 Saul David, *The Force: The Legendary Special Ops Unit and WWII's Mission Impossible* (New York: Hachette Books, 2019) 147.

8 Max Hastings, *All Hell Let Loose: The World at War* (London: Harper Press, 2011) 454.

9 RG 24, v. 10787, 224C1.093 (D3), RCAF Participation in the Italian Campaign, September 3rd to December 31st, 1943.

10 For Canada's role in Italy, see G.W.L. Nicholson, *The Canadians in Italy, 1943–1945: Official History of the Canadian Army in the Second World War, volume II* (Ottawa: Queen's Printer, 1957).

11 David Pugliese, The Devil's Brigade," *Canada's History* (February-March 2023) 30–31.

12 Springer, *The Black Devil Brigade*, 91.

13 LAC, RG 24, v. 12540, file Organization and Administration, Lt.-Gen Mark W. Clark to Commanding Officer, FSSF, 10 December 1943.

14 Robert Burhans, *The First Special Service Force* (Battery Press, 1981), 124.

15 Peter Layton Cottingham, *Once Upon a Wartime: A Canadian Who Survived the Devil's Brigade* (self-published, 1996) 104.

16 Springer, *The Black Devil Brigade*, 153.

17 John Nadler, *A Perfect Hell: The Forgotten Story of the Canadian Commandos of the Second World War* (Toronto: Doubleday Canada, 2005) 200.

18 Whitney Lackenbauer, "A Hell of a Warrior: Remembering Sergeant Thomas George Prince," *Journal of Historical Biography* 1.1 (Sprint 2007) 26–79.

19 Clinton B. Conger, "Allies Reveal Record of Special Service Force," *The Salt Lake Tribune* (Utah), 22 August 1944, 4.

20 Ibid.

21 Sholto Watt, "Crack Mixed Force is Gradually Becoming American," *The Montreal Star*, 9 April 1944.

22 Cottingham, *Once Upon a Wartime*, 128.

23 Nicholson, *The Canadians in Italy*, 678.

24 Douglas Porch, *The Path to Victory: The Mediterranean Theater in World War II* (New York: Farrar, Straus, and Giroux, 2004) 656.

25 Dominic Graham and Shelford Bidwell, *Tug of War: The Battle for Italy, 1943–1945* (London: Hodder & Stoughton, 1986) 402; Lee Windsor, "Anatomy of Victory: Allied Containment Strategy and the Battle for the Gothic Line" (Ph.D. dissertation: University of New Brunswick, 2006) 46–47.

26 Springer, *The Black Devil Brigade*, 253.

27 Wood, *We Move Only Forward*, 118.

CHAPTER 19: THE ALLIED AIR WAR

1 Stephen M. Fochuk, "Magee's War—John Gillespie Magee's One and Only Time he engaged the Luftwaffe," *Air Force Magazine* 41.3 (2017) 44, 49.

2 For the poem's endurance, see *High Flight: The Life and Poetry of Pilot Officer John Gillespie Magee* (Roger Cole: Fighting High Publishing, 2014).

3 *The Industrial Front* (Ottawa: King's Printer, 1944) 84.

4 W.L. Mackenzie King, *The British Commonwealth Air Training Plan* (Ottawa: King's Printer, 1939).

5 R.V. Manning, "Graduation of the First Pilot Course, BCATP," *Roundel* 12 (October 1960) 14–5; Hatch, *Aerodrome of Democracy*, 55–56.

6 Memorandum from Prime Minister to Under-Secretary of State for External Affairs, 7 May 1940, in *DCER*, vol. 8, 39.

7 Simon Theobald, "No So Black and White: Black Canadians and the RCAF's Recruiting Policy during the Second World War," *Canadian Military History* 21.1 (2015) 35–43.

8 McNeil, *Voices of a War Remembered*, 65.

9 J. Douglas Harvey, *Boys, Bombs and Brussels Sprouts: A Knees-Up, Wheels-Up Chronicle of WWII* (Toronto: McClelland & Stewart, 1981) 116.

10 Minister in the United States to Under-Secretary of State for External Affairs, 4 November 1940, in *DCER*, vol. 8, 49–50.

11 LAC, RG 24, v. 5368, HQ 45-10-2 contains several memorandums on the issue; Reid, *Radical Mandarin*, 140.

12 Memorandum from Under-Secretary of State for External Affairs to Prime Minister, 21 November 1940, in *DCER*, vol. 8, 55.

13 Douglas, et al., *Creation of a National Air Force*, 640–41.

14 J.L. Granatstein, "The American Influence on the Canadian Military, 1939–1963," in B.D Hunt and R.G. Haycock (eds.), *Canada's Defence: Perspectives on Policy in the Twentieth Century* (Toronto: Copp Clark Pitman, 1993) 131.

15 DHH, 171.009 (D219), HQS 8906, F.D. 9, 9 April 1942.

16 DHH, 80/478, Canadian American Military Board, n.d. [ca. June 1942].

17 Dickon, *Americans at War in Foreign Forces*, 92.

18 "Americans Here Surprised, Elated," *The Winnipeg Tribune*, 8 December 1941, 8.

19 W. Hays Parks, "'Precision' and 'Area' Bombing: Who Did Which and When?" *Journal of Strategic Studies* 18.1 (1995) 145–74.

20 Richard Overy, "Allied Bombing and the Destruction of German Cities," in Roger Chickering, et al., *A World at Total War: Global Conflict and the Politics of Destruction, 1937–1945* (Cambridge: Cambridge University Press, 2005) 277.

21 Alfred C. Mierzejewski, *The Collapse of the German War Economy, 1944–1945* (Chapel Hill: The University of North Carolina Press, 1988) 17–18.

22 Brereton Greenhous, S.J. Harris, William Rawling, and W.C. Johnston, *The Crucible of War: The Official History of the Royal Canadian Air Force*, vol. 3 (Ottawa: Department of National Defense, 1994).

23 Williamson Murray, *Strategy for Defeat: The Luftwaffe, 1933–1945* (Alabama: Air University Press, 1983) 190.

24 Robert C. Skipper, *I Never Got to be a Teenager* (self-published, 1996) 163–65.

25 Dickon, *Americans at War in Foreign Forces*.

26 Tami Davis Biddle, *Rhetoric and Reality in Air Warfare: The Evolution of British and American Ideas about Strategic Bombing 1914–1945* (Princeton: Princeton University Press, 2022) 211–13, 243; W.F. Craven and James Lea Cate, *The Army Air Forces in World War II*, volume 3 (Chicago: University of Chicago Press, 1958) 723.

27 Greenhous, *Crucible of War*, introduction, 14.

28 *The Canadians at War, 1939/45*, volume II (Reader's Digest, 1969) 539.

29 Stacey, *Arms, Men and Governments*, 290.

30 W.A.B. Douglas, "Alliance Warfare, 1939–1945: Canada's Maritime Forces," in *Revue Internationale d'Histoire Militaire* 51 (1982) 160.

31 Walter A. Irwin, *World War II Memoirs of Walter A. Irwin* (self-published, 1998) 17.

32 Jack Singer, *Grandpa's War in Bomber Command* (self-published, 1998) 173.

33 Cook, *The Necessary War*, 316–17.

34 A.G. "Red" Sherwood, *Flying 40 Missions with Red* (Penticton: Durango Publishing, 2005) 127.

35 Adam Tooze, *The Wages of Destruction: The Making and Breaking of the Nazi Economy* (London: Allen Lane, 2006) 597–602.

36 Phillips Payson O'Brien, *How the War was Won: Air-Sea Power and Allied Victory in World War II* (Cambridge: Cambridge University Press, 2015) 3.

37 Robert Gellately, *Backing Hitler: Consent and Coercion in Nazi Germany* (New York: Oxford University Press, 2001).

38 W.A.B. Douglas and Brereton Greenhous, *Out of the Shadows: Canada in the Second World War* (Toronto: Dundurn Press, 1995) 189.

39 Randall Wakelam, "Bomber Harris and Precision Bombing—No Oxymoron Here," *Journal of Military and Strategic Studies* 14.1 (Fall 2011) 12; Williamson Murray and Allan R. Millett, *A War to be Won: Fighting the Second World War* (Cambridge: Harvard University Press, 2000) 413.

40 O'Brien, *How the War was Won*, 290.

41 Hayword S. Hanswell Jr., *The Air Plan that Defeated Hitler* (Atlanta: Higgins, 1972) 281–82; Williamson Murray, *Strategy for Defeat: The Luftwaffe, 1933–1945* (Maxwell Air Force Base: Air University Press, 1983) 182.

42 Greenhous, et al., *The Crucible of War*, 864.

CHAPTER 20: LIBERATION

1 Joyce Hibbert, *Fragments of War: Stories from Survivors of World War II* (Toronto: Dundurn Press, 1985) 92.

2 L.S.B. Shapiro, "Invasion Chief," *Maclean's*, 15 March 1944.

3 Michael Howeard, *Strategic Deception* (London: Cambridge University Press, 1990) 71–83.

4 For the RCN's roles, see W.A.B. Douglas, et al., *A Blue Water Navy: The Official Operational History of the Royal Canadian Navy in the Second World War, 1939–1945, volume II, part II* (St. Catharines: Vanwell Publishing, 2007).

5 Michael Whitby, "There Must Be No Holes in Our Sweeping": The 31st Canadian Minesweeping Flotilla on D-Day," *Canadian Military History* 3.1 (1994) 61–66.

6 Jean Portugal (ed.), *We Were There: A Record for Canada*, volume I (Shelburne: Battered Silicon Dispatch Box, 1998) 14.

7 King diary, 15 March 1943.

8 King diary, 6 June 1944; Pickersgill, *Seeing Canada Whole*, 238.

ENDNOTES

9 Granatstein, *The Generals*, 109.

10 Daniel P. Malone, "Breaking Down the Wall: Bombarding FORCE E and Naval Fire Support on JUNO Beach," (Master's thesis, University of New Brunswick, 2005) 44–45.

11 Olivier Wieviorka, *Normandy: The Landings to the Liberation of Paris* (Cambridge: The Belknap Press of Harvard University Press, 2008) 179.

12 LAC, RG 24, v. 15233, War Diary, Royal Winnipeg Rifles, 6 June 1944.

13 Ross Laver, "Operation Overlord," *Maclean's* (11 June 1984) 25.

14 C.P. Stacey, *The Victory Campaign: The Operations in North-West Europe, 1944–1945, Official History of the Canadian Army in the Second World War* (Ottawa: Queen's Own Printer, 1960) 650. For a breakdown by unit, see LAC, RG 24, v. 18569, 133.01 (D1), Canadian Casualties, 6 June 1944, Appendix 1.

15 "The Invasion Launched," *The Charlottetown Guardian*, 7 June 1944, 4.

16 "The Invasion Launched," *The Charlottetown Guardian*, 7 June 1944, 4.

17 John D. Long (ed.), *We Will Remember Them: An Accounting of the D-Day Fallen* (Virginia: National D-Day Memorial Foundation, 2019).

18 RG 24, v. 10913, 235.C3.056 (D1), Operation Overlord, Administrative Plan, 11 May 1944.

19 CWM Oral History, 31D1 HARPER, Burton Harper.

20 "The Technique of the Assault: The Canadian Army on D-Day After-action Reports by Commanders," *Canadian Military History* 14.3 (2005) 69.

21 Michel Reynolds, *Steel Inferno: 1 SS Panzer Corps in Normandy* (New York: Sarpedon, 1997) 60.

22 John English, *Surrender Invites Death: Fighting the Waffen SS in Normandy* (Mechanicsburg: Stackpole Books, 2011) 55.

23 Howard Margolian, *Conduct Unbecoming: The Story of the Murder of Canadian Prisoners of War in Normandy* (Toronto: University of Toronto Press, 1998) 57–74; LAC, Harry Crerar papers, MG 30 E157, v. 5, 958C.009 (D132), First Canadian Army in the Field to all commanders, 1 August 1944.

24 LAC, RG 24, v. 20348, 952.013 (D71), "Report on Experiences of a Panzer Division," 26 August 1944.

25 LAC, RG 24, v. 13766, War Diary, 3rd Division, Comments on Operation Overlord, 21 June 1944; for the Canadian defence, see Marc Milner, *Stopping the Panzers: The Untold Story of D-Day* (Kansas: University of Kansas Press, 2014).

26 LAC, RG 24, v. 10553, 215.A21.093 (D2), No. 2 Operational Research Section, "21st Army Group and Operational Research Section, 2nd Tactical Air Force"; Ibid, Joint Report No. 3, "Rocket-Firing Typhoons in Close Support of Military Operations."

27 RG 24, v. 10799, 225.C2.012 (D8), Lessons Learned from Ops during War, by Lt-General G.G. Simonds, 1 July 1944.

28 RG 24, v. 10912, 235.C3.035 (D4), Headquarters, 3 Canadian Infantry Division, 12 July 1944; Reader's Digest, *The Canadians at War, 1939/45*, 362.

29 Powley, *Broadcast from the Front*, 100.

30 Stacey, *The Victory Campaign*, 163–64.

31 Ian Baxter, *Operation Bagration: The Soviet Destruction of German Army Group Center, 1944* (London: Casemate, 2020).

32 For Montgomery and Crerar, see John A. English, *Monty and the Canadian Army* (Toronto: University of Toronto Press, 2021).

33 Cook, *Fight to the Finish*, 223.

34 Stacey, *The Victory Campaign*, 183–85.

35 Mike Bechthold, "Spitfires, Typhoons, and Mustangs: RCAF Fighters in Normandy," *Royal Canadian Air Force Journal* 8.2 (Spring 2019) 60.

36 Brian A. Reid, *No Holding Back: Operation Totalize: Normandy, August 1944* (Toronto: Robin Brass Studio, 2005).

37 Granatstein, *The Best Little Army*, 109; Jody Perrun, "Best-Laid Plans: Guy Simonds and Operation Totalize, 7–10 August 1944," *Journal of Military History* 67.1 (January 2003) 167–68.

38 LAC, RG 24, v. 11001, 215C1.011 (D1), First Canadian Army Report, 7 August to 23 August 1944, by Gen H.D.G. Crerar.

39 Ian Gooderson, *Air Power at the Battlefront: Allied Close Air Support in Europe 1943–45* (London: Frank Cass, 1998).

40 McNeil, *Voices of a War*, 245.

41 Omar Bradley, *A Soldier's Story* (New York: Holt, 1951) 304–305.

42 RG 24, v. 10685, 215C1.98 (D137), Interrogation report of 12th SS prisoners of war, 17 August 1944.

43 Captain Harold MacDonald, "In the Heat of Battle: Letters from the Normandy Campaign," *Canadian Military History* 11.2 (Spring 2002) 41.

44 Murray and Millett, *A War to Be Won*, 445.

45 On Canadian casualties, see Terry Copp, "To the Last Canadian? Casualties in 21st Army Group," *Canadian Military History* 18.1 (Winter 2009) 3–6, Table 1.

CHAPTER 21: DEFEATING THE NAZIS

1 LAC, Harry Crerar papers, MG 30 E157, v. 7, D156, Crerar to Lett, 24 August 1944.

2 Carlo D'Este, *Eisenhower: A Soldiers' Life* (New York: Holt, 2003) 585.

3 Donald Pearce, *Journal of a War: North-West Europe, 1944–1945* (Toronto: Macmillan of Canada, 1965) 61.

ENDNOTES

4 John Buckley, *Monty's Men: The British Army and the Liberation of Europe* (New Haven: Yale University Press, 2013) 200–2.

5 Murray and Millett, *A War to be Won*, 438.

6 John A. Mimms (ed.), *The Cinderella Army: Canada's First Army in Europe 1944* (Barrie: Ram Press, 1993) 17.

7 Martin Middlebrook and Chris Everitt, *The Bomber Command War Diaries* (Harmondsworth: Penguin Books, 1985) 585.

8 LAC, RG 24, v. 10907, 235.C3.013 (2), Capture of Boulogne, Operation Wellhit, 17–22 September 1944, 28; Stacey, *The Victory Campaign*, 343.

9 Sebastian Ritchie, *Arnhem: Myth and Reality* (London: Robert Hale, 2010) 132–33.

10 Kennedy, *The American People in World War II*, 312.

11 LAC, RG 24, v. 10911, 235.C3.021 (D1), Interrogation of Maj–Gen Eberding, 64th Division, 1 November 1944; Stacey, *The Victory Campaign*, 424–45.

12 RG 24, v. 10907, 235C3.013 (D3), Report on Operation Switchback by historical officer, 3rd Division, n.d. [ca. January 1945].

13 Granatstein, *Canada's Army*, 285.

14 LAC, RG 24, v. 10907, 235.C3.013 (D3), Report on Operation Switchback, 3rd Division, 8; RG 24, v. 10911, 235.C3.021 (D1), Interrogation of Maj-Gen Eberding, 64th Division, 1 November 1944.

15 Pearce, *Journal of a War*, 87.

16 Powley, *Broadcast from the Front*, 135.

17 LAC, RG 24, v. 10636, 215.C1.013 (D1), Simonds to Crerar, 22 November 1944, 2.

18 LAC, RG 24, v. 15169, War Diary, Queen's Own Rifles of Canada, 28 October 1944.

19 LAC, RG 24, v. 10907, 235.C3.013 (D3), Report on Operation Switchback, 3rd Division.

20 Cameron Pulsifer (ed.), "Pursuit: The Letters of Captain Harold Macdonald, North Shore Regiment, from Normandy to the Scheldt," *Canadian Military History* 11.4 (Summer 2003) 50.

21 Terry Copp and Robert Vogel, *Maple Leaf Route: Scheldt* (Alma: Maple Leaf Route, 1985) 28–32.

22 Copp, *Fields of Fire*, 123; Terry Copp and Bill McAndrew, *Battle Exhaustion: Soldiers and Psychiatrists in the Canadian Army, 1939–1945* (Montreal: McGill-Queen's University Press, 1990).

23 Carol Field McKee, *Letters from Bert* (self-published, 2012) 133.

24 LAC, RG 24, v. 10637, 215.C1.013 (D22), Operation Infatuate, 17–1–9/Ops, 26 September 1944.

25 LAC, RG 24, v. 10985, 265.C5.011 (D1), The Capture of Zuid Beveland, 5th Brigade operations, interview with Brigadier W.J. Megill, [ca. December 1944].

26 Leo Arthur Hoegh and Howard J. Doyle, *Timberwolf Tracks: The History of the 104th Infantry Division, 1942–1945* (Washington, DC: Infantry Journal Press, 1946).

27 Major Nicholas Wheeler, "Forgotten Battle: A Command Analysis of Lieutenant-General Sir John Crocker GoC I British Corps, 23 September–8 November 1944," *Journal of Military and Strategic Studies* 18.4 (2018) 28.

28 LAC, Harry Crerar papers, v. 5, 958C.009 (D107), The Campaign in North West Europe from the 'Break Out' South of Caen to 31 December 1944; LAC, RG 24, v. 10636, 215.C1.013 (D1), Simonds to Crerar, 22 November 1944.

29 Morton and Granatstein, *A Nation forged in Fire*, 228.

30 Stacey, *The Victory Campaign*, 284.

31 E.L.M. Burns, *Manpower in the Canadian Army, 1939–1945* (Toronto: Clarke, Irwin, 1956).

32 King diary, 30 April 1940. Also see, King diary, 9 June 1944; Pickersgill and Foster, *The Mackenzie King Record*, Volume 2, 19.

33 For a detailed account, see Granatstein, *Canada's War*.

34 Mélanie Morin-Pelletier, «‹J'ai combattu le bon combat, j'ai achevé ma course, j'ai gardé la foi› : Récit de guerre d'un conscrit néo-brunswickois, 1943–1945,» *Canadian Military History* 22.4 (2013) 45–58.

35 Greenhous, et al., *The Crucible of War*, 867.

36 David Bashow, *None but the Brave: The Essential Contributions of RAF Bomber Command to Allied Victory during the Second World War* (Kingston: Canadian Defence Academy Press, 2009) 148.

37 Anthony Beevor, *The Second World War* (New York: Little, Brown and Co., 2012) 671.

38 Rick Atkinson, *The Guns at Last Light: The War in Western Europe, 1944–1945* (New York: Henry Holt, 2013) 96.

39 L.S.B. Shapiro. "Canadians Hail Yank Soldiers," *The Charlotte Observer* (North Carolina), 31 October 1944, 3.

40 RG 24, v. 10636, 215.C1.013 (D1), Crerar to McNaughton, 5 April 1945, 3.

41 Robert C. Engen, *Stranger in Arms*: Combat Motivation in the Canadian Army, 1943–1945 (Montreal: McGill-Queen's University Press, 2016) 168.

42 Terry Copp, *Cinderella Army: The Canadians in Northwest Europe, 1944–1945* (Toronto: University of Toronto Press, 2006) 225–26.

43 RG 24, v. 10986, 265.C7.011 (D3) The Clearing of Moyland Wood, historical report.

44 Granatstein, *The Best Little Army*, 208.

ENDNOTES

45 Dickson, *A Thoroughly Canadian General*, 335.

46 Henri A van der Zee, *The Hunger Winter: Occupied Holland, 1944–45* (London: J. Norman and Hobhouse, 1982) 307.

47 Bob Moore, *Victims and Survivors: The Nazi Persecution of the Jews in the Netherlands, 1940–1945* (London: Arnold, 1997) 2.

48 David Kaufman and Michael Horn, *A Liberation Album: Canadians in the Netherlands, 1944–1945* (Toronto: McGraw-Hill, 1980) 9.

49 LAC, RG 24, v. 18715, 133.065 (D358), First Cdn Army, Battle Casualties, 12 Mar–5 May 45.

50 Ray W. Lane, *In Chariots of Iron* (Edmonton: Espresso Books, 2009) 16. On the grim encounter, see Mark Celinscak, *Distance from the Belsen Heap: Allied Forces and the Liberation of a Nazi Concentration Camp* (Toronto: University of Toronto Press, 2015).

51 Dave McIntosh, *Terror in the Starboard Seat* (Don Mills: General Publishing, 1980) 108.

CHAPTER 22: WAR AGAINST JAPAN

1 LAC, RG 2, v. 32, file D-19-1 (Asia), aide memoire by Power, 10 February 1944.

2 Pickersgill, *Mackenzie King Record*, volume 1, 636–41.

3 *House of Commons Debates*, 31 January 1944, 41–42; Perras, "Aleutian Allusions," 15.

4 Ross Coen, *Fu-Go: The Curious History of Japan's Balloon Bomb Attack on America* (Lincoln: University of Nebraska Press, 2014).

5 Stacey, *Six Years of War*, 509; Andrew Brown, "The Canadian Army's Observer Program in the Asia-Pacific Region, 1944–45," *Canadian Military History* 28.1 (2019) 1–36.

6 John Alexander Swettenham, *McNaughton*, volume 3 (Toronto: Ryerson Press, 1968) 171.

7 DHH, file 82/1125 JP (44), Employment of Canadian Forces After the Defeat of Germany, 24 July 1944.

8 Stacey, *Arms, Men and Governments*, 58.

9 Pickersgill and Foster, *The Mackenzie King Record*, volume 2, 60.

10 Brian L. Villa, "Alliance Politics and Atomic Collaboration, 1941–1943," in Sidney Aster (ed.), *The Second World War as a National Experience* (Ottawa: The Canadian Committee for the History of the Second World War, 1981) 152.

11 Donald Avery, *The Science of War: Canadian Scientists and Allied Military Technology during the Second World War* (Toronto: University of Toronto Press, 1998) 266.

12 Richard Rhodes, *Making of the Atomic Bomb* (New York: Simon and Schuster, 1988) 44.

13 Robert Bothwell, *Eldorado: Canada's National Uranium Company* (Toronto: University of Toronto Press, 1984).

14 Martin Sherwin, *A World Destroyed: The Atomic Bomb and the Grand Alliance* (New York: Knopf, 1975) 36–53.

15 Stacey, *Historical Documents of Canada, Volume V*, 648.

16 Robert Bothwell, *Your Country, My Country: A Unified History of the United States and Canada* (Oxford: Oxford University Press, 2015) 215–16.

17 James Eayrs, *In Defence of Canada: Peacemaking and Deterrence* (Toronto: University of Toronto Press, 1972) 238; Stacey, *Arms, Men and Governments*, 518.

18 See Daniel Macfarlane, *Natural Allies: Environment, Energy, and the History of US–Canada Relations* (Montreal: McGill University Press, 2023).

19 Pickersgill and Foster, *The Mackenzie King Record*, vol. 2, 314.

20 Bill Rawling, "A Lonely Ambassador: HMCS *Uganda* and the War in the Pacific," *The Northern Mariner* 8.1 (January 1998) 52–53.

21 Douglas E. Delaney, *The Soldier's General: Bert Hoffmeister at War* (Vancouver: UBC Press, 2005) 222–24.

22 Atholl Sutherland Brown, "Forgotten Squadron: Canadian Aircrew in Southeast Asia, 1942–1945," *Canadian Military History* 8.2 (Spring 1999) 59.

23 "Democracy Carries On," *The Globe and Mail*, 14 April 1945, 6.

24 Pickersgill and Foster, *The Mackenzie King Record*, Volume 2, 365.

25 FDR Library, file PSF 1 Diplomatic Correspondence—Canada, Roosevelt to King, 5 November 1941.

26 Alonzo L. Hamby, *Man of the People: A Life of Harry S. Truman* (New York: Oxford University Press, 1995) 293.

27 Kennedy, *The American People in World War II*, 136.

28 On the bombing, see James M. Scott, *Black Snow: Curtis LeMay, the Firebombing of Tokyo, and the Road to the Atomic Bomb* (New York: Norton, 2022).

29 On the invasion, see Dennis Giangreco, *Hell to Pay: Operation Downfall and the Invasion of Japan, 1945–1947* (Annapolis, MD: Naval Institute Press, 2009).

30 Barrett Tillman, *Whirlwind: The Air War Against Japan, 1942–1945* (New York City: Simon & Schuster, 2010) 256.

31 Kenneth Cambon, *Guest of Hirohito* (Vancouver: PW Press, 1990) 97.

32 CWM, online exhibition, War Against Japan, Canada at War Against Japan, 1941–1945 (warmuseum.ca); CWM, 20070017-074_14a. And see Nathan

Greenfield, *The Damned: The Canadians at the Battle of Hong Kong and the POW Experience, 1941–45* (Toronto: HarperCollins Canada, 2010).

CHAPTER 23: THE LEGACIES OF WAR

1   LAC, RG 24, v. 6530, file HQ 512-27-1, D.F. Davis, 11 November 1927; Holt, *Filling the Ranks*, 86–87; RG 24, v. 1753, file DHS-7-25, part 1, Cross of Sacrifice, Persons Born in the United States Enlisted in CEF.

2   Gaffen, *Cross-Border Warriors*, 50; LAC, RG 24, v. 18826, file 133.065 D667, Recruiting in the United State of American, 1945.

3   LAC, RG 24, v. 18569, file 133.009 (D131), Americans in Canada's Armed Forces, WWII.

4   "Canadian Wins Highest U.S. Award for Valour," *The Legionary* (October 1945) 10.

5   Rana Mitter, *Forgotten Ally: China's World War II, 1937–1945* (New York: Houghton Mifflin Harcourt, 2013) 378.

6   Hastings, *All Hell Let Loose*, 669; Jurgen Forster, "From 'Blitzkrieg' to 'Total War': Germany's War in Europe," in Chickering, et al., *A World at Total War*, 102.

7   Cook, *Fight to the Finish*, 74–88; RG 24, v. 18715, 133.065 (D351), Total Wounded (Battle Casualties Only), from War Service Records, 21 September 1949.

8   Laurence F. Wilmot, *Through the Hitler Line: Memoirs of an Infantry Chaplain* (Waterloo: Wilfrid Laurier University Press, 2003) 55.

9   Reid, *Radical Mandarin*, 112.

10 Cook, *Warlords*, 338; Hall and Wrigley, *Studies of Overseas Supply*, 46.

11 On surveys, see John English, "Politics and the War: Aspects of the Canadian National Experience," in Sidney Aster (ed.), *The Second World War as a National Experience* (Ottawa: The Canadian Committee for the History of the Second World War, 1981) 52–66.

12 Peter Neary, *On to Civvy Street: Canada's Rehabilitation Program for Veterans of the Second World War* (McGill-Queen's University Press, 2011) 117.

13 On veterans, see Neary, *On to Civvy Street* and Cook, *The Fight for History*.

14 On Canada's population, see Stacey, *Historical Documents of Canada*, 138; Doug Owram, *Born at the Right Time: A History of the Baby Boom Generation* (Toronto: University of Toronto Press, 1996).

15 Robert Bothwell, *The Penguin History of Canada* (Toronto: Penguin, 2006) 365.

16 King diary, 10 September 1944.

17 Desmond Morton and J.L. Granatstein, *Victory 1945: Canadians from War to Peace* (Toronto: HarperCollins, 1995) 223.

18 Kimball, *Forged in Fire*, 268.
19 Martin Gilbert, *Road to Victory: 1941–1945* (Toronto: Stoddart, 1986) 1155.
20 Kennedy, *The American People in World War I*, 188.
21 Caroline Kennedy-Pipe, *Russia and the World, 1917–1991* (London: Bloomsbury, 1998) 84.
22 For the international impact, see Amy Knight, *How the Cold War Began: The Gouzenko Affair and the Hunt for Soviet Spies* (Toronto: McClelland & Stewart, 2005).
23 Bothwell, *Alliance and Illusion*, 43; and for King's public comments, *House of Commons Debates*, 18 March 1946, 47.
24 Reg Whitaker and Gary Marcuse, *Cold War Canada: The Making of a National Insecurity State, 1945–1957* (Toronto: University of Toronto Press, 1994) 29.
25 Gary Kinsman and Patrizia Gentile, *The Canadian War on Queers: National Security As Sexual Regulation* (Vancouver: UBC Press, 2010).
26 Michael R. Bechloss, *The Conquerors: Roosevelt, Truman and the Destruction of Hitler's Germany* (New York: Simon and Schuster, 2002) 159.
27 See Andrew Burtch and Tim Cook (eds.), *Canada and the Korean War: Histories and Legacies of a Cold War Conflict* (Vancouver: UBC Press, 2024).
28 Cited in Aronsen, "From World War to Limited War," 216.
29 Hector Mackenzie, That Path to Temptation, The Negotiation of Canada's Reconstruction Loan to Britian in 1946, *Historical Papers* 17.1 (1982) 205.
30 Granatstein, *A Man of Influence*, 136.
31 Hector Mackenzie, "Sinews of War and Peace: The Politics of Economic Aid to Britain, 1939–1945," *International Journal*, 54.4 (Autumn 1999) 648–70; Granatstein, *Yankee Go Home?*, 90.
32 Morton and Granatstein, *Victory 1945*, 182.
33 Ryan Touhey, *Conflicting Visions: Canada and India in the Cold War World, 1946–76* (Vancouver: UBC Press, 2015).
34 Peter Dean, Stephan Fruhling and Brendan Taylor (eds.), *Australia's American Alliance* (Melbourne: Melbourne University Press, 2023).
35 Robert Cuff and J.L. Granatstein, "The Rise and Fall of Canadian Free Trade, 1947–1948," *The Canadian Historical Review* 58 (December 1977) 459–82; Pickersgill, *The Mackenzie King Record*, volume IV, 273.
36 Keenleyside, *Memoirs of Hugh L. Keenleyside*, 179.
37 *DCER* 9, 1139.
38 Hector Mackenzie, "Shades of Gray: 'The Foundations of Canadian Policy in World Affairs' in Context," *American Review of Canadian Studies*, 37.4 (Winter 2007) 459–73.

ENDNOTES

39 John English and Norman Hillmer, "Canada's Alliances," in *Revue Internationale d'Histoire Militaire* 51 (1982) 38.

40 James B. Reston, "Arctic Vital to Warfare, Experts Say," *The Globe and Mail*, 13 February 1947, 1.

41 DHH, 112.3M2(D213), "Sovereignty in the Canadian Arctic in Relation to Joint Defence Undertakings," 29 May 1946. And see LAC, RG 25, file 52-C(s), "Post-War Canadian Defence Relationship with the United States, General Considerations," 2 March 1945.

42 See Shelagh Grant, *Sovereignty or Security? Government Policy in the Canadian North, 1936–1950* (Vancouver: UBC Press, 1988); Joseph T. Jockel, "The Canada–United States Military Co-Operation Committee and Continental Air Defence, 1946," *Canadian Historical Review* 64.3 (1983) 352–77.

43 Stacey, *Canada and the Age of Conflict*, 395.

44 Joseph T. Jockel and Joel J. Sokolsky, *Canada in NATO, 1949–2019* (Montreal: McGill-Queen's University Press, 2021) 37.

45 Norman Hillmer, "Canada, the North Atlantic Treaty Organization and the Boundaries of Alignment," in Ann-Sofie Dahl and Norman Hillmer (eds.), *Activism and (Non)Alignment: The Relationship Between Foreign Policy and Security Doctrine* (Stockholm: The Swedish Institute of International Affairs, 2002) 55–70; quote in Ignatieff, "A.G.L. McNaughton," 403.

46 James B. Lamb, *The Corvette Navy: True Stories from Canada's Atlantic War* (Halifax: Nimbus, 2010) 92.

47 Pope, *Soldiers and Politicians*, 178.

48 Roy Miki and Cassandra Kobayashi, *Justice in Our Time: The Japanese Canadian Redress Settlement* (Vancouver: Talonbooks, 1991).

49 Kaufman and Horn, *A Liberation Album*, 164.

50 See Greg Donaghy, *Grit: The Life and Politics of Paul Martin Sr.* (Vancouver: UBC Press, 2015); Robertson, *Memoirs of a Very Civil Servant*, 57.

51 Granatstein, *How Britain's Weakness . . .* , 24, 39.

52 Paul Litt, *The Muses, The Masses, and the Massey Commission* (Toronto: University of Toronto Press, 1992).

CONCLUSION

1 LAC, Maurice Pope papers, v. 1, Pope's diary, 9 August 1943.

2 Lawrence Martin, *The Presidents and the Prime Ministers: Washington and Ottawa Face to Face: The Myth of Bilateral Bliss, 1867–1982* (Toronto: Doubleday, 1982) 147.

3 See Greg Donaghy, *Tolerant Allies: Canada and the United States, 1963–1968* (Montreal: McGill-Queen's University Press, 1963).

547

4 For the 1960s, see Granatstein, *Yankee Go Home?*
5 On the memory of the war in Canada, Cook, *The Fight for History.*
6 For a new book on the importance of American alliances, see Mira Rapp-Hooper, *Shields of the Republic: The Triumph and Peril of America's Alliances* (Harvard: Harvard University Press, 2020). Canada is barely mentioned, as is the country's fate in almost every single US-focused diplomatic history.

ACKNOWLEDGMENTS

Every book has a question to be answered and an argument to be made. *The Good Allies* has those, and its origin was in many conversations over the years with American colleagues. They often did not know that Canada fought in the Second World War—so absent was it from the history books and documentaries—let alone that it participated significantly in the military operations that took the fight to the fascists overseas. Such is the dominance of American contributions in the narrative promoted by mass media over many decades. If little is known in the US about Canada's substantial war effort in multiple land, sea, and air campaigns, almost nothing has been remembered about its role in the defence of North America or its massive military industrial output. I don't blame Americans for that. It is our job in Canada to tell our history. I've tried to do that here, for both Americans and Canadians.

I remain indebted to the many colleagues and friends who shared with me their knowledge of war and conflict. Every day at the Canadian War Museum I learn something new, and I am thankful for the opportunity to serve Canadians as a public historian. As with past books, in shaping this one I turned to friends to read draft chapters and offer advice. *The Good Allies* is better for the time these gifted historians took to read and reflect on the ideas presented in it. My appreciation goes to Drs. Mike Bechthold, J.L. Granatstein, Steve Harris, Norman Hillmer, Duncan

Macdowell, John Macfarlane, Peter Macleod, Bill Stewart, and Ryan Touhey.

Nick Garrison, my editor at Penguin Random House, was a cheerful friend and skilled adviser as we swapped emails about our kids playing hockey and the value of history. The team at Penguin remains dedicated and responsive to writers. My closest interactions are with Shona Cook, who works magic to publicize books. Rick Broadhead, my literary agent, has been a friend and confidant for almost twenty years; our long conversations span business, health, and the trials of life. And this book is the eleventh with Tara Tovell, the best line and copy editor in the business. I've learned much from her patient editing, and I'm grateful for her expert knowledge that she channels into making better books—for me and many other lucky authors.

This book was partially written during another battle with cancer, and I wish to thank the many doctors and nurses at the Ottawa General Hospital who once again worked together in saving my life. I am lucky to have friends, near and far, who sent prayers, well wishes, good thoughts, and positive energy.

My greatest support comes from my family. My father, Dr. Terry Cook, who passed away ten years ago, not only instilled in me a great passion for history but also taught me how to be a writer and how to be a good dad. Graham and I miss him very much, and we both have come to understand his lesson that family should be central in one's life. Graham is lucky to have Ankai, and they both heap love on Hannah. Dr. Sharon Cook remains a rock in our families, a joyful light for all who benefit from her kindness, support, and love. My mom has never wavered in her support for her kids, grandkids, and those in her wide network. A nod (and bone) go to Bear and Walter, two four-legged friends who were never worried about things like COVID or cancer, and who continue to share affection unconditionally for the price of a head scratch. Sarah and I are better people for our three daughters, Chloe, Emma, and Paige, who have grown up in a house of history but have more immediate concerns and interests. That's okay. We know that they understand Canada and its place in the world better than most young adults their age and that they may one day find themselves browsing our many bookshelves to find their new passion. Until that time, their parents could not be happier to have seen them grow up to be the outstanding ladies that they are today. Rarely has the parenting of three teenagers been done with so much ease or joy. And much of the credit for that success goes to Sarah, who juggles an intense career in archives with keeping the family on the right track. My love to you. I am lucky to have found you in this world, and to be with you as we march along, hand in hand, with a rich past and a richer future, together.

CREDITS

The Author has been collecting images from multiple sources for over two decades. All of the images here are his own unless otherwise stated.

Page 21: Library and Archives Canada (LAC), C-016768
Page 24: LAC, PA-119007
Page 58: McCord Stewart Museum
Page 75: McCord Stewart Museum
Page 94: McCord Stewart Museum
Page 130: LAC, 0760877
Page 136: LAC, 3630689
Page 176: LAC, e010695747
Page 184: LAC, PA-187835
Page 235: McCord Stewart Museum
Page 246: McCord Stewart Museum
Page 255: LAC, PA-110825
Page 334: LAC, PA-163408
Page 357: LAC, C-031186
Page 359: Courtesy of Paige Cook
Page 373: LAC, A128986
Page 380: McCord Stewart Museum
Page 464: Courtesy of Emma Cook
Page 483: LAC, e010750727

INDEX

INDEX